Why another book on predestina
struggle with these great biblical docu...
Venema on the subject? Because he is one of the clea...
systematic theologians today. Why read this book rather than an older
one? Because Venema applies old texts and old doctrines to contemporary
questions. Are you sold yet?

Ryan M. McGraw
Morton H. Smith Professor of Systematic Theology,
Greenville Presbyterian Theological Seminary, South Carolina

As a doctoral student I found Professor Venema's work on predestination
during the Reformation period immensely helpful. But this book brings
abundant exegesis and theological argument to bear on a controversial
but wonderful truth. I'm delighted to commend such a learned and
helpful work.

Michael Horton
J. Gresham Machen Professor of Systematic Theology & Apologetics,
Westminster Seminary California, Escondido, California

This is a magnificent discussion of predestination and election. It
exemplifies the thorough Biblical exegesis and careful historical and
theological analysis that we have come to expect from Dr Venema.
I can think of no better resource, for not only does it address the usual
questions surrounding this difficult but vital topic but it does so with
close attention to the Biblical text and in dialogue with the history of
thought from Augustine to the present day.

Robert Letham
Professor of Systematic and Historical Theology,
Union School of Theology, Bridgend, Wales

Cornel Venema had given us a careful, thoughtful, and very helpful study
of predestination: its biblical foundations, its historical development in
Augustine and the Reformation, its modern challenges from Arminius,
Barth, and open-theism, and its pastoral significance. Throughout
Venema provides an excellent exposition and defense of the Reformed
doctrine of election.

W. Robert Godfrey
President Emeritus and Professor Emeritus of Church History,
Westminster Seminary California, Escondido, California

Vigilant in explanation and polemic, Venema serves up the classic Reformed doctrine of predestination for a new generation of readers. Those readers will here find an intelligent overview of the most relevant biblical materials, along with a careful survey of select authors who have shaped this doctrine to the present day. Taking measure of some modern rivals to the Reformed confessional consensus, Venema contests Barth's revision of the doctrine. But, more importantly, against Open Theism, and in conversation with some of the Reformed tradition's best teachers, he wages a fresh defense of the conquering grace of God—which is to say, he defends 'the old, old story of Jesus and His love.'

J. Mark Beach
Professor of Doctrinal and Ministerial Studies,
Mid-America Reformed Seminary, Dyer, Indiana

This is an important book for the lucid and instructive treatment of predestination it provides. Composed of in-depth biblical, historical, and theological discussions with some concluding pastoral reflections, it will greatly benefit all who are interested in this doctrine and the crucial issues involved—issues, the author shows convincingly, that concern nothing less than the heart of the gospel.

Richard B. Gaffin, Jr.
Professor Emeritus of Biblical and Systematic Theology,
Westminster Theological Seminary, Glenside, Pennsylvania

R.E.D.S.

REFORMED,
EXEGETICAL
AND
DOCTRINAL
STUDIES

CHOSENinCHRIST

REVISITING THE CONTOURS OF PREDESTINATION

Cornelis Venema

MENTOR
Encouraging Christians to Think

Copyright © Cornelis Venema 2019

paperback ISBN 978-1-5271-0235-4
epub ISBN 978-1-5271-0319-1
mobi ISBN 978-1-5271-0320-7

10 9 8 7 6 5 4 3 2 1

Published in 2019
in the
Mentor Imprint
by
Christian Focus Publications Ltd,
Geanies House, Fearn, Ross-shire,
IV20 1TW, Great Britain.

www.christianfocus.com

Cover design
by Pete Barnsley

Printed
by
Bell & Bain, Glasgow

CONTENTS

To my wife Nancy,
And all our children and grandchildren.

ABBREVIATIONS

APC   Benjamin B. Warfield, 'Augustine and the Pelagian Controversy,' in *The Works of Benjamin B. Warfield*, vol. 4: *Studies in Tertullian and Augustine*. Reprint. Grand Rapids: Baker Book House, 1981

BDE   H. H. Rowley, *The Biblical Doctrine of Election*. London: James Clarke and Co., 1950

BECNT   Baker Exegetical Commentary on the New Testament

BNTCS   Black's New Testament Commentary Series

CC   *Calvin's Commentaries*. Grand Rapids: Baker, 1981

CD   Richard A. Muller, *Christ and the Decree: Christology and Predestination in Reformed Theology from Calvin to Perkins*. Studies in Historical Theology 2. Reprint. Grand Rapids: Baker Academic, 1988

CD II/2   Karl Barth, *Church Dogmatics*, vol. II/2: *The Doctrine of God*. Ed. G. W. Bromiley and T. F. Torrance. Edinburgh: T & T Clark, 1957

CNTC   *Calvin's New Testament Commentaries*, 12 vols. Ed. David W. Torrance and Thomas F. Torrance. Grand Rapids: Eerdmans, 1960

CO   *Calvini Opera (Ioannis Calvini opera quae supersunt omnia)*. Ed. G. Baum, E. Cunitz, E. Reuss, et al., 59 vol. Brunsvigae, Schwetschke, 1862–1900

CTJ   *Calvin Theological Journal*

DSHR   D. A. Carson, *Divine Sovereignty and Human Responsibility: Biblical Perspectives in Tension*. Grand Rapids: Baker Book House, 1981, 1994

EEC   Evangelical Exegetical Commentary

GCP   Richard A. Muller, *God, Creation, and Providence in the Thought of Jacob Arminius: Sources and Directions of Scholastic Protestantism in the Era of Early Reformed Orthodoxy*. Grand Rapids: Baker Publishing, 1991

GECC   Richard A. Muller, 'Grace, Election, and Contingent Choice: Arminius' Gambit and the Reformed Response,' in *The Grace of God, the Bondage of the Will*, vol. 1: *Biblical and Practical Perspectives on Calvinism*. Ed. Thomas R. Schreiner and Bruce A. Ware. Grand Rapids: Baker Books, 1995

GGBW   Schreiner, Thomas, and Bruce A. Ware, eds. *The Grace of God, the Bondage of the Will*, vol. 1: *Biblical and Practical Perspectives on Calvinism*. Grand Rapids, Baker Books, 1995

GGWM   Clark H. Pinnock, ed., *The Grace of God, the Will of Man: A Case for Arminianism*. Grand Rapids: Zondervan, 1989

HC   Heidelberg Catechism

ICC   International Critical Commentary

Institutes John Calvin, *Institutes of the Christian Religion*, 2 vols. Ed. John T. McNeill. Trans. Ford Lewis Battles. Vols. 20–21: Library of Christian Classics. Philadelphia: Westminster Press, 1960

IVPNCS   The IVP New Testament Commentary Series

JES   *Journal of Ecumenical Studies*

JETS   *Journal of the Evangelical Theological Society*

LCC   The Library of Christian Classics

LW   *Luther's Works*. Ed. Jaroslav Pelikan and Helmut T. Lehmann. American ed. 82 vols (projected). Philadelphia: Fortress; St. Louis, MO: Concordia, 1957–

MAJT   *Mid-America Journal of Theology*

MSJ   *The Master's Seminary Journal*

NICNT   The New International Commentary on the New Testament

NIGTC   The New International Greek Testament Commentary

NT   New Testament

NTL   The New Testament Library

OS   John Calvin, *Opera Selecta*, 5 vol. Ed. P. Barth and G. Niesel. München: Kaiser, 1926–52

OT   Old Testament

PNTC   The Pillar New Testament Commentary

R&R   *Reformation and Revival*

RD   Herman Bavinck, *Reformed Dogmatics*, 4 vols. Trans. John Vriend. Ed. John Bolt. Grand Rapids: Baker Academic, 2003, 2004, 2006, 2008

SCJ   *The Sixteenth Century Journal*

SJT   *The Scottish Journal of Theology*

SLNPNF   A Select Library of the Nicene and Post-Nicene Fathers of the Church

TECT   Dempsey, Michael T., ed, *Trinity and Election in Contemporary Theology*. Grand Rapids: Eerdmans, 2011

TNTC   Tyndale New Testament Commentaries

WCF   Westminster Confession of Faith

WJA   *The Works of James Arminius*. Trans. James Nichols and William Nichols, 3 vols. Reprint. Grand Rapids: Baker, 1986

WTJ   *The Westminster Theological Journal*

Acknowledgments

WHILE working on this book, I was reminded frequently of my dependence upon the help of others. The topic of election is one with which the church of Jesus Christ has wrestled throughout its history. It can scarcely be addressed without careful engagement with, as well as reliance upon, the formulations of the church's confessions and most gifted theologians. I am aware that my study on election will be published on the four-hundredth anniversary of the convening of the Synod of Dort in 1618 A.D. Readers of this book will discover that I make grateful use of the Canons of Dort, which offer one of the finest confessional summaries of the Scriptures' teaching on election. They will also discover that I stand in the line of those, like the authors of the Canons, who are indebted to the great church father, Augustine, whose writings on the subject of election have had a formative influence upon Christian theology.

I would like to express more particularly my gratitude to a number of people without whom this book could not have been written or completed. I thank Matthew Barrett and John V. Fesko, the editors of the R.E.D.S. series, for inviting me to write a new study on the doctrine of election. Throughout the process of writing the book,

Matthew and John offered timely and helpful advice and steered the project to completion. I am also grateful for my faculty colleagues at Mid-America Reformed Seminary with whom I have enjoyed camaraderie for many years and from whom I have learned much along the way. I am especially thankful for the editorial assistance of J. Mark Beach and Ruben Zartman, who read some parts of this study that were first published as articles in the *Mid-America Journal of Theology*. I am also grateful for the assistance of Glenda Mathes, who willingly edited the entire manuscript; Daniel Ragusa, who worked readily and patiently on preparing a table of abbreviations, a glossary and a select bibliography; and Tim Scheuers who read the chapter on Karl Barth's doctrine of election and offered suggestions for improvement. I also want to thank those at Christian Focus, especially Willie MacKenzie, for their commitment to the R.E.D.S. series and willingness to publish this book.

I owe a special debt to the Board of Trustees of Mid-America Reformed Seminary for granting me a sabbatical during the fall term of 2017. Without the Board's willingness to grant this sabbatical, I could not have completed the book within the time frame suggested by the editors.

Last, but by no means least, I would like to acknowledge my gratitude for my wife, Nancy, whose encouragement, companionship, and music, have enriched my life for more than four decades. I am deeply grateful for her, as well as for the four children and twelve grandchildren that the Lord has given to us. All of them are a constant reminder of the truth of 1 Corinthians 4:7 ('What do you have that you have not received?'), a text that reminds us that God's grace alone is the source of every blessing in our lives. I dedicate this book to them.

Introduction

NEARLY every author who tackles the biblical teaching regarding predestination and election begins by noting the controversial nature of the topic, as well as the dangers that often accompany any treatment of it. During the course of my preparation of this volume on election, I occasionally wondered about the wisdom of writing yet another book on the subject. Some of the most gifted and faithful theologians in the history of the church have wrestled with this subject, and yet none seems to have provided a completely persuasive account of the Scriptures' teaching. Certainly, none of them has put an end to the divisions this theme often provokes. Nor have they provided a resolution of questions likely to continue arising in Christian theology's ongoing conversation regarding the doctrine. No feature of biblical teaching affords a more compelling proof that theology in this time between the times of our Lord's first and second comings will remain a 'theology of pilgrims' (*theologia viatorum*). On this subject, as well as many others, we must recognize with humility how much we do not know, and even what we know is seen through a glass darkly (1 Cor. 13:12). No doubt, we will be reminded of this again and again as we make our way through this study.

However, even though the task is daunting, we are obliged to continue to reflect upon the doctrine of election for several reasons.

In the first place, it is impossible to marginalize the Scripture's teaching on the subject of election. Try as we may to avoid the topic, it is scarcely possible to listen carefully and humbly to the teaching of Scripture without bumping up against a story whose main Actor is the triune God, whose gracious initiatives throughout the long course of redemptive history are born out of a deep-rooted determination to redeem His people in Christ. Whether it be in the Old Testament's account of God's election of His people Israel, or in the New Testament narrative of Christ's coming in the fullness of time as God's chosen Servant through whom the blessings of salvation will extend to all the peoples of the earth, God is always the One who directs the course of events in a way that fulfills His saving purposes. Anyone who attends to the biblical story of redemption can hardly fail to ask the question to which the doctrine of election provides an answer: What ultimately lies behind these gracious initiatives of God?

Even if the biblical account didn't expressly answer this question by pointing us to look deep within the eternal counsel of God for the redemption of His people in Christ, we would not be able to repress such questions as: When did this story begin, within God's eternal counsel or in the course of history? Why does God choose to act in the manner in which He does? Does the story of redemption that unfolds in the Scriptures begin and end with God's grace in Jesus Christ? Or is the story of redemption merely an afterword, a kind of second story that only begins after God's first work, creation, is unexpectedly undone by the introduction of sin into a world originally created good? In what way does the story of redemption fulfill God's original purposes in creation, including the destiny of human life in fellowship with Him? What we will discover in this study is how the biblical answers to these questions inevitably take us back to God's own eternal counsel and will, which are revealed and unfolded to us through the whole course of the history of redemption and revelation. What we will see is that the doctrine of election, far from being an obscure and speculative subject to be reserved to the playground of theologians, lies before and underneath the whole course of the triune God's redemptive actions throughout the course of history.

In addition to the integral place of the doctrine of election in the biblical understanding of redemptive history, it is remarkable to observe how this theme is often linked in the Scriptures with two, closely interrelated, motifs. The first of these is the believer's humility in the presence of God's merciful election in Christ. Nothing more starkly expresses the truth that salvation is God's gift in Christ to all who believe than the teaching of God's gracious election of His people in Christ. The scriptural teaching that salvation finds its source in God's free and sovereign purpose of election nullifies any view that ascribes any part in salvation to human merit or worthiness. The second of these motifs complements the first. If the salvation of sinners does not depend upon human merit, but upon God's grace alone, then all praise and honor for salvation belong exclusively to God. No room remains to boast in anything we do to make ourselves worthy recipients of what God alone graciously grants to us. For this reason, in the scriptural presentation of election, we hear a recurring 'hymn of praise and gratitude for the foundation of salvation' in God's merciful election, and not a fear or foreboding that steals from believers their thanksgiving to God for His unspeakable gift.[1] Accordingly, any biblically-faithful engagement with the doctrine of election ought to encourage humility as well as hearty thanksgiving on the part of those who acknowledge God's grace toward them in Christ. If these responses are not provoked by our contemplation of God's gracious purpose of election, then we have reason to ask whether or not we have handled the topic properly or harbor some residue of pride in our own merit before God's presence.

Despite the centrality of the doctrine of election in the Scriptures, as well as the humility and thanksgiving it ordinarily ought to produce in us, we must frankly admit that the theme of election also provokes considerable uneasiness on the part of many. This uneasiness has at least two occasions.

---

1. G. C. Berkouwer, *Divine Election* (Grand Rapids: Eerdmans, 1960), 13. Berkouwer rightly observes that in Scripture 'the certainty of salvation is never threatened or cast in shadows because of the fact of election. Rather, we always read of the joy of God's election and of election as the profound, unassailable and strong foundation for man's salvation, both for time and eternity.'

On the one hand, the doctrine of election seems for many to raise the specter of God's 'secret' and 'inscrutable' will to save some and not others. If salvation ultimately depends upon God's free decision to save some fallen sinners in and through Christ, how can we obtain any certainty or assurance of our salvation? Since we do not know (as God alone knows) those who are elect (2 Tim. 2:19), doesn't the doctrine of election inevitably confront us with a hidden or unknown will of God that casts a dark shadow over the revelation of His grace in Jesus Christ? Although the scriptural presentation of election is invariably linked with thanksgiving and praise to God for His undeserved mercy in Christ, the history of Christian theological reflection on election often seems to have aggravated the problem of assurance. If election in the Scriptures is inseparably joined to the gospel of salvation through faith in Christ, how do we explain the disjunction between what is said about God's grace and mercy as these are revealed in Christ and the inscrutable, hidden will of God in respect to those toward whom He elects not to show mercy? Certainly, in the modern period, theological reflection upon the doctrine of election has often been preoccupied with the question of the assurance we may have of God's grace toward us in Christ.[2] We will have occasion to see how this has come to expression in the course of our study. But it undoubtedly constitutes one of the most vexing features of the doctrine of election, which cannot be avoided in any contemporary treatment of it.

On the other hand, the doctrine of election raises questions regarding divine sovereignty and human freedom. If salvation or non-salvation ultimately depend upon God's purpose of election, then how are we to understand the responsibility of sinners in relation to the summons of the gospel to faith in Jesus Christ? For many, the doctrine of predestination and election, which emphasizes God's unconditional choice to save His people in Christ from before

---

2. When I treat Karl Barth's revision of the Reformed understanding of election in chapter 7, I will note how his view is driven in significant measure by a desire to address this question. In Berkouwer's introduction to his study on the doctrine of election, he clearly identifies the question of the certainty of salvation as 'the most important' question that needs to be addressed. As he puts it, 'Can we really speak of the consolation of election, or must we conclude that this doctrine undermines the basic foundations of our lives, devastating all certainty and stability?' (ibid., 12).

the foundation of the world, seems to diminish, even nullify, the choices fallen sinners make in response to the gospel summons to believe in Christ for salvation. The idea of God's pre-temporal foreordination of what will come to pass in time, especially in respect to the salvation of fallen human beings who are called to faith and repentance, seems incompatible with the freedom of human beings to choose for or against God. In the history of Christian theology, the doctrine of election has inevitably provoked questions regarding human freedom and the implications of the doctrine of original sin for the ability of sinners to respond properly in faith to the call of the gospel. If God's choice determines who will be saved and who will not be saved, can we still maintain the freedom and responsibility of fallen human beings to respond to the gospel's obligations? Not a few theologians in the history of the church have regarded a robust doctrine of God's merciful election to be incoherent with what we know about human responsibility. In their judgment, if God's choice to save some does not depend upon what fallen sinners do in response to the call of the gospel, then fallen sinners are no more responsible for their decisions than a robot is for doing what it was programmed to do. We are left with a view of redemption's history that looks more like the playing out of a script by actors, all of whose actions and decisions are not their own but pre-determined by the divine author and playwright. If the salvation of believers ultimately depends upon God's sovereign choice to save them and not others, fatalism is introduced into the order of salvation.

While these questions concerning divine sovereignty and human freedom have recurred throughout the history of theology, they have become especially acute in the context of the modern world. Although generalizations regarding what some call the 'post-modern mind' are often unduly simplistic, two broad convictions predominate among many people who live in the secularized, post-Christian cultures and societies of the West. Both of these convictions are hostile to the biblical teaching of election and to the most common formulations of this teaching that have held sway throughout the history of the Christian church. In the language of David Wells, a keen analyst of the postmodern mind, the two great foci of the postmodern mind are a 'decentered world' and the 'autonomous self.'[3] A decentered world is one in which God is radically marginalized and no longer viewed as the One who lies at the center of what transpires in history. Because the modern mind has dethroned God, the world and its history have no ultimate meaning, and the future becomes unknown and unknowable. The postmodern world is one in which anything is possible, and hence everyone is at risk of what the future may bring in the way of random changes. The decentered world of the modern mind corresponds to its deep-seated commitment to human autonomy, the freedom of human beings to do as they will, to think as they please, and to fashion a 'god' small enough to accommodate their autonomous selves. From the perspective of the autonomous self, the future depends in large measure upon what we choose to make it, at least within the little world that lies within our sovereign control.

It is not difficult to see how these assumptions of the postmodern mind are incompatible with the traditional Christian doctrine of God in general and anything like a traditional understanding of the doctrine of election in particular. In the biblical worldview, God is the transcendent Creator of all things and the providential Lord over all that transpires within the created order. The first article of the Belgic Confession, one of the great confessions of the Protestant Reformation, offers a typical statement regarding God that represents the common view of the historic Christian church: 'there is one only simple and spiritual Being, which we call God; and … he is eternal, incomprehensible, invisible, immutable, infinite, almighty, perfectly wise, just, good, and the overflowing fountain of all good.' Within the framework of this biblical understanding of who God is, the doctrine of election has its proper home. When God is at the center of all things,

---

3. David F. Wells, *Above All Earthly Pow'rs: Christ in a Postmodern World* (Grand Rapids: Eerdmans, 2005), 233-62. Wells recognizes that the language of 'postmodernism' is rather elusive, and that many of the tenets of what is called postmodernism find their origins earlier in the modern period, especially in the period of the Enlightenment. In a companion volume, *The Courage to Be Protestant: Reformation Faith in Today's World* (2nd ed.; Grand Rapids: Eerdmans, 2008, 2017), Wells uses the language of an 'inside' and 'outside' God to express the way God's transcendent otherness and governance of history has been replaced in the modern era by a therapeutic god who answers to our felt needs (67-103). As Wells observes, only a transcendent God, who is 'outside' of us, 'rules over all of life, [and] guides it toward the end he has in mind for it' (91).

the One in whom 'we live and move and have our being' (Acts 17:28), it is not surprising that He should lie at the center not only of the creation as a whole but also of all that takes place in the course of history. Nor is it surprising that, in respect to the salvation of human beings who bear His image and fell into sin through the disobedience of Adam, God should lie at the center of their redemption. That God works all things according to the counsel of His will (cf. Eph. 1:11), and that the salvation of fallen sinners depends upon His saving purpose, makes eminently good sense within the framework of the biblical assumptions that shaped the formulation of the doctrine of election throughout the history of the church. But it makes no sense within the framework of the postmodern worldview with its convictions about a decentered world and the autonomous self. From the postmodern perspective, the doctrine of election is not only inconceivable, but radically opposed to what is most prized, namely, the freedom of human beings to shape their own future and decide for themselves what kind of 'god' answers to their aspirations for human well-being. The postmodern mind can only be inhospitable to any doctrine of election that views the salvation of fallen sinners to depend wholly upon God's grace in Christ. Consequently, when modern theologians allow themselves to 'make peace with the culture of modernity', they are obliged to revise the doctrine of election in a way that diminishes God and enlarges human autonomy.[4]

For all of these reasons, and especially in view of the inhospitable cultural context in which the doctrine of election must be presented today, I believe revisiting the biblical doctrine of election will prove beneficial and timely. Because the doctrine of election is a central theme in the Scriptures, it has intrinsic and perennial importance as a topic for Christian theology. But especially in the contemporary context, Christian theology needs to present the biblical doctrine of election as the only satisfactory answer to the baleful consequences

---

4. See Clark H. Pinnock, 'From Augustine to Arminius: A Pilgrimage in Theology,' in *The Grace of God, the Will of Man: A Case for Arminianism,* ed. Clark H. Pinnock (Grand Rapids: Zondervan, 1989), 27. According to Pinnock, the doctrine of election requires radical modification in order to make peace 'with the culture of modernity'. In Chapter 8 of this study, I treat the 'open theist' view of election, which is the 'radical modification' that Pinnock believes will help to make peace between Christian theology and modernity.

of the postmodern mind. Rather than make peace with modernity, the doctrine of election needs to be formulated as a radical challenge and alternative to the obvious vulnerabilities of postmodernism – a little god who cannot really help us, and an autonomous self with insufficient resources to handle a world where anything is possible but nothing is certain. Whereas postmodernism can only produce a meaningless world and an uncertain future, the biblical doctrine of election focuses our hearts and minds upon God's immeasurable and deep-rooted love for fallen sinners in Jesus Christ. In the biblical view of election, we meet the true and living God, who has graciously chosen to save His people in Christ. The doctrine of election introduces us to the God and Father of Jesus Christ, who alone promises to work all things together for good in the lives of those who love Him and are called according to His purpose (Rom. 8:31-39). From the standpoint of the biblical doctrine of election, rather than living in a decentered world occupied with autonomous selves, we find ourselves the beneficiaries of God's undeserved mercy in Jesus Christ. Rather than being left to our meager resources or devices, we find the God who is for us in Christ, and whose gracious purposes are certain to be fulfilled. While we may still have unresolved questions, we will not be left as fatherless orphans to face them. Rather, we will be able to face them as those whom God has lovingly predestined to adoption as sons (Eph. 1:4-5).

Predestination and Election: A Preliminary Definition of Terms

Before turning to the plan I propose to follow in this study, a brief definition of terms that will recur throughout is necessary. In any theological reflection upon the teaching of Scripture, we must always remember the dictum, 'he who distinguishes well, teaches well' (*qui bene distinguit, bene docet*). Part of what is required for distinguishing well is the recognition of the meaning of terms and their proper use. While I will treat a considerable number of additional terms during the course of this study of the doctrine of election, a few key terms require comment before we engage the topic directly.

The two terms that I will use most often are 'predestination' and 'election'. The first term, 'predestination,' derives from a Latin root, *praedestinatio*, which is a composite of *prae-*, 'before,' and *destinare*, 'to destine' or 'to ordain'.[5] Within the framework of historic Christian theology, the doctrine of predestination concerns God's eternal purpose or will for the salvation or the non-salvation of fallen sinners. Whereas the 'general decree of God' (*decretum Dei generale*) in its comprehensive meaning refers to all God wills respecting creation and providence, predestination is the 'special decree of God' (*decretum Dei speciale*) respecting the salvation or damnation of fallen human beings.[6] Traditionally, the doctrine of predestination was treated in the system of theology as a part of the broader doctrine of providence (as a 'special providence', *specialis providentia*). Whereas the doctrine of providence deals with God's sustenance and governance of all created things, the doctrine of predestination especially focuses on God's eternal purpose regarding the salvation of fallen human beings. The doctrine fundamentally assumes that all things occur within history according to God's eternal purpose and decree(s). In the Christian distinction between the triune God, who is the Creator of all things and the sole Redeemer of His people, and the created world, the entire creation in its existence and history is governed by God's counsel and not by chance or fate.

In the history of theology, predestination is ordinarily viewed as consisting of two parts, 'election' and 'reprobation' (double predestination or *gemina praedestinatio*). Election, from the Latin word *eligere*, 'to choose out of,' refers to God's choice to save some fallen sinners and to grant them faith in Jesus Christ as Savior.[7] Reprobation, from the Latin word *reprobare*, 'to reject,' refers to God's choice not to save others but to leave them in their sins.[8] The decree or purpose of God to elect or to reprobate expresses God's sovereign freedom either to save and grant faith in Jesus Christ to some or to not save and thus to leave others in their

---

5. See Richard A. Muller, *Dictionary of Latin and Greek Theological Terms: Drawn Principally from Protestant Scholastic Theology*, (2nd ed.; Grand Rapids: Baker Academic, 1985, 2017), q.v. *praedestinatio*, 274-6. My definition of terms in this section makes free use of Muller's fine dictionary, but deliberately simplifies his far more subtle and scholastically-defined definitions.

6. ibid., q.v. *decretum*, 287.

7. ibid., q.v. *electio*, 104.

8. ibid., q.v. *reprobatio*, 312-13.

sins. A distinction is also often drawn between election, which is a positive expression of God's gracious will to grant salvation to otherwise undeserving sinners, and reprobation, which is a negative expression of God's just determination to 'pass by' some of the fallen human race, all of whose members are justly worthy of condemnation and death for their sins. In this understanding, reprobation, which manifests God's justice, is not exactly parallel to election, which is rooted in God's undeserved mercy. For this reason, a distinction is sometimes drawn between what is termed 'preterition' (from the Lat. *praeterire*, 'to pass by'), which expresses God's negative will not to save the reprobate, and 'condemnation,' which expresses God's justice in punishing the reprobate for their sins.[9] Although God's will is the ultimate reason for the salvation of some and the non-salvation of others, the proximate reason for the non-salvation of the reprobate is their own sinfulness.[10] Because my interest in this study is primarily upon God's gracious and positive will to elect His people in Christ unto salvation, not His just will to leave others in their sins, I will most commonly use the term 'election' rather than 'predestination'.

In the history of Christian theology, two related terms are employed to distinguish the doctrine of predestination and election from alternative views regarding God's work in the salvation of sinners. Since a robust doctrine of predestination and election accents the truth that salvation is grounded in God's gracious and sovereign choice, this doctrine is a form of *monergism*. The only effective cause in the initiating of conversion is God's sovereign grace. This stands in contrast to *synergism*, which teaches that the divine and human wills co-operate in the believer's response to the gospel. Synergism implies that the salvation of believers is not solely authored by God in consequence of His electing purpose. Instead, salvation ultimately

---

9. ibid., q.v. *praeteritio,* 285-6.

10. The definitions provided in this paragraph do not necessarily entail a particular view of the 'order of God's decrees' (*ordo decretorum Dei*). Nor do they prejudge the question whether or not the topic of the order of God's decrees is a legitimate topic for theological reflection. Later in this study, I will identify the two most common views on this order in Reformed theology ('infralapsarianism' and 'supralapsarianism') and offer an opinion on the question. To define these views at this point would be premature.

depends on the free and independent co-operation of the human will in embracing the gospel promise of salvation in Christ.

The Aim and Plan of the Book

As the subtitle of this book indicates, my aim is to treat the doctrine of election in biblical, historical, theological, and pastoral perspective. These perspectives roughly correspond to the sequence of the three main parts of the study, as well as the specific chapters in each part.

In the first and foundational part of the study, I dedicate three chapters to a broad overview of the scriptural teaching regarding the doctrine of election. My purpose in providing this summary is to provide background for subsequent parts of the study, which address the history of theological reflection upon the doctrine of election and more recent attempts to revise traditional formulations. Despite the effort on the part of some to marginalize the doctrine of election, suggesting that it may only be a principal theme in some of the writings of the apostle Paul, these chapters illustrate how pervasive the theme of God's gracious election is in the Scriptures, beginning in the Old Testament with the election of His people Israel, and then fulfilled in the person and work of Christ according to the witness of the New Testament. Since the theme of God's gracious purpose of election receives its most thorough and extensive treatment in the epistles of the apostle Paul, I reserve a separate chapter for summarizing the doctrine of election in them. While these chapters on the biblical foundations for the doctrine of election deliberately avoid much direct engagement with formulations produced throughout the history of theological reflection on the Scripture's teaching, they provide a touchstone by which to evaluate the biblical fidelity of these historical developments and formulations.

The second part of the study consists of three chapters, each of which focuses upon a particular theologian or period that is of special significance in the history of theological reflection on the doctrine of election. In the early history of theology, the first period of significant reflection is associated with the names of Pelagius and especially Augustine, the arch-opponent of Pelagius and Pelagianism. No name in the history of Christian theology deserves to be more closely associated with the doctrine of election and predestination than that of Augustine. In many respects, Augustine's formulation of the doctrine of election has served as a kind of benchmark for all subsequent developments, including the re-emergence of a broad Augustinian consensus in the Protestant Reformation of the sixteenth-century. For this reason, a separate chapter is devoted to Augustine's formulation of the doctrine in his anti-Pelagian writings, as well as the abiding influence of these writings during the medieval period. After I treat Augustine's formulation, separate chapters are devoted to the formulation of the doctrine of election in the period of the Reformation and in the post-Reformation response of Reformed theology to the writings of Arminius. The chapter devoted to the Reformation view of election seeks to demonstrate that the leading Reformers, both Lutheran and Reformed, broadly adhered to an Augustinian view of election in opposition to developments in late medieval theology that leaned toward a semi-Pelagian doctrine. Though there is some diversity of formulation among the Reformers regarding the doctrine of election, they commonly appealed to Augustine's anti-Pelagian writings to demonstrate that their emphasis upon salvation by grace alone through the work of Christ alone was the prevalent view of the ancient catholic church. I conclude the historical part of the study with a chapter on Arminius and the Reformed response to his views at the Synod of Dort. My purpose with this chapter is to establish the parameters for developments in the modern period that reflect the ongoing debate between an Augustinian/Calvinist and an Arminian/semi-Pelagian formulation of the doctrine of election.

In the third and last major part of the study, I consider two revisionist views on the doctrine of election, each of which illustrates the abiding influence of the Augustinian and Arminian alternatives on the theme of election. The first of these revisionist views is associated with the name of Karl Barth, whose doctrine of election was intentionally formulated to redress certain problems that he detected in the more classical Augustinian/Calvinist view. Barth's revision of the doctrine of election represents one of the most important developments in the history of Reformed theology in the modern period. No contemporary treatment of the doctrine of election may bypass Barth's view, which represents perhaps the most extensive consideration of the topic since Augustine's engagement with Pelagianism in the patristic period and then the Reformers', especially Calvin's, appropriation of Augustine's teaching in the period of the Reformation. Whereas Barth's doctrine of election involves a revision of classic Augustinianism, the second of these revisionist formulations, 'open theism,' aims to build upon and draw out more rigorously the implications of an Arminian view of human freedom for the doctrine of election. Since the open theist revision of Arminianism especially aims to accommodate the doctrine of election to modern views of human freedom and autonomy, it provides a striking illustration of the challenges to the doctrine of election faced by Christian theology in the modern era.

In the concluding chapter of the book, I address a number of issues that often arise in any reflection on the doctrine of election. Rather than simply summarizing the findings of the three main parts of the book's treatment of election, this chapter aims to apply the book's findings to several questions of a more practical, homiletical, and pastoral nature. These questions include, among others: Does the doctrine of election unnecessarily complicate the simplicity of the gospel message? Is God unjust or unfair in electing to save some fallen sinners and not others? Does election diminish the urgency of gospel proclamation and evangelism? What about the well-meant offer of the gospel? How can believers be assured of their election? While many of these questions are extraordinarily difficult to answer, I believe they need to be addressed, even though we will have to admit that our best answers do not provide a full resolution. These questions remind us of the way the doctrine of election intersects with a variety of theological topics, and of the ongoing task of Christian theology to provide a faithful account of the Scripture's teaching.

CHAPTER 1

The Doctrine of Election in the Old Testament

'And because he loved your fathers and chose their offspring after them and brought you out of Egypt with his own presence, by his great power, driving out before you nations greater and mightier than yourselves, to bring you in, to give you their land for an inheritance, as it is this day, know therefore today, and lay it to your heart, that the Lord is God in heaven above and on the earth beneath; there is no other.' DEUT. 4:37-39

THE doctrine of election taught in the New Testament can only be understood against the background of the story of Israel's redemption recounted in the Old Testament. Though God's gracious election of His people to salvation is often mistakenly viewed as a uniquely New Testament (and Pauline) theme, it is scarcely possible to follow the great drama of redemption that unfolds throughout the Scriptures without recognizing that its main Author and Actor is the true and living God. The biblical story of redemption is one in which God graciously initiates and ceaselessly works to restore His people to fellowship with Himself. At the heart of this redeeming work lies God's purpose to gather His chosen people to Himself and grant them salvation. While the New Testament sheds greater light upon the theme of the triune God's merciful election of His people in Christ, the Old Testament provides a compelling background to its testimony.

Consequently, before we consider the teaching of the New Testament on the subject of election, we need to identify the most important features of the Old Testament's teaching. Without recognizing these, we cannot expect to understand what is taught in the New. These features include the following: (1) the Old Testament's understanding of God's all-comprehensive counsel and providence; (2) the election of Israel from among all peoples and nations; (3) the election of particular persons or individuals among the people of Israel who are the special recipients of God's promises; (4) the election of a 'remnant' from among the people of Israel; and (5) the election of the Messianic King and Servant through whom God's promises will be fulfilled.[1]

In this chapter, I will examine these themes largely within the boundaries of the Old Testament. At some points, it will be necessary to make reference to the way Old Testament themes and passages are interpreted and applied by New Testament authors. Even at those points, however, I will endeavor to treat the Old Testament's teaching as background to the New Testament's teaching. In doing so, I will resist the temptation to appeal too quickly to what we know from the New Testament. Though it is true that the 'new is in the old concealed, and the old is in the new revealed', my aim in following this approach is to recognize the progressive nature of scriptural revelation and teaching.

God's Counsel and All-Comprehensive Providence

Before discussing the Old Testament's view of God's election of Israel as His chosen people, it is important to observe that this view is a corollary of the general Old Testament understanding of God's counsel and all-comprehensive providence. The Old Testament reveals God as a personal being whose actions in history are rooted in His counsel or plan for all that transpires in the world that He has created. The Old Testament begins with an account of creation, which represents the

---

1. For surveys of the Old Testament's teaching regarding the doctrine of election, see Th. C. Vriezen, *Die Erwählung Israels nach dem Alten Testament* (Zürich, 1953); H. H. Rowley, *The Biblical Doctrine of Election* (London: James Clarke and Co., 1950); Horst Dietrich Preuss, *Old Testament Theology,* vol. 1, trans. Leo G. Perdue (Louisville, KY: Westminster John Knox Press, 1995); Joel S. Kaminsky, *Yet I Loved Jacob: Reclaiming the Biblical Concept of Election* (Eugene, OR: Wipf & Stock, 2007); D. A. Carson, *Divine Sovereignty and Human Responsibility: Biblical Perspectives in Tension* (Grand Rapids: Baker Book House, 1994 [1981]), 9-40; William W. Klein, *The New Chosen People: A Corporate View of Election* (Grand Rapids: Zondervan, 1990), 25-41; Robert A. Peterson, *Election and Free Will: God's Gracious Choice and Our Responsibility* (Phillipsburg, NJ: Presbyterian & Reformed, 2007), 37-52; and Stephen N. Williams, *The Election of Grace: A Riddle without a Resolution?* (Grand Rapids: Eerdmans, 2015), 13-58.

covenant Lord of Israel as the One who calls the heavens and earth into existence by means of a series of royal decrees (cf. Gen. 1:3ff., 'let there be light,' etc.). On the sixth day of creation, God's creation of man in His own image and likeness is portrayed as the outcome of God's taking counsel within Himself (Gen. 1:26, 'Let us make man in our image, after our likeness ...'). Whatever the significance of the plural form of the verb in this passage, it clearly presents God as acting in a way that is purposeful and expressive of willful deliberation.[2] Then, in chapters 2 and 3 of Genesis, the stage is set for the biblical story of redemption to unfold. When the relationship or covenant that the Lord God establishes between Himself and the human race in Adam is broken through the fall into sin, we are told in the 'mother promise' (the *protevangelium*) of Genesis 3:15 that God intends to 'put enmity' between the seed of the serpent and the seed of the woman, and that the seed of the woman will 'crush' the head of the serpent. In this first word and promise of God after the fall into sin, we are given a kind of prequel of the redemption story that will find its fulfillment in the coming of Christ in the fullness of time. Adam's fall into sin and liability to God's judgment-curse is not the end of God's purposes in history, but the occasion for the commencement of a great work of redemption in which He will restore the seed of the woman to fellowship with Himself.

It must be admitted that the biblical narrative in the early chapters of Genesis does not expressly speak of God's eternal purpose in its account of creation, the fall, and the beginning of redemption's history. Indeed, it may be acknowledged that the Old Testament nowhere speaks as fulsomely as the New Testament about the eternal plan and foreknowledge of God (cf. e.g., Acts 2:23). In the Old Testament, God's actions in the course of history, particularly His initiatives in redeeming His people Israel, are in the foreground.[3] What God does to

---

2. In the history of interpretation, opinions vary regarding the significance of the plural subject in the Hebrew. Some interpreters regard it as a 'plural of majesty'. Others suggest that it represents God's kingly deliberation in the presence of the heavenly host of angels. In the Patristic period, it was commonly viewed as an intimation of the Trinity.

3. Herman Bavinck, *Reformed Dogmatics,* vol. 2: *God and Creation,* ed. John Bolt, trans. John Vriend (Grand Rapids: Baker Academic, 2004), 343: 'Scripture as such does not offer us an abstract description of these decrees; instead, they are made

achieve His good purposes receives most of the attention. Nevertheless, the Old Testament represents God's actions as the expression of His will and intention. God acts in time to realize His eternal plan for the world He has created and for the redemption of His people.[4]

Accordingly, before we turn more directly to the Old Testament theme of God's election of His chosen people Israel, it is important to recognize that this theme finds its place within the larger framework of the Old Testament's teaching regarding God's eternal counsel and all-comprehensive providence.[5] The covenant Lord of Israel is the God who creates, preserves, and rules over all things by His Spirit and Word (Pss. 33:6; 103:19; 104:24; 121; Job 38; Prov. 8, etc.). He knows all things, including the future course of history, and He knows them because He is their Creator and Sovereign King. For this reason, Israel's covenant Lord can prophecy what will take place in the future and how it will occur (Gen. 3:14ff.; 6:13; 9:25ff.; 12:2ff.; 15:13ff.; 25:23; 49:8ff.). Since God exhaustively knows the future, He is able to declare in advance what will take place in various circumstances (Isa. 41:21-3; 42:9; 43:9-12; 44:7; 46:10; 48:3ff.; Amos 3:7). According to the Psalmist, a person's days are numbered before they occur, and they are recorded in God's book 'when as yet there were none of them' (Ps. 139:16; cf. Pss. 31:15; 39:5; Job 14:5). Consistent with this teaching of God's exhaustive knowledge of all things, past, present, and future, the Old Testament anticipates the New Testament's language of the 'book of life' that records the names of those whom God wills to save (Isa. 4:3; Dan. 12:1; cf. Rev. 17:8; 21:27). In the same way that the names of a city's inhabitants or a nation's citizens are recorded in

visible to us in the progression of history itself.' For similar assessments, see Preuss, *Old Testament Theology*, 37; and Carson, *DSHR*, 30-34.

4. This could even be said of God's work of creation. As the creation account in Genesis 1 intimates, God 'elects' to create the world and human beings as His image-bearers. To speak this way seems to be a good and necessary consequence of all the Old Testament tells us about God's wisdom, knowledge, power, and person.

5. Carson, *DSHR, 35*: 'The idea that God really is the sovereign disposer of all is consistently woven into the fabric of the Old Testament, even if there is relatively infrequent explicit reflection on the sovereignty-responsibility tension.' Carson's study is a comprehensive reflection upon the way this theme is correlated with an equal emphasis upon the responsibility of human beings who bear God's image. Though these themes may seem to us incompatible, they are both taught throughout the Old Testament and as well in the New.

a registry, the names of God's people, the righteous, are recorded by God in this book of life.

Thus, the Old Testament's testimony to the sovereign rule of God over all things also includes the idea of God's plan or counsel for all things. When God sovereignly acts to accomplish His purposes, He does so in accordance with His wise, just, good, and beneficent plan for His creatures. God's acts in history express His power and understanding (Job 12:13; Prov. 8:14; Isa. 9:6; 11:2; 28:29; Jer. 32:19). The course of history is determined neither by fate nor blind chance. Rather, history unfolds in accord with God's own wisdom and counsel. God always chooses the most suitable means to accomplish His ends, and He does so without consulting any creature (Isa. 40:13; Jer. 23:18, 22; Ps. 89:7-9). God's decree represents His self-determination and intention to act in a particular way in order to realize His purposes and, as such, is not liable to change or frustration (Isa. 14:24-27; 46:10; Ps. 33:11; Prov. 19:21; Dan. 4:24). In this respect, God's counsel is radically dissimilar to the counsels of His creatures, especially His enemies, that are always nullified when they resist Him (Neh. 4:15; Ps. 33:10; Prov. 21:30; Jer. 19:7).

The Election of Israel as God's 'Chosen' People

Within the context of the Old Testament's pervasive teaching that the God of Israel is the creator of all things and the sovereign Lord of history, the centerpiece of redemption's history is God's election of Israel as His 'chosen' people. In the words of G. E. Wright, 'The Old Testament doctrine of a chosen people, one selected by God "for his own possession above all the people that are on the face of the earth" (Deut. 7:6), is the chief clue for the understanding of the meaning and significance of Israel.'[6] The theme of God's gracious election of Israel runs like a thread throughout the course of the Old Testament's account of the history of redemption subsequent to the fall into sin.

Though Israel's election is often associated with what might be called the 'formal establishment' of the covenant of grace at the time God called Abraham from Ur of Chaldees (see esp. Gen. 12; 15; 17), its roots are deeper than that. The story of God's gracious election of Israel is

---

6. G. E. Wright, *The Old Testament Against Its Environment* (London: SCM, 1957), 47. Cf. Charles H. H. Scobie, *The Ways of Our God: an Approach to Biblical Theology* (Grand Rapids: Eerdmans, 2003), 470.

anticipated already before the time of the Old Testament Patriarchs.[7] After Adam's fall into sin and subsequent expulsion from the garden of Eden, the story of redemption proceeds in a way that anticipates God's sovereign and gracious choice of Abraham. In the Genesis account of the early history of redemption, the story is arranged according to the sequence and order of the generations after Adam (cf. Gen. 5:1; 6:9; 10:1). Consistent with the mother promise of Genesis 3:15, God separates the human race into two communities, the one community in whom the promise of blessing is realized and the other community in whom sinful alienation from God increases. The line of God's blessing and favor proceeds from Seth until Noah, and the line of His judgment and disfavor proceeds from Cain until the generations contemporary with Noah. After the great flood-judgment in the days of Noah, the history of redemption continues to move forward in the same way. God blesses Shem and Japheth, but pronounces His curse upon Canaan (Gen. 9:25-7). The history of Israel as God's chosen people is of a piece with the history of the Patriarchs. Just as God bestowed His favor upon Seth and his descendants after him, so at the formal beginning of Israel's history God chooses to show His favor to Abraham and his descendants after him.

Though the Old Testament often speaks of God's election of specific individuals who play a distinct role, the dominant use of the language of election refers to His gracious choice to bless the people of Israel among all the nations of the earth. For this reason, I will consider in this section some important Old Testament passages that speak of God's election of Israel. However, when I take up the theme of God's election of particular persons in the next section, it will become apparent that the distinction between God's election of Israel and His election of particular individuals is somewhat artificial.[8]

---

7. Cf. Kaminsky, *Yet I Loved Jacob*, who begins his treatment of election with the stories in Genesis of Cain and Abel, Ishmael and Isaac, Jacob and Esau, and Joseph and his brothers.

8. For a survey of the use of the language of election, especially the Hebrew term *bāḥar* ('to choose') and related expressions, see Klein, *The New Chosen People*, 26-7, fn5; and Preuss, *Old Testament Theology*, 1:27-36. These surveys illustrate how variously the theme of 'election' is understood in the Old Testament. It not only includes the election of the people of Israel, but also the election of specific individuals, places, and institutions through which God's purposes are realized in the history of redemption.

God's gracious election of Israel only occurs by means of His election of particular individuals who play a particular role in Israel's history. Throughout the Old Testament, God's election of His chosen people Israel is demonstrated by two great events in the course of redemption's history: the calling of Abraham and Israel's redemption in the exodus under Moses.[9] These events are constitutive for Israel's entire history. They were formative for the Old Testament's teaching regarding election set forth in the Pentateuch, the prophets, and the writings.

Several key passages in the book of Deuteronomy strikingly summarize the testimony of the Old Testament to God's election of Israel:

> And because he loved your fathers and chose their offspring after them and brought you out of Egypt with his own presence, by his great power, driving out before you nations greater and mightier than yourselves, to bring you in, to give you their land as an inheritance, as it is this day. (Deut. 4:37-8)

> For you are a people holy to the LORD your God. The LORD your God has chosen you to be a people for his treasured possession, out of all the peoples who are on the face of the earth. It was not because you were more in number than any other people that the LORD set his love on you and chose you, for you were the fewest of all peoples, but it is because the LORD loves you and is keeping the oath that he swore to your fathers, that the LORD has brought you out with a mighty hand and redeemed you from the house of slavery, from the hand of Pharaoh king of Egypt. (Deut. 7:6-8)

> Behold, to the LORD your God belong heaven and the heaven of heavens, the earth with all that is in it. Yet the LORD set his heart in love on your fathers and chose their offspring after them, you above all peoples, as you are this day. (Deut. 10:14-15)

---

9. See Rowley, *BDE*, 19-24, who embraces a long-standing consensus among Old Testament scholars in the 'critical' school that these two instances of election in the history of Israel, first of the patriarchs and then of Israel in the period of Moses, were originally two disparate, independent traditions. Despite his adherence to this critical view, Rowley does recognize that the Old Testament views these two events together as belonging to a single history. Rowley acknowledges that Israel's exodus under Moses was a fulfillment and continuation of the promises God made earlier to Abraham (23).

> For you are a people holy to the LORD your God, and the LORD has chosen you to be a people for his treasured possession, out of all the peoples who are on the face of the earth. (Deut. 14:2)

In these descriptions of God's election of Israel to be His people, several themes stand out. God's choice of Israel is born out of His love for her. The unique privileges that Israel enjoys flow from God's good pleasure to call Israel into fellowship with Himself, and to grant her a unique status as His treasured possession. Whatever blessings Israel enjoys in distinction from all other nations stem from God's distinguishing affection toward her. All of God's redeeming acts on Israel's behalf – His promises to and calling of her fathers, His mighty acts of redemption in Israel's exodus from Egypt, His embracing of Israel as His peculiar people and possession – find their source in God's electing love and grace.[10] Because Israel's existence and privilege are wholly based upon God's loving election of her, she is expressly reminded that her election was unmerited. Though other nations were mightier than Israel, God nonetheless set His love upon her in particular. God's election of Israel was not dependent upon anything Israel possessed that would make her deserving of God's choice. To the contrary, Israel is represented as a most unlikely recipient of God's electing love.[11]

Another prominent theme associated with Israel's election is the responsibility that corresponds to Israel's privileged status. Though God does not choose Israel to be His people because she is holy, He does choose her in order that she might be holy. This theme is especially prominent in Deuteronomy 7. Israel is called out from among the nations as a 'people holy to the LORD your God' (Deut. 7:6). By virtue of Israel's election, she has become

---

10. The Old Testament's emphasis upon the way Israel's election was born out of God's peculiar love for her is echoed in the New Testament, which associates God's purpose of election with His love toward those whom He chooses (see, e.g., Eph. 1:4-5; 2 Tim. 1:9). This theme also finds its echo in the New Testament's understanding of God's surprising choice of those who are weak and powerless by worldly standards (cf. 1 Cor. 1:27-9).

11. Rowley, *BDE,* 18. The Old Testament also associates God's election of Israel as His chosen people with His granting of the promised land as her inheritance (Exod. 3:6-10; Deut. 6:21-3; Ezek. 20:5-6; Ps. 105:5-11), and His election of Jerusalem as His peculiar dwelling place (Zech. 2:11ff.; Ps. 78:68ff.).

God's 'treasured possession' and as such she has the obligation to serve the Lord and not the gods of the nations surrounding her (Deut. 7:1-5). This privilege undergirds Israel's obligation to live in accordance with the Lord's commandments (Deut. 7:11). For this reason, when the prophets indict the Israelites for their disobedience, they recall Israel's status as God's chosen people (e.g. Ezek. 20:5). The responsibility that status entails is sometimes expressed in the Old Testament by what might be termed an 'elective' use of the verb 'to know' (*yāda'*).[12] In the prophecy of Amos, for example, the people of Israel are reminded of God's electing love toward them, which distinguished them from all other families: 'You only have I known of all the families of the earth.' This reminder underscores the prophet's warning that the Lord's judgment will fall upon them for their iniquities. The language of God's 'knowing' Israel in a distinctive way is equivalent to saying that Israel is His chosen people. Israel's election heightens her responsibility to live as a holy people. Or to put it negatively, Israel's election, and the privileges that this entails, only magnify the seriousness of her failure to live as God's treasured possession.

The Election of Specific Individuals for Salvation and Service

In the Old Testament, the election of Israel as God's chosen people is closely linked to the election of specific individuals. God's election of Israel does not mean that all members of the elect community are necessarily the beneficiaries of God's blessing or the instruments through whom God's saving purpose will be fulfilled. As we noted earlier, the line of the promised seed in Genesis is one that passes from Seth to Noah and eventually to Abraham. But even among Abraham's seed, God's election distinguishes between Isaac and Ishmael, as well as between Jacob and Esau. Not all who belong to the people of Israel are equally the recipients of the blessings of the

---

12. See Klein, *The New Chosen People,* 31. Klein's study is burdened by his insistence that God's election to salvation is always corporate, the election of a people, some of whose members are saved when they choose to believe and obey God. According to Klein, when God elects individuals, He only elects them to a particular kind of service, and not to salvation.

covenant of grace that God establishes with Israel. To illustrate the way the Old Testament's teaching about election also includes the particular choice of individuals for salvation and service, we will consider the election of Abraham, Isaac, and Jacob.

The Election of Abraham

The story of Israel's election as God's people has its foundation in the election of Abraham. In Nehemiah 9:7, we are told that Abraham's calling from Ur of the Chaldees was rooted in his election by the Lord: 'You are the LORD, the God who chose Abram and brought him out of Ur of the Chaldeans and gave him the name Abraham' (cf. Josh. 24:2-3). The gracious covenant God established with Abraham and his seed was, according to this passage, the fruit of God's choice of Abraham.

In the accounts of God's calling of Abraham in Genesis 12, 15, and 17, it is clear that there was nothing about Abraham that distinguished him as a worthy recipient of God's choice. Prior to God's gracious initiative in calling Abraham, he was a member of a family who had no special relationship with the living God. In Genesis 12, we are told how God summoned Abraham to leave his country, his family, and his father's house and go to a land that God would show him (v. 1). God also promises to make Abraham into a 'great nation', blessing him and making his name great so that he would become one through whom 'all the families of the earth shall be blessed' (v. 3). In the subsequent accounts of God's covenant with Abraham, these promises are reiterated and further elaborated. God promises to be Abraham's 'shield' who will protect him and grant him a great 'reward' (Gen. 15:1). Lest Abraham should doubt the truth of His promise, God also enters into a solemn covenant with him, swearing by means of a self-maledictory oath that God would bear the curse Himself for breaking the covenant rather than fail to fulfill His promise (Gen. 15:12-19). In the last of the Genesis accounts of God's formal establishment of His covenant with Abraham, God changes his name from Abram ('exalted father') to Abraham ('father of many'), indicating that the blessing promised to Abraham would be granted not only to him but also to his 'seed' or offspring:

Behold, my covenant is with you, and you shall be the father of a multitude of nations. No longer shall your name be called Abram, but your name shall be Abraham, for I have made you the father of a multitude of nations. I will make you exceedingly fruitful, and I will make you into nations, and kings shall come from you. And I will establish my covenant between me and you and your offspring after you throughout their generations for an everlasting covenant, to be God to you and your offspring after you. And I will give to you and to your offspring after you the land of your sojournings, all the land of Canaan, for an everlasting possession, and I will be their God. (Gen. 17:4-8)

The accounts of God's calling of and covenant with Abraham confirm the sheer graciousness of God's election of him. All the blessings of the covenant relationship that the Lord establishes between Himself and Abraham, together with his seed after him, find their source in God's gracious choice and unmerited favor. Abraham does not take the initiative or in any way commend himself to God's favor. God takes the initiative to favor Abraham by calling him into covenant fellowship. These accounts also illustrate the intimate interplay between God's election of Israel as a people and His election of Abraham as an individual. Israel's status as a chosen nation finds its historical occasion in the election of a specific person who will become, according to God's promise, the father of a great nation and one through whose seed all the families of the earth will be blessed. Though God's choice of Abraham and the people of Israel is *exclusive* – no others share in the blessings and privileges that it entails – this choice also includes the promise that God's salvation will reach *all* people of the earth. The *particularism* of God's elective choice does not mitigate the *universal* reach of God's grace, which He intends to extend *through* Abraham and his seed *to* all the nations of the world.

The Election of Isaac

Immediately after the story of Abraham's election, Genesis recounts the story of God's election and calling of his son Isaac. In Genesis 17, which concludes the narrative of God's covenant with Abraham and his seed after him, we read that God will provide Abraham and Sarah a son through whom the blessings of the covenant will be conveyed:

'And God said to Abraham, "As for Sarai your wife, you shall not call her name Sarai, but Sarah shall be her name. I will bless her, and moreover, I will give you a son by her. I will bless her, and she shall become nations; kings of peoples shall come from her"' (vv. 15-16). In this passage, God makes clear that the blessings promised Abraham will only come in the line of the child whom He has chosen to grant to him and Sarah.

Remarkably, when God makes this promise to Abraham, we are told that Abraham fell on his face and laughed (Gen. 17:17). Abraham's laughter in response to God's promise is born from his conviction that Sarah's barrenness was divinely caused (cf. Gen. 16:2), and that he and his wife were too old to have a son (Gen. 17:17). And so Abraham proposes to the Lord that Ishmael, his offspring born of Sarah's concubine, Hagar, should be the one through whom the blessings of the covenant would come. God responds, however, by clearly designating Isaac, who would be born of Abraham and Sarah, as the child of promise through whom the covenant's blessings would be granted: 'God said, "No, but Sarah your wife shall bear you a son, and you shall call his name Isaac. I will establish my covenant with him as an everlasting covenant for his offspring after him"' (v. 19). In Genesis 18, we are told that God visited Abraham again and once more declared that He would grant a son to him and Sarah, and that this son would be the offspring who would inherit the promised blessing. On this occasion, Abraham and Sarah are told that Isaac would be born to them the following year. Though the birth of this child lies wholly outside the reach of human possibility, the Lord reminds Abraham and Sarah that nothing is too 'hard' or 'wonderful' for the Lord (Gen. 18:9-15).[13] Against the backdrop of God's promises to Abraham, the birth of Isaac is reported in Genesis 21:1-2: 'The LORD visited Sarah as he had said, and the LORD did to Sarah as he had promised. And Sarah conceived and bore Abraham a son in his old age at the time of which God had spoken to him.'

---

13. In the New Testament, we find a fulfillment and confirmation of this demonstration of God's surprising, invincible grace in the angelic announcement of Jesus' birth (Luke 1:37) and Paul's description of Abraham's paradigmatic faith in God's gracious promises (Rom. 4:13-25).

In this brief summary of the election of Isaac, we see how God's election of Israel as His chosen people includes the election of particular individuals to whom the promises of covenant blessing are granted. Although Abraham's offspring includes Ishmael, God chooses Isaac as the one through whom Abraham's offspring 'will be named' (Gen. 21:12).[14] Abraham, and now Isaac, are recipients of the covenant promises in a way that it is not true of Ishmael. Although it may seem premature at this point in our Old Testament summary to consider the apostle Paul's appeal to the election of Isaac rather than Ishmael (see Rom. 9:6-9), it undeniably underscores that God elects some to be recipients of covenant promises in a way not true of others. We also see in the election of Isaac that the blessings of the covenant do not come by human strength or ingenuity. Rather, they come by God's power, grace, and faithfulness to His promises. For this reason, the apostle Paul properly appeals to Abraham's faith in the promised birth of Isaac as an example of the kind of faith that rests only in God's gracious provision, and not in human ability (cf. Rom. 4:13-25). Or, as the apostle Paul argues in his Galatians 3–4 allegory regarding Sarah and Hagar, God's promised blessings are not obtained through human works or initiative, but solely by trusting in His promises.

The Election of Jacob

Perhaps the most dramatic instance of God's election of a particular person to blessing and salvation is His election of Jacob. Just as was true of Abraham and Isaac, God's election of Jacob emphasizes not only His election of a specific individual but also the election of Israel as His people. But in the case of Jacob, we are given the clearest testimony to the sheer graciousness of God's electing purpose.

The account in Genesis of the generations of Isaac begins by telling the reader that, when Isaac was forty years old, he took Rebekah to be his wife. Rebekah was barren, however, so Isaac asked the Lord to grant them a child (Gen. 25:19-21). After the Lord answered Isaac's

---

14. For this reason, God's election of Isaac, together with Abraham before him and Jacob after him, is celebrated and remembered in Psalm 105:6-9: 'O offspring of Abraham, his servant, children of Jacob, his chosen ones! He is the LORD our God; his judgments are in all the earth. He remembers his covenant forever, the word that he commanded for a thousand generations, the covenant that he made with Abraham, his sworn promise to Isaac.'

prayer and enabled Rebekah to conceive children, Rebekah inquired of the Lord why the children in her womb were 'struggling together within her' (v. 22). The Lord responds by saying: 'Two nations are in your womb, and two peoples from within you shall be divided; the one shall be stronger than the other, the older shall serve the younger' (v. 23). In his response, the Lord declares something that could only be true by virtue of His choice and purpose: though the older of the twin sons would be stronger than the younger, he would nonetheless serve the younger. Rebekah's younger son, Jacob, would be the recipient of God's favor in a way that would not be true of the older son, Esau. After the birth of Esau and Jacob, the story in Genesis 25–35 demonstrates how God's election of Jacob continues the pattern witnessed in the earlier accounts of Abraham and Isaac. At the end of the narrative of Isaac's generations, God appears to Jacob and declares that from henceforth his name will be 'Israel'. At the close of the story of Jacob, it becomes clear that, in the same way God chose Abraham and Isaac to be recipients of the promise, so He has now chosen Jacob. Israel's election to be God's people focuses upon God's election of Abraham, Isaac, and Jacob. The promised seed will be in the line of Jacob, who like Abraham and Isaac before him, will be fruitful and multiply as one from whom 'a nation and a company of nations shall come'. The covenant inheritance earlier promised to Abraham, including the land God will give to him, will find its fulfillment through Jacob and his offspring after him (Gen. 35:10-12).

The account of Jacob's election illustrates two features of the Old Testament's teaching. In the first place, it shows in the most dramatic way possible that God's election is not dependent upon any merit or work in the person or people whom He elects. Even if the apostle Paul's appeal to the account of Jacob's election were not in the Scriptures, it would be evident that God's choice was not based upon anything Jacob had done, whether good or bad (cf. Rom. 9:11). Jacob's election was not based upon his 'works' but upon his 'call' by God's gracious initiative.[15] In the second place, it illustrates the close connection

---

15. Cf. J. Barton Payne, *The Theology of the Older Testament* (Grand Rapids: Zondervan, 1962), 179: 'He was chosen before birth. He was one of twins, so humanly equal. He was the younger of the two and, in his personal character, he was an unethical trickster—from his very birth in fact.'

between God's election of specific persons and His election of a community of persons. In the Old Testament, the election of Jacob and the non-election of Esau also represent God's election of two nations. This is clear from the account in Genesis 25 where the twin sons of Rebekah are described as 'two nations' in her womb (v. 23). In the prophecy of Malachi 1:2-3, which the apostle Paul quotes in Romans 9:13, Esau is identified with the nation of Edom and Jacob with the nation of Israel. However, it would be a mistake to conclude that Jacob and Esau are not also individual persons whom God chooses to bless in a special way. Though they may represent two nations, they are also two individuals, one of whom God chooses to treat as a special recipient of His love and heir of the promises of the covenant, the other of whom God chooses not to grant His favor. As the apostle Paul observes in Romans 9:11, God chose Jacob in order that 'his purpose of election might continue, not because of works but because of his call.'[16]

Election for Salvation or for Service?

In the context of our treatment thus far of the election of Israel as God's chosen people, and its teaching of the election of particular individuals, it is necessary to address a question often raised in discussions of the Old Testament's teaching. Although this question is variously articulated, it can be expressed in these terms: Does the Old Testament teaching of election primarily focus upon an election unto salvation or an election unto service? Was God's election of Israel as His chosen people intended to grant her a privileged status that included the blessing of saving communion with Himself? Or was God's election of Israel exclusively an election to a particular role in the course of redemptive history? The same question could be put in respect to the individuals whom the Old Testament distinguishes as the particular objects of God's electing favor. Were they merely elected to special service in the course of redemptive history, or

---

16. God's election of Abraham, Isaac, and Jacob illustrates not only the error of those who oppose the 'corporate' election of Israel to the 'particular' election of individuals, but also forms a necessary background to our discussion of the apostle Paul's argument in Romans 9–11, which we will treat at some length in a subsequent chapter. Geerhardus Vos, in his *Biblical Theology: Old and New Testaments* (Grand Rapids: Eerdmans, 1948), 79, offers an important comment on the interplay between corporate and individual election in both the Old and New Testaments.

were they elected to enjoy the blessing of saving communion with the Lord God?[17]

Many interpreters of the Old Testament's view of election have argued that Israel's election was to special service in the history of redemption, not to salvation in the strict sense of the term. Perhaps the most vigorous proponent of the view that Israel's election was merely an election to service is H. H. Rowley, the author of an influential study of the biblical doctrine of election.[18] According to Rowley, Israel's election to service consisted of three elements: (1) receiving and cherishing the revelation of God that was entrusted to her; (2) living a life of holiness that reflected the character and will of God; and (3) mediating the law of God to all the nations and spreading the heritage of her faith to the whole world.[19] Rowley offers a similar interpretation of the Old Testament view of the election of specific individuals. The election of such individuals, like the election of the people of Israel, is exclusively an election to service. To suggest that Israel or specific individuals were also elected to the blessing of salvation, while those whom God did not elect were thereby excluded from God's saving blessing, is to encumber the Old Testament view with a notion alien to its teaching.

> Whom God chooses, He chooses for service. There is a variety of service, but it is all service, and it is all service for God. Whom God destroys, He finds no longer serviceable. Hence the use of this metaphor only supports the view that the Divine election concerns exclusively the Divine service.[20]

There is an element of truth in this view. As we have seen, God's purpose in the election of His people Israel was not merely to grant her the blessing of being His favored people. It also included a call

---

17. There are, of course, a number of instances in the Old Testament where God elects nations, as well as specific individuals, to a task, but there is no suggestion that this is an election unto salvation. For a helpful treatment of such instances, see Rowley, *BDE,* 121-38. Rowley treats these instances as a form of 'election without covenant', and cites the examples of God's election of the Assyrians, the Chaldeans, and Cyrus to serve His purposes of judgment and blessing toward His people Israel.

18. See Rowley *BDE,* 161.

19. Rowley, *ibid.,* 161-5.

20. Rowley, *ibid.,* 42.

to holiness and obedience to His statutes. Israel's privileged status heightened, rather than diminished, her responsibility to live as God's treasured possession. Furthermore, Israel's election included the promise that she would be a people through whom the blessing of fellowship with God would extend to all peoples of the earth. God's saving blessings would flow to the nations *through* Israel, and in this sense Israel's election would serve the universal extension of salvation to all peoples. Likewise, the election and calling of specific individuals throughout Israel's history were not at odds with this larger reach of God's saving favor. Throughout the course of Israel's history, God's design to use His elect people to bring blessing to the ends of the earth is never forgotten.[21] Indeed, the prophets who ministered before and during Israel's exile frequently speak of a future day of blessing and salvation, not only for Israel but also for all nations.

There are, however, at least three serious problems with the view that Israel's election was exclusively an election for service.

First, the view that Israel's election was merely for service posits a false dichotomy between Israel's privileges as an elect people and her corresponding obligations. That Israel was elected to fulfill a mission in service to the nations is undeniable. The exclusivism of God's choice of Israel to be His people was never divorced from His wider intention to extend the blessings of salvation to all nations. But Israel's fulfillment of this mission depended upon her possession of saving privileges that belonged inherently to her as an elect people. In order for Israel to serve as an instrument of blessing to the nations, she had to possess blessings that were not yet extended to these nations.

---

21. For this reason, some recent missiological treatments of Israel's election tend to echo Rowley's insistence that election in the Old Testament is not an election to saving blessings but merely to service. In this approach, Israel's election was not unto saving privileges, but to a particular task in serving God's greater mission to bring blessing to all nations and peoples. For examples of this tendency in contemporary missiology, see Lesslie Newbigin, *The Open Secret: An Introduction to the Theology of Mission* (London: SPCK, 1978); and Christopher J. H. Wright, *The Mission of God: Unlocking the Bible's Grand Narrative* (Downers Grove, IL: IVP Academic, 2006), 191-264. Wright's account of the election of Israel is more balanced than Newbigin's, since it also affirms the soteriological nature of election. In his summary of the nature of Israel's election, Wright (*The Mission of God,* 264) maintains that 'Election is of course, in the light of the whole Bible, election unto salvation. But it is *first of all* election unto mission' (emphasis mine).

It makes little sense to say that Israel was commissioned to be a blessing to the nations, unless she already possessed saving blessings not yet communicated to other peoples. After all, what was Israel commissioned to convey to the nations, if she was not a people who enjoyed the privilege of salvation? There is something odd, even contradictory, about a view that equates Israel's election merely with her special calling, while denying that Israel actually possessed the blessings of salvation she was to convey to others. Moreover, the election of Israel would in this way come to depend finally upon her faithfulness in fulfilling the task assigned to her. No longer would God's election of Israel be grounded in His undeserved favor toward her and His resolute accomplishment of the salvation of His people. Rather, it would ultimately come to depend upon the degree to which Israel successfully carried out her assignment in the course of redemptive history.

Second, the view that Israel's election was merely for service is unnecessarily reductionistic.[22] The privileges granted to Israel by virtue of her election included what can only be described as *saving* blessings. The history recounted in the Old Testament is a history of redemption. The blessings God promises His elect people include not only an inheritance in the land of promise, but fellowship with the true and living God. The great covenant promise God makes to His elect people throughout this history is that He will be Israel's God, and Israel will be His treasured possession. This covenant promise contains in seed form all the blessings God granted to Israel, including the provision of the Levitical priesthood, the guilt and sin offerings of the Levitical sacrifices, the temple as a symbolic representation of God's choice to dwell in the midst of His people, and the like. Israel's Psalter is replete with expressions of praise and thanksgiving for all the saving blessings that stem from God's gracious election of His people Israel. Though not all the individuals who belong to Israel as a corporate people enjoy these blessings, those who believe

---

22. Kaminsky, *Yet I Loved Jacob,* 156, calls this a merely 'instrumental' view of Israel's election, which fails to recognize the 'intrinsic' significance of election as a manifestation of God's saving love for His people: 'While election reaches its greatest heights when the elect humbly submit to the divine service God has placed upon them, it is not reducible to service. Rather, it flows out of God's mysterious love for those chosen.'

God's promises and embrace them with thanksgiving certainly do. In the Psalms, these saving blessings include communion with God (Ps. 73:23-26), dwelling in the presence of God (Ps. 16:10-11; Ps. 46:4-5; Ps. 90:1), the forgiveness of sins (Ps. 32; Ps. 51:1-2; Ps. 103:3), redemption from the dominion of sin, righteousness and peace (Ps. 1), the indwelling of the Spirit of God (Ps. 51:10-11), and much more. As Stephen N. Williams expresses it:

> At all levels of election, whatever its instrumental necessity in God's hands for carrying out his particular historical purposes, it carries with it the peculiar privilege of the elect – the privilege of communion. If the Lord is our life (Deut. 30:20), there is no higher privilege, and if he is God of the living, it is also an eschatological privilege which goes beyond the length of earthly days mentioned in Deuteronomy, according to the power of the Lord, who is the God of the living.[23]

And third, the claim that election in the Old Testament is exclusively for service contradicts the New Testament's interpretation of God's promises to Israel that are now fulfilled in Christ. The Gospel of Matthew, for example, opens with a record of the genealogy of Jesus Christ, who is identified as the 'son of Abraham' and the 'son of David'. The evangelist Matthew wants to make clear that the birth of Jesus Christ is a fulfillment of God's promises to Israel, and that He comes to 'save his people from their sins' (Matt. 1:21; cf. 1 Tim. 1:15). In the epistles of the apostle Paul, we are told that 'all of the promises of God' that were made to Israel now find their 'yes' and 'Amen' in Christ (2 Cor. 1:20); that Abraham, the father of all believers, was justified by faith in God's promise just as believers in the new covenant (Rom. 4; cf. Gal. 3:16-18); that believers in Jesus Christ enjoy the privilege of adoption, and are 'Abraham's offspring, heirs according to promise' (Gal. 3:29); that believers in Jesus Christ are 'grafted into' the one 'olive tree' of God's people, inclusive of all believing Jews and Gentiles (Rom. 11:17-24). The assumption of these and many other passages is that the election and salvation of Israel finds its fulfillment in the election and salvation of all believers in

---

23. Williams, *The Election of Grace*, 34-35. Williams offers this comment in the context of a sustained critique of the claim that the Old Testament view of election is merely one of election unto service, and not unto salvation.

Jesus Christ, whether Jews or Gentiles. In the same way, the author of the book of Hebrews argues that Christ's prophetic, priestly, and kingly work as Mediator is a fulfillment of the types and shadows of the Old Testament economy.

The point here is not to provide an exhaustive account of the myriad ways in which the New Testament regards Christ's coming as a fulfillment of the promises first made to Israel under the old covenant. It is simply to demonstrate that the promises of God to His elect people Israel included not only temporal blessings and privileges but also saving blessings. These blessings are the common inheritance of God's people Israel and the New Testament church (cf. 1 Pet. 2:9-10). The promises of salvation made to Israel in the Old Testament find their fulfillment in the fullness of saving blessings granted to those who belong to Christ by faith.

The Election of a 'Remnant' Within Israel

Another theme in the Old Testament's teaching about election requiring our attention is that of an 'elect remnant' within Israel. This theme is present throughout the entire course of God's dealings with His people Israel, but it becomes increasingly prominent in the period leading up to the exile. The fact that God already, in the period of the Patriarchs, elected Abraham, Isaac, and Jacob to receive the blessings of the covenant reveals how His electing purpose distinguishes between Israel in the broader sense of a corporate people and in the narrower sense of particular recipients of the promise. Accordingly, the distinction between Isaac and Ishmael, as well as the distinction between Jacob and Esau, establishes a pattern in the Old Testament's increasing focus upon the theme of an elect remnant within Israel.[24]

Throughout the Old Testament history of Israel as a chosen nation, it is evident from the earliest beginnings that not all members of the community enjoyed the promised blessings. As we have already noted, Israel's privilege as an elect people heightened her obligation to respond to God's grace in faith and obedience. Thus, all throughout Israel's history, failure to believe God's covenant promises or to obey

---

24. Rowley, *BDE*, 71.

His statutes invited God's judgment. Ultimately, Israel's failure to keep covenant with God would bring upon her the great judgment of exile from the land of promise. However, at no time during Israel's history does God ever fail to ensure that His purpose of election is realized. One of the most striking illustrations of God's preservation of a faithful remnant among His people occurs during the period of the reign of King Ahab. When Elijah the prophet declares that he alone remains faithful among the people of God, the Lord assures him that He 'will leave seven thousand in Israel, all the knees that have not bowed to Baal, and every mouth that has not kissed him' (1 Kings 19:18). The Lord's preservation of a righteous remnant during this period of Israel's history becomes paradigmatic for the theme of an elect remnant that is preserved throughout the entirety of Israel's history (cf. Rom. 11:1-6).

Not surprisingly, the theme of an elect remnant within the people of Israel becomes increasingly prominent in the period of the prophets before and during the exile. According to these prophets, God's preservation of a remnant among His people confirms that His promises to Israel will continue to be fulfilled (Isa. 41:8ff.; 43:4ff.; Jer. 51:5). Though the people of Israel as a whole may lie under God's judgment, the remnant within Israel continues to testify to God's purpose in electing Israel (Isa. 65:8-10; Amos 9:8-15). Those who constitute this remnant are the genuinely elect of God (Isa. 1:21-6; 4:2-6; 10:20ff.). For the sake of this elect remnant, God will restore Israel after the period of the exile (Jer. 31:33; 32:37-41; 50:5; Isa. 55:3). God's purpose through Israel to extend His saving blessing to the nations will be realized through His preservation of this faithful remnant. The existence of this remnant will be due solely to God's electing purpose and gracious work. God's electing grace alone will preserve and equip the remnant for its calling. This elect remnant will not serve God's purpose or be chosen because of their inherent worthiness. Rather, God alone will enable His covenant promises to be fulfilled through the restoration of this remnant, through the 'new covenant' that He will establish with them (Jer. 31:31-4). To this remnant, God will grant a heart of flesh, pouring out His Spirit upon them, and gathering them to Himself (Jer. 31:31-4; Ezek. 11:16-21; 36:22-32). Only upon the basis of God's unmerited and sovereign favor will this remnant be constituted, preserved, and equipped to fulfill God's purposes.

A Brief Excursus on Election and Covenant

If the election of Israel as God's chosen people was an election to salvation, and not merely to a particular task in redemption's history, the question of the relation between Israel's election and God's covenant with her becomes pressing. Furthermore, the theme of an elect remnant within the broader community of God's elect people, Israel, requires some explanation regarding how election and covenant are related in the Old Testament's account of God's dealings with the people of Israel.

On the one hand, it is apparent that divine election and covenant are closely linked. For when God elects Israel to be His chosen people, He chooses to establish a gracious covenant with this people, a covenant that consists of promises of blessing and corresponding obligations of obedience. As we have observed, the election and calling of Abraham constitute the basis for the covenant God makes with him and his descendants. The same can be said of God's election of Isaac and then Jacob. God's election of these Patriarchs comes to expression in the covenant promises that He makes to them, as well as in the covenant obligations these promises entail. Because divine election and gracious covenant are so closely joined in Israel's history, they seem to coalesce entirely, as though they were two aspects of one, indivisible reality. The people whom God elects seem to coincide exactly with the people with whom God covenants.

On the other hand, it is evident throughout Israel's history, from the time of the Patriarchs until the close of the Old Testament, that not all of those who are members of the nation of Israel with whom God covenants, are equally partakers in the saving blessings that Israel's election entails. Though there is a sense in which Ishmael and Esau are embraced within the promises and obligations of the covenant, they are not the divinely-intended recipients of the covenant's blessings in the way Isaac and Jacob are. Furthermore, because the covenant consists of both promises and obligations, there is always the real possibility, often realized throughout Israel's history, that some of those with whom God covenants do not enjoy or retain the blessings of the covenant. Among the children of Israel, there are those who prove unfaithful and disobedient, and who come under God's judgment and the curse of the covenant. Israel's exile at the close of the period of the divided kingdom is a dramatic confirmation of this truth. Only through a portion of Israel, the elect remnant, will God's gracious election and covenant be brought to fruition.

The most helpful way to resolve the question regarding the relation between election and covenant is by distinguishing between *the historical election of the people of Israel* and *the saving election of those among this people who are divinely-intended recipients of the covenant's blessings.*[25] Though the Old Testament does not provide as explicit a statement of this distinction as the apostle Paul does in Romans 9:6, the rudiments are already present for Paul's claim that 'not all who are descended from Israel belong to Israel'. When Israel's history is viewed in the strict sense of God's 'purpose of election', it becomes evident that the election of the people of Israel does not entail the election unto salvation of all those who belong to Israel and with whom God establishes His covenant in history. What moves Israel's history forward, despite her oft-repeated periods of unbelief and disobedience, is God's resolute purpose through Israel to bring salvation to the elect among this people who are 'children of the promise' in a unique way. In terms of this distinction, the election of Israel as a people, as well as the covenant that was established with her, is wider in circumference than the circle of the true Israel whom God elects to save. Though the covenant in its administration serves God's purpose of election, it does not coincide with it. Indeed, the only way God's purpose of election can be achieved is through

---

25. See Calvin, *Institutes,* 3.21.6, who distinguishes between different 'degrees' of election: 'We must now add a second, more limited degree of election, or one in which God's more special grace was evident, that is, when from the same race of Abraham God rejected some but showed that he kept others among his sons by cherishing them in the church'; and idem, *Institutes,* 3.21.7, where Calvin refers to a 'a special mode of election [that] is employed for a part of them, so that he does not with indiscriminate grace effectually elect all.' Cf. John Frame, *The Doctrine of God* (Phillipsburg, NJ: Presbyterian & Reformed, 2002), 317-30, who distinguishes 'eternal' from 'historical' election. For an extensive treatment of the relation between the biblical themes of election and covenant, see Cornelis P. Venema, *Christ and Covenant Theology: Essays on Election, Republication, and the Covenants* (Phillipsburg, NJ: Presbyterian & Reformed, 2017), 147-255.

God's invincible grace and faithfulness, not through the faithfulness and obedience of its beneficiaries. The covenant God makes with Israel is instrumental to the furtherance of God's saving election of some among this people who truly enter into and enjoy what the covenant promises. Only those whom God chooses to save receive the covenant's promises in full. And they receive these promises, not upon the basis of their own achievement, but upon the basis of God's gracious work on their behalf.

The Election of the Lord's Messianic 'Servant'

In our survey of the Old Testament's teaching, we noted the way God's gracious election often focuses upon specific individuals through whom His saving purposes will be achieved. Not all of those who belong to the elect people of Israel are equally the recipients of the blessings of saving communion with God, or are regarded as belonging in the strict sense to the 'seed' of the covenant. One often neglected feature of the Old Testament's understanding of election is God's choice of a King to rule over and shepherd His people, Israel. In the prophecy of Isaiah, which contains a number of prophetic passages regarding the coming Messiah (cf. Isa. 9:2-7; 11:1-16), the Lord expressly speaks of His 'chosen' or 'elected' servant: 'Behold, my servant, whom I uphold, my chosen, in whom my soul delights, I have put my Spirit upon him, he will bring forth justice to the nations' (Isa. 42:1-3). If the election of this servant is associated with the Old Testament promises of a coming Messianic King, we have the basis for speaking of God's election of this Messianic Servant for a special task or service in the history of redemption.[26]

The earliest instances of the Old Testament's promise of a coming Messianic King go all the way back to the period of the Patriarchs. In

---

26. I use the conditional *if* here to acknowledge that many critical interpreters of the Old Testament are not prepared to acknowledge that the Old Testament provides a composite, and coherent, promise of a single Messianic King and Servant of the Lord who corresponds to the New Testament's claims regarding Jesus Christ. I do not mean thereby to express any doubt as to whether this is the case. For extensive treatments of the Messianic teaching of the Old Testament, see Ernst Wilhelm Hengstenberg, *Christology of the Old Testament and a Commentary on the Messianic Predictions,* 4 vols. (reprint; Grand Rapids: Kregel, 1956 [1854]); and Gerard Van Gronigen, *Messianic Revelation in the Old Testament* (Grand Rapids: Baker Book House, 1990).

the Patriarchal narratives in Genesis, which frequently focus upon the 'seed' of promise whom God elects to bless, we are told that among the children of Jacob, Judah was singled out as one through whom God's purposes will be especially fulfilled: 'The scepter shall not depart from Judah, nor the ruler's staff from between his feet, until tribute comes to him and to him shall be the obedience of the peoples.' In the period of the establishment of the monarchy in Israel, God chooses David, who is from the line of Judah (1 Sam. 16:1-13; cf. Ruth 4:13-22; Matt. 1:3-6), to be Israel's Shepherd-King. In 2 Samuel 7, the Lord covenants with David and his house, promising that He will establish his kingdom forever:

> Moreover, the LORD declares to you that the LORD will make you a house. When your days are fulfilled and you lie down with your fathers, I will raise up your offspring after you, who shall come from your body, and I will establish his kingdom. He will build a house for my name, and I will establish the throne of his kingdom forever. (2 Sam. 7:11-13)

The election of David and his house, together with the covenant the Lord makes with him, provides the basis throughout the period of the monarchy for the anticipation of a Messianic King who would sit on the throne of his father David. Despite the failures and disobedience of the kings after David, the election of David's house by the Lord shapes the expectation of Israel for a future fulfillment of the Lord's promise. Indeed, even in the period leading up to and during Israel's exile, the prophets continue to declare, sometimes in increasingly bold and clear notes, that the house of David would be restored.

In the prophecies of Isaiah, we find a number of passages directly or indirectly related to this Messianic King and chosen Servant of the Lord.[27] If the election of the Lord's servant in Isaiah 42 is viewed firstly within the prophecy of Isaiah itself, it is clear that He is elected to represent and act on behalf of the people of Israel. Through the ministry of the Lord's chosen Servant, justice will be brought to the nations (Isa. 42:1). Like Jeremiah the prophet, this servant of the Lord will be chosen from birth for the Lord's service (Isa. 49:5). He will 'bring Jacob back to [the Lord]' (Isa. 49:5). Through His

---

27. For an extensive treatment of these passages, see Rowley, *BDE*, 111-20; and Van Gronigen, *Messianic Revelation in the Old Testament*, 516-666.

service Israel will become 'as a light for the nations' so that the Lord's 'salvation may reach to the end of the earth' (Isa. 49:6). The epitome of His obedience will be His suffering and death in the place of His people with whom He willingly identifies Himself, shouldering the burden of their sin and suffering the punishment due them in order to obtain their peace (Isa. 52:13–53:12). Through the obedience of the Lord's chosen Servant, Israel's service as a light to the nations will be realized. Through the election of this Servant, God's election of Israel will find its fulfillment, and the blessing of salvation that He intends to extend through Israel to the nations will come to fruition.

While the rich implications of God's election of David's house and His chosen Servant are not fully disclosed in the Old Testament, the New Testament clearly views the coming of Christ as the fulfillment of the promises regarding the Messianic Servant of the Lord. In the Gospel of Matthew, Isaiah's prophecy regarding the Lord's chosen Servant is directly applied to Jesus Christ. After Jesus' miracle of healing a man with a withered hand on the Sabbath, which provokes the Pharisees to seek to destroy Him, Matthew appeals to Isaiah 42:1-3. According to Matthew, Jesus is the 'chosen' servant of the Lord, who comes to proclaim justice to the Gentiles and who responds to those who oppose Him in meekness. Jesus is the true servant of the Lord, the One through whom God chooses to bring salvation to all peoples. Consistent with the teaching of the New Testament generally, all of the promises concerning the Messiah and Servant of the Lord are understood to find their fulfillment in Jesus Christ. Unlike other individuals whom the Lord elects to salvation and service, the Messianic Servant will be the unique instrument through whom salvation will come to Israel and the nations.[28]

Summary
Though it is generally recognized that the Old Testament's teaching regarding election focuses upon the history of redemption, particularly God's election of His chosen people, Israel, the fundamental assumption of the Old Testament is that God is the Sovereign Lord

---

28. Cf. Peterson, *Election and Free Will,* 45.

of creation and history. What takes place in the course of history does not occur fortuitously, but in accordance with God's plan and purpose. While the Old Testament primarily tells the story of God's redeeming acts in respect to Israel, the narrative presumes that these acts find their deepest source in God's eternal counsel. As B. B. Warfield observes:

> Throughout the Old Testament, behind the processes of nature, the march of history and the fortunes of each individual life alike, there is steadily kept in view the governing hand of God working out His preconceived plan—a plan broad enough to embrace the whole universe of things, minute enough to concern itself with the smallest details, and actualizing itself with inevitable certainty in every event that comes to pass.[29]

For this reason, even though the Old Testament seldom speaks overtly about God's eternal decree in relation to the salvation of His people, the rudiments for a more developed formulation of this doctrine are clearly present.

The principal theme in the Old Testament view of election is God's sovereign, loving choice of His people Israel. Throughout the patriarchal narratives in Genesis and in the subsequent history of God's dealings with the nation of Israel, the theme of God's electing favor toward His people is pervasive. All of God's acts in respect to Israel find their deepest source in the distinguishing love and favor that He chooses to display toward this people. God's election of Israel is commonly explained as an act that has no other basis than God's sheer grace and undeserved love. Israel was not chosen because she was great in number or because she had commended herself to God's favor. Rather, God chose to grant her the privilege of being set apart for His possession, and called her to Himself as a treasured people. The calling of Abraham, Isaac, and Jacob attest that God's election is born out of His sovereign and free decision to embrace this people as His own. Though the election of Israel undergirds her calling to be consecrated to God's service, Israel was not chosen upon the basis of her holiness or any other circumstance that would distinguish her as worthy of this privilege.

---

29. Benjamin B. Warfield, 'Predestination,' in *The Works of Benjamin B. Warfield,* vol. 2: *Biblical Doctrines* (reprint; Grand Rapids: Baker Book House, 1981 [1929]), 13.

In recent treatments of the Old Testament's teaching regarding election, it is often argued that God's election of Israel was the election of a corporate people, and not the election of particular individuals. Furthermore, it is alleged that Israel's election was solely an election to service. Israel was elected in order to be an instrument of God's blessing to all the families and peoples of the earth, and not to enjoy the blessings of saving communion with God and all that such communion entails in the way of privilege.

The problem with these claims, however, is that they unnecessarily posit a dichotomy between corporate and individual election, as well as between an election to salvation and an election to service. The Old Testament clearly teaches that God's election of Israel included the election of particular individuals to saving blessings. Not all who belong to Israel corporately are in the narrower and more precise sense of the term elected unto saving blessings. From the beginning of God's dealings with His people Israel, it is evident that the promise of salvation is peculiarly extended, for example, to Isaac rather than Ishmael, and to Jacob rather than Esau. Consistent with this distinction between corporate Israel and those among this people who were the peculiar objects of God's electing favor, the theme of an 'elect remnant' becomes increasingly prominent throughout Israel's history, especially in the latter prophets. Perhaps the most dramatic illustration of this emphasis upon an elect remnant is the teaching regarding God's election of His 'chosen Servant' through whom His promises to Israel would be fulfilled. None of this militates against the truth that God's election of Israel would ultimately be the means by which all of the families of the earth would know the blessing of salvation. But it does illustrate how the election of Israel as a corporate people is not inconsistent with the election of particular individuals among this people for special favor. Nor is it inconsistent with the larger theme of God's intention to extend His grace to all the peoples of the earth through the instrument of His people Israel.

In the next two chapters, which summarize the New Testament's teaching regarding election, we will see how these features of the Old Testament's teaching are appropriated and clarified. Though the New Testament offers a more developed doctrine of election, we will discover that the principal features of its teaching on election are a further elaboration of themes already present in the Old Testament.

CHAPTER 2

The Doctrine of Election in the New Testament

B. B. WARFIELD employed a striking analogy about the doctrine of election. He wrote that the teaching in the Old Testament is like a richly furnished but dimly lit room compared to the same room, which is brightly lit in the New Testament.[1] His point is that all the features are already present in the Old Testament's teaching, but cannot be clearly seen without the brighter light of the New Testament. The Old Testament's teaching regarding God's purpose in the election of Israel is preparatory to the fulfillment of that purpose in the coming of Christ in the New Testament. The New Testament continues redemption's story as it culminates in the coming of Jesus Christ and clarifies the roots of this story in God's eternal plan. While the Old Testament doctrine of election stays largely within the boundaries of what takes place in redemptive history, the New Testament teaches more overtly that this history accords with God's eternal purpose to save His people in and for the sake of the work of Jesus Christ.

In my summary of the teaching of the New Testament, I will roughly follow the arrangement of the New Testament canon.[2] In this chapter,

---

1. Benjamin Breckinridge Warfield, *The Works of Benjamin B. Warfield,* vol. 2: *Biblical Doctrines* (reprint; Grand Rapids: Baker Book House, 1981 [1929]), 141.

2. For surveys of the New Testament's teaching regarding the doctrine of election, see Klein, *The New Chosen People,* 63-256; Peterson, *Election and Free Will,* 53-124; Williams, *The Election of Grace,* 59-102; Warfield, *The Works of Benjamin B. Warfield,* 2:32-67; Thomas R. Schreiner and Bruce A. Ware, eds. *The Grace of God, the Bondage of the Will,* (Grand Rapids: Baker Books, 1995), 47-200; and Steven J.

I will begin with a survey of the doctrine of election in the Synoptic Gospels, the book of Acts, the Gospel of John, the general epistles, and the book of Revelation. Because Paul's epistles contain the most extensive treatments of election found anywhere in the Scriptures, they warrant particular attention and will be examined in the next chapter.

Election in the Synoptic Gospels and Acts

Though the Synoptic Gospels (Matthew, Mark, and Luke) and the book of Acts do not speak often or at length regarding election, they do include a number of important references to God's gracious choice to save His elect people. These references evidence how God's gracious election accounts for the fact that those called to faith in Jesus Christ, whether Jews or Gentiles, are brought to faith and preserved in it by virtue of God's gracious choice to grant them salvation. In a comprehensive fashion, the Synoptic Gospels uniformly represent the person and work of Christ as a fulfillment of Old Testament promises. God's election of His chosen people Israel finds its culmination in the sending and electing of His Son, the true Messianic King and chosen Servant, through whom God's gracious purposes of redemption for all nations will be realized. The book of Acts, the account of the apostles' ministry, demonstrates that the gathering of the church, beginning in Jerusalem but eventually extending to the ends of the earth, is entirely a work of God's grace in Christ by the power of the Spirit. All who respond to the gospel in faith and repentance do so in consequence of God's having elected and appointed them to eternal life.

For the purpose of my survey, I will begin with a consideration of three types of passages in the Synoptic Gospels that are of particular importance to the doctrine of election. I will then treat two passages in Acts that view the salvation of believers as rooted in God's sovereign and gracious appointment of them to eternal life.

Many are Called, Few Are Chosen (Matthew 22:14)

Jesus' parable of the wedding banquet in Matthew 22:1-14 is one among a number of similar parables in the Synoptic Gospels. Like those in Luke 14:7-24 and Luke 15:11-32, this parable compares the joy

Lawson, *Foundations of Grace,* vol. 1: *A Long Line of Godly Men* (Lake Mary, FL: Reformation Trust, 2006), 241-440.

of restored fellowship with God in His kingdom to the celebration of a wedding feast. The kingdom of God is likened to a king who sends his servants out to extend a gracious invitation to a wedding feast he has prepared for them. Though some refuse the king's invitation, others respond favorably and join the king at the feast. At the conclusion of Matthew's account of Jesus' parable, we are told that the king discovers a man among the invited guests who is not dressed in an appropriate wedding garment. The parable concludes with the king instructing his attendants to cast this man out of the banquet hall into 'outer darkness' where there will be 'weeping and gnashing of teeth' (v. 13). Jesus then draws a contrast between those whom the king graciously invited to the feast, the 'many' who were 'called' [*kletoi*], and those who properly belong at the feast, the 'few' who were 'chosen' [*eklektoi*] (v. 14).

Within the context of the Gospel of Matthew, this parable is clearly to be read against the background of the opposition to Jesus' ministry and teaching on the part of the chief priests, Pharisees, and Sadducees (Matt. 21:45-46; 22:15, 23). The failure of many to respond properly to the king's gracious invitation represents the failure of many among the people of Israel to respond in faith to Jesus' teaching. In this respect, the parable accents the way God graciously summons many to the banquet feast, but among those invited there are some who prove unwilling to come in response to the invitation extended to them. Even among those who come to the feast, some do not come dressed in the wedding garment provided for the king's guests. Because the parable clearly emphasizes the responsibility of those invited to come to the banquet, some interpreters argue that the distinction between those 'called' and those 'chosen' at the end of the parable says nothing about God's sovereign election. For example, commenting on this passage, William Klein argues that

> The chosen ones are marked out because they alone responded to the invitation *in the proper way*. ... People acquire 'chosenness' at some point in their lives. The Jews had every opportunity to enter the sphere of the elect, but they refused God's invitations. The disciples accepted the invitation and therefore are among the chosen few.[3]

---

3. Klein, *The New Chosen People,* 56.

While Klein is undoubtedly correct in his emphasis upon the necessity of a proper response to the king's invitation, his explanation of the reason some respond improperly whereas others respond properly does not do justice to the language Jesus uses at the end of the parable. Klein's interpretation fails to adequately appreciate the contrast in language between those who are 'called' and those who are 'chosen'. Contrary to Klein's view, the actor in both the 'calling' of many and the 'choosing' of a few is the king. Just as the king takes the initiative in extending the call to the banquet he has prepared, so the king takes the initiative in electing a few to enjoy that blessing. In Klein's view, the king doesn't really 'elect' anyone. The king only ratifies after the fact the good response of the few who accept his invitation. Rather than electing some from among the larger number of those whom he invites, the king merely acknowledges those who meet the requirements for admission.

Admittedly, the parable in Matthew 22 does not give a fulsome statement of God's purpose of election. But it does give a clear indication that the same God who issues a gracious summons to the banquet also chooses to grant some of those He invites to receive this invitation with gladness and enjoy the benefits that it promises.

The Preservation of the Elect in the Midst of Tribulation

Another significant passage in the Synoptic Gospels on the subject of election is the well-known 'Olivet Discourse' in Mark 13:20-27 (and its parallel in Matthew 24:22, 24, 31). This passage records the discourse of Jesus on the Mount of Olives in answer to His disciples' question about His prophecy of the temple's impending destruction. It is sometimes termed the 'Little Apocalypse', as it comprehensively describes the signs that will precede and accompany the temple's destruction, as well as the circumstances at Christ's coming and the end of the present age.

While the Olivet Discourse is notoriously difficult to interpret, our interest in it stems from the way Jesus speaks three times in this passage of the 'elect' people of God. According to Jesus' teaching, when the temple is destroyed, the faithful will experience 'such tribulation as has not been from the beginning of the world that God created until now, and never will be' (v. 19). After this prophecy of the tribulation God's people will experience, Jesus assures His disciples that God will graciously 'shorten' these days to ensure the salvation of 'the elect': 'And if the Lord had not cut short the days, no human being would be saved. But for the sake of the elect, whom he chose, he shortened the days' (v. 20). Though the severe tribulation that will accompany the temple's destruction will threaten the salvation of anyone who endures it, God will intervene in such a way as to preserve the elect.

After this initial reference to the elect, Jesus adds another warning that 'false Christs' and 'false prophets' will arise in the future. These false Christs and prophets will 'perform signs and wonders to lead astray, if possible, the elect' (v. 22). After this warning, Jesus encourages His listeners to be on their guard. To be forewarned is to be forearmed. He does not teach that the elect will in fact be led astray. He issues the warning to reassure His audience that God's elect will be protected and kept in the salvation that God has granted to them. While some interpreters of this passage argue that it leaves open the possibility that even God's elect could be led astray and lose their salvation,[4] Jesus' language expresses His confidence that this will not be possible. Though the deceivers may seek to lead the elect astray, Jesus' words declare His conviction that this eventuality is impossible. Because God's elect are kept from being deceived by these false teachers and their performance of powerful signs and wonders, they will not be led away by them.[5]

---

4. Cf., e.g., I. Howard Marshall, *Kept by the Power of God: A Study of Perseverance and Falling Away* (London: Epworth Press, 1969), 54: 'The possibility that the elect may be led astray cannot be ruled out, although the form of expression certainly suggests that the possibility is a remote one.' According to Marshall, the interpretation of Jesus' words depends upon whether the language, 'if possible,' expresses the opinion of the deceivers or the opinion of Jesus. In the first instance, the deceivers clearly believe that the possibility of apostasy is real; otherwise they would not seek to deceive the elect. Though this is undoubtedly true, the language, 'if it be possible,' is Jesus' way of expressing His opinion that such a possibility is ruled out by God's gracious election and its consequences.

5. Leon Morris, *The Gospel According to Matthew*, PNTC (Grand Rapids: Eerdmans, 1992), 607: 'Since the elect are God's own, and are kept by the power of God, it will not be possible for them to be led away by these charlatans.' Cf. Peterson, *Election and Free Will*, 54: 'The words "if possible" are more naturally interpreted as expressing Jesus' mind. I say this because Jesus is the speaker for Mark 13:14-20 and he carefully introduces words of deceivers in v. 21.'

The third statement in the Olivet Discourse supports this understanding of Jesus' teaching about the circumstances at the time of the 'coming' of the Son of Man 'in clouds with great power and glory' (v. 26). When the Son of Man comes in the latter days, the creation itself will be caught up in the momentous consummation of God's saving work: 'the sun will be darkened and the moon will not give its light, and the stars will be falling from heaven, and the powers in the heavens will be shaken' (v. 25). Despite the tumult and shaking that will accompany the coming of the Son of Man, Jesus assures His audience again that God's elect will not be shaken or lose their salvation. For at His coming, the Son of Man will send out His angels 'and gather the elect from the four winds, from the ends of the earth to the ends of heaven' (v. 27).[6] By means of this prophecy, Jesus reinforces what He has already prophesied regarding the preservation of God's elect. Despite all the tribulation and deception that faces God's elect, nothing will cause them to fall away through unbelief and lose the salvation that they have received. God will so superintend what takes place that they will be guarded unto the time of Christ's coming. As the beneficiaries of God's electing and preserving grace, they will not be lost or deprived of the salvation to which they are called.

Three aspects of Jesus' teaching about election in this passage are worthy of notice. First, when Jesus speaks of the 'elect' or those whom God has chosen, He does not offer an explanation of this language, as though it were unfamiliar to Him or to His audience. He simply assumes that His listeners are familiar with the common Old Testament teaching regarding God's election of His chosen people for salvation. Second, though Jesus is speaking directly to His disciples, who represent the nucleus of the New Testament church as the true Israel of God, He describes the elect in terms that imply they are drawn from all nations and peoples of the earth. This is consistent with Jesus' earlier declaration that the 'gospel of the kingdom will be proclaimed throughout the whole world as a testimony to the nations,

---

6. Though dispensationalists interpret the 'elect' in this passage to refer to elect Jews in a future millennial period that follows Christ's second coming, I am convinced that Jesus is referring to all the elect, Jews and Gentiles alike, who will be gathered together at the time of Christ's second coming. For a critical assessment of the dispensational position, see Cornelis P. Venema, *The Promise of the Future* (Edinburgh: The Banner of Truth Trust, 2000), 245-95.

and then the end will come' (Matt. 24:14). Upon the foundation of the apostles' teaching, Christ will build His church of the elect from all peoples of the earth (cf. Matt. 16:13-20), whom the angels will gather from the 'four winds' at the coming of the Son of Man. Within the setting of the Gospel of Matthew, Jesus' description of this gathering can only be understood as a confirmation that He is the Son of Man who fulfills the Old Testament promises regarding the gathering of God's elect, whether Jews or Gentiles, from all the nations. And third, Jesus' teaching in this passage is consistent with a theme that we observed in our treatment of the Old Testament's teaching about election. Though there is a legitimate sense in which we may speak of the election of Israel and of the church as a corporate election of a people, this passage clearly emphasizes the specific persons among Israel and other peoples who are the peculiar objects of God's electing grace. Not all of the people of Israel are included in the elect. Nor are all members of the nations of the earth regarded as the elect. In this parable, Jesus views the elect in the precise sense of the true members of the church whom God elects to save in the proper sense of the word.

The Election of Christ

The teaching of the Synoptic Gospels regarding election also includes God's choice of Jesus Christ as His beloved Son and Servant through whom His saving purpose is accomplished. In our treatment of the Old Testament's teaching about election, we noted that it included the election of a Messianic King from the house of David who would be the Lord's chosen Servant through whom salvation would come to Israel and to all the nations of the earth. In the Synoptic Gospels, we are told that the Old Testament promise of the Messianic King and chosen Servant of the Lord finds its fulfillment in God's Son and His ministry on behalf of His people. The election of Christ is not an election unto salvation, but an election to service in accomplishing God's gracious purpose of election for all those whom He came to save. Three passages in the Synoptic Gospels speak expressly of the election of Christ in these terms.

The first of these passages is Matthew 12:15-21, which associates Jesus' ministry with the promise in Isaiah 42:1-3 regarding the Lord's 'chosen Servant'. The setting of this passage is Jesus' miraculous healing on the Sabbath of a man who came to Him with a withered hand. When the Pharisees in the synagogue witness this act, they began to conspire against Jesus and plot ways to destroy Him. Jesus responds to the Pharisees' opposition by withdrawing from the synagogue, healing many who followed after Him, and instructing His disciples not to make Him known. In his account of these events, Matthew declares that it all occurred in fulfillment of what the Lord had promised through Isaiah:

> This was to fulfill what was spoken by the prophet Isaiah: 'Behold, my servant whom I have chosen, my beloved with whom my soul is well pleased. I will put my Spirit upon him and he will proclaim justice to the Gentiles.'

According to Matthew, Jesus is the elect Servant of God whom He chose as His instrument to bring justice to the Gentiles, and in whom the Gentiles will place their hope (Matt. 12:21). Through the ministry of Jesus, the promise the Lord made to His people in the days of Isaiah are now being fulfilled. Through the Servant whom the Lord appointed, and with whom He is well pleased, God's gracious intention to save His people, Jews and Gentiles alike, is being brought to fruition.

The second passage, Luke 9:35, occurs within the context of Jesus' transfiguration. The event occurs at an important moment in Jesus' ministry. Prior to it, Luke records Peter's crucial confession that He is 'the Christ of God', as well as Jesus' prophecy of His impending death and subsequent resurrection on the third day. In the immediate context, Luke also records Jesus' call to His disciples to take up their cross and follow Him, a call buttressed by a warning that Jesus will be ashamed of those who are ashamed of Him when He comes as the Son of Man 'in his glory and the glory of the Father and of the holy angels' (Luke 9:18-27). Luke introduces his account of the transfiguration by noting that it was 'about eight days after these sayings that he took with him Peter and John and James and went up on the mountain to pray' (v. 28). The transfiguration is an event that takes place against the background of these sayings, and it confirms Jesus' true identity as the Son of God.

According to Luke's account, while Jesus and the disciples with Him were praying on the mountain, Jesus' appearance was 'altered, and his clothing became dazzling white' (v. 29). Concomitant with this alteration of Jesus' appearance, two men are seen to join Jesus, Moses and Elijah, the two great and paradigmatic prophets of the Old Testament economy. When Peter and those with Jesus awaken from a deep sleep into which they had fallen, they see Jesus' glorious appearance and the two who are with Him. As Peter suggests that three tents be built for Jesus, Moses and Elijah, 'a cloud came and overshadowed them, and they were afraid as they entered the cloud. And a voice came out of the cloud, saying, "This is my Son, my Chosen One, listen to him!"' (vv. 34-35).

The significance of this passage cannot be overstated. At a critical point in Jesus' ministry, the transfiguration authenticates Jesus' claim to be the Son of God, who was sent into the world in order to accomplish His saving purpose. God Himself descends in the form of a glory cloud and testifies that Jesus is indeed His Son, the One whom He has chosen to be the great Redeemer who will fulfill what was promised through the prophets of the Old Testament. The Father's declaration concerning Jesus as His chosen One also identifies Him as a prophet greater than Moses or Elijah or any Old Testament prophet.[7] Because Jesus is the Son of God, the One whom the Father has chosen and sent into the world as the Redeemer and Prophet of God, He is to be received as such. He is elected to be the instrument through whom God will save His people and who bears the Father's imprimatur. Remarkably, the Father's testimony regarding His 'chosen' One follows the appearance of Moses and Elijah, the two representatives of God's Old Testament prophets, whom Luke tells us were speaking together of Jesus' impending 'departure' (v. 31). The term used for 'departure' in the Greek literally describes Jesus' death as His *exodus*.[8] The history of God's chosen people Israel is, therefore, regarded as a kind of typological prefigurement of God's Son, the true Israelite, who was chosen to bring His people out of their bondage in sin and redeem them for God's own possession.

---

7. Though it is not expressly stated, the language, 'listen to him,' recalls the promise of Deuteronomy 18:15 that the Lord would send to His people Israel a prophet greater than Moses to whom they were to listen.

8. Cf. Peterson, *Election and Free Will*, 58: 'Jesus' death is the New Testament *exodus* that will redeem all who believe in Christ.'

The third passage in the Synoptic Gospels that speaks of Jesus' election is Luke 23:35. This passage is also located at a particularly important moment in the course of Jesus' ministry. Luke records that while the people witnessed Jesus' crucifixion, 'the rulers scoffed at him, saying, "He saved others; let him save himself, if he is the Christ of God, his Chosen One!"' Though none of the other Gospels single out the rulers of the people in their accounts of the mockery Jesus endured upon the cross, Luke does so to remind his readers of the way these rulers offer unwitting testimony to the truth concerning Jesus' identity and work. These rulers recall the witness of the Father concerning His Son whom He elected to be the Redeemer of His people. Though their mockery is born of unbelief, Luke's account of it underscores that Jesus' death (and resurrection on the third day) took place according to the Father's gracious purpose to provide salvation for this people.[9] Jesus is truly the Christ of God, the Messianic King whom the Father elected to be the Savior of His people.

These passages testifying to the Father's election of Christ can only be fully appreciated against the background of the Old Testament's teaching and are consistent with the general claim of the New Testament Gospels that Christ is the promised Messiah and Servant of God. In the coming and ministry of Jesus Christ, God's election of Israel, and especially of the chosen Servant through whom redemption would come through Israel to all the peoples, finds its fulfillment. Consistent with the Old Testament promise of the coming Messiah and Servant of God, Jesus Christ's election is, strictly speaking, an election to service. He is the chosen Son and Servant of God who will be the instrument through whom redemption will be accomplished for God's elect people. Unlike the election of God's people to salvation in Christ, the election of Christ is an election to a particular ministry. While Christ's election highlights the Father's sovereign freedom in choosing Him for His appointed ministry, it is not in His case an election to salvation.[10] Rather, it is His election to be the One through whom God's elect obtain salvation.

---

9. Interestingly, Luke later provides an account of how many of these rulers came to faith and salvation in Christ (cf. Acts 6:7).

10. Paul Jewett, *Election and Predestination* (Grand Rapids: Eerdmans, 1985), 55, offers a helpful description of the dissimilarity and similarity between the election

Election in the Book of Acts

The book of Acts bears the title, 'The Acts of the Apostles,' because it recounts the foundational epoch of Jesus Christ gathering the church from among the nations through the ministry of His chosen apostles. Though this title accurately reflects the book's content, it is clear from the narrative in Acts that this church-gathering work is comprehensively the work of the triune God. Luke begins his account by describing the way the risen Christ, prior to His ascension into heaven and departure, gives 'commands through the Holy Spirit to the apostles whom he had chosen' (Acts 1:2). Though these commands are not explicitly identified, the context makes clear that they focused upon Christ's commission to make disciples in His name from among all the nations. The apostles are instructed to wait in Jerusalem for the fulfillment of the Father's promise that they would be 'baptized with the Spirit' (Acts 1:5). When the apostles inquire whether Jesus will immediately 'restore the kingdom to Israel,' they are told that it is not for them to know the 'times or season that the Father has fixed by his own authority' (Acts 1:7). Jesus' implication becomes clear when He speaks of the Spirit's outpouring upon them that will empower them to be His witnesses: 'But you will receive power when the Holy Spirit has come upon you, and you will be my witnesses in Jerusalem and in all Judea and Samaria, and to the end of the earth' (Acts 1:8). After Jesus makes this promise, Luke gives an account of Jesus' ascension and the subsequent gathering of the believers in Jerusalem to wait for Pentecost and the fulfillment of His promise. The baptism of the Holy Spirit, recorded in chapter 2, completes what might be described as the introduction to the story that unfolds throughout the book of Acts.

---

of Christ and the election of God's people: 'It is not what we are *delivered from* but what we are *elected to* that is the element common to the election of Christ and his people. As we are elected to life, so is Christ our Lord, who triumphed over death in the resurrection. Yet there is obviously a difference between the Head and the members of the body in this respect as in all others. We are elect as living stones, but Christ is elect and precious as the chief Cornerstone' (emphasis his). Cf. also Calvin, *Institutes,* 3.22.1, who draws a comparison between the Father's free and sovereign election of His Son to His office as incarnate Redeemer and the free and sovereign election of His people to salvation in Him. As we shall see in a subsequent chapter, Augustine was fond of citing the election of Christ as an illustration of the gratuitous, non-meritorious nature of the election of believers. Though Christ's election was an election to service, it was nonetheless a free and sovereign act of God the Father.

This brief summary of the opening of Acts sets the stage for our consideration of two key passages in the book that speak of God's gracious purpose of election. Though these two passages are of special importance to the subject of election, they do not stand alone within the story recounted in the book of Acts. Rather, they are at home within the framework of Luke's emphasis upon the gathering of the church as a comprehensive work of the triune God. The ministry of Christ's apostles is carried out in the power of the Spirit who is poured out upon the whole church (cf. Acts 2:1-4). Without the empowerment of the Spirit, whom the Father promised and the Son bestowed, the preaching and teaching of the gospel of the kingdom would bear no fruit. Christ Himself gathers His church and sends His Spirit to make the apostles' witness powerful unto salvation for those who believe and repent. Consistent with this emphasis upon the gathering of the church as a work of the triune God – rooted in the Father's promise, based upon the ascended Christ's granting of the Spirit, and effected in the power of the Spirit of the ascended Christ – the apostle Peter declares in his Pentecost sermon that this work has its source in the 'definite plan and foreknowledge of God' (Acts 2:23).[11] The story that is told in the book of Acts is, accordingly, a story that unfolds according to the eternal purposes of the triune God. What takes place in redemption's history, now culminating in gathering the church from all nations, occurs by God's gracious initiative and sovereign power. The gathering of the church in this epochal period (and ever since) is God's achievement, even though it takes place through the ministry of apostles whom Christ has commissioned and empowered for the task.[12]

Within the framework of this view of the gathering of the church, it is not surprising the book of Acts includes two passages that expressly speak of God's gracious purpose of election in relation to the salvation

---

11. Calvin, *The Acts of the Apostles,* CNTC, 6:65, offers the following helpful comment on this language: 'From this we may deduce a general doctrine that God shows forth His providence no less in governing the whole world than in ordaining the death of Christ. It therefore belongs to God not only to foreknow the future, but of His own will to ordain what He will have take place.'

12. Cf. Harry Boer, *Pentecost and Missions* (Grand Rapids: Eerdmans, 1961), 109-10: 'It is *at Pentecost* that the witness of the Church began, and it is *in the power of the Pentecostal Spirit* that this witness continues to be carried forward' (emphasis his).

of those who believe and repent at the preaching of the gospel. These passages provide the deepest explanation for the way the book of Acts describes the Lord's work in adding daily to the church 'those who were being saved' (Acts 2:47; cf. Acts 5:14; 6:7; 11:18; 12:24; 16:5, 14; 19:20).

The first of these passages, Acts 13:48, is found at the mid-point of the story told in Acts. Consistent with Christ's promise regarding the way the Holy Spirit would empower the apostolic ministry of the gospel, this passage is within the context of the gospel's reach beyond Jerusalem and Samaria to Pisidian Antioch. Even though many among God's ancient people, Israel, were resisting the gospel message in unbelief, Paul and Barnabas boldly pressed on and were increasingly 'turning to the Gentiles' (Acts 13:46). Noting that the salvation of the Gentiles was a fulfillment of the Lord's promise to Israel, Paul and Barnabas appeal to the prophecy of Isaiah 49:6: 'I have made you a light for the Gentiles, that you may bring salvation to the ends of the earth' (Acts 13:47). When the Gentiles hear these words, Luke records that they began to rejoice and glorify the word of God 'and as many as were appointed to eternal life believed. And the word of the Lord was spreading through the whole region' (Acts 13:48-49). In a simple, straightforward way, Luke views the fact that many Gentiles believed to be evidence that God had appointed them to believe and thereby be saved. Although Luke's language does not expressly speak of God's 'electing' them to salvation, he clearly conveys the same idea: they believed in consequence of God's having appointed or elected them to believe and so be saved.

While this passage seems straightforward upon first reading, some interpreters do not concede that it teaches God's ordination of some Gentiles to faith and salvation. Among these, William G. MacDonald notes that the verbal form Luke uses, *tetagmenoi,* could be translated in the passive ('were appointed') or middle voice ('appointed themselves'). If we opt for the middle voice, then Luke is only saying that 'as many as were putting themselves in a position for eternal life believe'.[13] On this translation of Luke's language, God does not appoint these Gentiles to believe the gospel and be saved. Rather,

---

13. William G. MacDonald, 'The Biblical Doctrine of Election,' in *GGWM,* 227. I am not aware of any reputable translations of Acts 13:48 that correspond to MacDonald's.

they appoint or position themselves in such a way that they come to believe the gospel message. This translation and interpretation turn the passage on its head, however, and are inconsistent with the way Acts describes God's gracious initiative in granting faith to those whom He calls and saves through the gospel Word.[14] The believing response to the gospel message of these Gentiles is indispensable to their salvation, but the response itself is the result of God's prior action in appointing them to believe.

Another interpreter, Howard Marshall, acknowledges that this text 'could be taken in the sense that God had predestined certain of them [Gentiles] to believe', but he suggests that this is subject to dispute in the light of alternative interpretations.[15] According to Marshall, these Gentiles were already proselytes and worshippers of God. Since there 'is no suggestion that they received salvation independently of their own act of conscious faith', he believes that this passage does not support the theological assumption that God's election or predestination is independent of, or prior to, their believing response.[16] While Marshall is undoubtedly correct in asserting that these Gentiles were saved as they believed the gospel message, he betrays his own dogmatic prejudice by denying that their faith was itself the result of God's prior appointment of them to this response.

The second important passage on election in the book of Acts is found in Acts 18:9-10. This passage is found within the context of

14. Williams, *The Election of Grace,* 64, fn13: 'The text in question should certainly not be interpreted independently of the wider Lukan witness.' See also F. F. Bruce, *Commentary on the Book of Acts,* IVPNCS (London and Edinburgh: Marshall, Morgan and Scott, 1954), 283fn62; and William J. Larkin, *Acts* (Downers Grove, IL: InterVarsity Press, 1995), 207.

15. *Acts* (Leicester: Intervarsity, 1980), 231. For a similar interpretation of this verse, see Matthew W. Bates, *Salvation by Allegiance Alone: Rethinking Faith, Works, and the Gospel of Jesus the King* (Grand Rapids: Baker Academic, 2017), 171fn11. Though Bates acknowledges that Acts 13:48 is the 'closest the Bible comes to affirming individual predestining election', he insists that the 'timing of this appointment is not specified other than that it is prior to or simultaneous with these individuals giving *pistis.*' Ironically, while Bates accuses the predestinarian interpretation of this text of ascribing 'inappropriate temporal and theological weight to it', his own interpretation reflects a theological bias when he suggests that the divine appointment of some to faith could be 'simultaneous' with their decision to believe. This is not what the text says, however. Those who believe do so in consequence of God's appointment of them to faith.

16. Marshall, *Acts,* 231.

Luke's account of Paul's preaching in Corinth, where the response to his preaching is similar to that in Pisidian Antioch. On the one hand, many Jewish members of the synagogue oppose and revile Paul for his preaching that Jesus was the Christ (Acts 18:5-6). On the other hand, many Gentiles in Corinth believe and are baptized. In this setting, Luke records that the Lord came to Paul in a vision and encouraged him to continue boldly preaching the gospel. Paul should do so, says the Lord, 'for I am with you, and no one will attack you to harm you, for I have many in this city who are my people' (Acts 18:9-10). In response to this encouragement, Paul remained in Corinth for a year and six months, preaching and teaching the Word of God. The Lord encourages Paul by sharing that He has many people marked out for salvation among the Corinthians. Paul should continue, therefore, for the sake of this people and in the confidence that they will respond favorably to his preaching. While this passage also does not speak expressly of God's election, it clearly teaches that God knows His people in Corinth before Paul preaches to them and they respond favorably to his preaching.

Though this passage, like Acts 13:48, seems fairly clear in its implications for the doctrine of election, it too has received a mixed reception among interpreters. According to some, the 'many people' in Corinth to whom the Lord refers are those whom the Lord foreknows will respond in faith to Paul's preaching. Because the Lord knows in advance who among the Corinthians will believe at Paul's preaching, He is able to encourage Paul by assuring him that He has many people in Corinth. In defense of this interpretation, Howard Marshall writes:

> 'I am with you ... I have many people in this city.' The 'many people' are usually and rightly regarded as people who would form Paul's field for evangelism and not as the many who had already believed (Acts 18:8). Hence the forces of evil would not prevent Paul from accomplishing the work given to him by God. Divine foreknowledge is accordingly taught in this verse, but it is not necessary to assume that a rigid predestination is present also.[17]

Marshall's comments about this passage are problematic in at least two respects. First, the Lord's encouragement to Paul does not mention

---

17. Marshall, *Kept by the Power of God,* 85.

anything about God's foreknowledge of their believing response to His message.[18] No doubt God knows in advance who among the Corinthians will respond in faith to Paul's preaching. It is also true that such a believing response is indispensable to their salvation. But the Lord's encouragement speaks of 'many in the city who are my people'. These people are identified as belonging to the Lord in advance of Paul's preaching to them, and therefore also in advance of their response to his apostolic preaching. The point of the Lord's encouragement is that there are many in Corinth who belong to Him, and because they belong to Him they will respond appropriately to the preaching of the gospel. Nothing is said to Paul about the Lord's knowing in advance that they will believe. They are not said to be His people because they believe, but they believe because they belong to God. And second, Marshall's interpretation pejoratively labels the alternative view a 'rigid predestinarianism'. Though Marshall does not elaborate on the meaning of this language, the alternative view does not deny the indispensability of Paul's preaching as well as the response of faith on the part of some Corinthians to the gospel's invitation. Rather, it merely insists that the Lord's encouragement to Paul is based upon the fact that there are many in Corinth whom He has purposed to save. Because this is the case, Paul can carry out his ministry without fear of failure. Paul can preach with the assurance that all those whom the Lord has already chosen will believingly respond to his message.

When these two passages are placed within the context of the story that is told in the book of Acts, it becomes apparent that the gathering of the church through the ministry of Christ's apostles is in the most profound sense a work of the triune God. In fulfillment of the Father's promise, Christ's Spirit empowers the apostles in their witness and draws those whom God has elected to save to respond in

---

18. Peterson, *Election and Free Will,* 71: 'It is true that the "many ... people" referred to in Acts 18:10 had not yet believed. But the text says nothing about God's foreseeing their faith. Rather, God reveals to Paul that many people in Corinth belonged to God even before they believed in order to embolden Paul to keep preaching the gospel there in difficult circumstances. Of course, they had not yet believed—but God had claimed them in advance by his grace; and when Paul preached to them, they would believe.' Cf. Larkin, *Acts,* 265: 'The Lord's predestination (13:48) not only guarantees an effective ministry but demands that Paul responsibly fulfill his obligation to witness.'

the way of faith and repentance. Just as God's determinate counsel and foreknowledge provides the ultimate explanation for the crucifixion of Christ on behalf of His people, so it provides the ultimate explanation for the gathering of His chosen people from all the nations and peoples of the earth.[19]

Election in the Gospel of John

Among the New Testament gospels, the Gospel of John provides some of the most rich and significant teaching regarding God's gracious purpose of election in Christ.[20] Though the Gospel of John is sometimes overlooked in deference to Paul's epistles, this Gospel testifies that Christ's coming into the world was an expression of God the Father's gracious plan and purpose to send Christ into the world to save those whom He chooses to give Him. Though the language of 'election' is not typically used in the Gospel of John, the idea of God's eternal purpose to save a particular people through the Word become flesh is a central theme throughout the fourth Gospel.

The Prologue (John 1)

The prologue to the Gospel of John is well-known. What is not so often recognized, however, is how this prologue locates the work of Christ within the framework of the Father's election to send His eternal Word into the world to save those who dwell in darkness.[21] The prologue's first words recall the opening verses of Genesis and serves as a kind of overture to God's work of creation: 'In the beginning was the Word, and the Word was with God, and the Word was God. He

---

19. The story told in the book of Acts reminds me of the Heidelberg Catechism, Question & Answer 54: 'What do you believe concerning the holy catholic church? That the Son of God, out of the whole human race, from the beginning to the end of the world, gathers, defends, and preserves for Himself, by His Spirit and Word, in the unity of the true faith, a Church chosen to everlasting life.'

20. For more extensive summaries of the teaching of the Gospel of John on the theme of election, see Bruce A. Ware, 'Divine Election to Salvation: Unconditional, Individual, and Infralapsarian,' in *Perspectives on Election,* ed. Chad Owen Brand (Nashville, TN: Broadman & Holman Academic, 2006), 1-58; and Robert W. Yarbrough, 'Divine Election in the Gospel of John,' in *GGBW,* 47-62.

21. When I take up Karl Barth's doctrine in a later chapter, we will see that Barth bases his revisionist doctrine of election in part upon a controversial interpretation of the prologue to John's Gospel.

was in the beginning with God' (v. 1). Just as God's work of creation is a work that He 'elects' to perform, so God's work in re-creation or redemption is a work that He elects to accomplish through the Word who 'became flesh and tabernacled among us' (v. 14). The eternal Word of God, in whom was life and whose life is 'the light of men', has shone forth into the darkness 'and the darkness has not overcome it' (v. 5). In a few short sentences, John's Gospel announces that God's work of redemption has its foundation in the self-determination of God the Father to send His eternal Word whose incarnation brings light to a world in darkness and life to a world under the sway of death. Through the witness of John the Baptist, whom God sent before Christ to announce His coming, the whole world was summoned to believe in the incarnate Word, and to behold 'his glory, glory as of the only Son from the Father, full of grace and truth' (v. 14).

In these well-known words of John's prologue, we glimpse what lies within the depths of God the Father's purposes of grace and truth, now revealed through the incarnation of the Word. Though no one has ever seen God as He is in Himself, the eternal Word, who is the 'only God, who is at the Father's side,' has made Him known (v. 18).[22] The intimate depths of God's grace and truth are openly displayed to us in the incarnation of the eternal Word, who is both the Creator of all things and the Savior of all who believe in Him. In the incarnation, God reveals Himself as the One who chooses to come to those dwelling in darkness. They have not taken the initiative to come to God but rather lie under the power of darkness, unwilling to receive Him (v. 11). Although the language of 'election' is not used, the idea is latent throughout the whole of John 1. Out of the depths of the intra-trinitarian communion between the Father, the eternal Word, and the Holy Spirit, God freely determines to make known His gracious purpose to save those who believe in the Son whom He has sent. What the incarnation reveals to humanity finds its source in the fullness of God's grace and truth that were known to the Son before His incarnation and communication of them to us.

---

22. The language, 'made him known,' could be rendered more literally, 'exegeted him.' The incarnate Son of God is the definitive 'exegesis' of the fullness of God's grace and truth.

But this is not all that John's prologue tells us about God's gracious election. We are also told that, when the Word became flesh, He was not received by all people. Even though He came into the world that He made, the world did not know Him. Indeed, though He came especially to 'his own people' (v. 11), they too did not receive Him. However, 'to all who did receive him, who believed in his name, he gave the right to become children of God, who were born, not of blood nor of the will of the flesh nor of the will of man, but of God' (vv. 12-13). In these remarkable words, which anticipate Christ's teaching in John 3:3-8 about the need for new birth through the Spirit, we see that those who receive Him do so by the will of God. Though it is necessary to believe in Him in order to have the right to be called children of God, no one believes in Him unless they are granted the new birth. This new birth is not the result of any human action or quality. It does not depend upon blood ties or natural descent from a common human father, such as Abraham (cf. John 8:33). Neither does it come about through an act of the will or decision to believe that lies within the power of the person who believes in Christ. Not at all. Even the power to believe is a free gift of God's gracious initiative. Unless God grants the new birth by His life-giving Spirit, no one would or could receive the fullness of grace and truth that are revealed through the Word.

John 6:35-45

While the prologue of the Gospel of John discloses the depths of God's grace and truth that led Him to send His Son in the fullness of time, there are also several passages in this Gospel that speak of the Father's eternal purpose to give to His Son those whom He has chosen to draw into fellowship with Himself.

The first of these passages is found in John 6:35-45, which records one of several 'I am' sayings of Jesus Christ, each of which confirms that He is the fulfillment of God's promises to the people of Israel. In this passage, John records Christ's declaration that 'it was not Moses who gave the bread from heaven, but my Father gives you the true bread from heaven. For the bread of God is he who comes down from heaven and gives life to the world' (vv. 32-33). When those who hear this declaration ask Jesus to give them this bread of life, He announces that 'I am the bread of life; whoever comes to me shall not hunger, and whoever believes in me shall never thirst' (v. 35).

Immediately after Jesus identifies Himself as the bread of life, He goes on to explain why some come to Him and others do not. Those who embrace Him as the bread of life are those whom the Father chooses to give to Him.

> All that the Father gives me will come to me, and whoever comes to me I will never cast out. For I have come down from heaven, not to do my own will but the will of him who sent me. And this is the will of him who sent me, that I should lose nothing of all that he has given me, but raise it up on the last day. For this is the will of my Father, that everyone who looks on the Son and believes in him, should have eternal life, and I will raise him up on the last day. (vv. 37-40)

In these striking words, Jesus offers an account of the reason some refuse to believe in Him while others come to Him in faith and obtain life. Although clearly emphasizing the responsibility of all to look to the Son and believe in Him unto eternal life, Jesus appeals to the 'will of the Father' to give to Him those whom He has purposed to save. What distinguishes those who come from those who do not come is the will of the Father. Furthermore, Jesus promises that those whom the Father gives to Him, and who therefore come to Him in faith, will not fall away. None of those persons whom the Father has purposed to give Him will be lost, for they will be raised up at the last day.[23] When many of the Jews grumble, Jesus reiterates the point that no one comes to Him unless drawn by the Father: 'No one can come to me unless the Father who sent me draws him. And I will raise him up on the last day' (v. 44). The failure of many to respond in faith to His claim to be the bread of life confirms the truth of His teaching. Though those who disbelieve are wholly culpable for their unwillingness to come to Him, their unbelief only underscores the point He wishes to make.[24]

---

23. Ware, 'Divine Election to Salvation,' 42-3, appeals to this passage as an especially clear instance of the teaching that God graciously elects specific persons to salvation: 'First, Jesus declares that *specific* persons are given to him by the Father. The point of Jesus saying what he does in verse 37 was so that the Jews who rejected Jesus would conclude that they have not been given to him. If they had been, they would have come.'

24. Cf. D. A. Carson, *The Gospel According to John,* PNTC (Grand Rapids: Eerdmans, 1991), 291: 'Divine sovereignty in salvation is a major theme in the Fourth Gospel. Morever [sic], the form of it in these verses, that there exists a group of people who have been given by the Father to the Son, and that this group will inevitably come

Those who come to Him in faith do so by virtue of the Father's will to give them to the Son and to keep them until the day of resurrection.[25]

John 10:1-30

In John 10:1-30, we find another discourse of Jesus that focuses upon one of His 'I am' sayings. The discourse begins by comparing those who belong to Jesus to sheep, all of whom enter through the sheepfold door provided by the shepherd. They are not like the thief who endeavors to obtain entry by climbing in 'by another way' (v. 1). Because the shepherd knows his sheep by name and they know his voice, those who belong to the shepherd respond to his voice and not to the voice of strangers (v. 5).

Upon hearing Jesus using this 'figure of speech', John notes that the crowd did not understand what Jesus was saying to them. And so Jesus offers them the following explanation:

> Truly, truly, I say to you, I am the door of the sheep. All who came before me are thieves and robbers, but the sheep did not listen to them. I am the door. If anyone enters by me, he will be saved and will go in and out and find pasture.... I am the good shepherd. The good shepherd lays down his life for his sheep.... I am the good shepherd. I know my own and my own know me, just as the Father knows me and I know the Father, and I lay down my life for the sheep. And I have other sheep that are not of this fold. I must bring them also, and they will listen to my voice. So there will be one flock, one shepherd. (John 10:7-16)

In the same way that a shepherd knows and loves his sheep, so Jesus knows and loves His sheep. His love for them is exhibited in His willingness to lay down His life for them. Indeed, in the same way the Father knows and loves the Son, the Son knows and loves His own. Likewise, the sheep know and respond to the voice of their shepherd

---

to the Son and be preserved by him, not only recurs in this chapter (v. 65) and perhaps in 10:29, but is strikingly central to the Lord's prayer in ch. 17 (vv. 1, 6, 9, 24 ...).'

25. Later in the discourse in John 6, Jesus says: 'No one can come to me unless the Father who sent me draws him. And I will raise him up on the last day' (v. 44). Yarbrough, 'Divine Election in the Gospel of John,' 50fn10, calls attention to the strong verb Jesus uses in this verse: '"Draw" in 6:44 translates the Greek *helkuō*.' Outside of John, it appears in the New Testament only at Acts 16:19: "they seized Paul and Silas and dragged them into the marketplace".... It is hard to avoid the impression that John 6:44 refers to a "forceful attraction" in bringing sinners to the Son.'

as those for whom Jesus lays down His life know and respond to His voice.

We are told that those who heard Jesus' words were eager for Him to explain Himself further. 'How long,' they ask, 'will you keep us in suspense? If you are the Christ, tell us plainly' (v. 24). Sensing that their question was not born of faith, but of unbelief, Jesus responds in a way that reveals the implications of what He had said about Himself as the Good Shepherd:

> The works that I do in my Father's name bear witness about me, but you do not believe because you are not part of my flock. My sheep hear my voice, and I know them, and they follow me. I give them eternal life, and they will never perish, and no one will snatch them out of my hand. My Father, who has given them to me, is greater than all, and no one is able to snatch them out of the Father's hand. I and the Father are one. (vv. 25-30)

With these words, Jesus clearly affirms that His Person and work are intimately joined with the Person and work of His Father. The Father, who knows and loves Him, has purposed to give to Him all those who belong to His sheepfold and for whom He lays down His life. By contrast, those who do not know Him, and who do not respond to His voice, are not of His sheepfold. Only His sheep hear His voice. Only those whom the Father chooses to give to Him will come to Him. Not one of those whom the Father gives Him will be snatched out of His Father's hand.

John 15:14-19

In John 15:14-19, yet another 'I am' passage provides some of Jesus' most explicit teaching on election in the Gospel of John. The passage opens with Jesus' statement, 'I am the true vine, and my Father is the vinedresser' (v. 1). When Jesus uses the image of the vine to describe those who belong to and abide in Him, He uses language familiar to His audience. In the Old Testament, God's chosen people, Israel, are the vine that God calls into existence and nurtures, pruning and providing for its life, nourishment and growth (Ps. 80; Isa. 3:14; 5:7). Thus, as with the other 'I am' sayings in the Gospel of John, this saying makes a sweeping claim regarding Jesus' Person and work. Jesus identifies Himself with the God of Israel and with the Lord's redemptive work throughout history until the time of His coming.

After Jesus identifies God as the vinedresser of His people who abide in Him, He tells His disciples that He lays down His life for His friends. 'Greater love has no one than this, that someone lays down his life for his friends. You are my friends if you do what I command you' (vv. 13-14). Jesus' willingness to lay down His life for those who are His friends carries with it their responsibility to respond in grateful obedience to His commands. However, this does not mean that the obedience of Jesus' disciples is a precondition for His love. Jesus follows this declaration of love for His friends by telling the disciples that they were 'elected' by Him. 'You did not choose me, but I chose you and appointed you that you should go and bear fruit and that your fruits should abide, so that whatever you ask the Father in my name, he will give it to you' (v. 16). Though the disciples' election and calling place them under an obligation to bear fruit, this obligation follows from their election and cannot therefore be the basis for their election. As D. A. Carson, puts it, commenting on this passage:

> The disciples cannot even legitimately boast that they are believers on the ground that they, unlike others, wisely made the right choice. On the contrary: Jesus chose them. Merit theology is thus totally savaged. On the other hand, that Jesus chose them does not entail a robot-like stance on the part of the disciples, but increased responsibility—responsibility to produce enduring fruit (15:16), to love each other (15:17). Election entails both privilege and responsibility.[26]

While the company of the disciples is the specific audience of Jesus' teaching about election in this passage, its teaching has broader application. All who are grafted into Christ, the true vine, are the beneficiaries of the gracious election of the Father and the Son. They do not choose to come to Christ, unless they are first chosen by Him.

Some interpreters of this passage, however, maintain that the election of the disciples was merely an election to a particular form of service to Jesus. Since we know that one of Jesus' disciples, Judas, would eventually betray Him and prove not to be a true disciple, Jesus' teaching about election in this passage is not about an election to salvation.[27]

---

26. Carson, *DSHR*, 191.
27. Klein, *The New Chosen People*, 132; and Roger T. Forster and V. Paul Marston, *God's Strategy in Human History* (Wheaton, IL: Tyndale House, 1973), 120.

In reply to those who maintain that Jesus speaks only of an election to privilege in John 15, it needs to be noted that Jesus identifies His disciples as those whom the world hates even as the world hates Him (v. 16). Since the disciples of whom He speaks are 'not of the world' but are 'chosen' by Christ, it should be expected that the world would hate them in the same way the world hates Christ Himself. The election of Jesus' disciples in John 15 is, therefore, an election to genuine fellowship with Christ, including fellowship with Him in His suffering. Admittedly, Jesus does speak elsewhere of an election of the twelve disciples (John 6:70), which includes Judas whom Jesus predicts would subsequently betray Him. For this reason, the election of which Jesus speaks in John 6:70 may not be identified with the election of which He speaks in John 15. In the former, it is indeed merely an election to service. This is evident not only from the prediction that Judas would betray Jesus, but also from a parallel passage in John 13:18 where, in the context of Jesus' washing of His disciples' feet, He distinguishes Judas from the other disciples by saying, 'I am not speaking of all of you; I know whom I have chosen' (cf. John 17:12) In this passage, Jesus distinguishes Judas whose election was to service as one of the twelve disciples from the other disciples whose election was both to salvation and service. By the time we come to Jesus' teaching in John 15, Judas has already left the company of the twelve in fulfillment of Jesus' prediction of His betrayal.[28]

John 17

The last passage in John's Gospel that bears upon the doctrine of election is John 17, which records what is commonly known as Jesus' 'high-priestly' prayer to His Father shortly before His arrest and crucifixion. This prayer echoes several themes already noted in the Gospel of John. Jesus identifies Himself as the One whom the Father has sent into the world to fulfill His saving purposes, which include the Father's determination to give Him a chosen people. Christ came

---

28. Peterson, *Election and Free Will*, 66-67: 'Jesus' choice in John 6:70 was a choice of twelve to be his disciples. His choice in 15:16, 19 is a choice of the eleven disciples "out of the world" that results in their no longer belonging to the world, but henceforth to Jesus. Furthermore, John 6:70 is not parallel to John 15:16, but it is parallel to John 13:18 where, after washing his disciples' feet, Jesus says, "I am not speaking to all of you; I know whom I have chosen."'

to accomplish the salvation of those people whom the Father wills to give to Him, and so He petitions the Father to fulfill this purpose by giving them to Him. Christ prays that the Father will grant eternal life to those elected to receive knowledge of Himself and the Son whom He has sent (John 17:3).

From the beginning to the end of His high-priestly prayer, Jesus' petitions are governed by a clear awareness of the Father's purpose in sending Him into the world. That purpose was to save those whom the Father elected to give to Him, and for whom He came into the world. In the opening words of the prayer, Jesus asks the Father to glorify Him that He might glorify the Father. He acknowledges He came into the world by the Father's authority to give eternal life 'to all whom you have given him'. As Jesus comes to the 'hour' of His death and an awareness that He has 'accomplished the work' the Father had given Him to do (v. 4), He now asks the Father to glorify Him with the glory that was His 'before the world existed' (v. 5) and that the fruit of His work be granted to those on whose behalf it was performed.

> I have manifested your name to the people whom you gave me out of the world. Yours they were, and you gave them to me, and they have kept your word. Now they know that everything that you have given me is from you. For I have given them the words that you gave me, and they have received them and have come to know in truth that I came from you; and they have believed that you sent me. I am praying for them. I am not praying for the world but for those whom you have given me, for they are yours. (John 17:6-9)

Even though the language of election is not used in His prayer, Jesus acknowledges that His work was accomplished in perfect conformity to God's purpose for sending Him into the world, namely, to make the Father known to those whom the Father has elected to give to Him.[29] He does not pray for the world in a general or non-specific manner. Rather, He prays explicitly and specifically for those whom the Father has willed to give to Him. By doing so, He affirms that the Father has elected to save only those whom He has determined

---

29. Carson, *DSHR*, 187. Cf. Ware, 'Divine Election to Salvation,' 6-7: 'And what identifies those select ones to whom this eternal life is given? Those "given Him" from the Father. ... The unconditional election of the Father accounts for those who receive eternal life from the Son.'

to give to Him, but not those who belong to the world and remain in their lost estate.

Because Jesus identifies the elect as those who have 'received' His words and 'believed' that the Father sent Him, some argue that Jesus does not imply a doctrine of 'pretemporal' election in this prayer. Since Jesus does not use the language of 'election,' they insist we may not infer that He is speaking of a purpose antedating His coming into the world. Moreover, because Jesus identifies those whom the Father gives him with those who believe in Him, the most important qualification for obtaining eternal life is that those who hear Jesus' words respond to Him in faith. Just as in John 3:16, which joins faith in Christ with the promise of eternal life, so in this prayer Jesus says that those who believe in Him will, *on that basis*, obtain eternal life. William Klein, for example, says in defense of this interpretation:

> As we saw in 6:37-40, both with *give* and God's *will*, faith in Jesus is the key to eternal life. Here Jesus gives no warrant to read in some pretemporal idea of predestination. In the context of John's gospel, the 'given ones' are believers, in contrast to the unbelieving world out of which they have come.[30]

The problem with this interpretation of John 17 is not that it acknowledges a connection between a believing reception of Jesus' words and being given by the Father to Jesus. Certainly, no one is able to obtain eternal life, unless they believe in Jesus and come to know the only true God through Him. Jesus explicitly says this in John 17:3, and it is the clear teaching of John 3:16 as well as many other passages in the Gospel of John and the New Testament writings. The problem is that this interpretation does not do justice to the over-riding theme of Jesus' high priestly prayer, namely, that He came into the world by the Father's commission to save those whom the Father had purposed to give Him.[31] The whole of Jesus'

---

30. *The New Chosen People,* 142.

31. Cf. Grant R. Osborne, 'Soteriology in the Gospel of John,' in *GGWM*, 243-61. Osborne argues that, because 'sovereignty and responsibility exist side by side' in John's Gospel (245), divine election works 'with one's faith decision'. Election does not produce faith, but depends upon it. Osborne describes his position as 'a modified Arminian theology that balances sovereignty and responsibility' (258). While Osborne properly recognizes the importance of human responsibility and faith in response to the gospel, he fails to do justice to divine election as the antecedent source and basis for the believer's response to the gospel. Those whom the Father gives to the Son,

high-priestly prayer is built upon the awareness that His incarnation and earthly mission were born out of the depths of the Father's self-determination to accomplish the redemption of those whom He had previously determined to give to Him. For this reason, D. A. Carson captures well the way the Father's purpose of election precedes and undergirds how believers receive eternal life, when they respond to Jesus and His work by believing in Him: 'The giving by the Father of certain men to the Son precedes their reception of eternal life, and governs the purpose of the Son's mission. There is no way to escape the implicit election.'[32] The point Carson is making is simple. Though John 17 does not explicitly speak of a pretemporal giving of some to Christ, it certainly speaks of a giving of some by the Father that precedes their coming to Him in faith. That some believe in Christ occurs as a result and consequence of God's prior determination to give them to Christ and to give Christ the authority to grant them eternal life through faith in Him (v. 2). Since Christ roots all of this within the will of His Father, who sent Him to accomplish the work He has performed, we are warranted in concluding that Christ's earthly mission was in fulfillment of a pretemporal plan. God's eternal purpose to give some persons to His Son precedes Christ's coming, and explains why some receive Him and believe His words. The specific petitions of Christ's high-priestly prayer arise out of His privileged knowledge of the Father's antecedent purpose and plan.

Jesus' high-priestly prayer in John 17 provides a compelling confirmation of what we have seen throughout the Gospel of John. Without using the express language of 'election' or 'predestination', the Gospel of John is pervaded by its emphasis upon God's eternal purpose of election. What God the Father has made known through the incarnation of the eternal Word is nothing less than His antecedent purpose in Christ to save those whom He has chosen to give to Him.

Election in the General Epistles and Revelation

The last part of the New Testament canon that we consider in this chapter is the teaching on election in the general epistles and the

---

and for whom the Son has come into the world, are precisely those who are drawn to respond in faith. For a critical evaluation of Osborne's view, see Yarbrough, 'Divine Election in the Gospel of John,' 56-60.

32. *DSHR*, 187. See also Carson, *The Gospel According to John,* 557-65.

book of Revelation. Here we find similar themes to those in other parts of the New Testament. These themes include God's gracious election of the church, comprised of Jews and Gentiles, as the fulfillment of His election of Israel in the Old Testament economy. They also confirm that God's election is unto salvation, has its roots in His eternal purpose and plan, and comes about through fellowship with Jesus Christ, whom God sent to be the Redeemer of His people. This portion of the New Testament, especially the book of Revelation, also clearly teaches that God's purpose of election is a central feature of His all-inclusive plan to realize His purposes in the course of history.

Election in the General Epistles

Among the general epistles, several instances in the letters of James, Peter, and John speak of God's gracious election of His people.

In the epistle of James, the theme of election is mentioned only once and in the practical context of his exhortation against the sin of partiality among God's people. According to James, it is inappropriate to favor the rich in the assembly of God's people. If a rich person is treated favorably and a poor person unfavorably when the church gathers, the church fails to act out of the awareness that God shows no such partiality in graciously choosing to save His people. In the face of such ungodly favoritism, James asks, 'Has not God chosen those who are poor in the world to be rich in faith and heirs of the kingdom, which he has promised to those who love him?' (James 2:5). Even though James' appeal to God's election of the poor appears within the context of practical exhortation regarding Christian conduct, it is instructive. While James is not teaching that all the poor are objects of God's choice or that God chooses no rich persons, he does affirm that salvation rests upon God's sovereign and gracious choice. He speaks of an election that brings about the salvation of some among those who are poor. In doing so, he offers more than a 'proverbial expression' that teaches only that God chooses those who are willing to obey and depend on Him in a way that others are not.[33] He declares

---

33. Klein, *The New Chosen People,* 226, uses the language 'proverbial expression' to avoid the implication that James is speaking of the election of such persons to salvation.

directly that the salvation of some who are poor in this world's goods depends upon God's gracious choice to save them.

In contrast to the single mention of election in the letter of James, the letters of Peter and John contain several important references to election. Some offer important testimony to the way God elects to save particular persons from among all people. Others refer to God's election of the church of Jesus Christ as the true Israel of God, the fulfillment and continuation of His purpose of election in the Old Testament epoch. Still others echo a theme we have seen in other parts of the New Testament, namely, that Jesus Christ is the chosen One through whom God provides for the salvation of His people.

The first and second letters of Peter mention election at several points. In the salutation with which the letter opens and the final greetings with which it closes, Peter identifies those to whom he writes as God's elect:

Peter, an apostle of Jesus Christ. To those who are elect exiles of the dispersion in Pontus, Galatia, Cappadocia, Asia and Bithynia, according to the foreknowledge of God the Father, in the sanctification of the Spirit, for obedience to Jesus Christ and for sprinkling with his blood. (1 Pet. 1:1-2)

She who is at Babylon, who is likewise chosen, sends you greetings, and so does Mark, my son. (1 Pet. 5:13)

Peter's salutation acknowledges that those to whom he writes were known to God as His elect people before they became beneficiaries of His saving work. Their salvation as God's elect accords with God the Father's foreknowledge,[34] the Spirit's sanctification of them, and the Son's bloody sacrifice on their behalf. His closing greetings

---

34. Because Peter uses the expression, 'according to the foreknowledge of God the Father,' some interpreters of this text understand it to teach divine election based merely upon God's foreknowledge of those who will choose to believe. Since this expression is paralleled by the Spirit's work of sanctification and the Son's atoning sacrifice, I believe it should be taken in the strong sense of 'foreloved' or 'loved in advance'. For a defense of this interpretation, see J. N. D. Kelly, *A Commentary on the Epistles of Peter and Jude,* BNTCS (London: A. & C. Black, 1969), 42-43; and Wayne Grudem, *1 Peter,* TNTC (Grand Rapids: Eerdmans, 1988), 50. I will consider the meaning of God's 'foreknowledge' in relation to divine election in the next chapter, which will explore the apostle Paul's teaching in Romans 8:28-30.

refer to the church in Rome as God's 'elect' and 'chosen'. Although some have argued that Peter is referring to his wife or a well-known woman in the church in Rome, it is likely that he is using the feminine pronoun to refer to the church as God's elect people.[35] In addition to these references, Peter also describes the New Testament church in language drawn from the Old Testament's teaching regarding Israel as God's elect nation and people (cf. Deut. 10:15; Isa. 43:20): 'But you are a chosen race, a royal priesthood, a holy nation, a people for his own possession, that you may proclaim the excellencies of him who called you out of darkness into his marvelous light' (1 Pet. 2:9). According to this passage, the election and calling of the church of the new covenant are a fulfillment and continuation of the election and calling of the people of Israel.

Perhaps the best known reference to election in Peter's epistles is found in 2 Peter 1:10, where he encourages his readers to 'be all the more diligent to make your calling and election sure'. Peter links the calling of believers with their election, as is also the case in Romans 8:30 and 9:22-24. Unlike the passages in Romans, however, Peter places calling before election due to his emphasis upon the cultivation of assurance. Assurance of election never grows apart from an awareness of God's gracious call to faith in Jesus Christ. Therefore, Peter encourages believers to fortify their assurance, not apart from a consideration of their calling, but in conjunction with it. When believers are encouraged to make their election sure, they are encouraged to do so in the remembrance of the gracious and powerful call that came to them through the gospel's invitation to believe in Christ.

Two references to election in Peter's epistles focus especially upon the election of Jesus Christ to accomplish the work necessary for those who are joined to Him by faith. The first passage is 1 Peter 1:20, which speaks of God's foreknowledge of Christ as the lamb whose precious blood was the ransom price for His people's redemption. Peter encourages readers to live in a way corresponding to their status

---

35. Cf. Peterson, *Election and Free Will,* 76. Peterson interprets this language to refer to God's 'corporate election of the church'. Though the visible church may include some who do not truly belong to the number of God's elect, the church as the community of God's people is nonetheless an elect community.

as those redeemed with 'the precious blood of Christ, like that of a lamb without blemish or spot' (v. 19). In this context, Peter reminds them that Christ was chosen for this work from all eternity: 'He was foreknown before the foundation of the world but was made manifest in the last times for your sake' (v. 20). Though interpreters debate the meaning of God's 'foreknowledge' of Christ, it seems evident that Peter is saying more than that God knew in advance when Christ would come. Because he joins God's eternal foreknowledge of Christ with His coming for the purpose of redeeming His people, Peter is describing what might be called God's determination for this to take place to save His people.[36]

The second passage in Peter's epistles speaking of the election of Christ is 1 Peter 2:4-6:

> As you come to him, a living stone rejected by men but in the sight of God chosen and precious, you yourselves like living stones are being built up as a spiritual house, to be a holy priesthood, to offer spiritual sacrifices acceptable to God through Jesus Christ. For it stands in Scripture: 'Behold, I am laying in Zion a stone, a cornerstone chosen and precious, and whoever believes in him will not be put to shame.'

Echoing Isaiah 28:16, Peter affirms that Christ is the fulfillment of God's promise to build a temple whose cornerstone, chosen and precious, is Jesus Christ. All who believe in Jesus are living stones being built up as a spiritual temple where God dwells and is praised. Whereas Jesus Christ is the chosen instrument through whom this house will be built, all who belong to Him by faith will become members of the house, enjoying the benefit of His saving work by virtue of their communion with Him.

In the epistles of John, there are two instances where the theme of election is mentioned. In 2 John 1, the apostle identifies the recipients of his letter as 'the elect lady and her children, whom I love in truth, and not only I, but also all who know the truth.' Then, at the close of his brief letter, which encourages its recipients to walk in truth and love, John extends greetings on behalf of their 'elect sister'. While these references are relatively incidental, they reflect John's conviction that the church's existence derives from God's gracious election of His

---

36. Peterson, *Election and Free Will,* 79.

people to salvation. Though 'the elect lady' in verse 1 may refer to a particular woman, John's use of the second person plural in the body of his letter suggests that he is identifying the church, and those who belong to her, as God's elect. Thus, John uses this term to identify those who belong to God in a way that corresponds to the common scriptural view that the church and her members are born out of God's purpose of election.

Election in the Book of Revelation

The last non-Pauline portion of the New Testament canon that we need to consider briefly is the book of Revelation. In this book, two themes are especially pertinent to the biblical understanding of election. The first of these themes is the encouragement that believers may derive from the registry of their names in what is called the 'book of life' (Rev. 3:5; 17:8; 20:12, 15) or 'the Lamb's book of life' (Rev. 21:27; cf. 13:8). A second and related theme is that the Lamb of God is alone 'worthy' to 'open the scroll and its seven seals' (Rev. 5:5).[37]

A principal theme of the book of Revelation is that Jesus Christ is the triumphant Lamb of God who purchased the redemption of His people by His death upon the cross and protects them in the midst of their present trials and persecutions. In order to buttress the hope of believers, the book of Revelation frequently speaks of the 'book of life' in which their names are registered:

> The one who conquers will be clothed thus in white garments, and I will never blot his name out of the book of life. I will confess his name before my Father and before his angels. (Rev. 3:5)

> And all who dwell on earth will worship it [the beast], everyone whose name has not been written before the foundation of the world in the book of life of the Lamb who was slain. (Rev. 13:8)

---

37. Peterson (ibid., 81) also cites Revelation 17:14 in his treatment of the doctrine of election in the book of Revelation. Revelation 17:14 identifies those who belong to the Lamb, and who are protected against the warfare of the 'ten kings' who align themselves with the 'beast'. They are described as those who are 'called and chosen and faithful'. Consistent with what we will see regarding those whose names are written in the Lamb's 'book of life', there is a close correlation between the calling, election, and faithfulness of those whom God has inscribed in this book.

And the dwellers on the earth whose names have not been written in the book of life from the foundation of the world will marvel to see the beast, because it was and is not and is to come. (Rev. 17:8)

And I saw the dead, great and small, standing before the throne, and books were opened. Then another book was opened, which is the book of life. ... And if anyone's name was not found written in the book of life, he was thrown into the lake of fire. (Rev. 20:12, 15)

But nothing unclean will ever enter it, nor anyone who does what is detestable or false, but only those who are written in the Lamb's book of life. (Rev. 21:27)

Several observations may be made regarding these passages. First, the contrast in Revelation between those whose names are written in the book and those who are not finds its roots in the Old Testament (see Dan. 12:1-2; 7:10ff.).[38] Second, with one possible exception (Rev. 3:5), all of these passages emphasize the certainty that those whose names are written in the book of life will be kept by God in the way of salvation, no matter what they may have to endure in their earthly pilgrimage. Third, the Author of this book of life is God Himself, who wrote the names of His people in this registry 'before the foundation of the world' (Rev. 17:8). The names recorded are not added or erased at a particular moment in the history of redemption. They were recorded by God Himself before creation and the historical unfolding of His purposes. And fourth, the protection afforded those whose names are written in this book is secured by the Lamb of God who was slain to purchase their redemption. Their protection is entirely dependent upon, and in consequence of, the work of Christ.[39] The cumulative force of these passages seems clearly to be that the salvation and preservation of believers finds its sure basis in God's

---

38. See G. K. Beale, *The Book of Revelation,* NIGTC (Grand Rapids: Eerdmans, 1999), 279, 701-2, 866-7, 1032-8. The theme of those whose names are inscribed in the book of life by God Himself is found elsewhere in the New Testament (cf. Luke 10:20; Phil. 4:3; Heb. 12:23).

39. Beale, *Revelation,* 866-7: 'Protection for those written in the book comes from the Lamb. This is borne out in 13:8 and 21:27, where τοῦ ἀρνίου ("of the lamb"), a genitive of either possession or source, further qualifies "the book of life." The genitive could be intentionally ambiguous and include both nuances: the Lamb both gives life and has sovereignty over who receives life and who does not.'

eternal and gracious decision to write their names in the book of life, and to provide for their salvation and preservation through the work of the Lamb.

While the implication of these passages for the teaching of election seems clear, some interpreters maintain that the language used in Revelation 3:5 opens the possibility that names in the book of life could be erased or blotted out. Since all of these passages occur within a context of exhortations to persevere in the face of tribulation, they include warnings against falling away through unbelief and disobedience. These warnings imply that some believers might lose their salvation. Grant Osborne, for example, appeals to the language of Revelation 3:5 to argue that some believers may have their names blotted out by virtue of their unfaithfulness or failure to persevere in the Christian life.

> Participation [in the book of life] depends on Christ's sacrificial death *and the believer's faithful perseverance in Christ.* ... The 'book of life' itself contains both the names and deeds of all who claim allegiance to Christ, and only those who remain faithful will stay in it. The verb ... I will blot out was often used of a name 'erased' from a written record ....[40]

Several considerations, however, speak against Osborne's interpretation.[41] First, none of the other passages in the book of Revelation speaking of the 'book of life' suggest that some of those whose names are recorded risk losing their salvation. Those whose names are registered in the 'book of life' are uniformly encouraged to be confident of their salvation, even in the face of tribulation. Second, in the book of Revelation, those whose names are in the 'book of life' are contrasted with those who finally prove to be unbelieving, whose names 'have not been written in the book of life' (Rev. 13:8; 17:8). The names of such persons are recorded in the 'books' of judgment

---

40. Grant R. Osborne, *Revelation,* BECNT (Grand Rapids: Baker, 2002), 180-1. For a similar argument, see Klein, *The New Chosen People,* 154. Cf. Beale, *Revelation,* 867: 'It could be asked why, if true saints are already protected because their name has been written in the book, it is necessary that they be warned not to worship the beast and exhorted to have wisdom to prevent deception. Theologically, from the divine perspective, the answer lies in the idea that God's plan to save his elect in the end includes the penultimate means of issuing them warnings and exhortations to which they respond positively on the basis of divine protective grace.'

41. For an elaboration of these considerations, see Beale, *Revelation,* 279-80.

(Rev. 20:12). And third, the theme of the 'names' of believers in Revelation 5 (vv. 4, 5a, 5b) suggests that they are authentic and true, and therefore not counted among those who prove to be inauthentic and false. By definition, those whose names are written in the 'book of life' are believers whose salvation will not be lost through unfaithfulness.

Further confirmation of this interpretation of the names written in the 'book of life' can be found in Revelation 5, which records the vision of the scroll and the Lamb. In this chapter, we do not read of a 'book of life', which contains only the names of those whom God has determined to save by the blood of the Lamb. Revelation 5 speaks rather of a 'scroll written within and on the back, sealed with seven seals.' Although there is considerable debate regarding the identity of this scroll, it likely represents a book authored by God as Creator and Redeemer, which details His eternal plan for the course of history. Unlike the book of life, this scroll not only identifies those whom God has purposed to grant salvation through the work of the Lamb, but also those unbelieving peoples and nations upon whom His judgment rests. In his commentary on the book of Revelation, G. K. Beale offers a helpful summary of the nature of this scroll:

> The 'book' [scroll] is best understood as containing God's plan of judgment and redemption, which has been set in motion by Christ's death and resurrection but has yet to be completed. The question asked by the angelic spokesman ['Who is worthy to open the scroll and break its seals?'] concerns who in the created order has sovereign authority over this plan.[42]

Though this scroll describes God's plan in comprehensive terms, including both judgment and redemption, it certainly portrays God's plan to save particularly those for whom the Lamb was slain and who were ransomed by His blood (Rev. 5:9). In this respect, the scroll has the character of a 'testament' that promises an inheritance in Christ to all those God has determined to save.

Summary
Though I will offer a more complete summary of the New Testament's teaching regarding the doctrine of election at the close of the next

---

42. Beale, *Revelation,* 340.

chapter on the Pauline epistles, there are several conclusions that may be drawn from what we have seen thus far.

In the first place, it is evident that the New Testament's teaching is very much in line with and a confirmation of what we witnessed in our survey of the Old Testament. In the Synoptic Gospels, Jesus' teaching includes clear testimony to the theme of divine election. The coming of Jesus Christ is presented as a fulfillment of God's promises to His chosen people Israel. As the 'chosen Servant' and Son of God, He has come to save His people from their sins and call them to faith and repentance in His name. Just as God elected and called His Old Testament people into fellowship with Himself, God has elected and called Jesus Christ to fulfill Israel's history and gather those whom He has chosen by His Word and Spirit.

In the Gospel of John, the sending of Jesus Christ fulfills the Father's gracious purpose to reveal His grace and truth, and to draw those whom He has willed to save into fellowship with Christ. Though the Gospel of John does not often use the express language of election, it is pervaded by the theme that Christ's coming and the salvation of those who believe in Him takes place according to the Father's purpose. No one comes to the Father through faith in His Son, unless they are numbered among those for whom Christ came and on whose behalf He laid down His life. While some interpreters deny that God's purpose of election includes the choice of specific persons, the language of two important passages in the Gospel of John (John 10 and 17) indicates that Christ laid down His life for His sheep whom He knows by name and who will not be snatched from His Father's hand. Accordingly, in His high-priestly prayer, Jesus prays for those whom the Father chooses to give to Him.

When the book of Acts tells the story of the gathering of the church in the foundational epoch of the apostles' ministry, it is clear that they minister in Christ's authority and the power of His outpoured Spirit. That some believe in response to the gospel summons is due wholly to the Spirit's powerful work. The Lord adds to the church those who are being saved, according to His purpose and plan. As many as were appointed unto eternal life are effectually called into and preserved within the church. Much like the Old Testament, the doctrine of election is not set forth in abstract terms in the gospels and the book of Acts. These portions of the New Testament record the historical-redemptive events associated with Christ's coming and His ministry, including His gathering of the church after Pentecost during the apostles' ministry. It is quite natural, therefore, that the doctrine of election is embedded within and forms the underlying premise of the New Testament narrative. But it is an unmistakable story of God's gracious initiative and powerful work in drawing those whom He chooses to salvation through faith in Christ. The broad reach of God's grace, which includes Jews and Gentiles alike, fulfills the Old Testament promise that all the families of the earth will experience God's saving grace.

In the non-Pauline epistles, the theme of God's sovereign election of His people is set forth in more general terms than in the narrative portions of the New Testament. In these epistles, we also find a clear and consistent emphasis upon God's election of some to salvation through faith in Jesus Christ. Though the church is sometimes described corporately as an 'elect' community, the language of election also includes the specific choice of some and not others. For this reason, in the book of Revelation, we find the language of the Lamb's 'book of life', language with roots in the Old Testament and found elsewhere in the New Testament. From before the foundation of the world, God registered the names of those whom He purposed to redeem through the blood of the Lamb. For the believing community, the theme of election, especially evident in the imagery of the 'book of life', provides assurance that God's grace will prevail in the lives of His chosen ones. And as was true in the Old Testament, election demonstrates that the salvation of believers is rooted in God's gracious choice, not human performance or achievement.

CHAPTER 3

The Doctrine of Election
in the Pauline Epistles

IN my survey thus far of the Old Testament and New Testament teaching about God's gracious purpose of election, we have seen that redemption's history is a transcript of the way the triune God acts to achieve His redemptive purpose to save those toward whom He chooses to show mercy. In the Old Testament, this purpose is realized through the election of Israel as God's chosen people, and the election of particular individuals as the special recipients of God's saving blessings. In the New Testament, God's purpose finds its fulfillment in Jesus Christ, the chosen Servant through whom God's promise to bless all the families of the earth is fulfilled. Although the Bible tells the story of redemption largely through a narrative of God's acts in time, these acts are deeply rooted within God's own eternal will and counsel.

While the scriptural teaching regarding election is most often set forth concretely in a narration of redemptive history, it is especially in Paul's epistles that we find the rudiments of a more systematic treatment of election and predestination. Though Paul's treatment of election clearly respects redemption's history, he provides a more overt formulation of God's eternal purpose that underlies and gives birth to this history in its progressive unfolding. Consequently, in the history of theological reflection upon and systematic formulation of the doctrine of election, it is not surprising to find that Paul's teaching on the subject has occupied the greatest attention. As William Klein observes:

When we think about the topic of election, our minds naturally fasten upon the writings of the apostle Paul. Paul's teaching about election has inspired and challenged all who have striven to understand this issue. To attempt to explain the theology of election requires that we zero in on what Paul wrote about the topic. Paul employs election concepts and terminology more than any other New Testament writer.[1]

Because Paul's treatment of the theme of election is more systematic than that of other biblical authors, it has always played an especially important role. In Paul's epistles, we find some of the most profound reflection upon the depths of God's redemptive purposes in His eternal counsel and will. According to Paul, what transpires in the course of the history of redemption is rooted in the eternal plan of God who works all things according to the counsel of His will (Eph. 1:11).[2]

While it is a daunting, if not impossible, task to give an adequate account of Paul's teaching on the topic of election, my summary of his teaching in this chapter will begin with a treatment of three especially important passages: (1) Romans 8:28-30; (2) Romans 9-11; and (3) Ephesians 1:3-14. After offering an interpretation of these passages, I will also consider several passages in the remaining Pauline epistles, including the pastoral letters to Timothy and Titus, which address the subject of election.

Romans 8:28-30: God Foreknew Those Whom He Foreordained

The first passage in the Pauline epistles that we consider is Romans 8:28-30, which has played a considerable role in the history of the

---

1. Klein, *The New Chosen People,* 158.

2. Cf. Williams, *The Election of Grace,* 73-4: 'In approaching the biblical material, we need to bring a hermeneutical rule to the forefront. ... The plea is that the story of Israel as narrated in Scripture (or the dramatic account of God and Israel) be permitted a heavy hand on the hermeneutical tiller.' Though I acknowledge that the biblical narrative plays an important role in ascertaining the meaning of God's electing acts, Williams does not adequately recognize that a doctrinal text, which treats the history of redemption as the unfolding of God's plan or counsel, has a unique hermeneutical status. On this issue, see Richard A. Muller, 'The Myth of "Decretal Theology",' *CTJ* 30, no. 1 (1995): 159-67. Regarding the relation between history and God's counsel or decree, Muller aptly observes: 'If, then, God did not ordain "whatsoever comes to pass," *nothing would come to pass. The eternal decree does not, therefore, abolish history—it makes history possible'* (165, emphasis his).

church's reflection on the doctrine of election. Since the apostle Paul correlates God's foreknowledge in this passage with His act of predestination, many interpreters conclude that Paul grounds God's act of predestining some people to be conformed to the image of His Son upon His foreknowledge of their faith. In the historic debates between Arminian and Reformed interpreters, which we will consider in subsequent chapters of this study, the key question raised by this passage is whether Paul is basing God's gracious election of some upon His foreknowledge of the way they will respond in faith to the call of the gospel (*praevisa fides*).

The first feature to note in this passage is the way it begins with a confident affirmation of God's care and providence in the lives of 'those who are called according to his purpose': 'And we know that for those who love God all things work together for good, for those who are called according to his purpose' (Rom. 8:28). With these words, Paul expresses a confidence that belongs to those whom God has graciously called to salvation through faith in Christ. This confidence derives from the assurance that God is carrying out His gracious 'purpose' in the believer's life and that He will superintend all that transpires in the believer's life for good. The same thought is expressed later in Romans 8, when Paul declares, 'If God is for us, who can be against us? He who did not spare his own Son but gave him up for us all, how will he not also with him graciously give us all things? Who shall bring any charge against God's elect?' (Rom. 8:31-33).

Consistent with the theme of God's gracious purpose and work in the life of those whom He has called, Paul goes on to explain why believers may have this confidence.

> For those whom he foreknew he also predestined to be conformed to the image of his Son, in order that he might be the firstborn among many brothers. And those whom he predestined he also called, and those whom he called he also justified, and those whom he justified he also glorified. (Rom. 8:29-30)

There are two questions that need to be addressed in order to interpret properly what Paul is teaching in this passage. The first question concerns the meaning of Paul's language about God's 'foreknowledge' in relation to His act of 'predestination'. Does this language mean no more than that God knew in advance how some persons would respond to the call of the gospel in faith or repentance? The second question, closely linked to the first, concerns what might be termed the 'object' of what God foreknows. Does this language refer to something that some persons will do in response to the call to believe in Christ, or does it rather refer to these persons themselves as the peculiar objects of God's foreknowledge and predestination?

Regarding the first question – what is meant by God's 'fore-knowledge'? – there are two observations pertinent to the interpretation of this passage. First, while it is true that God in His omniscience knows all that will take place in advance of its occurrence, the Scriptures often speak of God's knowledge of His people in a far richer and more relational manner.[3] We have previously noted that in the Old Testament there is what might be termed an 'elective' use of God's knowledge of His chosen people. In Amos 3:2, the prophet declares to Israel by the word of the Lord, 'You only have I known of all the families of the earth.' Similarly, in Jeremiah 1:5, the Lord declares that He 'knew' the prophet before he was born or appointed as a prophet to the nations. In the New Testament as well, the language of God's 'knowledge' in relation to His people expresses His peculiar commitment to and affection toward those who are the objects of this knowledge (cf. Matt. 7:23; John 10:14). In these passages, God's knowledge is not merely a factual knowledge or cognition of certain persons, but it is a knowledge that includes a disposition of favor toward those whom God knows.[4] And second, there is an indication in the broader context of Paul's letter to the Romans that this conception of God's knowledge is in Paul's purview. In the opening section of

---

3. S. M. Baugh, 'The Meaning of Foreknowledge,' in *GGBW*, 191-92, offers an obvious reason the language of God's foreknowledge in this passage cannot mean God's simple cognition of what will take place in the future: 'One way to hone one's understanding of a word is to contrast it with its antonym. That "he foreknew" in Romans 8:29 cannot refer to mere intellectual apprehension is demonstrated by use of negation: "Those of whom God was not previously cognizant are the ones he did not predestine…" This is clearly not the corollary of what Paul does say. Was it through God's ignorance of them that some people were not predestined to glory?'

4. See Ware, 'Divine Election to Salvation,' 26-7; and Baugh, 'The Meaning of Foreknowledge,' 192-5. Baugh appeals to the Old Testament usage of God's 'knowledge' of His chosen people Israel, and concludes that it expresses the idea of a 'relationship of commitment'.

Romans 11, Paul declares that 'God has not rejected his people whom he foreknew' (v. 2). The apostle adduces God's 'foreknowledge' of His chosen people, Israel, to support his claim that there is at the present time a 'remnant [within Israel], chosen by grace' (Rom. 11:2-5). Paul clearly uses the language of God's 'foreknowledge' to refer to God's particular choice and saving affection for those among the people of Israel whom He elected to save.[5] When Paul speaks of God's 'foreknowledge' in Romans 8:29, it is most likely that he is using this language in the same way as in Romans 11:2. God's foreknowledge is His prior (pre-temporal) commitment to treat those whom He predestines with special favor.

Further confirmation of this understanding of God's foreknowledge can be derived from a consideration of the second question. The focus of God's foreknowledge in this passage is not something that certain persons do in response to the gospel call. Rather, the object of God's foreknowledge is consistently those persons whom God beforehand distinguishes as the special recipients of His favor. Paul does not say anything about those whom God foreknows and predestines that would distinguish them from others. He does not say that God foreknows how these persons will respond in faith and repentance, when the gospel comes to them. Nor does he say that they will act in a certain way that makes them the peculiar objects of God's foreknowledge.[6] He simply says that there are certain persons whom God foreknows and whom He predestines. Furthermore, in the language of verse 30, which describes what is often termed the 'golden chain of salvation', he sets forth a sequence of parallel statements, each of which begins with 'those whom' and ends with a statement of God's action with respect to them. The way Paul crafts this sequence of parallel statements, including his use of a past tense (Aorist) verb

5. Ware, ibid., 27: 'Now, if we applied the Arminian notion of foreknowledge here, this text [Rom. 11:2] would mean, 'God has not rejected His people *whom He knew in advance would choose Him.*' But clearly this is not the case! God chose Israel, from all the nations of the world, even though she was the smallest and weakest of the lot (Deut. 7:6-8; 14:2)!'

6. Baugh, 'The Meaning of Foreknowledge,' 194: 'Paul does not say: "whose faith he foreknew," but "whom he foreknew." He foreknew us…. But in Romans 8:29, predestination is not dependent on faith; rather, God predestines us on the basis of his gracious commitment to us before the world was.'

in each case ('predestined,' 'called,' 'justified,' 'glorified'), confirms that the salvation of believers depends upon God's gracious action from beginning to end, and not upon the diverse response of those to whom the gospel call is extended.[7]

While Romans 8:28-30 is often interpreted, especially by Arminian theologians, to mean no more than that God has a prior knowledge of the conditions some will fulfill in order to be saved, this interpretation does not stand up to careful scrutiny.[8] Such an interpretation does not do justice to the biblical sense in which God 'knows' those who are His own. When God's knowledge refers to His relationship with His people, it typically describes His commitment to treat them with special grace. What may be unusual in Paul's language is that the apostle expressly speaks of this commitment as preceding its expression in actual history. God's foreknowledge is the basis and occasion for His gracious predestination. And this foreknowledge and corresponding act of fore-ordination are what undergirds His acts of calling, justifying, and glorifying. In a concise and compelling way, Romans 8:28-30 teaches that the whole of the believer's salvation, from beginning to end, is rooted in God's pre-temporal, gracious self-determination to grant salvation to those who are the chosen objects

---

7. Commenting on the construction of this passage, Robert A. Peterson (*Election and Free Will*, 114-15) notes that there 'are breaks in the chain of verbs. Paul uses a literary device called "climax," brought out well by the NASB: "For *whom* He foreknew, He also predestined...; and *whom* He predestined, *these* He also called; and *whom* He called, *these* He also justified; and *whom* He justified, *these* He also glorified" (Rom. 8:29-30). ... Paul does not make salvation contingent on human faithfulness, but on divine grace from beginning to end. When Arminians add conditions to Paul's words to make the passage better fit their theology, they change the meaning of the apostle's words.'

8. For a critical evaluation of various attempts by Arminian interpreters to avoid the implications of this passage, see Peterson, *Election and Free Will*, 112-15. Although Peterson identifies four different Arminian approaches to this passage, they all have one thing in common, namely, the redefinition of the object of God's foreknowledge. Though Paul speaks of 'those whom' God foreknows and predestines, Arminian interpreters invariably add the idea of faith and repentance as (pre-) conditions for God's actions. For examples of this Arminian approach, see Grant R. Osborne, 'Exegetical Notes on Calvinist Texts,' in *Grace Unlimited*, ed. Clark H. Pinnock (Eugene, OR: Wipf & Stock, 1999), 508; J. Kenneth Grider, *A Wesleyan-Holiness Theology* (Kansas City: Beacon Hill Press, 1994), 249-51; and Jerry L. Walls and Joseph R. Dongell, *Why I Am Not a Calvinist* (Downers Grove, IL: InterVarsity Press, 2004), 83.

of His favor. In a compact manner, this passage provides a scriptural basis for affirming God's unconditional, pre-temporal, and gracious decision to grant salvation to those whom He chooses.[9]

Romans 9–11: 'He Has Mercy On Whomever He Wills'

The apostle Paul's treatment of the doctrine of election in Romans 9–11 is arguably the most extensive treatment of the topic in all of Scripture. Though the theme of God's gracious election of His people is found throughout the Scriptures, Paul's engagement with God's 'purpose of election' in Romans 9–11 presents the matter in the boldest possible light. Due to Paul's extensive treatment in this passage, the interpretation of Romans 9–11 has invariably played a crucial role in theological reflection on the Scripture's teaching.

Following the lead of the influential church father, Augustine, Reformed theology's historic interpretation of Romans 9–11 is understood to teach the unconditional election of a particular number of persons unto salvation.[10] Although this interpretation is commonplace in the Augustinian understanding of divine election, it has met with considerable resistance in more recent treatments of the passage. Resistance to this view is frequently expressed not only by Arminian theologians, but also among biblical theologians who believe Paul's argument here should be read less individualistically. Though the arguments against the historic Reformed interpretation are diverse, they often coalesce around the claim that the traditional interpretation reads Paul's argument too abstractly. For these interpreters, Romans 9 does not present us with a non-historical treatment of God's eternal decree, which focuses upon the specific

9. Cf. Ware, 'Divine Election to Salvation,' 26-8, who argues that this passage offers compelling evidence for a doctrine of divine election to salvation that is 'unconditional, individual, and infralapsarian.' Although I have purposely avoided introducing technical theological categories in my overview of the scriptural teaching of election, I believe Ware's conclusion is warranted. In my treatment in subsequent chapters of the history of theological reflection on the scriptural teaching regarding election, I will have occasion to define these terms further.

10. Augustine's doctrine of election will be considered extensively in the next chapter, which is the first of several chapters on the understanding of election in the history of Christian theology up to the modern period.

persons whom He graciously chooses to save. Rather, Romans 9 addresses a more comprehensive question in the history of redemption, namely, the respective place of the corporate people of Israel and the Gentiles in God's gracious purposes as these are realized within history.[11]

The dissatisfaction with the traditional interpretation can be expressed in two closely related questions. First, does Paul focus in Romans 9–11 upon God's 'purpose of election' in respect to the salvation of individual persons or corporate peoples (Israel and the Gentiles)? And second, is Paul addressing the topic of God's election of particular persons to whom He chooses to grant salvation, or is he addressing the topic of the particular role that Israel and the Gentiles play in the history of redemption? While my aim in this section will be to offer my own interpretation of Paul's argument throughout Romans 9–11, I will do so with these questions in mind.

The Problem Posed in Romans 9:1-6: Have God's Word and Promise Failed?

To understand the argument related to these chapters, it is necessary to begin with a clear understanding of the problem posed in Romans 9:1-6, which constitutes the occasion for the apostle Paul's lengthy exposition of God's redemptive purposes, not only for the Gentiles but especially for the people of Israel. Put concisely, the problem Paul addresses is whether the Word and promises of God have failed with respect to the people of Israel.

---

11. For an extensive treatment of this claim, see Cornelis P. Venema, "'Jacob I Loved, But Esau I Hated": Corporate or Individual Election in Paul's Argument in Romans 9?' *MAJT* 26 (2015): 7-58. The 'corporate election' interpretation has considerable representation among recent biblical-theological treatments of Romans 9. See, e.g., C. E. B. Cranfield, *A Critical and Exegetical Commentary on the Epistle to the Romans,* 2 vols., ICC (Edinburgh: T & T Clark, 1979), 444-79; Paul J. Achtemeier, *Romans,* Interpretation (Atlanta: John Knox Press, 1985), 153-63; Klein, *The New Chosen People,* 158-212; Herman Ridderbos, *Paul: An Outline of His Theology,* trans. John R. de Witt (Grand Rapids: Eerdmans, 1959), 203-31; A. Chadwick Thornhill, *The Chosen People: Election, Paul and Second Temple Judaism* (Downers Grove, IL: IVP Academic, 2015), 229-53; N. T. Wright, *Paul and the Faithfulness of God,* Parts 2 & 3 (Minneapolis, MN: Fortress, 2013), 774-1042; Brian J. Abasciano, *Paul's Use of the Old Testament in Romans 9.10-18* (London: T & T Clark, 2005); idem, 'Corporate Election in Romans 9: A Reply to Thomas Schreiner,' *JETS* 49, no. 2 (2006): 351-71; and Bates, *Salvation by Allegiance Alone,* 170-75.

Paul's query at the outset of Romans 9 arises within the setting of his exultant conclusion of Romans 8. After an extended exposition of God's mercy and grace in salvation, the apostle rejoices that nothing can separate those who have been called according to God's purpose from His love for them in Christ Jesus (Rom. 8:28-39). Paul's peroration on God's invincible love seems a fitting conclusion to which the entire argument in Romans 1–8 leads. Though all people are by nature sinners, deserving of the wrath and judgment of God (Rom. 1–3), a way of salvation is provided for all who believe in Jesus Christ (Rom. 4–8). Although the wrath of God is being revealed from heaven against all the ungodliness of men who suppress the truth in unrighteousness (Rom. 1:18-32) and though 'none is righteous, no, not one' (Rom. 3:10), the mercy of God in the free justification of sinners is the hope of all believers. Therefore, Romans 8 concludes with a climactic affirmation of the victory of God's grace in Christ for all who believe.

However, this confidence in God's grace in Christ poses an inescapable problem for the apostle Paul. How can he exult in the triumph of God's grace in Christ through faith, when this grace seems to have so little effect among the people of Israel in his day? If God's promises to Israel have ended in unbelief, how can he affirm that the gospel is the power of God unto salvation to the Jew first and also to the Greek (Rom. 1:16)? Indeed, if God's Word has failed with respect to Israel, can we have confidence that God's promises will not likewise fail in regard to the Gentiles? This is the great problem that presses in upon the apostle at the outset of Romans 9–11, as the opening words of chapter 9 eloquently attest:

> I am telling the truth in Christ, I am not lying, my conscience bearing me witness in the Holy Spirit, that I have great sorrow and unceasing grief in my heart. For I could wish that I myself were accursed, separated from Christ for the sake of my brethren, my kinsmen according to the flesh, who are Israelites, to whom belongs the adoption as sons and the glory and the covenants and the giving of the Law and the temple service and the promises, whose are the fathers, and from whom is the Christ according to the flesh, who is over all, God blessed forever. Amen. (Rom. 9:1-5)

The pressing question to which the entire argument of Romans 9–11 is addressed, then, is whether the Word and promise of God have failed by virtue of the evident unbelief of many of the children of Israel, Paul's 'kinsmen according to the flesh.'

God's 'Purpose of Election' Prevails

To this troublesome question, Paul's comprehensive answer throughout Romans 9:6-29 and into chapter 10 is a resounding 'no'. Paul argues that God's purpose of election for His people Israel was, and continues to be, accomplished. He maintains that the Word of God has in no wise failed. Rather, 'God's purpose according to election' prevailed in the past history of Israel and continues to do so in the present (Rom. 9:11). Just as God's purpose of election discriminated in the past between some who were children of Israel only according to the flesh, and others who were true children according to the promise and purpose of God, so this purpose of election continues to be realized in the salvation of some to whom God chooses to show mercy and others to whom He chooses not to show mercy.

Thus, the apostle Paul answers generally the question regarding the supposed failure of God's promise by arguing that throughout the whole history of the Lord's dealings with His people Israel, some were brought to salvation and others were hardened in their unbelief according to God's purpose. He also argues at some length in Romans 9:30 through chapter 10 that the occasion for the failure of many Israelites to be saved lies in their unbelieving efforts to obtain salvation, not in the way of faith, but upon the basis of works (Rom. 9:30–10:4). Though many of the children of Israel were zealous for God, their zeal was not according to knowledge. Rather than submitting to God's righteousness, which is revealed through Christ who is the 'end of the law for righteousness to everyone who believes' (Rom. 10:4), they sought to establish their own righteousness in obedience to the law. Consequently, the prophecy of Isaiah is being fulfilled, namely, that Christ has become to them a 'stone of stumbling, and a rock of offense' (Rom. 9:33). The way of salvation for Jew and Gentile alike is the same: only those who, upon hearing the Word of the gospel preached, believe with their heart and call upon the name of the Lord, will be saved.

Though it is not necessary to trace all the steps in the apostle's argument in chapters 9 and 10, it is evident that his fundamental response to the question regarding Israel's apostasy is to appeal to

God's electing purpose, which has not and cannot fail. In the language the apostle uses at the outset of chapter 11, God's purpose of election was realized through a 'remnant, chosen by grace' from among the broader company of the children of Israel (Rom. 11:5).

God's Merciful Election of Isaac and Jacob: Romans 9:6-13

In order to demonstrate the unfailing power of God's Word and promise in respect to His people Israel, Paul appeals specifically to the way God's 'purpose of election' was evident in His choice of Isaac and Jacob. According to Paul, not all who belonged to God's chosen people as descendants of Abraham were truly 'children of the promise' in the same sense: 'For not all who are descended from Israel belong to Israel, and not all are children of Abraham because they are his offspring' (Rom. 9:6-7). A distinction must be made between those who are children of Israel according to the flesh and those who are genuinely the recipients of God's gracious promise of salvation in Christ.[12] To illustrate this distinction, Paul adduces the important instances of God's gracious election of Isaac rather than Ishmael, and of Jacob rather than Esau.

Concerning God's choice of Isaac, Paul appeals to the Old Testament narrative regarding Isaac and Ishmael, which recounts how God elected Isaac as the one through whom His promise to Abraham would be realized. God's choice of Isaac illustrates that not all who belonged to the people of Israel as a whole were in the same way the objects of God's favor.

> 'Through Isaac shall your offspring be named' [Gen. 21:12]. This means that it is not the children of the flesh who are the children of God, but the children of the promise are counted as offspring. For this is what the promise said: 'About this time next year I will return and Sarah shall have a son' [Gen. 18:10]. (Rom. 9:7b-9)

Paul appeals to the story of God's choice of Isaac rather than Ishmael to confirm that not all who are children of Israel according to the flesh are among the offspring of Abraham who will enjoy God's covenant blessings. The choice of Isaac rather than Ishmael confirms that a

---

12. See Schreiner, 'Does Romans 9 Teach Individual Election Unto Salvation?,' 92.

distinction must be made between Abraham's descendants according to the flesh and those among these descendants who properly belong to Israel (Rom. 9:6).

In addition to the case of God's election of Isaac, Paul then adds the further, and even more remarkable, case of Jacob and Esau. In the case of God's choice of Jacob rather than Esau, we see a most dramatic illustration of God's purpose of election.

> And not only so, but also when Rebecca had conceived children by one man, our forefather Isaac, though they were not yet born and had done nothing either good or bad—in order that God's purpose of election might continue, not because of works but because of his call—she was told, 'The older will serve the younger' [Gen. 25:23]. As it is written, 'Jacob I loved, but Esau I hated' [Mal. 1:2, 3]. (Rom. 9:10-13)

Despite a long history of dispute among interpreters regarding the meaning of these words, it seems clear that Paul is citing the example of God's choice of Jacob, not Esau, to demonstrate how God's purpose of election is unfailing. This choice was not based upon any condition that distinguished Jacob from Esau as a more suitable object of His mercy. Before the boys were born, and therefore before either had done anything good or bad, God declared that the younger would serve the older. In the language of theology, God's choice of Jacob was 'unconditional' and therefore unmerited. What ultimately distinguishes Jacob is that God elected to grant him blessings that He chose not to grant Esau.

Two Objections: Romans 9:14-26

After citing these two examples of God's purpose of election, Paul goes on to identify two objections that he anticipates will be brought against what he has said.

The first objection is that God's decision to show mercy to some and not others is unjust. Utilizing the rhetorical form of diatribe, Paul responds to the question of God's injustice.

> What shall we say then? Is there injustice on God's part? By no means! For he says to Moses, 'I will have mercy on whom I have mercy, and I will have compassion on whom I have compassion.' So then it depends not on human will or exertion, but on God, who has mercy. For the Scripture says to Pharaoh, 'For this very purpose I have raised you up, that I might show my power in you, and that my name might be proclaimed in all

the earth.' So then he has mercy on whomever he wills, and he hardens whomever he wills. (Rom. 9:14-18)

The objection Paul identifies is that God's choice to show mercy to some and not others conflicts with the dictates of justice. While some question whether the standard of justice that gives rise to this objection is a common notion of impartiality or a particular view of God's faithfulness to the promises He makes to His people Israel, Paul's answer is clear:[13] God is free to have mercy upon those whom He chooses. God's gracious election of Isaac and Jacob is not an act of justice but an act of mercy, which accords with God's own character and testimony regarding Himself. The mercy God shows to Isaac and Jacob is an unmerited and sovereignly granted favor. Whereas justice demands that everyone receive what is properly due to them (as a *quid pro quo*), God's choice of Isaac and Jacob was born out of His free determination to show mercy rather than treat them as they deserve. In support of this answer, Paul appeals to God's own self-testimony to Moses in Exodus 33:19 and to Pharaoh in Exodus 9:16. The ultimate standard for evaluating God's decision to show mercy to some and not to others can only be God's own testimony regarding His freedom to bestow mercy upon those whom He chooses.[14]

The second objection that Paul anticipates follows closely upon the heels of the first. If what Paul says is true – that God is free to show mercy to whom He wills, as His own self-testimony in Scripture attests – then doesn't it follow that God has no basis for finding fault with those toward whom He does not will to show mercy?

You will say to me then, 'Why does he still find fault? For who can resist his will?' But who are you, O man, to answer back to God? Will what is molded say to its molder, 'Why have you made me like this?' Has the potter no right over the clay, to make out of the same lump one vessel for honorable use and another for dishonorable use? What if God,

---

13. For a helpful discussion of what this objection might assume regarding the standard of 'justice' as it applies to God's choice, see Douglas J. Moo, *The Epistle to the Romans*, NICNT (Grand Rapids: Eerdmans, 1996), 591-2.

14. Moo, *Romans*, 592: 'Justifiably, Paul finds in God's words to Moses a revelation of one of God's basic characteristics: his freedom to bestow mercy on whomever he chooses. It is against this ultimate standard, not the penultimate standard of God's covenant with Israel, that God's "righteousness" must be measured.'

desiring to show his wrath and to make known his power, has endured
with much patience vessels of wrath prepared for destruction, in order
to make known the riches of his glory for vessels of mercy, which he has
prepared beforehand for glory—even us whom he has called, not from
the Jews only but also from the Gentiles? (Rom. 9:19-24)

In Paul's response to the objection that God has no basis for faulting
those who resist His will, he does not shrink back from his previous
teaching that God is free to show mercy to some and not to others.

Paul begins with an appeal to Isaiah 29:16. He wants to impress upon
his interlocutor that he is in no position as a creature to 'answer back'
to God. While it is one thing for a creature to seek an answer from God
that explains His ways, it is another thing for a creature to presume to
judge God's ways and find them to be unjust by human standards.[15] Paul
also calls to mind the imagery of Isaiah 29:16 and 45:9, which describes
God as a divine potter who has the right to make from one lump of clay
both a vessel of honor and a vessel of dishonor. Just as the clay has no
right to object to the potter by saying, 'why have you made me like this?'
so human beings have no right to object to God's sovereign decision 'to
make out of the same lump one vessel for honorable use and another
for dishonorable use' (v. 21). God is free, if He so desires, to display His
wrath and power by enduring with much patience those 'vessels of wrath
prepared for destruction', and in so doing to 'make known the riches
of his glory for vessels of mercy, which he has prepared beforehand for
glory.' God's decision to call those whom He pleases from among the
Jews as well as Gentiles is consistent, therefore, with His prerogatives
as the sovereign Lord and Redeemer of His people.

In the history of interpretation of Paul's answer to this second
objection, some discussion has taken place regarding his description
of those toward whom God chooses to display His wrath and power.
According to some interpreters, Paul's use of the verb 'prepared'
in the expression, 'vessels of wrath prepared for destruction,' could
be taken to mean that these vessels 'prepared themselves' or 'made

---

15. Cf. Moo, *Romans,* 602: 'Paul is not here denying the validity of that kind of
questioning of God which arises from sincere desire to understand God's ways and an
honest willingness to accept whatever answer he might give. It is the attitude of the
creature presuming to judge the ways of the creator—to "answer back"—that Paul
implicitly rebukes.'

themselves ripe' for destruction.[16] On this reading, these vessels are responsible for making themselves into vessels that are suited for destruction. If this is Paul's meaning, then God's role in 'preparing' them for destruction is significantly diminished. Other interpreters note that this reading does not do justice to the obvious role of God's sovereign power in preparing some to be vessels of wrath, and in distinguishing them from those whom He prepares to be vessels of mercy. In my judgment, John Murray strikes a good balance in his comments on this language:

> The hardening, it should be remembered, is of a judicial character. It presupposes ill-desert and, in the case of Pharaoh, particularly the ill-desert of his self-hardening. Hardening may never be abstracted from the guilt of which it is the wages. It might appear that the judicial character of hardening interferes with the sovereign will of God upon which the accent falls in this text. It would be sufficient to say that this cannot be the case in the counsel with which the apostle is dealing. It is impossible to suppress or tone down the sovereign determination of God's will any more than in the first part of the verse, as noted earlier. But it should also be observed that the sin and ill-desert presupposed in hardening is also presupposed in the exercise of mercy.[17]

Murray's point is that God does not directly act to make those who are vessels of wrath worthy of condemnation and death. He does not cause them to become unworthy or justly liable to punishment. In this respect, God's will toward those who are vessels of wrath is distinguished from His will with respect to those whom He prepares beforehand to become vessels of mercy.

An Election to Salvation, Not Merely to Service

Now that we have summarized Paul's argument in Romans 9, we are in a position to return to the two questions often raised regarding his teaching in more recent interpretations of Romans 9.

---

16. See, e.g., Leon Morris, *The Epistle to the Romans,* PNTC (Grand Rapids: Eerdmans, 1988), 368; and John R. W. Stott, *Romans: God's Good News for the World* (Downers Grove, IL: IVP, 1994), 272,

17. Murray, *The Epistle to the Romans*, vol. 2, NICNT (reprint; Grand Rapids: Eerdmans, 1975[1959]), 2:29. Cf. Moo, *Romans,* 606-09; and Thomas R. Schreiner, *Romans,* BECNT (Grand Rapids: Baker, 1998), 522.

With respect to the first question – whether Paul is addressing God's election of some to salvation or to service – there are several observations that support the first view. While God's purpose of election may include an election of some persons to a special role in the course of redemptive history, in this passage Paul seems clearly to be speaking of God's purpose of election to save those whom He chooses.

First, it seems evident from Paul's language in Romans 9:1-5 that he is addressing the question of the salvation of his fellow Israelites. If Paul's argument does not address God's purpose to elect some to salvation, Paul's language in these verses would appear to be unduly exaggerated. How else could we understand his 'great sorrow and unceasing anguish' (Rom. 9:2) at the unbelief of his kinsmen according to the flesh? Or how could we make sense of his language about 'being accursed or cut off from Christ for the sake of my brothers' (Rom. 9:3)? Such language would be little more than a remarkable case of theological shadow-boxing, if Paul were not addressing the issue of salvation in its deepest sense. Paul would not be addressing the problem identified in the opening section of Romans 9, and to which he now aims to provide a resolution. However, when his argument is viewed against the backdrop of the question raised at the outset of Romans 9, the whole point of Paul's exposition of God's purpose of election throughout this section of Romans is to show that God's Word has not failed (and will not fail) to accomplish its purpose in the salvation of those who are the recipients of His sovereign mercy and grace.[18]

Second, when the broader context and subsequent argument of Paul in Romans 10–11 are borne in mind, it becomes apparent that Paul is not merely concerned with the particular service or vocation of Israel in the history of redemption. In the larger context of his argument in Romans 9–11, Paul addresses the issue of eschatological salvation or damnation. Paul is not restricting his interest to the function Israel played in redemption's history. Nor is he restricting his comments to general or non-salvific privileges that Isaac may have enjoyed rather

---

18. Remarkably, Cranfield, after acknowledging that Paul is focusing upon the question of the salvation of his fellow Israelites, nonetheless maintains that Paul's interest in Romans 9:6ff. is only focused upon the 'historical function' of Israel in the realization of God's plan of redemption (*Romans,* 479). This is remarkable in view of Cranfield's admission that Paul does raise the issue of the salvation of many of his fellow Israelites at the beginning of Romans 9.

than Ishmael, or Jacob may have received but not Esau. This can be seen in several ways.

Throughout Romans 10–11 Paul repeatedly makes clear that he is dealing with the theme of salvation in the ultimate sense, not of general blessings that are extended to all those who belonged to the people of Israel without exception. After closing the first main part of his argument in Romans 9, Paul notes that the prophet Isaiah foretold that 'only a remnant of them [the sons of Israel in general] will be saved' (Rom. 9:27). In chapter 10, after Paul expresses his heartfelt prayer to God and desire that his fellow Israelites might be 'saved' (verse 1), he enlarges upon the reason for their failure to obtain salvation. This failure stems from their unwillingness to believe in Jesus Christ. Because many of his fellow Israelites have not believed the gospel Word, they have cut themselves off from Christ and the promise of salvation in Him. Thereafter in chapter 11, Paul expands upon the way Israel's unbelief was the occasion within God's gracious purpose for the gospel to be extended to the Gentiles. And he argues further that the engrafting of the Gentiles into the 'olive tree' of God's people will in turn provoke Israel to jealousy, and that this will issue in the salvation ultimately of 'all Israel' (Rom. 11:26). Even though the interpretation of Paul's argument, especially the meaning of the expression 'all Israel', is notoriously difficult and much disputed among commentators on the book of Romans, for our purpose here the point is clear: throughout the entirety of Paul's argument as it is unfolded in Romans 9–11, the question of God's purpose of election in respect to Israel and the Gentiles is a question that has everything to do with their salvation or non-salvation. It is not merely a question of the respective role or destiny of the people of Israel or the church in the course of redemptive history.[19]

Furthermore, it is telling to observe that later in Romans 9, in the section immediately after Paul's reference to Jacob and Esau, Paul speaks of some who are 'vessels of wrath prepared for destruction'

---

19. Schreiner, *Romans,* 502: 'That Paul has not restricted himself to issues of temporal destiny is evident from the terms he uses.' Contra Aaron Sherwood, *The Word of God Has Not Failed: Paul's Use of the Old Testament in Romans 9* (Bellingham, WA: Lexham Press, 2015), 145. Sherwood claims that 'it does not appear that in at least Romans 9:6-29 Paul is discussing salvation as such at all, whether of individuals or corporate groups.'

(Rom. 9:22) and of others who are 'vessels of mercy, which he [God] has prepared beforehand for glory' (Rom. 9:23). The language Paul uses to describe God's purpose of election with respect to the twin sons of Rebecca and Isaac, Jacob and Esau, is language that Paul typically uses when speaking of the salvation of believers. According to Paul, 'though they were not yet born and had done nothing either good or bad – in order that God's purpose of election might continue, not because of works but because of him who calls – she was told, "The older will serve the younger"' (Rom. 9:11-12). In this description, Paul adduces God's purpose to show mercy to the younger rather than the older, to confirm that God's call and grace are not granted 'because of works.' Within the argument of the book of Romans as a whole, this kind of language clearly implies that Paul is speaking about the salvation of the one to whom God shows mercy and the non-salvation of the one to whom God does not show mercy. An attentive reader of Romans in particular, or Paul's epistles in general, would immediately recall Paul's emphasis upon the justification of believers by faith 'apart from works' or 'the works of the law' (e.g. Rom. 3:20, 27-8; 4:2, 6; 9:32; 11:6; Gal. 2:16; 3:2, 5, 10; Eph. 2:9; 2 Tim. 1:9; Titus 3:5).

Corporate or Individual Election?

If Paul in Romans 9:6-29 is addressing the issue of the salvation of those who are truly 'children of Abraham', the peculiar recipients of the gracious promise of the gospel of Jesus Christ, the second question that remains to be addressed is this: Are these recipients a corporate people, whether Israel or the church? Or are they specific individuals from among a larger body of persons toward whom God has chosen to be merciful? Using the language of Paul in this passage, are we to understand his references to God's choice of Isaac rather than Ishmael, or of Jacob rather than Esau, to be references to the destiny of two groups or of two individuals?[20]

In my judgment, there are several aspects of Paul's argument in Romans 9 that require the idea of God's gracious choice to save some individual persons from among a larger body. However, I also believe

---

20. Cranfield's formulation of the corporate election reading of Romans 9 is representative (*Romans,* 479).

that Paul's argument cannot be adequately treated solely in individual terms. There are broad features of God's purpose of election in the course of redemptive history, specifically His abiding purpose to show mercy to 'all Israel', that remain an integral part of Paul's interest in the entirety of the argument in Romans 9–11. When properly defined, it is permissible to affirm both the individual and corporate features of Paul's doctrine of election, without losing the inescapably specific identity of those persons whom God is pleased to save in Christ, whether from among the people of Israel or the Gentiles. Due to the complexity of this, I will develop my case by way of several observations.

First, the whole of Paul's argument in Romans 9:6-16 depends upon the validity of the distinction that he draws between Israel as an elect people and the *true* Israel. In order to prove that God's Word to Israel has not failed, Paul notes the difference between the election of Israel to covenant privilege and the election of some within Israel to salvation. This difference is described as a difference between *elect Israel* and *the elect of Israel*, the children of Abraham *by natural descent* and the children of Israel *according to God's purpose of election*. The distinction Paul makes throughout the course of his argument in Romans 9 answers the question posed by Israel's unbelief, namely, whether or not the Word of God has failed in their case. Because God's Word has proven fruitful in the case of *the elect remnant* within Israel, it is impossible to charge God with failure because of the unbelief of many among the Israelites. The significance of this fundamental feature of Paul's argument with respect to the question of corporate or individual election, is transparent: if Isaac and Esau are not representatives of those among the larger company of Israelites in whom God's purpose of election is realized, then Paul's answer to his problem would amount to nothing more than a restatement of it! In this case, Paul's answer would say no more than that God has elected to save the people of Israel, and that his unbelieving kinsmen are from this people. This would offer no solution to the problem of the unbelief of Paul's kinsmen, since the corporate election of Israel is *the specific occasion* for Paul's argument in Romans 9:6-16, not its resolution.[21]

---

21. Cf. Murray, *Romans,* 2:18.

Second, the distinction Paul makes between elect Israel and the elect of Israel, between the children of Abraham by natural descent and the children of Abraham according to God's promise, is also important for sorting out the implications of Paul's appeal to the distinction between Isaac and Ishmael, and between Jacob and Esau.

Advocates of the corporate-election-of-Israel position commonly note that the Old Testament passages to which Paul refers (Gen. 21:12 and Mal. 1:1-5 [cf. also Gen. 25:33]) clearly refer to corporate peoples. While it is undeniable that the two individuals, Jacob and Esau, are closely linked in the history of redemption with two peoples, it is most important to consider why Paul in this instance appeals to God's merciful choice of Jacob instead of Esau. In the interpretation of Paul's argument in Romans 9, priority has to be given to the way Paul appeals to Malachi's prophecy, not to its meaning solely in terms of its original Old Testament setting.[22] Since Paul uses the example of Jacob and Esau to make a point regarding God's purpose of election, which distinguishes between those who are true children of the promise and those who are not, it is impossible to deny the particularity of God's choice of Jacob, the younger of the twin sons of Isaac and Rebecca. Undoubtedly, God's merciful choice of Jacob has implications for His purpose with respect to all who belong to the true Israel. This was true in the Old Testament history, and it remains true, as Paul argues more extensively throughout the entirety of Romans 9–11. But the purpose of God in the salvation of all the elect from among the people of Israel more generally can only be understood when it is recognized that this purpose issues in the salvation of specific persons to whom God is pleased to show His mercy.[23] When Paul adduces the example of God's choice of Jacob, he reinforces what he has already established in the case of Isaac. Because God's Word has always been effective unto salvation in the case of those who were the recipients of God's mercy

---

22. A similar point can be made regarding Paul's use of Hosea 2:23 and 1:10 in Romans 9:25-26. Although the point Paul makes in his use of Hosea is not materially different from the point made in the original context of the prophecy of Hosea (God's unmerited love is an amazing demonstration of His grace), he does use Hosea's words in a way that is peculiar to his own argument in Romans 9. Just as God graciously called Israel to be His people, so He now graciously calls the Gentiles to salvation and incorporation into the number of His people.

23. Cf. Moo, *Romans,* 585-86.

according to His purpose of election, God's promises to the people of Israel are not void or ineffectual. Just as the distinction between Isaac and Ishmael is grounded in God's gracious choice, so the distinction between Jacob and Esau illustrates the sheer graciousness of God's undeserved mercy toward those whom He saves. Because they were twin sons of one father and distinguished within God's purpose of election before they were born, this point becomes most clear.

And third, the usual way in which the choice between corporate election and individual election is posed in interpretations of Romans 9, needs to be more carefully analyzed. In my reading of Paul's argument in Romans 9, I have thus far stressed the inescapably individual nature of God's purpose of election. When Paul speaks of God's choice with respect to Isaac and Jacob, he is speaking of specific persons from among a larger group, the elect nation of Israel, upon whom God sets His saving mercy in Christ. However, there is no conflict between affirming the election of specific persons and the election of a community, provided the latter is properly defined.[24]

In the broader context of Paul's argument in Romans 9–11, those whom God saves in virtue of His purpose of election are described by Paul as 'a remnant' from among the larger community of Israel (Rom. 9:27). When Paul describes God's dealings with His people Israel throughout the Old Testament epoch, he notes how this history always proceeded in a way that confirmed the power of God's Word to save those whom He purposed to save. For example, in Romans 11:5-6, he says: 'So too at the present time, there is a remnant, chosen by grace. But if it is by grace, it is no longer on the basis of works; otherwise grace would no longer be grace.' Even though what Paul means toward the end of Romans 11, where he speaks of the eschatological salvation of 'all Israel' and of the large embrace of

---

24. In fairness to Calvin, it must be observed that he recognizes the legitimate sense in which the election of Jacob was not merely individual, but the election of a people in him. Cf. Calvin, *Comm.* Rom. 9:13, CNTC, 8.202, where he acknowledges that the conferral of the birthright upon Jacob is regarded in Malachi 1 as a declaration of the Lord's 'kindness to the Jews'. Cf. also Calvin, *Institutes,* 3.21.7: 'The statement "I have loved Jacob" applies to the whole offspring of the patriarch, whom the prophet there contrasts to the posterity of Esau. *Still this does not gainsay the fact that there was set before us in the person of one man an example of election that cannot fail to accomplish its purpose*' (emphasis mine).

God's mercy toward 'all' (11:32), is open to debate, it is evident that he does not view the election of particular persons from among the people of Israel in a way that denies God's great purpose to save an elect community. The reach of God's mercy in Christ will ultimately embrace the fullness of a community of persons, both Jews and Gentiles, whom God will save according to His gracious purpose. The implication of the broader argument in Romans 9–11 is that God's mercy will be extended, not merely to a few persons here and there who constitute a remnant chosen from a larger group, but to a great number of persons who will be brought into the one community of Christ or 'olive tree'. For Paul, there is no conflict between an affirmation of the particular election of individual persons and the gathering of a world-wide church of Jews and Gentiles alike who are all the recipients of God's undeserved mercy.[25]

And fourth, the emphasis upon the corporate nature of God's purpose of election leads, ironically, to an abstract or formal view of the objects of God's electing choice. Even if it is granted that the persons whom God elects comprise a community, it makes no sense to speak of this community in the abstract. At no point throughout the extended argument of Paul in Romans 9–11 are we dealing with nameless persons, or with an indefinite concept of the community of God.[26] In Romans 9, Paul speaks of 'Isaac' and 'Ishmael', of 'Jacob' and 'Esau', of those who are 'vessels of mercy' and those who are

---

25. Bavinck, *Reformed Dogmatics,* 2:404, offers a helpful statement of the consistency between an affirmation of God's merciful election of specific persons and His election of the organic unity of a new humanity in Christ: 'So it is not a random aggregate of things but an organic whole that is known by God in election and saved by Christ's redemption.... In an aggregate the number of its parts is totally immaterial. But an organism must by its very nature be based on measure and number.'

26. Schreiner, 'Does Romans 9 Teach Individual Election Unto Salvation?,' 102: '[T]hose who advocate corporate election do not stress adequately enough that God chose a group of people, and if he chose one group of people (and not just a concept or an abstract entity) rather than another group, then the corporate view of election does not make God any less arbitrary that the view of those who say God chose certain individuals.' I concur with Schreiner's point that it does not make sense to speak of the election of a group, if this group is not composed of any particular persons but is simply an abstraction whose identity remains indefinite. The problem here is not solved by emphasizing that Paul's argument focuses upon the history of redemption rather than the salvation of individuals in history. Expressed theologically, *historia salutis* does not diminish *ordo salutis,* but provides its basis and context.

'vessels of wrath'. In Romans 9:15, the personal pronoun is used twice to identify the one who is shown mercy and the one who is not. In the description of the failure of many fellow Israelites to believe in Romans 10, Paul describes real persons who are not obtaining salvation through faith in Christ, and who are not numbered among the 'remnant' of those who will be saved. And in Romans 11, Paul's language continues to describe those who are brought to salvation through faith in Christ by virtue of God's purpose to show them mercy. None of these descriptions is compatible with a basic assumption of the corporate election view, namely, that God's purpose of election does not involve His merciful choice of specific individuals.[27]

Upon the basis of my interpretation of Paul's argument in Romans 9, especially verses 6-16, I do not believe the recent endeavor to interpret this passage as teaching exclusively the corporate-election-of-Israel is tenable. Even though advocates of this interpretation properly emphasize the redemptive-historical setting for Paul's argument, they fail to do justice to the context and specifics of Paul's case. The occasion for Paul's treatment of God's purpose of election in this passage is undoubtedly the question of God's electing purpose with respect to the people of Israel in distinction from the Gentiles. However, when Paul raises the question whether or not the Word of God has failed to effect the salvation of many of his kinsmen according to the flesh, he is not merely asking whether or not Israel has lived up to its calling in the course of the history of redemption. He is asking whether or not God's Word of promise, which is demonstrated in the person and work of Christ, has and will achieve God's gracious and merciful purpose of election in respect to his fellow Israelites. Nothing less than the eschatological salvation or non-salvation of his fellow Israelites is at issue.

The particular answer that Paul gives to this question in Romans 9 is that God's Word has certainly not failed by virtue of the unbelief of

---

27. Cf. Williams, *The Election of Grace,* 70: 'Surely God's dealings are too personal, too particular, too intimate to permit a construction of the corporate which reduces the significance of the individual in this connection. When Paul, for example, speaks of those called from among the Gentiles (Rom. 9:24), ... there would seem to be a discrimination here which cannot be explained as the product of individuals autonomously inserting themselves into a class and, if that is not what is happening, they are incorporated into the body of the church by divine predestination, as the particular individuals that they are.'

many among the people of Israel. For in the course of God's redemptive dealings with Israel, God's purpose of election was – and continues to be – achieved among an elect remnant toward whom God has chosen to show His mercy. The core of Paul's answer requires that a distinction be drawn between Israel as an elect people and those among this people who are 'children of the promise' in terms of God's purpose of election. Paul's appeal to God's choice of Isaac rather than Ishmael, and of Jacob rather than Esau, constitutes an essential part of his argument for this distinction. Since the corporate-election-of-Israel position is unable to accommodate this distinction, which plays such a fundamental role in the way Paul makes his case in Romans 9, it glosses over the most decisive feature of Paul's argument. Even though proponents of the corporate-election-of-Israel view are warranted in their emphasis upon the pre-eminence and wide embrace of God's mercy in redemptive history, they are not warranted in their claim that Paul's argument includes no reference to God's just severity in choosing not to show mercy to all. The corporate-election-of-Israel reading of this passage is finally unable to give a plausible explanation for Paul's question in Romans 9:14: 'What shall we say then? Is there injustice on God's part?' This question is occasioned by Paul's appeal to God's merciful choice of some but not all of the children of Israel according to the flesh. It finds its basis in the fact that God distinguishes, according to His purpose of election, between Isaac and Ishmael, and between Jacob and Esau. Within the framework of a corporate-election-of-Israel reading, this question has none of the urgency it transparently has for Paul. For in the corporate election view, this distinction is always a penultimate one, which has to do only with Israel's role in the history of redemption.

Romans 11 and the Salvation of 'All Israel'[28]

Paul's answer to the enigma of the unbelief of many of his kinsmen, however, does not conclude at the end of chapter 9 or 10. Though chapter 10 ends on a sobering note – the Lord has been found by those who did not seek Him, as Isaiah formerly prophesied, but

---

28. For a more extensive treatment of the debate regarding the meaning of Romans 11:26, including a summary of various interpretations, see Cornelis P. Venema, '"In this Way All Israel Will Be Saved": A Study of Romans 11:26,' *MAJT* 22 (2011):19-40.

among Israel there has been a persistent disobedience to the Lord's gracious overtures – chapter 11 continues to address the problem of Israel's unbelief and offers a resolution that goes beyond what is said in chapters 9 and 10. The argument of this chapter leads Paul to the conclusion set forth in verse 26, 'And in this way all Israel will be saved,' which provokes him to burst forth in a doxology of praise to God for the depth of the riches of both His wisdom and knowledge (11:33).

Before we offer an interpretation of the argument in chapter 11, it should be noted that there are, broadly speaking, three views regarding the meaning of 'all Israel' that have been advanced throughout the history of interpretation of this passage.[29]

The first view takes this phrase to refer to the people of Israel as a totality (though not necessarily every individual Jew) who will be converted at some time after the fullness of the Gentiles has been gathered. Among those who take this view, three distinct forms of it are often defended: first, dispensational interpreters link this conversion of Israel as a totality within God's special program for the Jews in the future millennium;[30] second, premillennial interpreters who are not dispensationalists understand it to refer to a future conversion of the Jewish nation toward the close of the present period of redemptive history prior to the future millennium of Revelation 20;[31] and third, some interpreters who are neither dispensationalists nor premillennialists take it to refer to a future conversion of the people of Israel, not as a separate nation or people, but as a large company of those among the Jewish people who will be gathered into

---

29. For a good, more detailed summary of the primary interpretations of the phrase, 'and in this way all Israel will be saved,' see J. A. Fitzmyer, *Romans: A New Translation with Introduction and Commentary,* Anchor Bible, vol. 33 (New York, Doubleday, 1993), 619-20.

30. For a presentation and defense of the dispensational form of this view, see John F. Walvoord, *The Millennial Kingdom* (Findlay, OH: Dunham, 1959), 167-92; J. Dwight Pentecost, *Things to Come,* (Findlay, OH: Dunham, 1958), 504-7; and Michael G. Vanlaningham, 'Romans 11:25-27 and the Future of Israel in Paul's Thought,' *MSJ* 3. no.3 (Fall 1992), 141-74.

31. For a presentation and defense of the premillennialist form of this view, see George E. Ladd, *A Theology of the New Testament* (Grand Rapids: Eerdmans, 1974), 561-3; Oscar Cullmann, *Christ and Time: The Primitive Christian Conception of Time and History,* trans. Floyd V. Filson (Philadelphia: Westminster, 1960), 78.

the church.[32] In all the diverse forms of this view, it is maintained that the fullness of Israel must refer to the special people of God who will be converted at some future time, as they are provoked to jealousy by the salvation of the Gentiles. In this view, the 'all Israel' of Romans 11:26 is understood to refer to a future conversion of the fullness of ethnic Israel within the redemptive purpose of God.

The second view takes this phrase to be a reference to the salvation of all the elect, Jew and Gentile alike, gathered through the preaching of the gospel in the whole course of redemption's history. John Calvin, for example, took this position and argued that Israel here refers, not to a distinct people among the peoples of the earth, but to the people of God in the general and comprehensive sense, embracing elect Jew and Gentile alike.[33]

The third view takes this phrase to be a reference to the total number of the elect from among the people of Israel. According to this view, the fullness of Israel refers to the sum total of the remnant of elect Jews whom God has gathered, is gathering, and will yet gather throughout the entire history of redemption until the time of Christ's second coming.[34]

---

32. For a presentation and defense of this third form of the first view, see Charles Hodge, *A Commentary on the Epistle to the Romans* (Philadelphia: Alfred Martien, 1873), *ad loc.*; S. Greijdanus, *De Brief Van Den Apostel Paulus Aan De Gemeente Te Rome,* vol. 2 (Amsterdam: H. A. Van Bottenburg, 1933), 515-17; Murray, *Romans,* 2.91-103; Geerhardus Vos, *The Pauline Eschatology* (Princeton: University Press, 1930), 89; Moo, *Romans, ad loc*; Keith A. Mathison, *Postmillennialism: An Eschatology of Hope* (Phillipsburg, NJ: Presbyterian & Reformed, 1999), 121-30; and Schreiner, *Romans,* 612-23. Though many defenders of this position are postmillennialists, this position is not as such a sufficient condition for taking a postmillennialist view for the kingdom.

33. *CNTC,* 8.255.

34. Cf. Anthony Hoekema, *The Bible and the Future* (Grand Rapids: Eerdmans, 1994), 139-47, who provides an able defense of this view. Others who take this view include: Herman Bavinck, *Reformed Dogmatics,* vol. 4: *Holy Spirit, Church, and New Creation* (Grand Rapids: Baker Academic, 2008), 668-72; Louis Berkhof, *Systematic Theology* (Grand Rapids: Eerdmans, 1939, 1941), 698-700; William Hendriksen, *Israel in Prophecy* (Grand Rapids: Baker, 1974), 39-52; idem, *New Testament Commentary: Exposition of Paul's Epistle to the Romans* (Grand Rapids: Baker, 1980, 1981), 379-82; Ridderbos, *Paul,* 354-61; O. Palmer Robertson, 'Is There a Distinctive Future for Ethnic Israel in Romans 11?' in *Perspectives on Evangelical Theology,* ed. K.S. Kantzer and S.N. Gundry (Grand Rapids: Baker, 1979), 209-27; Robert B. Strimple, 'Amillennialism,' in *Three Views of the Millennium and Beyond,* ed. Darrell L. Bock (Grand Rapids: Zondervan, 1999), 112-18. O. Palmer Robertson, *The Israel of God:*

The diversity of interpretations of Romans 11 suggests that undue dogmatism is inadvisable regarding Paul's teaching. However, I am persuaded that Paul is affirming God's mercy will triumph in the salvation of the 'fullness' of Israel, when many among his kinsmen according to the flesh are provoked to jealousy by the gathering in the Gentiles. In addition to his earlier emphasis upon God's salvation of a remnant among the people of Israel, Paul also teaches that in the future God will display a richer measure of His mercy in the salvation, not merely of a remnant, but of the fullness of Israel. Though I do not concur with the dispensational and pre-millennial versions of this interpretation, I find this expectation of the salvation of Israel's fullness to be on balance the most satisfying interpretation of Paul's argument in Romans 11. There are several considerations that support this interpretation.

First, the meaning of 'Israel' in verse 26 can hardly be the sum total of all elect persons whether Jew or Gentile. In the immediate and more distant setting that leads to the conclusion of this verse, the apostle Paul has consistently used (eleven times) the term Israel in reference to the theocratic adoption of the people of Israel, the descendants of Abraham whom he describes as 'kinsmen according to the flesh' (9:3). Furthermore, the parallel between verse 26 and the verse that precedes it would be senseless, were 'Israel' in this verse to include Gentiles as well as Jews who will be saved within God's purposes of redemption. The distinction between Israel as a particular people and the Gentiles governs the argument throughout the chapter and indeed throughout Romans 9–11 as a whole.

Second, there are important clues in the context that the apostle is not referring simply to the sum of the remnant among the people

Yesterday, Today, and Tomorrow (Phillipsburg, NJ: Presbyterian & Reformed, 2000), 167-92, offers a slightly revised version of his earlier argument for this position. In his revised article, Robertson ultimately regards 'all Israel' to refer to the whole church of God, the one olive tree, comprised of elect Jews and Gentiles. Consequently, his present position seems closer to that of Calvin than the other views I have identified. In this article, Robertson also identifies at least five different interpretations of 'all Israel': '(1) all ethnic descendants of Abraham, (2) all ethnic descendants of Abraham living when God initiates a special working among the Jewish people, (3) the mass or at least the majority of Jews living at the time of a special saving activity of God, (4) all elect Israelites within the community of Israel, or (5) both Jews and Gentiles who together constitute the church of Christ, the Israel of God' (183).

of Israel. The sum of a remnant is still a remnant, and this would not advance the argument beyond the point Paul initially makes in chapter 9 and again in chapter 10 and again at the beginning of chapter 11. The context speaks of a contrast between Israel's trespass and loss on the one hand, and the 'fullness' of the Gentiles on the other (Rom. 11:11-12). It also speaks of Israel's 'life from the dead' and 'acceptance', which stands in marked contrast with her circumstance at present, which is one of unbelief and diminished blessing (Rom. 11:15). Within the context of the sustained argument of chapter 11, it would be an extraordinary anti-climax for Paul to conclude that Israel's restoration, acceptance, and life from the dead will amount to nothing more than the salvation of a small remnant.

Third, since the main point of verse 25 is that Israel's hardening is not final, but will hold true 'until the fullness of the Gentiles has come in', the conclusion of verse 26 would naturally suggest that Paul is now referring to a reversal of the pattern of Israel's unbelief and hardening that has been the occasion for the enlargement of blessing among the Gentiles. John Murray well summarizes this reversal:

> If we keep in mind the theme of this chapter and the sustained emphasis on the restoration of Israel, there is no other alternative than to conclude that the proposition, 'all Israel shall be saved,' is to be interpreted in terms of the fullness, the receiving, the engrafting of Israel as a people, the restoration of Israel to gospel favour and blessing and the correlative turning of Israel from unbelief to faith and repentance. When the preceding verses are related to verse 26, the salvation of Israel must be conceived of on a scale that is commensurate with their trespass, their loss, their casting away, their breaking off, and their hardening, commensurate, of course, in the opposite direction. This is plainly the implication of the contrasts intimated in fullness, receiving, grafting in, and salvation. In a word, it is the salvation of the mass of Israel that the apostle affirms.[35]

And fourth, this interpretation also fits well with the apostle's appeal in verses 26-27, which adduce prophecies from Isaiah 59:20, 21 and Jeremiah 31:34 to prove that this kind of salvation of all Israel, her restoration to blessing and salvation, was promised in the Old

---

35. Murray, *Romans,* 2:98.

Testament. The fulfillment of these Old Testament promises of Israel's future restoration confirms, as the apostle then reminds his readers, that God's 'election' of Israel and her 'gifts and calling of God' are 'irrevocable'. This language in verse 26 takes readers back to the question initially posed in chapter 9 and provides a culminating answer. Israel will by no means fall away irrevocably through unbelief, since God will ultimately save 'all Israel'. Just as Israel's unbelief occasioned the salvation of the Gentiles, so the salvation of the Gentiles will now occasion the salvation of all Israel. In this manner, God's mercy will be shown to 'all' (v. 32).

The cumulative weight of these considerations warrants the conclusion that Paul is likely describing a future restoration of Israel in which an abundance of blessing and salvation will be granted to her. Though God's electing purpose may be particular, it will ultimately issue in the salvation not only of the fullness of the Gentiles but also of the fullness of Israel.

Ephesians 1:3-14: Election in Christ Before the Foundation of the World

In the opening chapter of Paul's epistle to the Ephesians, we find one of the most profound statements of God's election of His people in Christ from before the foundation of the world. Within the context of an opening doxological celebration of the spiritual blessings granted to believers in Christ, Paul offers a clear and indisputable affirmation of God's sovereign, eternal, and loving election of His people in Christ. Ephesians 1:3-14 is one long and complex sentence, compactly summarizing God's grand purpose to unite all things in heaven and on earth under the headship of Jesus Christ, but we will only consider the passage's features that bear most directly upon the doctrine of election.

Eternal Election

After beginning with a benediction, which blesses God for all the spiritual blessings that He bestows upon His people in Christ, Paul focuses upon the root from which these blessings stem. The blessings of salvation in Christ find their ultimate and original source within God's eternal purpose of election. They derive from the fact that God graciously chose His people in Christ from 'before the foundation of the world'.

> Blessed be the God and Father of our Lord Jesus Christ, who has blessed us in Christ with every spiritual blessing in the heavenly places, even as he chose us in him before the foundation of the world, that we should be holy and blameless before him. In love he predestined us for adoption through Jesus Christ, according to the purpose of his will .... (Eph. 1:3-5)

According to this passage, the foremost blessing that should provoke believers to praise God is God's pre-temporal election of His people to salvation in Christ. When Paul follows his benediction in verse 3 with the expression 'even as' in verse 4, he intends to direct his audience to the blessings that are theirs in Christ and for which God should be praised. Foremost among those blessings are God's election of His people before the world was even created and His loving pre-destination of them for adoption through Christ.

What is especially noteworthy in this passage is that God's election and predestination took place before God called the world and its inhabitants into existence. When Paul uses the expression, 'before the foundation of the world,' he utilizes a common idiom for God's act of creating the world.[36] He clearly means to affirm that God's election and predestination of His people are not to be understood as acts in time or history, but as acts that belong to God's eternal purpose from before creation.

Unconditional Election

Paul's emphasis upon God's pre-temporal act of election has significant implications for the question of the ground for God's election of some to salvation. If God's purpose of election precedes the creation of the world and its inhabitants, it cannot be based upon any condition in those whom God chooses. In this respect, Paul's teaching in this passage goes even beyond what he says in Romans 9:11-12. While that text clearly places God's election of Jacob rather than Esau before they were born, it does not expressly say that God's purpose of election was

---

36. Frank Thielman, *Ephesians,* BECNT (Grand Rapids: Baker Academic, 2010), 48: 'The phrase καταβολῆ κόσμου was a common expression in Second Temple Judaism and early Christianity for God's creation of the world (e.g., Matt. 25:34; Luke 11:50; John 17:24; Heb. 4:3; 1 Pet. 1:20; Rev. 13:8 ...), and the idea that God chose his people before the world's foundation was well known.'

established before the world even existed. Both passages point out that God's election depends solely upon God's will to show mercy and not upon any merit in the person He elects, but Ephesians 1 emphasizes unconditional election in a remarkable way.

Paul's teaching of this doctrine in this passage is also confirmed by the way he describes the results of God's election. It is an election unto holiness. God does not elect those who are blameless, but rather elects His people in order that they might become 'holy and blameless before him' (v. 4). With this language, Paul clearly echoes the Old Testament teaching that God chose Israel in order that she might be separated unto Him as a holy people (cf. Deut. 7:1-6; 14:2).[37] God does not elect His people on account of any holiness in them, or by virtue of their having done anything that would commend them to His favor. Rather, God elects those who are undeserving and unholy in order that they may become holy. In a similar way, when Paul speaks of God predestining some in love,[38] he declares that He did this in order to realize His purpose to adopt them as His children. God's gracious election and loving predestination form the fountainhead from which flow all of the blessings of redemption in Christ that become the inheritance of believers in time. The sheer graciousness (or undeservedness) of God's act of election is confirmed by Paul's emphasis upon the way believers are to testify to God's grace. Those whom God called 'according to his purpose' are called 'to the praise of his glorious grace' (Eph. 1:6). God's predestination removes any possible occasion for boasting, or acting as though salvation were in any way dependent upon what believers do or have done.[39] Salvation

37. Stephen E. Fowl, *Ephesians*, NTL (Louisville, KY: Westminster John Knox, 2012), 29: 'In the light of this text [Deut. 7:6-8], it appears that Paul is telling or reminding the Ephesians that through Christ they have become participants in God's election of Israel, when God chose Abraham from among all people and graciously made a covenant with him.'

38. Commentators differ on whether the phrase 'in love' should be taken to modify the preceding clause ('holy and blameless before him in love') or the following sentence ('in love he predestined'). Though the placement of this clause leaves some ambiguity, I believe the latter is more likely due to the proximity of this clause to the verb 'predestined'. On this question, see S. M. Baugh, *Ephesians*, EEC, gen. ed. H. Wayne House (Bellingham, WA: Lexham Press, 2016), 82-3; and Fowl, *Ephesians*, 41.

39. Cf. Jack Cottrell, 'Conditional Election,' in *Grace Unlimited*, 61, who interprets this passage to teach that 'God foreknows whether an individual will meet the

in Christ from first to last, with all its consequent blessings, is an extravagant display of 'the riches of his grace', which God 'lavishes' upon His people (Eph. 1:7-8).

Though Paul emphasizes God's sovereign will as the sole ground for the election of His people in Christ, he does not represent God's will in an abstract or arbitrary manner. Predestination is an act of God's unconditional love toward those whom He elects unto salvation. While it is a free act of His will, it reveals God's grace and love for His own in Christ. God predestines those whom He loves 'according to the purpose of his will' (Eph. 1:5). Toward the end of Ephesians 1:3-14, Paul offers a comprehensive statement of how this accords with God's sovereignty. Those whom God elects to grant an inheritance in Christ 'have been predestined according to the purpose of him who works all things according the counsel of his will, so that we who were the first to hope in Christ might be to the praise of his glory' (Eph. 1:11-12). This sweeping statement underscores the theme of God's sovereignty, running like a thread throughout this passage. But Paul accents God's love, grace, and mercy so richly lavished upon those whom He is pleased to save. Though the ultimate ground for the salvation of the elect is God's will alone, God's sovereign election of His people is born out of His love. For this reason, the doctrine of predestination must always engender in those who believe a profound sense of gratitude for what God freely grants to them in and through Christ.

Election 'in Christ'

The final feature of Paul's teaching on election in Ephesians 1:3-14 that requires comment is his repeated use of the language 'in Christ.' Ordinarily in Paul's epistles, the language of union with Christ refers to the actual union that takes place as Christ's Spirit works through

---

conditions for salvation which he has sovereignly imposed.... The basis and all-encompassing condition is whether a person is *in Christ,* namely whether one has entered into a saving union with Christ by way of which he shares in all the benefits of Christ's redeeming work' (emphasis his). Cottrell's interpretation of this passage imports a typical Arminian claim that God's act of election is based upon His foreknowledge of those persons who will meet the conditions for salvation through faith in Christ. This interpretation undermines the point that Paul is making, namely, that the salvation of those who are joined to Christ is wholly based upon God's loving purpose and gives rise to the believer's praise to God for His unmerited grace.

the gospel to call believers to faith. This is also true in Ephesians 1:3-14 (vv. 3, 6, 7, 9, 13). However, in this passage Paul speaks of a union with Christ that belongs to God's act of election before the foundation of the world (vv. 4, 11). The fact that believers are called into fellowship with Christ through the gospel ministry finds its ultimate source within God's pre-temporal counsel and purpose.

When Paul speaks in this passage of election 'in Christ,' he is not teaching that Christ is the specific object of God's act of election. The beneficiaries of God's election are clearly identified in Ephesians 1:4-5 by the first person plural noun (v. 4, 'chose us'; v. 5, 'predestined us'). The beneficiaries of God's acts of election and predestination are those whom God has purposed to save, not Christ. Paul uses the prepositional phrases 'in him' and 'through him' to emphasize how God's act of election takes place in and not apart from Christ. God elects to save His people in Christ, who is accordingly the foundation, executor and source of the salvation that He is pleased to grant them. God does not elect His people to salvation without also electing Christ as the One through whom His purpose of election will be accomplished. The significance of this is well expressed by Peter O'Brien in his commentary on Ephesians:

> God's choice of his people 'in Christ' is the new element in election. He is the Chosen One par excellence (Luke 9:35; 23:35). The statement, however, does not mean that because Christians are *conscious* of being 'in Christ' they know themselves to be elect (even though this may be true on other grounds). Rather, it is objective, signifying that *in him* the people of God are chosen. If all things were created 'in him' (Col. 1:16), then it is no less true to say that earlier still it was *in him* that our election took place. [40]

---

40. O'Brien, *The Letter to the Ephesians,* PNTC (Grand Rapids: Eerdmans, 1999), 99-100. Cf. Harold Hoehner, *Ephesians: An Exegetical Commentary* (Grand Rapids: Baker Academic, 2002), 192. 'The ἡμᾶς, "us," is the object of the verb "he chose" and the prepositional phrase "in Christ" may refer to the sphere of the election or more likely it could be the relational or instrumental idea that God chose believers in connection with or through Christ's work of redemption. [Karl] Barth's construct is that Christ is the elect, and since all human beings are in Christ, then all are elect. This is completely foreign to the context of this passage as well as the entire NT. Certainly, Christ was chosen as the means to carry our [sic] God's plan of salvation, but that is not classified as election.' With these comments, Hoehner is opposing the position of Karl Barth and his son Markus Barth. We will address this issue in a

When Paul describes the believer's election 'in Christ', he means to teach that God's purpose of election is joined to, and therefore contemplates, His election of Christ as the One through whom His saving purpose for His elect will be achieved. For this reason, God may be said to elect His people in, through, and on account of Christ the Redeemer. When believers are united to Christ in time, they enter into the spiritual benefits of Christ's work of salvation that were already contemplated within God's pre-temporal decision to save His elect.[41]

That God's purpose of election contemplates the work of Christ as mediator is of particular importance to the question of the believer's assurance of God's grace in Christ. Since God elects to save those who will enter into the benefits of Christ's saving work on their behalf, believers derive their assurance of God's grace and mercy toward them by looking to Christ. In the person and work of Christ, believers find a sure basis for assurance of God's favor. They do not need to probe behind what God reveals in the person and work of Christ to be confirmed in God's favor. Since the salvation of the elect was inseparably joined to Christ's person and work in God's pre-temporal act, believers are warranted in finding Christ and His work to be sufficient for confidence in God's mercy.

---

subsequent chapter, which treats and evaluates Barth's revision of the doctrine of election. For Markus Barth's view, see his *Ephesians: Introduction, Translation, and Commentary on Chapters 1-3* (Garden City, NY: Doubleday, 1974), 'Election in Christ vs. Determinism,' 105-9.

41. Cf. Walls and Dongell, *Why I Am Not a Calvinist,* 76. Walls and Dongell argue that Jesus Christ is the One whom God elects, and that those who believe in Him come to enjoy salvation on the basis of Christ's work for them. In their view, Paul is merely teaching that God elects the class of persons who come to benefit from His saving work by their faith. For a similar claim, see Bates, *Salvation by Allegiance Alone,* 170-75. Bates argues that an emphasis upon God's election of particular persons 'runs roughshod over *the election story* the Bible wants to tell: God's election of the Messiah through Israel's election in order to save Jew and gentile alike within his elect church. In fact, there is not a single statement in the Bible that unambiguously indicates that God preselects *specific individuals* before they are born (apart from the Son) for eternal salvation' (emphasis his). However, Paul expressly declares in this passage that God elects those persons whom He sovereignly determines to save, and He elects them in and on account of Christ's work performed on their behalf. Bates erects a straw man when he speaks of the election of individuals 'apart from the Son'. I am not aware of any competent defender of God's gracious election of particular individuals who would separate this act from Christ.

Additional Evidence in the Pauline Epistles

After such an extensive treatment of the three most important Pauline passages on the doctrine of election, it may seem unnecessary to discuss any additional evidence for his teaching of God's choice to save the elect in Christ. However, other passages in Paul's writings are worth briefly noting before concluding the discussion of this doctrine in the New Testament.

Some of these passages simply identify particular believers or the community of believers as those whom God has chosen in Christ and called into fellowship with Himself. In the closing greetings of Romans 16:13, Paul identifies Rufus as 'chosen in the Lord'. Though this is a relatively incidental greeting, set in a series of similar ones to the church at Rome, it confirms the apostle's profound sense that those who truly belong to the church are members by virtue of God's gracious election. Similarly, in Colossians 3:12, Paul exhorts believers to 'put on then, as God's *chosen ones*, holy and beloved, compassion, kindness, humility, meekness, and patience' (emphasis added). In this passage, Paul describes believers in terms of God's election, which is set in parallel with their status as those whom God has set apart for Himself and whom He dearly loves. Election is unto salvation, but as is commonly the case throughout the Scriptures, it also carries with it the responsibility to live in accordance with this privilege.

In his letters to the church in Thessalonica, Paul refers to election in three places. In 1 Thessalonians 1:4-5, Paul greets the church with an expression of thanks to God for having chosen them and brought them to faith and obedience to God: 'For we know, brothers loved by God, that he has chosen you, because our gospel came to you not only in word, but also in power and in the Holy Spirit and with full conviction.' The emphasis of Paul's greeting lies upon the way we can have confidence that believers are God's elect. Paul does not appeal to God's hidden purposes for assurance, but rather to how the Thessalonians responded to the gospel call that he preached to them. Because they responded in the Spirit with faith and conviction, Paul is confident that this is a manifest token of God's electing grace bearing fruit in their lives.[42]

---

42. Peterson, *Election and Free Will*, 94.

Toward the close of his first epistle to the Thessalonians, Paul also expresses his confidence that the believers to whom he is writing will be preserved in the faith until the time of Christ's coming: 'For God has not destined us for wrath, but to obtain salvation through our Lord Jesus Christ' (1 Thess. 5:9). Paul's confidence is based upon the conviction that these believers were 'destined' or 'appointed' to salvation, and on that basis he urgently exhorts them to wait patiently and eagerly for the Lord's coming. He adduces the doctrine of election not only to assure them of their salvation, but also to undergird his exhortations to them. The third reference to election in Paul's epistles to the Thessalonians combines in a similar fashion confidence regarding their election and encouragement to continue steadfast in their profession. After instructing them regarding the coming of Christ, Paul expresses his gratitude 'because God chose you as the firstfruits to be saved, through sanctification by the Spirit and belief in the truth' (2 Thess. 2:13). The expression that Paul uses, *aparchēn,* which the ESV renders as 'first fruits' might be rendered more literally as 'from the beginning' in the sense of 'from the beginning of time'.[43] However this expression is translated, Paul clearly expresses the conviction in this verse that the Thessalonian believers were chosen by God, and that this election was evident in their calling to faith and continuance in the way of sanctification.

The pastoral epistles of Paul also contain three important references to the doctrine of election. In 2 Timothy 1:9-10, Paul follows his encouragement to Timothy not to be ashamed of the gospel by reminding him of the extraordinary privilege of being a beneficiary of God's grace in Christ. Timothy must remember, says Paul, that God 'saved us and called us to a holy calling, not because of our works but because of his own purpose and grace, which he gave us in Christ Jesus before the ages began, and which now has been manifested through the appearing of our Savior Christ Jesus.' This passage compactly affirms that the salvation of believers through faith in Christ Jesus is wholly a work of God's grace, which finds its

---

43. Charles A. Wanamaker, *Epistle to the Thessalonians: A Commentary on the Greek Text,* NIGTC (Grand Rapids: Eerdmans, 1990), 266. While Wanamaker acknowledges that Paul nowhere else uses this expression to mean 'from the beginning of time', it does make 'good sense in the context'.

fountainhead within God's eternal plan and purpose to grant salvation in Christ to those whom He wills to save. Though the language is different than that of Ephesians 1:4, the sentiment is the same: what transpires in time, when believers are called to faith in and union with Christ, is grounded in God's gracious purpose in Christ to grant them salvation.

In the second of these passages, 2 Timothy 2:10, Paul does not give as elaborate a statement of what election means. But he does appeal to the theme of election to explain what motivates him in his own apostolic ministry: 'Therefore I endure everything for the sake of the elect, that they also may obtain the salvation that is in Christ Jesus with eternal glory.' Far from undermining his sense of urgency or zeal to preach the gospel, Paul regards the fact that his ministry will serve to bring the elect to salvation as the most compelling reason to engage in the task, however difficult it may be.[44]

The third passage in the pastoral epistles that speaks of election, Titus 1:1, likewise links the theme of election with Paul's resolution to carry out the apostolic commission to preach the gospel: 'Paul, a servant of God and an apostle of Jesus Christ, for the sake of the faith of God's elect and their knowledge of the truth, which accords with godliness.' While this passage simply describes the ministry of the apostle Paul, it also links his self-denying labor to his desire to be an instrument whereby those whom God elects are saved through a knowledge of the truth. What motivates Paul's ministry is the prospect that God will be pleased to use him as a means to call the elect to salvation through faith in Christ.

Summary

To summarize the apostle Paul's teaching on election poses a special challenge. Even though Paul addresses the subject more extensively than any other biblical author, he never deals with it in an abstract manner. In Romans 9–11, Paul treats God's purpose of election within the context of His comprehensive purposes in the course of redemptive history, from the election of His people Israel to the calling of the Gentiles through the gospel, and then the salvation of all

---

44. Cf. Peterson, *Election and Free Will,* 96: 'Although God's choices are not based on foreseen faithfulness, his choices are compatible with exhortations to faithfulness.'

Israel. Undeniably, Paul does not present the doctrine of election out of excessive theological curiosity. He presents God's merciful election of His people in Christ as an answer to the pressing existential question: Has the Word of God failed? Upon the answer to this question hangs the confidence that believers have in God's unfailing love toward them in Christ. For if God's Word and promise have failed, the testimony of Paul to the gospel of Jesus Christ loses its luster. Accordingly, when Paul concludes his case at the end of Romans 11, he breaks forth in a doxology brimming with praise for God's unfathomable wisdom, power, and overflowing mercy.

Several features of Paul's formulation of God's purpose of election are especially noteworthy. Each of these has figured prominently in the long history of theological reflection on the biblical doctrine of election.

First, more explicitly than any other biblical author, Paul views the course of redemptive history comprehensively as the unfolding of God's eternal purpose to elect His people to salvation in Christ. Before the foundation of the world, God eternally, sovereignly, and graciously determined in Christ to show mercy to a great number of sinners (though not all) who are fallen in Adam, Jew and Gentile alike. All the blessings of salvation – effectual calling, justification, glorification, conformity to Christ, gracious adoption, sanctification – find their source in God's eternal purpose of election (Rom. 8:29-30; Eph. 1:3-6).

Second, just as the theme of free justification by faith accents the truth that fallen sinners owe their salvation to God's grace and not to their own works, so the theme of God's purpose of election in Christ accents God's sheer grace in the salvation of His people. Nothing more clearly magnifies God's grace alone in the salvation of fallen sinners than God's choice to show mercy to those whom He wills. In several key passages, Paul appeals to God's sovereign and gracious election of His people to demonstrate that salvation does not depend upon any human performance that distinguishes some from others (Rom. 9:11; Eph. 1:3-10). Though Paul does not employ the language of 'unconditional' election, this is undoubtedly what he teaches. When he appeals to the examples of Isaac and Jacob in Romans 9, his intention is to illustrate how their election was altogether undeserved.

Nothing distinguished those whom God elects that would make them worthy or properly the objects of God's unmerited favor.

Third, while Paul's primary emphasis is on God's undeserved mercy in the election of some to salvation in Christ, he also insists that those whom God does not choose to save have no ground to complain that He is unjust. For Paul, God displays His undeserved mercy in electing to save some, and He displays His justice in electing not to save others. Although the language is anachronistic, Paul speaks of God's purpose of election in terms that are broadly 'infralapsarian'. The persons whom God elects in Christ are fallen sinners in Adam, all of whom are worthy of condemnation and death. While it would be inappropriate to suggest that Paul anticipates later debates in Christian theology about the 'order of God's decrees' (*ordo decretorum Dei*), Romans 9:19-24 makes clear that God's purpose of election contemplates the whole human race in its fallen condition. For this reason, Paul compares the human race to a 'lump of clay' from which God is free to make 'one vessel for honorable use and another for dishonorable use' (v. 21). The implication of this language is that God is not only free to show mercy to some and not others, but He also acts justly when He 'endures with much patience vessels of wrath prepared for destruction' (v. 22). Paul's teaching regarding God's election of some and non-election of others amounts to what later theologians call 'double predestination', but this language must be carefully used when describing his view. For Paul, the primary emphasis lies upon the marvel of God's rich mercy toward all whom He wills to save, not upon the corollary truth that God justly withholds His mercy from others whom He leaves in their sin.

Fourth, despite the concerted efforts of many modern interpreters, it is also clear that Paul's doctrine of election addresses the issue of eschatological salvation, and that it involves God's election to save a particular number of sinners. While it is certainly true that the reach of His mercy encompasses the salvation of many from all nations, Jew and Gentile alike, God's election to save is always particular, and not universal, in its scope. Contrary to the claim that Paul knows only an election of a corporate people in Christ, we have seen that this claim is inconsistent with Paul's argument throughout Romans 9–11 and elsewhere. Even the assertion that Paul views Jesus Christ as the proper object of God's election is commonly overstated. In Ephesians 1:4, the passage often cited in support of this claim, Paul clearly identifies the objects of God's election as those whom He wills to bring to salvation through the work of Christ. God elects them 'in Christ', that is, in respect to Christ as their Redeemer and source of every saving blessing. Nowhere does Paul teach that God elected Christ and in Him an indefinite number of nameless persons who choose to enjoy fellowship with Him by faith.

And fifth, in Paul's teaching regarding election, there are always two emphases in the foreground: the praise due to God for His grace and mercy in Jesus Christ, and the confident persuasion of that grace and mercy on the part of those who embrace Christ by faith. Nowhere is this more evident than in Romans 8–11, where Paul's triumphant peroration on the love of God toward His own in Christ (Rom. 8) is followed by Paul's demonstration of God's rich mercy in saving the fullness of the Gentiles and his own kinsmen according to the flesh (Rom. 9–11).

CHAPTER 4

Augustine's Doctrine of Election: 'What Do You Have That You Have Not Received?'

IN view of its pervasiveness in the biblical witness, it is not surprising that the doctrine of election has received considerable attention throughout the history of Christian theology. The theme of the triune God's gracious election to save His people through the work of Christ is central to the biblical witness, and Christian theologians cannot escape the obligation to articulate this theme in a way that conforms to scriptural teaching and opposes erroneous formulations. Unhappily, in the course of theological history, no doctrine has occasioned more controversy or elicited more negative press than that of election.

My purpose in the second part of our study will be to provide a summary of how Christian theologians have articulated the doctrine of election at critical moments in the history of the church. Though there is often a tendency in modern theology to neglect the study of history, any contemporary presentation of the doctrine of election must be informed by the way theologians have grappled with the biblical data in the face of various challenges and aberrant views. Because contemporary interpreters of Scripture are members of the catholic church, they are obligated to listen to and learn from voices in the past. The enterprise of Christian theology is more than a simple and direct engagement with the scriptural witness. It always involves a responsibility to engage the history of doctrinal formulations.[1] The formulation of the doctrine of election requires a fresh engagement with scriptural teaching, but it also requires the humility to learn from those teachers of the church who have previously sought to summarize faithfully what the Word of God teaches regarding this subject.

The obvious place to begin a summary of the doctrine of election in the history of Christian theology is with the great church father, Augustine (354-430), bishop of Hippo in North Africa. No name is more inextricably linked with the doctrine of election. Augustine was compelled by the challenges of Pelagianism and semi-Pelagianism to defend what he termed the 'catholic' teaching of the church, namely, that fallen sinners in Adam are saved by the prevenient and electing grace of God, not by virtue of any human works or merits.

It is almost impossible to exaggerate the importance of Augustine's contribution to the controversial history of debate regarding the doctrine of election and predestination. In the same way that Augustine's most important writings on election were born in the heat of controversy with Pelagianism, the history of the church's reflection on the doctrine of election has often been marked by controversy. One feature of this history, however, is undeniable: subsequent attempts to articulate the biblical doctrine of election may not ignore Augustine's powerful polemic against any teaching that denies the sheer graciousness of God's saving work in Christ or ascribes to human merit a role, however large or small, as a basis for the salvation of fallen human beings. In many respects, the long history of theological reflection in the Christian church through the centuries has always had to reckon with the position Augustine espoused in the conflict with Pelagianism.[2] In subsequent chapters, which detail this history in the period of the sixteenth century and its aftermath,

---

1. For a defense of this approach to doctrinal formulation and a theological interpretation of Scripture, see Michael Allen and Scott R. Swain, *Reformed Catholicity: The Promise of Retrieval for Theology and Biblical Interpretation* (Grand Rapids: Baker Academic, 2015); and Carl R. Trueman, *The Creedal Imperative* (Wheaton, IL: Crossway, 2012).

2. Cf. Jaroslav Pelikan, *The Christian Tradition: A History of the Development of Doctrine,* vol. 1: *The Emergence of the Catholic Tradition (100-600)* (Chicago: The University of Chicago Press, 1971), 330.

as well as more recent discussions of the doctrine, we will see how Augustine's formulations often set the terms of the debates and serve as a point of departure for new perspectives.

The Challenge of Pelagianism and Semi-Pelagianism

Before considering Augustine's writings on the subject of election, we need to identify the occasion for them. Though Augustine is commonly known as a defender of a robust doctrine of election and predestination, it must be remembered that he was compelled to defend this doctrine in the face of the challenge of Pelagianism. The core issue in Augustine's articulation of the doctrine of election is well-expressed by his common moniker, the 'Doctor of Grace'.[3] The starting point for Augustine's formulation of the doctrine of election was not an abstract theory of God's sovereignty. Rather, Augustine was provoked to set forth the theme of election to combat the Pelagian denial that God's grace underlies, or is prevenient to, the salvation of all believers who embrace the gospel promise in Christ.

The provocateur of Augustine was Pelagius, a native of the British Isles who became an influential teacher in Rome late in the fourth century.[4] Although Pelagius was a zealous ascetic and advocate of a strict morality, the popular opinion that he was a monk is uncertain.

---

3. Gerald Bonner, *St Augustine of Hippo: Life and Controversies* (Philadelphia: The Westminster Press, 1963), 314.

4. For a more detailed summary of Pelagius' views and the history of Augustine's engagement with Pelagianism, see Bonner, *St. Augustine of Hippo,* 312-93; *idem, Freedom and Necessity: St. Augustine's Teaching on Divine Power and Human Freedom* (Washington, D.C.: The Catholic University of America Press, 2007); J. B. Mozley, *A Treatise on the Augustinian Doctrine of Predestination* (3rd ed.; London: John Murray, 1883), esp. 46-99, 126-232; 'Pelagius, Pelagianism,' in *The New Schaff-Herzog Encyclopedia of Religious Knowledge,* ed. Samuel M. Jackson, vol. 8 (Grand Rapids: Baker Book House, 1950), 438-444; and Benjamin Breckinridge Warfield, 'Augustine and the Pelagian Controversy,' in *The Works of Benjamin B. Warfield,* vol. 4: *Studies in Tertullian and Augustine* (reprint; Grand Rapids: Baker Book House, 1981 [1930]), 289-412. Of these studies, Bonner's are the least sympathetic toward Augustine's position. The exact dates of Pelagius' birth and death are not known. Though I describe Pelagius as Augustine's 'provocateur', it could also be said that Augustine was the provocateur of Pelagius. After spending a number of years in Rome, Pelagius left in A.D. 409 and took up residence in Palestine where his views obtained a more congenial reception.

Consistent with his desire to encourage Christian obedience and moral conduct, Pelagius was a fierce opponent of the 'fatalism' associated with Manichaeism. Its dualism distinguished good and evil, light and darkness, into two eternally co-existing realities. On that basis, Manichaeism repudiated radically the idea that all human beings retain the freedom to do what the holy law of God requires. For Pelagius, the Manichaen view of good and evil undermined encouragement to holy living through the ability to do what people ought to do. In Pelagius' estimation, if the principle of evil so dominates the lives of fallen human beings, then all exhortations to live well become futile.

During the period of his teaching in Rome, Pelagius first became aware of Augustine's teaching through consulting his anti-Manichaean writings. While Pelagius was disturbed by the implications for moral conduct of these anti-Manichaen writings, he became especially alarmed with Augustine's view in A.D. 405 upon hearing a bishop reading a passage in the tenth book of Augustine's *Confessions*. Augustine used the expression in prayer to God, 'Give what you command, and command what you will [*Da quod iubes, et iube quod vis*]':

> All my hope is found solely in your exceeding great mercy. Give what you command, and command what you will. You enjoin continence. 'And as I knew,' says a certain man, 'that no one could be continent except God gave it, and this also was a point of wisdom to know whose gift it was.'... O Love, who are forever aflame and are never extinguished, O Charity, my God, set me aflame! You enjoin continence: give what you command, and command what you will.[5]

Upon hearing this passage of Augustine, Pelagius was greatly agitated by the way it seemed to support the common excuse of those whom he taught and earnestly called to a life of holiness. Whereas Augustine's aim in this passage was to express his dependence upon God's gracious aid, Pelagius took it as a form of quietism that excuses disobedience by expressing human inability to do what God requires.

---

5. *The Confessions of St. Augustine,* trans. John K. Ryan, Book X, xix, 255-6. For an account of this event, see Bonner, *St. Augustine of Hippo,* 317; and Warfield, APC, 292-93.

In the subsequent course of the dispute between Pelagius and Augustine, several features of Pelagius' teaching became more pronounced. These features and the views of Pelagius' followers provoked Augustine in the last period of his life to write a series of anti-Pelagian writings in which he articulated his understanding of the scriptural doctrine of election.[6]

Undoubtedly, the first feature of Pelagius' teaching was his basic conviction that what God commands in His righteous law must be within the reach of human ability. If the law's demands are unable to be kept by human beings to whom they are communicated, then human beings are no longer responsible for their moral failures. Human responsibility assumes a corresponding ability. In reply to those who would excuse their disobedience to the law by saying, 'it is hard' or 'we are not able, being mere men,' Pelagius' response was to affirm the plenary ability of human beings to do what is required of them:

> Blind folly and profane rashness! We accuse the God of knowledge of a twofold ignorance, so that He seems to be ignorant of what He has done or what He has commanded—as if, unmindful of human frailty, whose author He Himself is, He has imposed commands upon man which man is not able to bear.[7]

In Pelagius' view, God would not require more from anyone in the way of obedience than he or she was able to do. Human responsibility only extends as far as human ability. Since God has given human beings the natural power to choose to do what He requires, 'whether we will, or whether we will not will, we have the capacity of not sinning.'[8] This means that all human beings retain the power of free will to obey the commands of God's law.

6. During his time in Rome, Pelagius converted a student, Coelestius, to his position. In the course of the controversy, Coelestius proved to be a capable and ardent proponent of Pelagius' views. In the later stages of the Pelagian and semi-Pelagian controversies, Julian, bishop of Eclanum, became the champion of a semi-Pelagian position.

7. Pelagius, *Epistle to Demetrias,* 16 (as quoted by Bonner, *St. Augustine of Hippo*, 361).

8. As quoted by Augustine, 'On Nature and Grace,' in SLNPNF, ed. Philip Schaff, vol. 5: *St. Augustine's Anti-Pelagian Works* (New York: The Christian Literature Company, 1887), chap 57. In subsequent footnotes, my citations from this volume will include the title, book (where applicable) and chapter numbers of Augustine's works.

The second feature of Pelagius' teaching was his insistence that, because human beings are in principle capable of keeping God's law in its entirety, they are able to live without sin. The capacity for perfect obedience to the commandments of God, which belongs to human nature as empowered and gifted by God, follows from Pelagius' view of human ability. If all the commandments of God are genuine exhortations to obedience, and if they presume the ability of human beings to perform what they require, perfect obedience to the law is possible for any person. While Pelagius acknowledged that most human beings commit discrete acts of disobedience to the law, he insisted that many Old Testament saints lived free from sin and that such perfection is possible for New Testament saints who have the help of the law and the example of Christ. Indeed, with the coming of Christ, whose sinless life is a principal example, perfection becomes even more likely.

The third feature of Pelagius' view was his repudiation of the doctrine of original sin. This doctrine traditionally taught that Adam's sin entailed the hereditary corruption of all his posterity. Original sin means that all human beings are born and conceived in sin, liable to condemnation and death, and in need of regeneration and renewal by God's prevenient grace. Pelagius recoiled against this doctrine and regarded it as an affront to divine justice. In Pelagius' view, Adam's sin is not transmitted to his posterity by any form of hereditary corruption, but solely by way of 'imitation'. The fact of human sin after Adam's fall must be accounted for by the way human beings voluntarily choose to follow his example of disobedience. For Pelagius, Adam's sin 'injured only himself, and not the human race,' so that 'infants at their birth are in the same state that Adam was before the transgression'.[9] In the strictest sense, no human being is born sinful. All are born sinless, neither virtuous nor evil (*ut sine virtute, ita sine vitio*).[10] That human beings sin is wholly a consequence of choices they make to do good or to do evil. In his summary of Pelagius' conception of sin, Warfield speaks of its 'peculiar individualism', which denies any real connection between Adam's sin and the sins of those who follow his bad example:

---

9. As quoted by Augustine, 'On Original Sin,' in SLNPNF, vol. 5, 11.

10. 'On Original Sin,' 14.

The peculiar individualism of the Pelagian view of the world comes out strongly in their failure to perceive the effect of habit on nature itself. Just as they conceived of virtue as a complex of virtuous acts, so they conceived of sin exclusively as an act, or series of disconnected acts. They appear not to have risen above the essentially heathen view which had no notion of holiness apart from a series of acts of holiness, or of sin apart from a like series of sinful acts. Thus the will was isolated from its acts, and the acts from each other, and all organic connection or continuity of life was not only overlooked but denied.[11]

The fourth feature of Pelagius' teaching was his attenuated view of God's grace in salvation. According to Pelagius, for human beings to do what the law of God requires, they need to be granted, and to retain by God's power, that freedom of will which belongs to their created nature. When Pelagius speaks of this aspect of God's grace, he means nothing more than the inalienable power of human beings to choose to do good or bad. In Pelagius' own description of this power, he declares, 'Everything good, and everything evil, on account of which we are either laudable or blameworthy, is not born with us but done by us: for we are born ... with a capacity for either conduct; and we are procreated as without virtue, so also without vice; and previous to the action of our own proper will, that alone is in man which God has formed.'[12] In addition to this basic dimension of God's grace (the bestowal of a created ability to choose to do good or evil), human beings also need the further grace of God's promise of forgiveness for past sins that cannot be undone, as well as the encouragement and instruction of His holy law and the good example of obedience that is provided in Christ. Though each of these aspects of God's grace provides a kind of 'external' encouragement to human beings, none of them involves an 'interior' or transformative work of God's grace that precedes and enables human beings to do what pleases God. Therefore, the salvation of human beings ultimately depends upon their voluntary choice to do what the law of God and the example of Christ encourage, namely, to perform holy acts that commend them to God's favor. Warfield's summary of Pelagius' view rightly illustrates

---

11. Warfield, APC, 295-96.

12. As quoted by Augustine, 'On Original Sin,' in SNLPNF, vol. 5, 14.

how he reduces the grace that saves human beings to little more than instruction in God's law and provision of Christ as an example:

> At first the light of nature was so strong that men by it alone could live in holiness. And it was only when men's manners became corrupt and tarnished nature began to be insufficient for holy living, that by God's grace the Law was given as an addition to mere nature; and by it 'the original lustre was restored to nature after its blush had been impaired.' And so again, after the habit of sinning once more prevailed among men, and 'the law became unequal to the task of curing it,' Christ was given furnishing men with forgiveness of sins, exhortations to imitation of the example and the holy example itself.[13]

In our exposition of Augustine's response to Pelagianism, we will clarify further these features of Pelagius' teaching. However, this summary of Pelagius' views provides a sufficient account of the occasion for Augustine's anti-Pelagian writings.

Augustine's Doctrine of Original Sin and Human Freedom

In the earliest phase of Augustine's engagement with Pelagianism, the topics of original sin and the nature of human freedom are his primary focus. In order to establish the context for understanding the necessity of God's prevenient grace, Augustine begins by expressing the underlying assumption of any biblical view, namely, that fallen sinners are not able to do what God requires of them (both in His holy law and in the gospel call to faith and repentance) because of the hereditary corruption they have received in Adam and the adverse effects of this corruption upon the exercise of the human will. For this reason, the first two treatises of Augustine against Pelagius, both of which were written in A.D. 412 ('On the Merits and Forgiveness of Sins, and On the Baptism of Infants' and 'On the Spirit and the Letter'), address the doctrine of original sin.[14] Although Augustine elaborates upon his arguments against Pelagianism in subsequent writings, these

---

13. Warfield, APC, 295. Warfield's quotes are from Augustine, 'On the Grace of Christ,' in SNLPNF, vol. 5, 43.

14. The first of these treatises, as its title indicates, was comprised of two distinct books. Hence, my references to it will include the book and chapter numbers.

two works provide important background for understanding his more mature statement regarding the doctrine of predestination.

In the first treatise, 'On the Merits and Forgiveness of Sins,' Augustine argues against the Pelagian attempt to separate the death of Adam and all his posterity from the fact that Adam fell from his original state of integrity. In Pelagius' view, Adam was 'so formed that he would even without any demerit of sin have died, not as a penalty of sin, but from the necessity of his being ....'[15] Augustine argues against this view. Though Adam was created mortal in the sense that he was capable of or liable to death should he fall into sin and disobedience, he was not created as one destined to die (*moriturus*).[16] The death of Adam was an 'accident' that did not belong to him by virtue of nature, but by virtue of his sin. Furthermore, the fact that Adam's posterity have become subject to the universal dominion of death follows from the way they are involved in and suffer the consequence of Adam's sin. Contrary to the Pelagian view that sin is solely transmitted to Adam's posterity by their 'imitation' of his sin, Augustine appeals to Romans 5:12 ('By one man sin entered into the world, and death by sin') to argue that the original sin of Adam is transmitted 'from the first man to other persons by natural descent.'[17] 'No doubt all they

---

15. 'On the Merits and Forgiveness of Sins,' I.2.

16. ibid., I.5.

17. ibid., I.9. Augustine holds what is often termed a 'realist' view of the relation between Adam and his posterity. In this view, God created one generic human nature that Adam possessed in such a way that his sin was not only his own but the sin of the whole human race. In his great work, *City of God* (*SLNPNF*, vol. 2, book 13, chapter 14), Augustine expresses this view succinctly: 'For we were all in that one man, since we all were that one man who fell into sin.... For not yet was the particular form created and distributed in us in which we as individuals were to live, but already the seminal nature was there from which we were to be propagated; and this being vitiated by sin, and bound by the chain of death, and justly condemned, man could not be born of man in any other state.' An alternative view, which prevailed among Reformed theologians in the post-Reformation period, is 'federalism'. As its name suggests (from *foedus*, covenant), federalism views Adam as the one whom God appointed as the 'head' or 'representative' of the whole human race. Because Adam sinned as a 'public' person, that is, as the covenant head of those whom he represented, his sin entails two consequences: (1) the guilt of Adam's sin is immediately imputed to all whom he represented; and (2) in consequence of their being implicated in the guilt of Adam's sin, all of Adam's posterity inherit a corrupted nature. For an extensive discussion of these two views, see G. C. Berkouwer, *Sin* (Grand Rapids: Eerdmans, 1971), 436-65.

imitate Adam who by disobedience transgress the commandment of God; but he is one thing as an example to those who sin because they choose; and another thing as the progenitor of all who are born with sin.'[18] Through the sin of Adam, every one of his progeny is 'depraved also in his own person ... by the hidden corruption of his own carnal concupiscence.'[19] The Pelagian view that sin is transmitted merely by human beings following Adam's example cannot do justice to the way the apostle Paul links the universal sway of death to Adam's original sin. All of Adam's progeny are subject to the power of death only in consequence of Adam's sin and the transmission of the corruption of his sin to all members of the human race.

In order to confirm this truth, Augustine appeals to the baptism of infants by which they are cleansed from the pollution of sin and delivered from condemnation and death. Since infants are baptized, though they 'have not yet become able to imitate any one', their baptism provides an irrefutable testimony to the reality of their inheritance of a corruption they receive by propagation from Adam.[20] Because Adam's original sin is a sufficient basis for the condemnation and death of all his progeny, it excludes not only adults but also infants from entrance into the kingdom of God. Only by God's grace is it possible for anyone, including infants, to be delivered from the power of sin and death. The baptism of infants, accordingly, is necessary to deliver them from the consequence of Adam's sin. While infants who are not baptized receive a 'milder condemnation' than those who add their actual sins to the original sin of Adam, they are nonetheless involved in that death and condemnation that is due to all of Adam's progeny.[21] Some followers of Pelagius attempt to escape this truth by saying that infants are baptized only for the remission of sins and

---

18. ibid., I.10.

19. ibid., I.10.

20. ibid., I.10.

21. ibid., I.20: 'It may therefore be correctly affirmed, that such infants as quit the body without being baptized will be involved in the mildest condemnation of all. That person, therefore, greatly deceives both himself and others, who teaches that they will not be involved in condemnation.' Augustine is compelled to this conclusion by virtue of his conviction that baptism is a necessary and effectual means of regeneration and redemption, apart from which no one can be saved. In the closing part of this chapter, I will comment on this conviction when assessing Augustine's view.

not for obtaining the kingdom of heaven, but this contradicts the universal teaching of the catholic church. According to the church's doctrine of baptism, no one can attain to eternal salvation 'without being born again in Christ, – [a result] which He meant to be effected through baptism.'[22] Thus, when infants are baptized, they are baptized as sinners who need to be delivered from 'the guilt of original sin which is healed in them by the grace of Him who saves them by the laver of regeneration.'[23] Though Augustine admits that it is hidden from our judgment why one is baptized and another is not, we may not question God's salvation of some, but not others. We must be content with the truth that God gratuitously grants salvation through baptism to some who have no 'prevenient merits for deserving it', while He justly withholds it from others.[24]

After rejecting the Pelagian view of original sin, Augustine turns to the topic of human freedom and the necessity of God's prevenient grace to enable fallen human beings to do any good. According to Augustine, the Pelagian view of human freedom, which affirms the ability of fallen human beings to live a perfect life of obedience, is incompatible with the biblical teaching regarding original sin and the necessity of God's grace to heal and renew fallen sinners. In response to Pelagius' position, Augustine argues the following points: (1) though it is possible for a fallen human being to live without sin, this possibility wholly depends upon God's gracious help to 'heal the facility of will' that was 'wounded' through the fall into sin; (2) though it is possible with God's help to live without sin, no fallen human being lives wholly without sin in this life; (3) the fact that fallen sinners fail to live a life of perfect obedience is due either to their failure to know what such obedience requires or to will accordingly; and (4) the only human being who has lived a perfect life of obedience is the Mediator, Christ.[25] Augustine's purpose in establishing each of these points is to show how fallen sinners can only be saved by a

---

22. ibid., I.22.

23. ibid., I.24.

24. ibid., I.29. Though Augustine does not directly address the theme of election and predestination in this treatise, his teaching at this point anticipates what he will say in subsequent treatises, which treat more directly the subject of election.

25. ibid., II.7-9, 26, 38.

mighty work of God's prevenient grace. Unless God graciously wills to grant to fallen sinners what is needed, namely, the healing of their wounded will and corrupted nature, no human being is able to do what is required of them for salvation.

The second of Augustine's early anti-Pelagian writings, 'A Treatise on the Spirit and the Letter,' provides an even sharper statement of Augustine's objections to Pelagianism. In this treatise, Augustine expands upon his argument that God's grace alone must precede anything that fallen sinners do in order to be saved. His particular focus is Pelagius' claim that the human will only needs the enlightenment and encouragement of God's law to know and will what is pleasing to God. According to Pelagius' teaching, human beings not only have the power of free will to live perfectly or advance in obedience, but they are also helped by God's giving His holy law to stimulate such obedience. In Augustine's words, the Pelagians teach that 'by means of the free-will naturally implanted within him, he [man] enters on the way which is pointed out to him, and by persevering in a just and pious course of life, deserves to attain the blessedness of eternal life.'[26]

Augustine argues that it is not enough for human beings to have a free will and be given a revelation of what the law of God requires in order to please God. What is needed is the 'Holy Ghost, by whom there is formed in his mind a delight in, and a love of, that supreme and unchangeable good which is God ... in order that by this gift to him of the earnest, as it were, of the free gift, he may conceive an ardent desire to cleave to his Maker, and may burn to enter upon the participation in that true light, that it may go well with him from Him to whom he owes his existence.'[27] Without the gift of God's love shed abroad in the heart of sinners, it is not possible for them to delight in and feel a genuine love for God. To know the law of God, but not the love of God, is akin to knowing the 'letter of the law that kills' but not the 'Spirit that gives life'.[28] While the law of God is able to give us a knowledge of God's will, it is not able by itself to implant within us the desire to will what is in accord with it. The law tells us what pleases God, but

---

26. 'On the Spirit and the Letter,' 4.

27. ibid., 5.

28. ibid., 6.

it cannot give us the requisite desire to do what pleases God. For this reason, the apostle Paul teaches that he would not have known what it is to covet, unless the law of God had said, 'you shall not covet.'[29]

After treating the role of God's law, which exposes but does not have the power to expunge sin, Augustine notes how Paul contrasts the righteousness of the law with the righteousness of faith. Both in the Old Testament and in the New Testament, righteousness comes only through faith as it receives God's grace. Unless the human will is healed by God's grace in Christ, it is unable to freely perform what God's law requires.

> For neither is the law fulfilled except by free will; but by the law is the knowledge of sin, by faith the acquisition of grace against sin, by grace the healing of the soul from the disease of sin, by the health of the soul freedom of will, by free will the love of righteousness, by love of righteousness the accomplishment of the law.[30]

Because grace 'cures the will', it does not oppose free will but empowers it for a true liberty.[31] Though fallen human beings retain the power of free will, this does not mean that they have the ability to believe or not to believe apart from God's grace.[32] To yield to the summons of the gospel is a 'function of our own will', but the ability to do so is given to us by God's grace.[33] Against the Pelagian view that the human will of fallen sinners is able in its own power to respond to God's grace, Augustine notes that

> this will is to be ascribed to the divine gift, not merely because it arises from our free will, which was created naturally with us; but also because God acts upon us by the incentives of our perceptions, to will and to

---

29. ibid.

30. ibid., 52.

31. ibid.

32. In a later treatise, 'On the Grace of Christ' (A.D. 418), Augustine rejects Pelagius' claim that fallen human beings retain three faculties by which to fulfill God's commandments: 'capacity' (*possibilitas*), 'will' (*velle*) and 'action' (*esse*). For Pelagius, the first of these is from God, while the second and third are entirely within our power. In Augustine's estimation, Pelagius wrongly reduces God's grace to what is ours merely by nature. Furthermore, Pelagius fails to acknowledge that the will to do what pleases God is also granted to us by grace.

33. ibid., 60.

believe, either externally by evangelical exhortations, where even the commands of the law also do something, if they so far admonish a man of his infirmity that he betakes himself to the grace that justifies by believing.... Since God, therefore, in such ways acts upon the reasonable soul in order that it may believe in Him ... it surely follows that it is God who both works in man the willing to believe, and in all things prevents [goes before] us with His mercy.[34]

Though Augustine wrote a number of anti-Pelagian writings after these two important works in A.D. 412, the main rudiments of his doctrine of original sin and the freedom of the will of fallen sinners are clearly evident in them. In his subsequent writings, Augustine was compelled to address several Pelagian objections to his doctrine that were raised in the course of the controversy. Though these objections do not lie at the heart of the controversy, two of them are worthy of brief notice.

The first focused upon Augustine's view of marriage as created by God. Because Augustine's doctrine of original sin included the idea that Adam's posterity were born and conceived in sin, advocates of Pelagianism accused him of treating marriage and sexual appetites as impure and unholy. To this accusation, Augustine responded by defending the sinless integrity of marriage and sexual appetites within it as originally created and given by God.[35] In Augustine's view, the perversion of human sexuality through 'fleshly concupiscence' after the fall is an 'accident' that arises from the fact of original sin. The guilt of such concupiscence is remitted through the grace of baptism, even though concupiscence itself is not altogether removed from those who are baptized. A second, related objection to Augustine's view of original sin was that it ascribed to God the creation of human souls that were corrupted through original sin and worthy of condemnation and death. Since the advocates of Pelagianism taught a doctrine of the direct, immediate creation of human souls, Augustine's doctrine

---

34. ibid. Cf. J.N.D. Kelly, *Early Christian Doctrines* (2nd ed.; New York: Harper & Row, 1958, 1960), 367-8: '[I]n the strict sense of free choice (*liberum arbitrium*), he holds that man is always free, that is, he can choose freely the course he will pursue; but since his will acts on motives and certain motives may press irresistibly on it, the range of choices which are "live options" for him is limited by the sort of man he is.'

35. 'On Marriage and Concupiscence.'

of original sin seemed in their view to make God the author of sin. In his reply to this objection, Augustine argued that Scripture's teaching regarding the creation of human souls does not clearly or necessarily favor the 'creationist' view of the origin of the human soul.[36] In Augustine's estimation, whether souls are directly created by God or produced through the natural process of procreation, the Scriptures clearly teach that all human beings who belong to Adam's posterity are born and conceived in sin and are therefore liable to condemnation and death.

Augustine's Doctrine of Election[37]

In the course of Augustine's early confrontation with Pelagianism, the focus of his attention was upon its denial of original sin and its assertion of the plenary ability of all human beings to do what God requires in His holy law. Though Augustine occasionally addresses the doctrine of election in his early anti-Pelagian writings, he increasingly does so in his later writings, especially in opposing a modified form of Pelagius' teaching known historically as semi-Pelagianism. Since the burden of Augustine's polemics against Pelagius was that he denies the necessity of God's prevenient grace to the salvation of fallen

---

36. 'A Treatise on the Soul and Its Origin,' 315-71. In the history of Christian theology, the origin of the human soul is usually explained either by 'creationism' or 'traducianism'. The creationist view ascribes the creation of the soul to a direct act of God, whereas the traducianist view regards the soul to be transmitted (*traduced*) through the mediate act of human procreation. The Pelagian accusation that Augustine's doctrine of original sin would make God the author of sin assumes that he espouses a creationist viewpoint, and expresses a common complaint against this view in the history of theology. For his part, Augustine declines to opt for one view or the other, declaring that the Scriptures do not clearly address the question. For an extensive discussion of 'creationism' and 'traducianism', see G. C. Berkouwer, *Man: The Image of God* (Grand Rapids: Eerdmans, 1962), 279-309.

37. For general treatments of Augustine's doctrine of election, see Bonner, *St. Augustine of Hippo,* 352-93; *idem, Freedom and Necessity*; Mozley, *The Augustinian Doctrine of Predestination*; Warfield, 'Augustine and the Pelagian Controversy'; Kelly, *Early Christian Doctrines,* 361-8; A. D. R. Polman, *De Praedestinatieleer van Augustinus, Thomas van Aquino en Calvijn: Een Dogmahistorische Studie* (Franeker: T. Wever, 1936), 27-186; Peter Brown, *Augustine of Hippo* (Los Angeles: University of California Press, 1967); Matthew Levering, *Predestination: Biblical and Theological Paths* (Oxford: Oxford University Press, 2011), 44-54; and *idem,* 'On the Predestination of the Saints,' in *The Theology of Augustine: An Introductory Guide to His Most Important Works* (Grand Rapids: Baker Academic, 2013), 71-88.

sinners, it is not surprising that Augustine increasingly turns to the doctrine of election to refute Pelagius' teaching. For if salvation is gratuitously given without any merit on the part of its recipient, then it ultimately depends upon God's gracious decision to grant faith to those whom He chooses to save.

'To Simplician': Augustine on Romans 9

Before I consider Augustine's fulsome statement of the doctrine of election in two of his later writings against Pelagianism, I want to begin by considering his first important formulation of the doctrine in an earlier work that preceded the Pelagian controversy. In A.D. 397, Augustine wrote a treatise to Simplician (d. 400), the successor of Ambrose as bishop of Milan, entitled 'To Simplician—On Various Questions.'[38] As the title of this work intimates, it was written by Augustine shortly after he had become coadjutor bishop of Hippo in order to answer several questions that Simplician had addressed to him. Two of Simplician's questions focused upon the interpretation of two difficult passages in Paul's epistle to the Romans: Romans 7:7-25 and Romans 9:10-29.[39] In his response regarding Romans 9, Augustine provides his first comprehensive statement of the doctrine of election and predestination. In this statement, Augustine anticipates the formulation of the doctrine that he subsequently set forth in his polemics with Pelagianism. Thus, it provides important evidence that the doctrine of grace Augustine propounded in his later controversy with Pelagianism was already held by him in a less-developed form prior to this controversy.

In his treatment of Romans 9:10-29, Augustine begins by noting that the passage, though 'rather obscure', must be interpreted in the light of the primary purpose of the apostle Paul throughout the book

---

38. *Augustine: Earlier Writings,* ed. J. H. S. Burleigh, LCC (Philadelphia: The Westminster Press, 1953), Book I, 372-406. In subsequent references, I will cite this source by part and section number (e.g. '2.2' refers to part 2, section 2).

39. In the first part of his letter, Augustine offers an interpretation of Romans 7:7-25 that emphasizes the impossibility for fallen human beings to do what the law of God requires. Only by God's grace are we able to desire and to act in a way that conforms to God's law, though even then we find ourselves in a state of tension between what we will to do and what we actually do. In the subsequent history of Christian theology, Augustine's interpretation of this passage, which views the struggle Paul describes in Romans 7:7-25 as one that characterizes the life of the regenerate believer, is commonly found among theologians who oppose Pelagianism and semi-Pelagianism.

of Romans. That purpose is 'that no man should glory in meritorious works', but rather should glory in the grace of God that precedes and makes possible the performance of good works.[40] Evangelical grace always precedes our good works, so that no one should 'think that he has received grace because he has done good works'.[41] This is the reason the apostle Paul adduces the examples of Isaac and Ishmael, and of Jacob and Esau. In the case of Isaac, God distinguished him as the peculiar object of the promise, apart from any preceding meritorious works. And in the case of Jacob, God likewise declared him to be a child of promise and the recipient of His grace apart from any preceding works. Since the twin sons of Isaac and Rebecca were still in their mother's womb when God declared that the 'elder should serve the younger', it could not be more clear that he became a co-heir of God's grace in Christ wholly by virtue of God's antecedent call and grace.[42] Before Jacob could do any good works, he was distinguished by God's grace and set apart for His mercy. In Augustine's estimation, these examples properly demonstrate that 'Grace is therefore of him who calls, and the consequent good works are of him who receives grace. Good works do not produce grace but are produced by grace.'[43] Nothing could confirm more starkly that the recipients of God's grace have no basis for boasting of their meritorious good works, as though they were the basis for God's gracious call.

After offering this explanation of Paul's purpose in Romans 9, Augustine pointedly acknowledges that God's choice of Isaac and Jacob raises an inescapable question: 'How can election be just, indeed how can there be any kind of election, where there is no difference?'[44] If nothing distinguished Jacob from Esau, what possible standard of equity or justice can account for God's election of Jacob on the one hand, and His non-election of Esau on the other hand? Since neither Jacob nor Esau had done any good or evil works, and since their natures as children of one father were indistinguishable, what

---

40. *To Simplician*, 2.2.
41. ibid.
42. ibid., 2.3.
43. ibid.
44. ibid., 2.4.

explanation, Augustine asks, can be given for God's choosing one and not the other?

To this probing question, Augustine responds by raising the possibility that God's election was by virtue of His 'foreknowledge' of Jacob's faith. Perhaps God 'foresaw the *faith* that was to be in Jacob even before he was born'.[45] While Augustine poses this as a possible answer to the question why God chose Jacob and not Esau, he quickly rejects it upon the basis of two considerations. First, Augustine notes that, if God's choice of Jacob was based upon His foreknowledge of Jacob's faith, it could equally be argued that it was based upon the good works that necessarily flow from faith. Surely God's foreknowledge includes His prior knowledge both of Jacob's faith and his works. Therefore, if God's choice was based upon what He foreknew Jacob would do, whether in believing or performing good works, then Paul wrongly maintains that God's choice was not according to works. The whole point of Paul's appeal to the case of God's choice of Jacob is that it preceded his birth, and therefore it preceded anything that he would do. Before Jacob believed or performed any good work, he was the special object of God's grace and His subsequent call to faith. For these reasons, the answer accounting for God's choice of one and not the other cannot lie in God's foreknowledge. What makes Jacob differ from Esau is God's purpose of election alone.

And second, Augustine notes how Paul ascribes Jacob's faith, and the faith of all who believe, to a work of God's prevenient grace. What distinguishes Jacob from Esau is that he was the object of God's sovereign mercy. For this reason, Paul cites God's words to Moses, 'I will have mercy on whom I will have mercy, and I will show compassion to him on whom I will have compassion.'[46] Though it is true that God's chosen people 'are those who have not despised him who calls, but have believed and followed him', it is also true that the will to believe and follow God is granted only to those to whom He wills to show mercy.[47]

> I do not know how it could be said that it is vain for God to have mercy unless we willingly consent. If God has mercy, we also will, for the

---

45. ibid., 2.5.
46. ibid., 2.9.
47. ibid., 2.10.

power to will is given with the mercy itself. It is God that worketh in us both to will and to do of his good pleasure. If we ask whether a good will is a gift of God, I should be surprised if anyone would venture to deny that. But because the good will does not precede calling, but calling precedes the good will, the fact that we have a good will is rightly attributed to God who calls us, and that fact that we are called cannot be attributed to ourselves. So the sentence, 'It is not of him that willeth, nor of him that runneth, but of God that hath mercy' cannot be taken to mean simply that we cannot attain what we wish without the aid of God, but rather that without his calling we cannot even will.[48]

For Augustine, God's prevenient grace toward those to whom He chooses to show mercy is the only explanation for the fact that some respond to the gospel in faith and are saved. Thus, it becomes all the more evident that we cannot explain God's choice of Jacob or others upon the basis of faith or good works. Since faith and good works are themselves the fruit of God's gracious choice, they cannot be the reason God chooses some and not others.[49]

At this point in Augustine's exposition of Romans 9, the question of the justice of God in choosing to show mercy to one and not another becomes especially acute. Augustine anticipates that someone might respond to his argument by asking, 'Why was not Esau called in such a way that he would be willing to obey?'[50] Since no one would

---

48. ibid., 2.12.

49. ibid., 2.13: 'Those are chosen who are effectually [*congruenter*] called. Those who are not effectually called and do not obey their calling are not chosen, for although they were called they did not follow.' Augustine's distinction between a general call of the gospel, which is extended to all to whom the gospel is preached, and an effectual call, which is extended to those whom God has chosen according to His purpose of election, is a commonplace in later Reformation and post-Reformation theology. I will discuss this distinction in later chapters on the doctrine of election in the period of the Reformation and post-Reformation orthodoxy. However, unlike later Reformed formulations of the doctrine of election, Augustine does not affirm that the call of the gospel is a 'sincere' or 'well-meant' offer, which expresses God's good-will toward those whom He has not chosen. Passages like 1 Tim. 2:4, which speaks of God's will that 'all men be saved', are interpreted by Augustine to refer to the fact that God wills the salvation of 'all types' of people who belong to the number of the elect. On this, see his *Enchiridion,* SLNPNF, 3.103; and Mathijs Lamberigts, 'Augustine on Predestination: Some *Questiones Disputatae* Revisited,' *Augustiniana* 54 (2004): 285-88. I will address this subject in a later chapter that treats the doctrine of election in the post-Reformation period.

50. ibid., 2.14.

affirm that God 'lacked a method of persuading even Esau to believe', what possible explanation answers whether it was equitable for God to withhold His mercy from Esau while choosing to extend mercy to Jacob? With respect to this question, Augustine offers three observations in defense of God's justice in choosing not to show mercy to some while showing mercy to others.

First, Augustine notes that there is a difference between God's will to show mercy toward some and His will to 'harden' those toward whom He chooses not to be merciful. In the case of God's will to show mercy to some, He acts positively to enable them to respond in faith to the call of the gospel. But when Paul says that God chooses not to show mercy but to 'harden' the hearts of others, he does not ascribe their hardness of heart to God, as if God positively acted so as to make them refuse the call of the gospel. According to Augustine, 'we must not think that anything is imposed by God whereby a man is made worse, but only that he provides nothing whereby a man is made better.'[51] In the instance of those toward whom God wills to show mercy, God graciously enables them to believe and be saved. But in the instance of those toward whom God wills not to show mercy, God merely withholds the grace that would lead them to believe and be saved.

Second, Augustine argues that we must affirm the justice of God in with-holding mercy from those whom He does not purpose to save. While 'this belongs to a certain hidden equity that cannot be searched out by any human standard of measurement', we must proceed upon the sure conviction that there is no unrighteousness with God.[52] In this connection, it is important to recognize the difference between justice and mercy. Even in human society, a creditor has the freedom to insist upon justice, exacting from a debtor what is owing to him or to show unmerited mercy by remitting the debt. For this reason, 'No one can be charged with unrighteousness who exacts what is owing to him. Nor certainly can he be charged with unrighteousness who is prepared to give up what is owing to him. This decision does not lie with those who are debtors but with the creditor.'[53] Likewise,

---

51. ibid., 2.15.
52. ibid., 2.16.
53. ibid.

when God, who is the 'Supreme Equity', chooses to require what is owed to Him from some of those who are in His debt and deserving of just punishment, He acts most justly. But this does not contradict His freedom to show mercy toward others from whom He does not demand what is owed to Him. That God chooses to show mercy toward some, but not toward others, does not imperil His justice.

And third, Augustine appeals to Paul's language in Romans 9 to show that all human beings who are fallen in Adam are worthy of condemnation and death. When Paul employs the familiar biblical imagery of God as the potter and the human race as a 'lump of clay', he proceeds from the conviction that 'all men are a mass of sin'.[54] 'To be sure, no one resists his will. He aids whom he will and he leaves whom he will. Both he who is aided and he who is left belong to the same mass of sin. Both deserve the punishment which is exacted from the one and remitted to the other.'[55] For this reason, when Paul speaks of God making 'one vessel unto honour and another unto dishonour', he presumes that all human beings belong to the same mass of corruption. And as such, all human beings are justly worthy of condemnation and death. Nevertheless, both to exhibit His justice and to magnify His mercy, God graciously chooses to grant to some what He justly withholds from others. There is no unrighteousness in this, since 'whether he remits or exacts the debt, he cannot rightly be charged with unrighteousness by him from whom he exacts it; and he who receives remission ought not to glory in his own merits. The former pays back nothing but what he owes, and the latter has nothing that he has not received.'[56] Furthermore, it must be noted that, when Paul speaks of God's 'hating' Esau, this must be understood of Esau as a 'sinner', and not of Esau as a human creature. Though God could not hate any good creature, He does 'hate impiety. In some He punishes it with damnation, in others he removes it by justification, doing what he judges right in his inscrutable judgments.'[57]

---

54. ibid., 2.17.
55. ibid., 2.16.
56. ibid., 2.17.
57. ibid., 2.18.

Two Treatises Against Semi-Pelagianism

Though Augustine's treatise, 'To Simplician,' evidences the presence of a developed understanding of election and predestination in his theology before the Pelagian controversy, there is no doubt that his clearest statement of the doctrine occurred at the end of this controversy. It is generally acknowledged that Augustine's last two treatises against semi-Pelagianism represent the most thorough statement of the doctrine in all of his writings.[58] These two treatises, 'On the Predestination of the Saints' and 'On the Gift of Perseverance' (428–429) were written as two parts of one work, which aimed to refute not only Pelagianism but also its modification in what became known as semi-Pelagianism.[59] Before we consider Augustine's formulation of the doctrine of predestination in these two works, a few brief comments on the semi-Pelagian position are in order.

While the label 'semi-Pelagianism' suggests a viewpoint that is more Pelagian than Augustinian, the semi-Pelagianism that surfaced late in the controversy with Pelagius was a kind of 'half-way' house between a full-blown Pelagianism and Augustine's robust doctrine of predestination. It could for this reason just as well be labelled a form of 'semi-Augustinianism'. Augustine was first apprised of this view by two laypeople, Prosper and Hilary, who alerted him to the differences between it and a more consistent Pelagianism. Warfield provides a helpful summary of the semi-Pelagian view:

> Its representatives were ready, as a rule, to admit that all men were lost in Adam, and no one could recover himself by his own free will, but all needed God's grace for salvation. But they objected to the doctrines of prevenient and irresistible grace; and asserted that man could initiate the process of salvation by turning first to God, that all men could resist God's grace, and no grace could be given which they could not reject, and especially they denied that the gifts of grace came irrespective of merits, actual or foreseen. They said that what Augustine taught as the calling of God's elect according to His own purpose was tantamount to fatalism, was contrary to the teaching of the fathers and the true Church doctrine,

---

58. On these two treatises, see Warfield, APC, 395-98.

59. Warfield, APC, 394-5. The label 'semi-Pelagianism' is a relatively modern expression, which was first officially used in the Lutheran *Formula of Concord* (1577).

and, even if true, should not be preached, because of its tendency to drive men into indifference or despair.[60]

As this summary of Warfield suggests, semi-Pelagianism rejects the idea that faith is a gift of God's grace that is granted to those toward whom God chooses to show mercy and effectively call through the gospel. Rather, faith, as the initial response to and acceptance of God's grace, finds its origin in a free act of the human will. Though God's grace invites, assists, and strengthens the initial act of faith in response to the gospel call, it does not effectually grant faith to those whom God sovereignly and undeservedly chooses to save. Semi-Pelagianism teaches that salvation begins, and ultimately depends upon, the co-operation of the human will with the grace of God. Though all human beings are fallen in Adam and could not save themselves apart from the assistance of God's grace, they cannot be saved unless they freely choose to co-operate with, and do not resist, the grace of God.

'On the Predestination of the Saints'

In the opening portion of 'On the Predestination of the Saints', Augustine begins by identifying the position of those who withdraw from a full-orbed Pelagianism. He commends them for their admission that the human will is 'anticipated by God's grace' and 'no one can suffice to himself either for beginning or for completing any good work'.[61] In this they distinguish themselves from the error of the Pelagians. However, he observes that their position still retains a crucial feature of the Pelagian error, namely, that 'we have faith itself of ourselves', though its 'increase is of God; as if faith were not given us by Him, but were only increased in us by Him, on the ground of the merit of its having begun from us.'[62] Against this claim, Augustine argues that faith itself is God's gift to those whom He saves. If we ascribe the beginning of faith to our own wills apart from the prevenient grace of God, then we will fall prey to presumption and

---

60. Warfield, APC, 395. Cf. G. C. Berkouwer, *Divine Election*, 30: 'It [semi-Pelagianism] taught that man retains his free will, but because it has been weakened by sin it is in need of God's helping grace, so that a cooperation between God's grace and man's freedom is necessary.'

61. 'On the Predestination of the Saints,' 2.

62. ibid., 3.

arrogance. In order for grace to be grace, the response of faith to the gospel call must also be given to us apart from any human merit. If we ascribe even a portion of faith to ourselves and a portion to God, or even worse, if we ascribe the 'beginning' of faith to ourselves and its subsequent increase to God's assistance, we make ourselves 'first' in the order of salvation and we relegate God to the 'second' position.[63]

While Augustine admits that in some of his earlier writings he had erred in his understanding of God's grace, he notes that he has come to understand more fully what the apostle Paul means by the election of grace. Even in its beginnings, faith is born of God's mercy. What especially convinced him of this was the apostolic testimony in 1 Corinthians 4:7, 'For who maketh thee to differ? And what hast thou that thou has not received? Now, if thou hast received it, why dost thou glory as if thou receivedst it not?'[64] By virtue of this testimony, it is impossible to affirm that faith is not itself received from God. Since it is God's grace that distinguishes one person from another, faith must be granted to some and not others by virtue of God's purpose of election. Though the capacity to have faith belongs to our natures as created by God, that some believe and others do not stems from the fact that God prepares the will of His elect to believe.[65] God shows mercy to some to whom He grants the gift of faith, and He demonstrates His justice toward those who are blind and unwilling to believe. As in his earlier treatise to Simplician, Augustine affirms that God's election of some is an act of His mercy, and His leaving others in their sins is altogether righteous, even if it is to us 'equally unsearchable'.[66]

To confirm that faith itself, even in its beginning, is God's gift to those whom He elects, Augustine appeals to a number of biblical passages that describe the calling of believers as an effect of God's prevenient grace. In the Gospel of John, for example, Christ teaches

---

63. ibid., 6.

64. ibid., 8: '[I]t was chiefly by this apostolic testimony that I myself had been convinced, when I thought otherwise concerning this matter.' At this point, Augustine mentions his earlier letter to Simplician. From my own reading of Augustine's voluminous writings against Pelagianism, it is evident that this passage plays a decisive role in Augustine's repeated denunciations of any affirmation of human merit in the salvation of fallen sinners.

65. ibid., 10.

66. ibid., 11.

us that all who come to the Father do so because the Father has determined to give them to Christ (6:37). Christ also declares that those who hear and learn from the Father come to Him (6:45).[67] These, and other passages like them, demonstrate that the response of faith to the call of the gospel is one that God Himself graciously gives to some, but not others. When the call of the Father is heard 'within', this occurs as the Father 'takes away the heart of stone and gives a heart of flesh'. In this way, the promise of God finds its fulfillment in those whom He 'makes children and vessels of mercy which He has prepared for glory'.[68] Indeed, the reason believers pray for those who are unbelieving is in order that the Father would perform this work in them, which He alone is able to accomplish.

> When, therefore, the gospel is preached, some believe, some believe not; but they who believe at the voice of the preacher from without, hear of the Father from within, and hear; while they who do not believe, hear outwardly, but inwardly do not hear nor learn;— that is to say, to the former it is given to believe; to the latter it is not given.[69]

For this reason, it is necessary to distinguish between the general call of the gospel that goes out to a great number of people, Jews and Gentiles alike, many of whom do not respond in faith, and the effectual call of the gospel that is 'according to God's purpose'.[70] Effectual calling is 'that calling wherewith a man is made a believer'.[71]

At this point in his response to the challenge of semi-Pelagianism, Augustine raises once more the issue regarding the justice of God's election of some to whom He grants the gift of faith and His non-election of others. In reply to this objection, he notes three things. First, it must always be remembered that all human beings are fallen in Adam and therefore properly worthy of condemnation. Accordingly, if God were to determine not to save any one, there 'would be no just cause for finding fault with God'.[72] Second, God's will to show mercy

---

67. ibid., 13.
68. ibid., 13.
69. ibid., 15.
70. ibid., 32.
71. ibid., 32.
72. ibid., 16.

to some and not others reminds believers of the 'great grace' that is granted to them, though they too are worthy of condemnation and death. Such grace removes any ground for believers to boast in their own merits. Rather, believers are taught to boast only in God and His grace toward them. And third, it is ultimately inappropriate for anyone to suppose that God could will anything that was unrighteous. We must proceed from the conviction that God's 'judgments are unsearchable, and His ways past finding out.'[73]

In the second half of this treatise, Augustine takes up three further issues regarding the doctrine of predestination: (1) the necessary distinction between God's foreknowledge and His act of predestination; (2) the illustration of unmerited election in the case of the Father's choice of Jesus Christ as Mediator; and (3) the relation between God's act of election and the holiness of those whom He elects.

On the distinction between God's foreknowledge and predestination, Augustine argues that foreknowledge 'may exist without predestination', but that predestination 'cannot exist without foreknowledge'.[74] God's foreknowledge, for example, includes His knowledge of 'those things He does not Himself do, – as all sins whatever.'[75] Though God judges sins, He does not predestine and author them by a positive act of His will. However, in the case of all that God predestines, He foreknows what will take place by virtue of His own will. This has immediate implications for the question of the relation between God's predestination of some to faith and salvation, and His foreknowledge that they will believe. God foreknows that some will believe because He has predestined them to salvation and salvation only comes by faith. The relation between God's predestination and faith is that between His 'preparation of grace' and 'the effect of that predestination'.[76] God's 'predestination is the preparation for grace, while grace is the donation itself.'[77] This distinction is important for an understanding of the relation between God's sovereign will to

---

73. ibid., 16.
74. ibid., 19.
75. ibid.
76. ibid.
77. ibid.

predestine some to salvation and His foreknowledge of their faith and whatever such faith produces in them. God does not base His act of predestination merely upon His foreknowledge of the faith of those who choose to respond to the gospel call in faith. Rather, God foreknows those who will choose to believe because He has predestined them to salvation, and this predestination is the source from which the gift of faith proceeds.

> Therefore they were elected before the foundation of the world with that predestination in which God foreknew what He Himself would do; but they were elected out of the world with that calling whereby God fulfilled that which He predestinated.[78]

In his argument for the claim that election and the gift of faith that flows from it are altogether unmerited, Augustine adduces the example of God's election of Jesus Christ as the Mediator. The man Christ Jesus is a singular illustration of the fact that God's election is wholly unmerited. Apart from any 'preceding merits of its own', Christ's human nature was chosen by God to be the instrument of the salvation of all who belong to Him by faith.[79]

> That man, whence did He deserve this, – to be assumed by the Word co-eternal with the Father into unity of person, and be the only-begotten Son of God? Was it because any kind of goodness in Him preceded? What did He do before? What did He believe? What did He ask, that He should attain to this unspeakable excellence?[80]

In this way, the predestination and election of Christ exemplify the way God's gracious election precedes any and all merit. Augustine also notes how the election of Christ confirms the harmony between God's act of predestination and the freedom of the human will. Christ was perfectly sinless, but this in no way mitigates the degree to which He was also perfectly free. Indeed, Christ was 'so much the more free in proportion to the greater impossibility of His becoming the servant of sin'.[81] In the predestination and election of Christ Jesus, the

---

78. ibid., 34.
79. ibid., 30.
80. ibid.
81. ibid.

eternal and only-begotten Son of God who became man and assumed our flesh, we witness in a paradigmatic way the predestination and election of those who are His members by faith. As Augustine puts it, God 'makes in men the beginning and the completion of the faith in Jesus who made the man Jesus the beginning and finisher of faith.'[82] Although the election of Jesus Christ was unlike ours in that He was not in need of salvation through the work of someone on His behalf, it was like ours in that it was a pure act of undeserved favor. The election of those whom God wills to save is, therefore, an election in, through, and on account of Christ whom God elected to the office of Mediator.

Augustine concludes the treatise with a treatment of Paul's teaching in Ephesians 1. When the apostle speaks of God's merciful election in this passage, he clearly affirms that 'God chose Christ's members in Him before the foundation of the world'.[83] Paul not only makes clear that God's election precedes the existence of those whom He chooses, but he also precludes the Pelagian idea that it was based upon God's foreknowledge of their holiness. According to the Pelagian view, God did not choose them in order to make them holy, but He chose them 'on account' of their holiness.[84] The problem with this view is that it openly conflicts with what the apostle says about the relation between God's act of election and the adoption and holiness of those whom He elects. For the apostle explicitly says that 'God chose us in Christ before the foundation of the world, predestinating us to the adoption of children, not because we were going to be of ourselves holy and immaculate, but He chose and predestinated us that we might be so.'[85] In the same way that God chose us, 'not because we believed, but that we might believe,' God chose us, not because we are holy, but that we might be holy.[86] God's election and calling are not based upon foreseen faith or holiness, but are the preparation and source for that faith and holiness that God grants to those whom He elects.

---

82. ibid., 31.
83. ibid., 35.
84. ibid.
85. ibid., 37.
86. ibid., 38.

'On the Gift of Perseverance'

As the title of the second part of Augustine's response to semi-Pelagianism suggests, the main burden of this treatise is to argue that God's predestination and election include not only the initial gift of faith but also the gift of perseverance in faith. The burden of Augustine's argument is to show that faith, both in its initiation and in its perseverance, is an unmerited gift of God granted to those whom He mercifully elects unto salvation. In the opening chapter, Augustine summarizes his main point: 'I assert ... that the perseverance by which we persevere in Christ even to the end is the gift of God; and I call that the end by which is finished that life wherein alone there is peril of falling. Therefore, it is uncertain whether any one has received this gift so long as he is still alive.'[87] As this statement makes clear, Augustine does not argue that believers can be assured of their perseverance in this life prior to death. He means only to argue that those whom God predestined to salvation will be granted the gift of a persevering faith.

In order to prove that the gift of perseverance is granted to those whom God elects unto salvation, Augustine appeals to the petitions of the Lord's Prayer, particularly as they are understood by such teachers as Cyprian. If perseverance were not a gift of God's grace, the prayers of Christians, especially as they are conformed to the Lord's Prayer, would not make sense. For almost all of the petitions of the Lord's Prayer, in one way or another, express the Christian's dependence upon God's grace to persevere in faith. When Christians pray this prayer, 'scarcely anything else is understood to be prayed for but perseverance.'[88] The foundation of this prayer is that God is able to grant what is asked of Him, namely, that His kingdom come, that His will be done on earth as in heaven, that He keep us from temptation, and that He give us our daily bread.[89] Because God is able to grant whatever we request of Him in prayer, we may be sure that none

---

87. 'On the Gift of Perseverance,' 1. Interestingly, Augustine notes that martyrdom for Christ's sake provides believers with the clearest confirmation that they were given a persevering faith according to God's purpose of election.

88. ibid., 3.

89. ibid., 7. Augustine understands this 'daily bread' as the Christian's communion in the body and blood of Christ through the sacrament of the Lord's Supper.

of those whom God has elected will fail to be given the power to continue in faith to the end. The grace of perseverance is not given according to merit, but is rather given according to God's purpose of election. If the question is asked, 'Why then is it not given to all?,' we have no other recourse than to say that God acts according to 'the good pleasure of his will' to deliver some from their deserved punishment. That God leaves others in their sin accords with His justice, since this is what is due to them.[90]

Although Augustine argues that the Lord's Prayer confirms how perseverance in faith is graciously granted God's elect, he does not affirm that believers can be sure they will be the recipients of this gift. Among those who 'in good faith' have worshipped God, there are some to whom the gift of perseverance is not given. To those who object to this, asking why God should not give to all believers the gift of perseverance to the end, Augustine notes that God has judged it better to 'mingle some who would not persevere with a certain number of His saints, so that those for whom security from temptation in this life is not desirable may not be secure.'[91] Believers are not granted the comfort of knowing in this life that they will persevere in faith in order that they may not become complacent.[92] In this way, believers are taught to look to God for help in times of temptation, and to be dependent always upon the grace that God alone can supply. For Augustine, it is even possible for some of those who have received the washing of regeneration in baptism to fail to persevere in faith. Why this is so belongs to God's inscrutable and just judgments.

---

90. ibid., 17: 'And although assuredly in the one case you see a most benignant benefactor, and in your own case a most righteous exactor, in neither case do you behold an unjust God. For although He would be righteous even if He were to punish both, he who is delivered has good ground for thankfulness, he who is condemned has no ground for finding fault.'

91. ibid., 19.

92. Augustine clearly denies that believers can have an assurance of their election and perseverance in faith in this life. Cf. 'On the Gift of Perseverance,' 33: 'To which calling there is no man that can be said by men with any certainty of affirmation to belong, until he has departed from this world; but in this life of man, which is a state of trial upon the earth, he who seems to stand must take heed lest he fall.' In this respect, Augustine's doctrine of election differs considerably from the later formulation of the doctrine in the Reformation and post-Reformation periods. In later Reformed reflection, the theme of assurance is an especially important feature of the doctrine.

> But of two pious men, why to the one should be given perseverance unto
> the end, and to the other it should not be given, God's judgments are even
> more inscrutable. Yet to believers it ought to be a most certain fact that
> the former is of the predestinated, the latter is not.[93]

Among those who were called, justified, and 'renewed through the
laver of regeneration' (baptism), there are some who subsequently
fall away through sin and lose the salvation that was once given
to them.[94] Regarding such persons, we must conclude that their
calling was not according to God's purpose of election. They were
not predestined from before the foundation of the world to salvation
and a persevering faith.

At this point in Augustine's treatment of the gift of perseverance,
he turns to a frequent objection by his Pelagian and semi-Pelagian
opponents. According to them, Augustine's teaching undermines the
preaching of the gospel. What purpose is served by preaching if all
of its precepts, exhortations, and rebukes are of no advantage to those
whom God does not choose to grant the gift of a persevering faith?

Augustine offers several responses to this objection. In the first
place, he notes that the same charge could be brought against Christ
Himself and the preaching of His apostles. Christ sought to persuade
many to believe and persevere in faith, though He also taught that
no one would believe in Him unless drawn by the Father. Similarly,
the apostles clearly teach the doctrine of predestination, namely, that
faith is a gift that God gives without merit to those whom He has
elected from before the foundation of the world.[95] Furthermore, since
God is pleased to communicate His grace through the gospel call to
faith, the preaching of the gospel is the means that God uses to grant
faith and perseverance. Although we do not know whom God has
elected to save, we may be sure that God will accompany the gospel
ministry with a work of His grace. With the gospel Word, God will
grant to His elect ears to hear the good message of the gospel.[96] Since
God is pleased to use the preaching of the gospel to grant faith, we

---

93. ibid., 21.
94. ibid.
95. ibid., 35.
96. ibid., 37.

must preach the gospel with the conviction that God will make such preaching effective to the salvation of His elect. While Augustine acknowledges that the topic of predestination must be handled discretely in preaching, he insists that it must be preached in order to magnify God's grace and to deny any merits to those who are saved.

In his response to the claim that predestination cannot be preached, Augustine does acknowledge that it is possible to preach the doctrine in a way that confuses some who are 'unskilled' or 'slow' to understand.[97] For example, if the preacher were to say, 'And if any of you obey, if you are predestinated to be rejected, the power of obeying will be withdrawn from you, that you cease to obey,' this would be 'abominable' and 'excessively harsh'.[98] Such preaching does not encourage believers to magnify God's grace or to deny all human merits, which should be the chief aim of the preacher who speaks of God's gracious purpose of election. When the preacher speaks this way – directly to the congregation in the second person ('you') – he discourages believers in their prayers that God would grant to them by grace what He alone can give them, namely, a faith that perseveres to the end. According to Augustine, when the topic of predestination is touched upon in preaching, the preacher ought to speak in the third person.

> For if any are not yet called whom by His grace He has predestinated to be elected, they will receive that grace whereby they may will to be elected, and may be so; and if any obey, but have not been predestinated to His kingdom and glory, they are for a season, and will not abide in the same obedience to the end.[99]

When the subject of predestination is handled properly, the congregation will be encouraged to look to God to provide that persevering faith that He alone can and does give according to His gracious purpose.

At the close of his fairly extended response to the question whether or not predestination can be preached, Augustine reiterates two points that we have seen in his previous writings on election. He once again argues that the prayers of the church and of believers are a compelling illustration of the gift of perseverance. When believers ask God to

97. ibid., 58.
98. ibid., 61.
99. ibid., 58.

grant faith to the unbelieving, they are not engaged in a 'perfunctory' exercise, as though God were not able to grant what is requested. They offer such prayers out of the conviction that God alone is able to grant faith and to grant a faith that perseveres. 'And if the Church has always prayed for these benefits, it has always believed them to be certainly God's gifts; nor was it ever right for it to deny that they were foreknown by Him.'[100] In addition to this proof that God alone gives what we ask of Him, Augustine concludes with the 'most eminent instance' of predestination, namely, the predestination of Christ Himself as Mediator. No more compelling proof is needed that God's grace precedes any human merit than the example of Christ. Just as Christ was predestined without any merit to His office as Mediator, so believers who persevere in faith are predestined to belong to Him, as members of the body who are joined to one head.[101]

Summary

Upon the basis of my survey of Augustine's engagement with Pelagianism and semi-Pelagianism, a number of observations may be made about his doctrine of election and predestination.

The starting point for Augustine's doctrine is clearly the conviction that the salvation of fallen human beings is wholly a work of God's grace. Augustine repeatedly appeals to Paul's language in 1 Corinthians 4:7 ('What do you have that you did not receive?') to underscore the sheer gratuity of God's gift of salvation in Jesus Christ. What especially offended Augustine was the failure of Pelagius and his followers to acknowledge that salvation is granted to sinners solely by grace, apart from any human initiative or merit. For Augustine, the salvation of sinners is only possible by God's prevenient grace, which precedes any human response to the gospel. Indeed, God's prevenient grace not only precedes faith and the good works that faith produces, but it also enables the elect to respond appropriately to the gospel call to faith and obedience.

Since the Pelagian view exalted the power and freedom of the human will to obey God's commandments, Augustine was compelled

---

100. ibid., 65.
101. ibid., 67.

to consider the implications of the doctrine of original sin for human freedom. According to Augustine, God created Adam as the organic and seminal head of the human race. In his original state of integrity, Adam possessed the power and ability to obey or disobey God. However, by virtue of Adam's free decision to disobey God, he plunged himself and all his posterity into sin. Through the sin of Adam, the whole human race became liable to condemnation and death. Though all human beings retain the freedom and power to choose to do as they will, the inherited corruption of original sin has so infected Adam's posterity that no fallen sinner is able and willing to do what pleases God, unless God's prevenient grace heals and renews their wills. The Pelagian teaching that all human beings retain the power, ability and will to do what God's holy law commands, amounts to a denial of the biblical doctrine of original sin. According to Pelagian teaching, grace is no longer grace but merely the created ability to do whatever God commands. The grace of God is reduced to God's provision of His holy law, which reveals what pleases Him, and the good example of the sinless life of Christ. In the Pelagian scheme, salvation comes through human merit, namely, free obedience to the commandments of God, which is stimulated through Christ's exemplary life. In order to refute the Pelagian view, Augustine repeatedly appeals to the way Christians are taught to petition God for His grace and love, which alone empower the Christian to believe and obey in response to the call of the gospel. He also adduces the practice of infant baptism as an irrefutable proof that all human beings are fallen in Adam and cannot be saved unless they receive the washing of regeneration and renewal.

Within the framework of his understanding of the necessity of God's prevenient grace, which alone grants to fallen human beings what is needed in order for them to be saved, Augustine appeals to the doctrine of God's sovereign and merciful election to confirm that salvation is a gift of God's unmerited grace. Just as Christ was 'elected' by God to be the Mediator, an election that was purely gratuitous and based upon nothing in His human nature that would merit God's choice, so God elects to show mercy to those whom He wills to save in and through Christ. For Augustine, the doctrine of election confirms that the salvation of believers is entirely an act of God's grace without any merit on the part of those who are saved.

In Augustine's formulation of the doctrine, election is God's eternal purpose or will to grant salvation in Christ to those whom He chooses out of the fallen human race. God grants faith and salvation to those to whom He wills to display His unmerited grace and mercy. For this reason, Augustine rejects any view of election that bases God's choice simply upon His foreknowledge of the faith and good works that some will produce in response to the gospel. Since faith and good works are themselves the fruits of God's merciful election, we must acknowledge that God's purpose of election is the source of all the fruits of the work of His grace in the lives of those whom He elects. What the gospel commands, God gives, and He gives according to His sovereign purpose to show mercy to those whom He will and to withhold His mercy from others. In the case of election, God displays His sovereign mercy. In the case of those whom God does not will to save, He displays His justice.

While God's decision not to save some may appear to be unjust, Augustine insists we remember that justice and mercy are not administered in the same way. Though God's will to withhold the blessing of salvation from some may be inscrutable to us, it fully accords with justice, which even in human affairs entails that a debtor be required to pay his creditor what is due. Since all fallen sinners are deserving of condemnation and death, God is free to leave them in their sins and to treat them according to what they deserve. However, God magnifies His grace and mercy by choosing to grant undeserved salvation to some, though not to all. When the call of the gospel is extended to the elect, God calls them according to His electing purpose and enables them to respond in the way of faith and obedience. Furthermore, since God's purpose of election is firm, He also grants to them the gift of perseverance so that they do not fall away through unbelief and disobedience.

In his treatment of God's purpose of election, Augustine repeatedly emphasizes what is often termed the 'asymmetry' between God's election of some and His non-election of others. Election is an act of God's will that must be carefully distinguished from God's act in relation to those whom He does not save. When God wills to save the elect, He positively purposes to save them through the work of Christ and the effectual call of the gospel. However, in the case of those whom

He does not elect, God's will is a permissive or passive one. He leaves them in their fallen condition and justly punishes them for their sins. For this reason, though the language is not Augustine's, it may be said that his formulation of the doctrine of election is 'infralapsarian' in form. In Augustine's view, the objects contemplated in God's merciful election are human beings whom He created but who are fallen in Adam.[102] When Augustine treats God's purpose of election, he describes the elect as those who belong to the 'mass of sinners' (*massa peccati*) or 'mass of perdition' (*massa perditionis*). When God elects to save some, He does so by electing to deliver them from out of the same 'lump of clay' to which they together with all fallen sinners belong.

Because Augustine strongly accents the asymmetry between God's active election to save some and His passive withholding of His saving grace from those whom He does not elect but leaves deservedly in their sins, the question has surfaced among interpreters of Augustine whether or not he teaches a doctrine of 'double predestination' (*gemina predestinatio*). Jaroslav Pelikan and Louis Berkhof, for example, conclude that Augustine does teach that God predestines some to salvation and others to destruction.[103] The preponderance of interpreters, however, argue that Augustine does not generally view the non-elect as the direct objects of God's predestinating will.[104] In

---

102. The language of 'infralapsarian' derives from a later point in history, when Reformed theologians debated the question of the order of elements within God's eternal counsel or decree/s (*ordo decretorum Dei*). Though it is somewhat anachronistic to use the language 'infralapsarian' to describe Augustine's view, he does certainly share the infralapsarian (lit. 'under' or 'after' the fall) conviction that the objects of God's eternal election are fallen human beings (*homo creatus et lapsus,* 'man as created and fallen'). For a treatment of this debate in Reformed theology, including a definition of terms, see J. V. Fesko, *Diversity Within the Reformed Tradition: Supra- and Infralapsarianism in Calvin, Dort, and Westminster* (Greenville, SC: Reformed Academic Press, 2001). I will address this debate more directly in later chapters.

103. Pelikan, *The Christian Tradition,* 1:293, 297-8; and Berkhof, *Systematic Theology,* 109. Though Berkhof acknowledges that Augustine views the non-elect as objects merely of God's 'foreknowledge' and not His act of 'predestination', he nonetheless maintains that 'there can be no doubt about it that he taught a double predestination'.

104. See, e.g., Adolph von Harnack, *The History of Dogma,* ed. T. K. Cheyne and A. B. Bruce, vol. 5 (3rd ed.; London: Williams & Norgate, 1898), 216; Emil Brunner, *Dogmatics,* vol. 1: *The Christian Doctrine of God,* trans. Olive Wyon (Philadelphia: The Westminster Press, 1949), 341; Karl Barth, *Church Dogmatics,* II/2, eds. G. W. Bromiley and T. F. Torrance, trans. G. W. Bromiley *et al.* (Edinburgh: T & T Clark, 1957), 16; Charles Hodge, *Systematic Theology,* vol. 2 (Grand Rapids: Eerdmans,

the judgment of these interpreters, Augustine articulates the doctrine of election in an 'infralapsarian' form, and regards God's act of predestination to be directed only to those whom He wills to save. In their view, Augustine teaches only the predestination of some to salvation, but not the predestination of others to destruction.

The reason interpreters come to such differing answers to the question whether Augustine taught double predestination is the ambiguity that surrounds what is meant by 'double' predestination. If 'double' predestination means that God predestines some to life and others to death *in the same way,* then Augustine clearly does not teach a doctrine of double predestination. Whereas God positively predestines some to salvation in Augustine's view, He does not positively predestine the non-elect to destruction. Though Augustine affirms that God chooses to show mercy to some who are otherwise undeserving, he does not affirm that God in a co-ordinate and parallel manner chooses not to show mercy to others. God's action with respect to the non-elect is His choice not to intervene in mercy in order to save them. Rather than speaking of the predestination of the non-elect to destruction, Augustine speaks of God's passive will to leave the non-elect in their lost condition. However, if 'double' predestination may include a position that affirms both God's positive choice to save some and His negative choice to leave others in their sin, Augustine's position amounts to a moderate, asymmetrical version of a double predestination view. The reason some argue that Augustine's view may be termed a doctrine of double predestination stems from the fact that he does acknowledge that the number of the elect and the non-elect is certain, and this accords with God's sovereign will. Since God's positive will of election involves His choice to save a definite number of persons out of the fallen mass of humanity, it also entails the non-election of those to whom He chooses not to show mercy.[105]

1993), 316; Fesko, *Diversity Within the Reformed Tradition,* 19. Fesko notes that 'The opinions of Harnack, Brunner, Barth, and Hodge are preferable to the analyses of Pelikan and Berkhof given that Augstine [*sic*] generally defines eternal rejection in terms of preterition ["passing over"] rather than predestination. Augustine, therefore is a single-predestinarian and an infralapsarian.'

105. Cf. Polman, *Praedestinatieleer,* 149: 'It is not so easy to give a categorical answer to the question whether Augustine taught a *gemina praedestinatio*' (trans. mine, CPV).

In addition to these general features of Augustine's doctrine of election, there are a few problematic elements that also require comment.

In his treatment of Augustine's doctrine of election, Warfield notes that Augustine's view limits the number of the elect to a 'comparatively few of the human race', and that this stems in part from his doctrine of the church and the sacrament of baptism.[106] Because Augustine taught the absolute necessity of baptism for salvation, he was obliged to limit the number of those who are saved to those who receive the washing of regeneration in baptism and thereafter persevere in faith and obedience.[107] Within the framework of this understanding of baptism, Augustine was compelled to exclude all unbaptized persons, including infants, from the number of those whom God elects to save.[108] Commenting on this aspect of Augustine's teaching, Warfield observes:

> The saddest corollary that flowed from this doctrine was that by which Augustine was forced to assert that all those who died unbaptized,

106. Warfield, APC, 410. Warfield has in mind Augustine's teaching that the number of the elect is limited to the number needed to replace the fallen angels who rebelled against God prior to the creation of the world, an idea that would later play a role in Anselm's formulation of the doctrine. Cf. Augustine, 'Enchiridion,' 29: 'We do not know the number either of the saints or of the devils; but we know that the children of the holy mother who was called barren on earth shall succeed to the place of the fallen angels ....' When treating the subject of election later in the same treatise, Augustine argues that 'it was right that those who are redeemed should be redeemed in such a way as to show, by the greater number who are unredeemed and left in their just condemnation, what the whole race deserved ...' ('Enchiridion,' 99).

107. See Augustine, 'On the Soul and its Origin,' I.11 and II.17, where he allows as an exception that martyred believers who die without baptism may be saved by a 'baptism of blood'; and Augustine, 'On the Merits and Remission of Sins,' II.46, where he notes that, 'if a man were to die immediately after baptism, he would have nothing at all left to hold him liable to punishment.'

108. In the later history of the Reformed and Presbyterian churches, the election and salvation of infants who do not undergo baptism are affirmed. The Canons of Dort, I/17, affirm the election and salvation of the children of believers who die in infancy. The Westminster Confession of Faith, chapter 10.3, speaks more generally of 'elect infants, dying in infancy,' who are 'saved by Christ, through the Spirit, who worketh when, and where, and how he pleaseth; so also are all other elect persons who are incapable of being outwardly called by the ministry of the Word.' These confessional affirmations allow for a much greater number to be included within God's purpose of election. For an extended treatment of these confessional statements, see Venema, *Christ and Covenant Theology,* 214-55.

including infants, are finally lost and depart into eternal punishment. He did not shrink from the inference, although he assigned the place of lightest punishment in hell to those who were guilty of no sin but original sin, but who had departed this life without having washed this away in the 'laver of regeneration.' This is the dark side of his soteriology; but it should be remembered that it was not his theology of grace, but the universal and traditional belief in the necessity of baptism for remission of sins, which he inherited in common with all of his time, that forced it upon him.[109]

In addition to this unhappy consequence of Augustine's doctrine of baptism for his view of the relative number of the elect, there is a further unfortunate aspect of Augustine's view that is also related to his doctrine of baptism. In the course of his treatment of the grace of perseverance, Augustine affirms that God's merciful election includes the grace of a persevering faith. However, he also acknowledges that there are many within the church who, though they were baptized and brought to true faith, are not ultimately to be numbered among those whom God has elected and to whom He grants the gift of perseverance. In this connection, Augustine also argues that the assurance of election and its corollary, perseverance, is not ordinarily given to believers in this life prior to their death. For this reason, he even maintains that martyrdom has the benefit of granting clear confirmation that the martyred believer was truly elect and a recipient accordingly of this benefit that flows from election. For Augustine, the fact that believers ordinarily are not able to be assured of their election and perseverance is beneficial to their sanctification, since it compels them to look to God for the grace to persevere in the face of temptation.

The problem that surfaces at this point in Augustine's doctrine is that, despite his emphasis upon God's grace and the certainty that God will enable elect believers to persevere, believers can have no confidence that the grace of perseverance will be granted to them. Believers can be truly regenerated, saved, and converted, but only for a season if they are not numbered among the elect. The consequence of this teaching is that Augustine can exalt God's merciful election

---

109. Warfield, APC, 410.

that removes from any believer a ground for boasting in their own merit. But he does not teach that the gift of grace given to some believers provides any basis for assurance. In this construction, the gift of grace and faith may not be joined to the gift of a persevering faith. Unlike the later formulation of the doctrine of election at the time of the Reformation, Augustine's doctrine provides a bulwark against any form of human boasting before God but does not produce any sure ground for the assurance that God's love toward His own in Christ is something from which the true believer will not be separated. In this respect, Augustine's formulation of the doctrine of election gives credence to the oft-repeated charge that the doctrine of election creates insoluble problems for the assurance of salvation. Since it is not possible to know or be assured that the believer's regeneration includes the promise of a persevering faith, it is not possible to be assured of salvation through the use of the means of grace, the preaching of the gospel, and the reception of the sacraments.

The Legacy of Augustinianism in Medieval Theology[110]

To close this chapter on Augustine's doctrine of election, I would like to offer a few remarks regarding the legacy of Augustinianism in medieval theology. Since the next chapter will treat the recovery of aspects of Augustine's teaching on election in the period of the Reformation, it is important to note that Augustine's doctrine loomed large as a point of reference for Christian theology throughout

---

110. For more extended treatments of the legacy of Augustinianism in medieval theology, see Harry Buis, *Historic Protestantism and Predestination* (Philadelphia: Presbyterian and Reformed, 1958) 14-27; Fesko, *Diversity Within the Reformed Tradition,* 21-56; Levering, *Predestination,* 68-97; and Mozley, *The Augustinian Doctrine of Predestination,* 259-93. In the fourteenth century, Augustine's views were embraced and defended by Thomas Bradwardine and Gregory of Rimini, who anticipated the views of the Reformers of the sixteenth century. For discussions of this development, see Heiko A. Oberman, *Archbishop Thomas Bradwardine, a Fourteenth-Century Augustinian: A Study of His Theology in Its Historical Context* (Utrecht: Kemink & Zoon, 1958); Gordon Leff, *Bradwardine and the Pelagians: A Study of His 'De Causa Dei' and Its Opponents* (Cambridge: Cambridge University Press, 1957); and P. Vigneaux, *Justification et predestination au XIVe siècle: Duns Scot, Pierre d'Auriole, Guillaume d'Occam, Gregoire de Rimini* (Paris: Librairie Philosophique J. Vrin, 1981).

the early and late medieval period. Though there were dissenters from Augustine's position during this period, a moderate form of Augustine's doctrine continued to be influential.

At the close of the Pelagian controversy, the ecumenical council of Ephesus in A.D. 431 condemned Pelagianism as incompatible with the Christian faith. Though this condemnation marked the end of any significant advocacy of a full-blown Pelagianism in the church, it did not mean that Augustine's position was fully embraced. Even though there was a general consensus that God's grace is necessary for salvation, the semi-Pelagian view that faith in its inception and perseverance depends upon the free co-operation of the will continued to enjoy support in the church. At the time of the Protestant Reformation in the sixteenth-century, this was in many respects the prevalent view of the Roman Catholic Church. After the condemnation of Pelagianism at Ephesus, further controversy emerged regarding the doctrine of election when the Scythian monks of Constantinople objected to Augustine's views. This new chapter of controversy was settled at the Synod of Orange in A.D. 529 Though this Synod condemned both Pelagianism and semi-Pelagianism, it also rejected some features of Augustine's position. While the Synod of Orange affirmed the necessity of God's grace for salvation, it did not clearly affirm Augustine's teaching that God's purpose of election ensures the salvation of all to whom He chooses to grant the gift of a persevering faith. The Synod also expressly rejected the predestination of some to eternal destruction.

For our purpose, it is important to observe that Augustine's doctrine of election nonetheless continued to exercise considerable influence.[111] Though there were dissenting voices in the church throughout the early and later medieval periods, the position of Augustine continued to be cogently defended by some of the principal theologians of the western church, including Peter Lombard, Bernard of Clairvaux, Anselm of Canterbury, Thomas Aquinas, Thomas

---

111. Mozley, *The Augustinian Doctrine of Predestination,* 234: 'The doctrine of S. Augustine reigned in the medieval Church, and moulded its authoritative teaching, till the Reformation produced a reaction; and the Roman church, apprehensive of the countenance which it gave to some prominent doctrines of the Reformers, and repelled by the use—sometimes unfair and fanatical—made of it, fell back upon a strong doctrine of freewill.'

Bradwardine and Gregory of Rimini, as well as others. Among these theologians, Thomas Aquinas was an especially influential figure who articulated the doctrine of election in an Augustinian manner. In his great work, the *Summa Theologica,* Aquinas devoted a chapter to the doctrine of predestination within the general context of his exposition of the doctrine of God and the particular context of his exposition of the doctrine of providence. After affirming that God's providence includes His ordering of all things in a way that serves His goodness, Aquinas argues that this includes especially God's predestination of some rational creatures to enjoy beatific communion with the Trinity.[112] Like Augustine, Aquinas distinguished God's positive and effective will to grant salvation to the elect and God's negative or permissive will to allow others to fall away.[113] According to Aquinas, God's act of predestination is not based upon His foreknowledge of human merit, and the number of the predestinated is certain.

While Augustine's legacy on the doctrine of election continued to exercise influence, especially in view of its defense by a theologian like Aquinas, it is noteworthy that the fourteenth century witnessed a resurgence of Augustinianism associated with the names of Thomas Bradwardine and Gregory of Rimini. Bradwardine, who was the archbishop of Canterbury and a Thomist in his theological orientation, wrote an important work *De Causa Dei,* which, as its full title indicates, was intended to be a refutation of his contemporaries who championed the cause of Pelagius.[114] In this work, Bradwardine exhibits a thorough acquaintance with and sympathy for Augustine's doctrine of election in opposition to the Pelagian teaching of human merit in salvation. In a similar way, Gregory of Rimini, an Augustinian friar who lectured on theology at the University of Paris from 1341 until 1351, defended Augustine's views on election in the context of a growing declension from his doctrine.

Much more could be said, of course, regarding the legacy of Augustine in the period of medieval theology. My purpose here,

---

112. Thomas Aquinas, *Summa Theologica,* vol. 1 (Westminster, MD: Christian Classics, 1981 [1920]), 1.23.5.

113. *Summa Theologica,* 1.23.3.

114. *De Causa Dei, Contra Pelagium et De Virtute Causarum, Ad Suos Mertonenses* (London: Ex Officina Nortoniana, 1618).

however, is to provide no more than a brief postscript in advance of the following chapter's treatment of the doctrine of election in the period of the sixteenth-century Reformation. In many respects, the Reformers of the sixteenth-century were able to appeal to Augustine's teaching in defense of their own opposition to semi-Pelagian views that continued to surface and find a footing within the church.

CHAPTER 5

The Doctrine of Election in Reformation Theology

A COMMONLY held prejudice regarding Reformation theology is that the doctrine of predestination and election was the peculiar focus of Reformed theologians, especially its leading theological figure, John Calvin. Although it is acknowledged that both the Lutheran and Reformed expressions of the Protestant Reformation emphasized the doctrine of free justification by grace alone through faith alone, some critics believe the Reformed branch was distinguished by its special interest in predestination. This prejudice has led some historians of Reformation theology to pit the Lutheran and Reformed traditions against each other: the Lutheran retaining a special focus on the doctrine of justification, which is the 'article of the standing and falling of the church' (*articulus stantis et cadentis ecclesiae*), and the Reformed substituting a kind of predestinarian metaphysic that deduces the entire corpus of theology from the governing principle of God's sovereign will. In this interpretation of the two traditions, the religious impulse of the Reformation – the rediscovery of the gospel of God's free acceptance of sinners on the basis of the righteousness of Christ alone – was imperiled by an austere and foreboding view of the absolute sovereignty of God. The fresh wind of Luther's rediscovery of justification by faith alone was threatened by a doctrine of predestination that removed the focus from God's revealed will in the gospel of Jesus Christ and replaced it with a focus on the hidden and inscrutable decree of the triune God.

I do not intend here to resolve this prejudice, which has played a significant role in the interpretation of Reformation theology. However, it deserves mention at the outset of this chapter on the doctrine of predestination and election in Reformation theology for at least three reasons.

First, since the Reformation was born out of a renewed attention to the teaching of Scripture, it was bound to include a renewed consideration of the scriptural teaching on predestination and election. Though the language does not belong to the sixteenth-century's theological vocabulary, historians of the Reformation period often speak of the doctrine of Scripture as its 'formal principle'. Over against the medieval Roman Catholic Church, which privileged the church's official interpretation of apostolic tradition (whether in written or unwritten form), the Reformers insisted that Christian theology must be normed by the teaching of Scripture, properly interpreted. The church's dogmatic pronouncements must always stand the test of Scripture and must be revised where they are at variance with scriptural teaching. For this reason, the leading theologians of the Protestant Reformation were obliged to address the doctrine of predestination and election. For example, since the apostle Paul's epistle to the Romans was a particularly important source for the Reformation's articulation of the doctrine of justification, it was scarcely possible that the Reformers could ignore the doctrine of predestination, which forms an important part of the teaching of Romans.

Second, the central theme of the Reformation, the doctrine of free justification, was born out of a rediscovery of the gospel of salvation by grace alone (*sola gratia*). Contrary to the medieval Roman Catholic Church's teaching that fallen human beings retain a free will that is able to 'co-operate' with God's grace and 'merit' further grace, even eternal life, the Reformers insisted that fallen human beings are incapable of performing any saving good.[1] According to the teaching of

---

1. The following statement of the Council of Trent, which treats the way in which fallen sinners can freely co-operate with God's grace and dispose themselves for justification, is representative of the Roman Catholic view: 'They, who by sins are alienated from God, may be disposed through his quickening and assisting grace, to convert themselves to their own justification, by freely assenting to and co-operating with that said grace' (Philip Schaff, *The Creeds of Christendom: With a History and Critical Notes, vol. 2: The Greek and Latin Creeds*, Rev. David S. Schaff [reprint; Grand Rapids: Baker, 1985], 92).

the leading Reformers, salvation begins and ends with God's gracious initiatives in Christ. Only those who are brought to faith through the work of the Holy Spirit and the word of the gospel are able to embrace the promise of the gospel, the forgiveness of sins, and free acceptance with God. Human merits, achievements, and performances contribute nothing to the salvation of fallen sinners. The Reformation doctrine of justification emphasized that the righteousness of Christ, freely granted and imputed to believers who embrace the gospel promise, is the sole basis for the believer's right standing with God. The Pelagian and semi-Pelagian teaching that fallen sinners have the wherewithal to co-operate freely with God's gracious initiative in Christ or the capacity to perform good works that constitute a partial basis for salvation was roundly condemned by Reformation theology.

These features of the Reformation doctrine of salvation were bound to raise the question that the doctrine of predestination and election addresses. After all, if fallen sinners are unable to save themselves or perform any works that contribute to their salvation, then their salvation is ultimately authored by God alone. As we shall observe in the course of expositing the Reformation views, the doctrine of predestination and election naturally finds its home within the context of acknowledging human inability and affirming the gospel of God's undeserved grace in Jesus Christ. The same theological emphases that gave impetus to the doctrine of justification undergirded the Reformation doctrine of election.

And third, although the Reformation was born from a renewed study of Scripture, it was also deeply rooted in a long-standing Augustinian legacy, especially in Western Christian theology. As argued in the previous chapter, the doctrine of predestination and election found its most thorough patristic expression in the great church father Augustine's polemical writings against Pelagianism and semi-Pelagianism. While Augustine's doctrine of justification did not coincide entirely with that of the sixteenth-century Reformers, his doctrine of predestination and election, as it was formulated over against Pelagianism, was an important source for the Reformation view.[2] Indeed, among most of

---

2. As noted in the previous chapter, in the fourteenth century Augustine's views were embraced and defended by Thomas Bradwardine and Gregory of Rimini, who in some ways anticipated the views of the Reformers of the sixteenth century.

the primary authors of Reformation theology, Augustine's doctrine of predestination and election was a key component in their polemic against medieval semi-Pelagianism and every form of a doctrine of salvation based (wholly or partly) on human works. The Reformers were biblical in their approach to theology, but they were also catholic and traditional in their claim to represent the historic teaching of the Christian church.[3] Invoking Augustine's teaching on the doctrine of predestination was, accordingly, an important component in their defense of the catholicity of the teachings both that salvation comes by grace alone and that salvation finds its source in the eternal counsel of the triune God.

For these reasons, it is not surprising that the Reformers, in the course of rediscovering the gospel of salvation by grace apart from any human works, also rediscovered the scriptural and Augustinian doctrine of predestination and election. The Reformation wanted to underscore the truth that God alone authors and accomplishes the redemption of His people through the work of Christ. In defending the truth of grace alone and Christ alone, they insisted that the work of Christ had deep roots in God's own loving determination from before the foundation of the world to save His elect people in Christ.

Luther and Lutheranism

Since Luther (1483–1546) and Lutheranism represent the first branch of the Protestant Reformation, it is appropriate to begin with a sketch of the doctrine of predestination as it was articulated by Luther and his followers. While Lutheranism is not ordinarily associated with the doctrine of predestination,[4] the topic does emerge expressly in two significant contexts: first, Luther's well-known treatise against

---

3. Cf. Heinrich Bullinger, *Der Alt Gloub* ('The Old Faith') (Zurich: Froschouer, 1537). Bullinger's treatise is a striking example of the Reformer's claim not to novelty but to a rediscovery of the 'old faith' of the Christian church. For a treatment of this essay and its significance, see Cornelis P. Venema, 'Heinrich Bullinger's *Der Alt Gloub* ("The Old Faith"): An Apology for the Reformation,' *MAJT 15* (2004): 11–32.

4. For example, Werner Elert claims that predestination was at best 'a merely auxiliary thought' in Luther's theology. Elert, *The Structure of Lutheranism*, trans. Walter A. Hansen (St. Louis, MO: Concordia, 1962), 1:123.

Erasmus, *The Bondage of the Will*,[5] and second, in subsequent debates within the developing Lutheran tradition regarding the freedom of the human will in receiving the grace of Jesus Christ.

Martin Luther: De Servo Arbitrio

The most important, and controversial, source for Martin Luther's treatment of the doctrine of predestination is undoubtedly *The Bondage of the Will*, his response to *The Freedom of the Will*,[6] written by Erasmus of Rotterdam (1466–1536) in 1524 as a criticism of Luther's teaching. Although Erasmus was committed to a moral and humanistic program of church reform, he was strongly opposed to Luther's early insistence that fallen human beings have no freedom of the will in respect to their response to the gospel.[7] In Erasmus' judgment, it was essential that human beings retain the freedom to respond favorably or unfavorably to the gospel. Without a clear emphasis on such freedom, the gospel could only be an occasion for human irresponsibility and antinomianism. If fallen sinners were unable to do (or to not do) what the gospel requires, God's favor toward believers or disfavor toward unbelievers would be baseless. Furthermore, if God were to condemn sinners who are incapable of performing what the gospel requires of them, He would be manifestly unjust.

---

5. For an English translation of this work, see *Luther's Works*, vol. 33, ed. Jaroslav Pelikan and Helmut T. Lehmann (Philadelphia: Fortress; St. Louis, MO: Concordia, 1957). For an extensive treatment of Luther's work, including a history of its reception in the developing Lutheran tradition, see Robert Kolb, *Bound Choice, Election, and Wittenberg Theological Method: From Martin Luther to the Formula of Concord*, Lutheran Quarterly Books (Grand Rapids: Eerdmans, 2005).

6. For an English translation of Erasmus's *De libero arbitrio*, see Ernst F. Winter, ed. and trans., *Erasmus-Luther: Discourse on Free Will* (New York: Continuum, 1961), 3–94. For recent studies of the exchange between Erasmus and Luther, written by respected Lutheran theologians, see Gerhard O. Forde, *The Captivation of the Will: Luther vs. Erasmus on Freedom and Bondage*, ed. Steven D. Paulson, Lutheran Quarterly Books (Grand Rapids: Eerdmans, 2005); and Kolb, *Bound Choice*, 11–28.

7. Even by 1521, Luther made the following claim in his Assertion of All Articles: 'It is a profound and blind error to teach that the will is by nature free and can, without grace, turn to the spirit, seek grace, and desire it. Actually, the will tries to escape from grace and rages against it when it is present.... These teachings [concerning free will] have been invented in order to insult and detract from the grace of God' (LW 32:93).

Luther's response to Erasmus is strikingly summarized in two significant passages from *The Bondage of the Will*:

> Christian faith is entirely extinguished, the promises of God and the whole gospel are completely destroyed, if we teach and believe that it is not for us to know the necessary foreknowledge of God and the necessity of the things that are come to pass. For this is the one supreme consolation of Christians in all adversities, to know that God does not lie, but does all things immutably, and that his will can neither be resisted nor changed nor hindered.[8]

> But now, since God has taken my salvation out of my hands into his, making it depend on his choice and not mine, and has promised to save me, not by my own work or exertion but by his grace and mercy, I am assured and certain both that he is faithful and will not lie to me, and also that he is too great and powerful for any demons or any adversities to be able to break him or to snatch me from him. 'No one,' he says, 'shall snatch them out of my hand because my Father who has given them to me is greater than all' [John 10:28–29]. So it comes about that, if not all, some and indeed many are saved, whereas by the power of free choice none at all would be saved, but all would perish together.[9]

Several aspects of Luther's view of predestination and election are present in these representative passages. In the first place, Luther started from the conviction that God is a personal God and the almighty Creator of all that exists. As the Creator and Lord of all creation, God is ultimately responsible for all that takes place in the world that He created and oversees by His providence. As Luther expressed it,

> He is God, and for his will there is no cause or reason that can be laid down as a rule or measure for it since there is nothing equal or superior to it, but it is itself the measure of all things. For if there were any rule or measure or cause or reason for it, it could no longer be the will of God.[10]

The God who reveals His mercy and grace in Jesus Christ in the fullness of time is at the same time the One who works His will and purpose in all things, including the salvation of fallen sinners:

---

8. Martin Luther, *The Bondage of the Will*, LW 33:43.

9. ibid., LW 33:289.

10. ibid., LW 33:181.

For the will of God is effectual and cannot be hindered, since it is the power of the divine nature itself; moreover it is wise, so that it cannot be deceived. Now, if his will is not hindered, there is nothing to prevent the work itself from being done, in the place, time, manner and measure that he himself both foresees and wills. If the will of God were such that, when the work was completed, the work remained but the will ceased – like the will of men, which ceases to will when the house they wanted is built, just as it also comes to an end in death – then it could be truly said that things happen contingently and mutably. But here the opposite happens; the work comes to an end and the will remains.[11]

In his presentation of God's sovereign, predestinating will, Luther frequently distinguished between God's 'hidden' and 'revealed' will, *Deus absconditus* and *Deus revelatus*. By means of this distinction, Luther aimed to emphasize that the all-governing will of God is perfect and righteous, even though it remains beyond our comprehension:

For if his righteousness were such that it could be judged to be righteous by human standards, it would clearly not be divine and would in no way differ from human righteousness. But since he is the one true God, and is wholly incomprehensible and inaccessible to human reason, it is proper and indeed necessary that his righteousness should be incomprehensible.[12]

While there is no discrepancy between what we know of God's will in the gospel concerning Christ and what remains inaccessible to us, we can never fully comprehend or fathom the depths of God's will.

In the argument of *The Bondage of the Will*, Luther rarely spoke explicitly of God's predestination or election. Interestingly, he did not even offer an exposition of passages like Romans 9 or Ephesians 1.[13] However, he did clearly teach that fallen sinners are incapable of

---

11. ibid., LW 33:38.

12. ibid., LW 33:290. For assessments of this distinction in Luther's theology, see Paul Althaus, *The Theology of Martin Luther*, trans. Robert C. Schultz (Philadelphia: Fortress, 1966), 274–86; and David C. Steinmetz, *Luther in Context* (2nd ed.; Grand Rapids: Baker Academic, 2002), 23–31.

13. See Steinmetz, *Luther in Context*, 12–22, for an insightful analysis of the difference between Luther and Augustine in their respective writings. Steinmetz identifies areas where Luther differs from Augustine's comments on Romans 9, especially Luther's concern that the doctrine of predestination might serve to undermine the believer's assurance of salvation.

turning themselves toward God in faith and repentance, unless God Himself graciously grants them these gifts according to His purpose of election. Predestination belongs to the gospel and not to the law because it refers to God's gracious choice of some fallen sinners to be His children through the work of Christ. In the spiritual realm of redemption, God alone is able to convert the will of fallen sinners so they embrace the gospel promise in faith. In this realm,

> man is not left in the hand of his own counsel but is directed and led by the choice and counsel of God, so that just as in his own realm he is directed by his own counsel, without regard to the precepts of another, so in the Kingdom of God he is directed by the precepts of another without regard to his own choice.[14]

While Luther emphasized the means of grace that the Spirit of God uses to draw sinners into fellowship with Christ and also insisted that the gospel always expresses God's desire for all sinners to be saved, his understanding of the sinful will's bondage led him to ascribe the salvation of believers entirely to the sovereign choice of God.

Philipp Melanchthon and Later Lutheranism

Next to Luther, Philipp Melanchthon (1497–1560) was arguably the most formative figure in the development of Lutheran theology during the sixteenth century. Melanchthon's growing reluctance to treat the doctrine of predestination and election and his apparent modification of the views Luther expressed in *The Bondage of the Will* contributed significantly to the muting of the doctrine in subsequent Lutheran theology.[15]

In the first edition (1521) of his principal theological work, *Loci Communes*, Melanchthon set forth a fairly robust form of the doctrine

---

14. Luther, *Bondage*, LW 33:118–19.

15. For a treatment of Melanchthon's relationship with Luther, see Timothy J. Wengert, 'Melanchthon and Luther/Luther and Melanchthon,' *Lutherjahrbuch* 66 (1999): 55–88, and Wengert, 'Philip Melanchthon's Contribution to Luther's Debate with Erasmus over the Bondage of the Will,' in *By Faith Alone: Essays on Justification in Honor of Gerhard O. Forde*, ed. Joseph A. Burgess and Marc Kolden (Grand Rapids: Eerdmans, 2004), 110–24. For a treatment of Melanchthon's early comments on predestination in Romans 9, see Robert Kolb, 'Melanchthon's Influence on the Exegesis of his Students,' in *Philip Melanchthon (1497–1560) and the Commentary*, ed. Timothy J. Wengert and M. Patrick Graham (Sheffield, England: Sheffield Academic Press, 1997), 194–215.

of predestination, which coincided with the view Luther espoused in *The Bondage of the Will*.[16] In this edition of the *Loci*, Melanchthon linked the doctrine directly with the gospel of justification by grace alone through the work of Christ alone. Salvation is by grace alone, and the work of Christ benefits only those whom God chooses to save by granting them faith in Christ. In subsequent editions of the *Loci* and in his other writings, however, Melanchthon began to view the doctrine with greater reserve. Fearful that the doctrine of predestination would undermine the presentation of the gospel promise in Word and sacrament, he shifted the doctrine's location to the doctrine of the church, and placed increasing emphasis on the universal promises of the gospel that are presented in the Word and sacraments. Furthermore, in his formulation of the doctrine of the bondage of the will, Melanchthon expressed views that modified the strong statements of Luther.

Melanchthon's reflections on the role of the will in the believer's response to the gospel engendered a protracted controversy about 'synergism' among Lutheran theologians that would be formally settled only by the Formula of Concord in 1576.[17] His emphasis on the co-operation of the human will in the believer's response to the gospel prompted considerable debate since it arguably compromised the sovereignty of God in granting faith to fallen sinners. Synergism emphasized the active co-operation of the human will in conversion, instead of God's sovereign work as the sole basis for the believer's response to the gospel. In the course of the synergism controversy, the Lutheran tradition stopped short of embracing Melanchthon's view and insisted that believers respond in faith to the gospel only by virtue of the Holy Spirit's sovereign work.[18]

---

16. Philipp Melanchthon, 'Loci Communes' (1521), in *Melanchthon and Bucer*, ed. Wilhelm Pauck, LCC 19 (Philadelphia: Westminster, 1969), 25–6: 'I think it makes considerable difference that young minds are immediately imbued with this idea that all things come to pass, not according to the plans and efforts of men but according to the will of God.'

17. For an extensive treatment of the controversy, see Kolb, *Bound Choice*, 106–34.

18. In the second and third editions of his *Loci Communes*, Melanchthon began to speak of 'three causes of good action': the Word of God, the Holy Spirit, and 'the human will which assents to and does not reject the Word of God.' *Melanchthons Werke in Auswahl*, ed. Robert Stupperich, vol. 2, bk. 1 (Gütersloh: Bertelsmann,

Rather than attempt to sort out the complicated history of Lutheran debates regarding the doctrine of predestination, the bondage of the will, and Melanchthon's modifications of Luther's insights, the Lutheran tradition's consensus on the doctrine can best be determined by considering the Augsburg Confession and the Formula of Concord.

Since Melanchthon was the principal author of the Augsburg Confession, the first and most formative of the confessional documents of the Lutheran tradition, a consideration of its teaching is instructive to ascertaining his view particularly and Lutheranism's generally. The Augsburg Confession does not explicitly mention the doctrine of predestination or election but does address it indirectly. An early article on the doctrine of justification emphasizes that sinners are justified before God by grace alone and not 'by their own powers, merits, or works.'[19] The confession then strongly repudiates the error of Pelagianism. An article treating the freedom of the will insists that fallen sinners have no freedom 'to work the righteousness of God, or a spiritual righteousness, without the Spirit of God; because the natural man receiveth not the things of the Spirit of God (1 Cor. 2:14). But this is wrought in the heart when men do receive the Spirit of God through the Word.'[20] The teaching of the Pelagians, namely, 'that by the powers of nature alone, without the Spirit of God, we are able to love God above all things,' is explicitly condemned. Though these statements do not expressly affirm the doctrine of God's election of some to salvation, they correspond closely to the burden of Luther's teaching that believers are saved by God's free decision and grace, not on the basis of their own works.

The Formula of Concord, written to settle doctrinal disputes within Lutheranism toward the end of the sixteenth century, is more relevant to understanding the Lutheran view of predestination and

---

1955), 243. See also Kolb, *Bound Choice*, 91–5. Employing Aristotle's scheme of causes, Melanchthon identified the Word of God as the 'instrumental', the Spirit as the 'creative', and the human will as the 'material' cause of conversion. Whether Melanchthon's formulations are truly synergistic remains a matter of debate among his interpreters.

19. 'The Augsburg Confession,' art. 4, in Schaff, *Creeds of Christendom, vol. 3, The Evangelical Protestant Creeds*, Rev. David S. Schaff (reprint; Grand Rapids: Baker, 1985) 10.

20. 'The Augsburg Confession,' art. 18, in Schaff, *Creeds of Christendom*, 3:18.

election despite not addressing the doctrine directly. It clearly views the nonsalvation of some fallen sinners who do not come to faith in a way that is asymmetrical with the salvation of those whom God wills to save. Whereas the salvation of believers is entirely the fruit of God's gracious initiative and the work of the Spirit, the nonsalvation of others is the result of their irresponsible refusal to embrace the free promises of the gospel.

In its handling of the synergistic controversy, however, the Formula of Concord offers a mild corrective to the followers of Melanchthon. Its descriptions of the work of God's grace in the salvation of believers and the bondage of the human will apart from the Spirit's work correspond significantly to the earlier themes of Luther's *Bondage of the Will*.[21] In article 2, which treats the controversy regarding the freedom of the will, the Formula rejects the teaching that fallen sinners can 'apply and prepare [themselves] unto the grace of God' in response to the Word and sacraments. Unless the Holy Spirit regenerates through the means of grace, the 'unregenerate will of man is not only averse from God, but has become even hostile to God, so that it only wishes and desires those things, and is delighted with them, which are evil and opposite to the divine will.'[22] The bondage of the will of fallen sinners prevents them from co-operating with God's grace ministered through the Word, unless the Spirit first draws them and makes them willing. In its defense of this view of the bondage of the will, the Formula of Concord cites Augustine's claim that God in the conversion 'of unwilling men makes willing men,' and it identifies only two 'efficient causes' in conversion, the Holy Spirit and the Word of God.[23] In doing so, the Formula of Concord took exception to Melanchthon's apparent synergism between the three causes of conversion, the Holy Spirit (the creative cause), the Word of God (the instrumental cause), and the consenting will of man (the material cause).

Therefore, although the Lutheran confessions do not directly affirm a doctrine of sovereign and gracious election, they do affirm that the salvation of fallen sinners, who are unable to convert themselves

---

21. Kolb, *Bound Choice*, 248–58.

22. 'The Formula of Concord,' art. 2, in Schaff, *Creeds of Christendom*, 3:107.

23. ibid., 3:113.

without a prior working of the Holy Spirit through the Word, happens entirely according to God's gracious purpose. The Lutheran tradition generally follows Melanchthon's reticence to speak of predestination and election, fearful this might mitigate the clarity of the gospel in distinction from the law. And yet, in clearly affirming salvation by grace alone through the gracious initiative of God in Christ, and in opposing any synergistic view of the relation between the work of God's grace and the will of fallen sinners, Lutheranism presents a moderate Augustinian monergism. To preserve the universal grace that is communicated in the gospel, however, the Lutheran tradition generally refrains from affirming any doctrine of reprobation or divine purpose to pass by nonelect persons, leaving them in their sins.

The Reformed Doctrine of Predestination and Election[24]

The leading theologians of the Reformed tradition in the sixteenth century did not share the Lutheran tradition's reticence to articulate a fulsome doctrine of predestination and election. Although Reformed theologians expressed a considerable diversity of formulation, their general consensus was that the salvation of fallen sinners is the fruit of God's gracious electing purpose. The principal confessional documents of the Reformed churches testify to this consensus. For the purpose of my survey of the Reformed doctrine of predestination, I will offer a summary of two leading figures, John Calvin of Geneva (1509–1564) and Heinrich Bullinger of Zurich (1504–1575). While these two theologians confirm a broad consensus of teaching among the Reformed theologians of the period, their differences also illustrate the diversity of opinion that remained on some points.

---

24. For general surveys of the doctrine of predestination in Reformed theology, see Buis, *Historic Protestantism and Predestination*; Richard A. Muller, *Christ and the Decree: Christology and Predestination in Reformed Theology from Calvin to Perkins, Studies in Historical Theology 2* (reprint; Grand Rapids: Baker, 1988 [1986]); Cornelis Graafland, *Van Calvijn tot Barth: Oorsprong en ontwikkeling van de leer der verkiezing in het Gereformeerd Protestantisme* ('From Calvin to Barth: The Origin and Development of the Doctrine of Election in Reformed Protestantism') ('s-Gravenhage, The Netherlands: Uitgeverij Boekencentrum, 1987); Pieter Rouwendal, 'The Doctrine of Predestination in Reformed Orthodoxy,' in *A Companion to Reformed Orthodoxy*, ed. Herman J. Selderhuis, *Brill's Companions to the Christian Tradition 40* (Leiden: Brill, 2013), 553–89.

Predestination in the Theology of John Calvin[25]

In the history of the interpretation of Calvin's theology, it has often been argued that predestination was the center and organizing principle of his theology. A number of nineteenth- and twentieth-century theologians regarded the doctrine of predestination as the 'central dogma' of Calvin's theology, the root from which all other doctrines were allegedly drawn.[26] Even in the popular imagination, the one feature of Calvin's theology that is most often emphasized is his doctrine of double predestination.

Despite a general assumption that predestination is at the center of Calvin's theology, it is noteworthy that Calvin treats the doctrine in his most important theological work, *Institutes of the Christian Religion*, toward the end of an extended discussion on the Holy Spirit's work in uniting believers to Christ and communicating to them the benefits of Christ's saving work.[27] Although Calvin originally

---

25. Among the many sources on Calvin's doctrine of predestination, the following are especially valuable: Muller, *CD*, 17–38; Paul Jacobs, *Prädestination und Verantwortlichkeit bei Calvin* (Kasel: Oncken, 1937); Fred H. Klooster, *Calvin's Doctrine of Predestination* (Grand Rapids: Baker, 1977); François Wendel, *Calvin: The Origins and Development of His Religious Thought* (New York: Harper & Row, 1963), 263–83; Carl R. Trueman, 'Election: Calvin's Theology of Election and Its Early Reception,' in *Calvin's Theology and Its Reception: Disputes, Developments, and New Possibilities*, ed. J. Todd Billings and I. John Hesselink (Louisville: Westminster John Knox, 2012), 97–120; R. Scott Clark, 'Election and Predestination: The Sovereign Expressions of God (3.21–24),' in *A Theological Guide to Calvin's Institutes: Essays and Analysis*, ed. David W. Hall and Peter A. Lillback, Calvin 500 Series (Phillipsburg, NJ: Presbyterian & Reformed, 2008), 90–122.

26. For representative presentations of the thesis that predestination is a 'central dogma' in Calvin's theology and in later Calvinism, see Alexander Schweizer, *Die Protestantischen Centraldogmen in ihrer Entwicklung innerhalb der reformierten Kirche*, 2 vols. (Zurich: Orell, Füssli, 1854-1856); Hans Emil Weber, *Reformation, Orthodoxie Und Rationalismus, vol. 1, pt. 1, Von Der Reformation Zur Orthodoxie* (Gütersloh: Gerd Mohn, 1937); Graafland, *Von Calvijn tot Barth*; Ernst Bizer, *Frühorthodoxie und Rationalismus* (Zurich: EVZ Verlag, 1963). For critical, persuasive refutations of this thesis, see Muller, *CD*, esp. 1–13, 177–82; idem., 'The Use and Abuse of a Document: Beza's Tabula Praedestinationis, the Bolsec Controversy, and the Origins of Reformed Orthodoxy,' in *Protestant Scholasticism: Essays in Reassessment*, ed. Carl R. Trueman and R. Scott Clark (Carlisle: Paternoster, 1999), 33–61; Willem J. van Asselt and Eef Dekker, 'Introduction,' in *Reformation and Scholasticism: An Ecumenical Enterprise*, ed. Willem J. van Asselt and Eef Dekker, *Texts and Studies in Reformation and Post-Reformation Thought* (Grand Rapids: Baker Academic, 2001), 11–43.

27. For helpful analyses of the significance of where Calvin placed the doctrine of predestination in the *Institutes*, see Richard A. Muller, 'The Placement of

treated the doctrine of predestination in the context of the doctrine of providence, in the final edition of the *Institutes* he discussed it within the context of soteriology (the doctrine of salvation) and ecclesiology (the doctrine of the church). In this way, Calvin emphasized how predestination confirms that the believer's salvation is born entirely of God's gracious purposes in Christ and how it undergirds the believer's assurance of God's favor.

Calvin opened his treatment of predestination by noting that 'the covenant of life is not preached equally among all men, and among those to whom it is preached, it does not gain the same acceptance either constantly or in equal degree.'[28] The topic of predestination and election is, therefore, unavoidable. How are we to explain that some respond to the call of the gospel in the way of faith, while others refuse to believe? The ultimate explanation must be found in God's 'free mercy' and 'eternal election', which form the fountainhead of all God's saving graces in Christ. If we fail to ascribe the difference between those who believe and are saved and those who remain unwilling to believe to 'God's mere generosity', we will dishonor God's sheer grace in saving us and fail to rest our comfort in God alone.[29] Consequently, Calvin argued that we must give attention to the scriptural doctrine of predestination and election. In doing so, we face two dangers. On the one hand, there is the danger of excessive curiosity regarding the doctrine, which can easily lead us to go beyond the limits of what Scripture reveals concerning God's eternal election. On the other hand, there is the danger of undue reticence, which fails to acknowledge that what God's Spirit has revealed in the Word is for our comfort and blessing.

Predestination in Reformed Theology: Issue or Non-Issue?' *CTJ* 40, no. 2 (2005): 184–210; Paul Helm, 'Calvin, the "Two Issues," and the Structure of the Institutes,' *CTJ* 42, no. 2 (2007): 341–48.

28. Calvin, *Institutes*, 3.21.1. In addition to Calvin's treatment of predestination in the *Institutes*, the following sources offer an extensive presentation of his view: *John Calvin, The Bondage and Liberation of the Will: A Defence of the Orthodox Doctrine of Human Choice against Pighius*, ed. A. N. S. Lane, trans. G. I. Davies, Texts and Studies in Reformation and Post-Reformation Thought 2 (Grand Rapids: Baker, 1996); Calvin, *Concerning the Eternal Predestination of God*, trans. J. K. S. Reid (Louisville: Westminster John Knox, 1997).

29. Calvin, *Institutes*, 3.21.1.

The title of Calvin's first chapter on the doctrine of predestination in the *Institutes* clearly identifies what is at issue: 'Eternal election, by which God has predestined some to salvation, others to destruction.'[30] The ultimate reason that some believe and are saved through Christ must be ascribed to God's purpose of election. While it is true that God is omniscient and knows all events prior to their occurrence, it is not true that election amounts to no more than God's foreknowledge of who will believe in response to gospel preaching. As Calvin defined it,

> We call predestination God's eternal decree, by which he compacted within himself what he willed to become of each man. For all are not created in equal condition; rather, eternal life is foreordained for some, eternal damnation for others. Therefore, as any man has been created to one or the other of these ends, we speak of him as predestined to life or to death.[31]

In the scriptural descriptions of God's purpose of election, a distinction may be drawn between 'degrees of election'. In the case of the people of Israel, God chose them corporately and granted to them many common blessings and privileges. However, to this general election of Israel as a people, we must 'add a second, more limited degree of election, or one in which God's more special grace was evident, that is, when from the same race of Abraham God rejected some but showed that he kept others among his sons by cherishing them in the church.'[32] When the apostle Paul speaks of God's 'purpose of election' in Romans 9–11, he speaks of this second, proper purpose of God to save a certain number of individuals from among the larger number of the people of Israel.

According to Calvin, God's decision to save some is based entirely on His 'freely given mercy', whereas His decision not to save others is based on His 'just and irreprehensible but incomprehensible judgment':

> As Scripture, then, clearly shows, we say that God once established by his eternal and unchangeable plan those whom he long before determined once for all to receive into salvation, and those whom, on the other hand, he would devote to destruction. We assert that, with respect to the elect,

---

30. ibid., 3.21.

31. ibid., 3.21.5.

32. ibid., 2.21.6.

this plan was founded upon his freely given mercy, without regard to human worth; but by his just and irreprehensible but incomprehensible judgment he has barred the door of life to those whom he has given over to damnation.[33]

When the apostle Paul treats the doctrine of election in Romans 9–11, he ascribes the salvation of some to God's undeserved mercy, which is revealed in His purpose of election, and he ascribes the nonsalvation of others to God's just decision to leave them in their sins. Contrary to those who affirmed election but not reprobation, Calvin argued that

> it will be highly absurd to say that others acquire by chance or obtain by their own effort what election alone confers on a few. Therefore, those whom God passes over, he condemns; and this he does for no other reason than that he wills to exclude them from the inheritance which he predestines for his own children.[34]

Although there is not an exact symmetry between election and reprobation – election reveals God's undeserved mercy, reprobation reveals God's justice in leaving some in their sin – the ultimate explanation for the salvation of some and not others rests in God's electing purpose.

In the concluding chapter of his relatively brief exposition of the doctrine of predestination in the *Institutes*, Calvin identified and responded to several common objections against the doctrine. Among these objections, two are of special importance.

The first objection was the claim that this doctrine makes God out to be a 'tyrant'. Calvin insisted that the will of God is perfectly just, even as God is just and is Himself the standard of all righteousness. Though we may not be able to fathom the depths of God's will, we may not regard it as arbitrary or unjust. When God chooses not to save some, it must always be remembered that the 'cause' of their condemnation lies in themselves.[35]

The second objection was that the doctrine of election takes the 'guilt and responsibility' away from sinners in respect to their salvation.

---

33. ibid., 3.21.7.

34. ibid., 3.23.1. In this passage, Calvin clearly has in view the Lutheran position, which affirms election but not reprobation.

35. ibid., 3.23.3.

According to this objection, if God's will is the ultimate reason for the nonsalvation of the reprobate, then 'why should God impute those things to men as sin, the necessity of which he has imposed by his predestination?'[36] In his reply to this objection, Calvin did not hesitate to insist that the nonsalvation of some sinners is due to God's foreordination, and that even the fall of the human race into sin was a result of God's decree.[37] For Calvin, it was not enough to say that God simply 'permitted' Adam's fall or that the nonsalvation of the reprobate had no other explanation than their own willful sinfulness. While it is true that the 'cause and occasion' for the nonsalvation of the reprobate must be 'found in themselves', Calvin declared, 'I shall not hesitate, then, simply to confess with Augustine that "the will of God is the necessity of things," and that what he has willed will of necessity come to pass, as those things which he has foreseen will truly come to pass.'[38] We must acknowledge that 'man falls according as God's providence ordains, but he falls by his own fault.'[39] God does indeed justly and freely determine not to save some. But this must not become the occasion for removing from the sinner the blame for his or her condemnation:

> By his own evil intention, then, man corrupted the pure nature he had received from the Lord; and by his fall he drew all his posterity with him into destruction. Accordingly, we should contemplate the evident cause of condemnation in the corrupt nature of humanity – which is closer to us – rather than seek a hidden and utterly incomprehensible cause in God's predestination.[40]

In Calvin's exposition of the doctrine of election, he placed special emphasis on the comfort that believers may derive from this doctrine. The doctrine of predestination and election must be handled judiciously and in a way that not only ascribes glory to God for His free grace in

---

36. Calvin, *Institutes*, 3.23.6.

37. Muller notes, 'Unlike many of his contemporaries and successors, Calvin did not shrink from the conclusion that permission and volition are one in the mind of an eternal and utterly sovereign God: reprobation could not be viewed simply as a passive act of God.... Nevertheless, in view of Calvin's emphasis on knowledge of God, reprobation does not appear the exact coordinate of election' (*CD*, 24–25).

38. Calvin, *Institutes*, 3.23.8.

39. ibid., 3.23.9.

40. ibid., 3.23.3.

Christ but also comforts believers and assures them of the certainty of their salvation. Since God's purpose of election is made known through the gracious call of the gospel, Christ is the 'mirror' of our election. Only as believers place their trust in Christ will they find the comfort and assurance that election properly affords them:

> If we seek God's fatherly mercy and kindly heart, we should turn our eyes to Christ, on whom alone God's Spirit rests.... Accordingly, those whom God has adopted as his sons are said to have been chosen not in themselves but in his Christ; for unless he could love them in him, he could not honor them with the inheritance of his Kingdom if they had not previously become partakers of him. But if we have been chosen in him, we shall not find assurance of our election in ourselves; and not even in God the Father, if we conceive him as severed from his Son. Christ, then, is the mirror wherein we must, and without self-deception may, contemplate our own election.[41]

As Calvin understood it, the scriptural teaching regarding predestination especially emphasizes that believers are saved by God's grace alone, and it affords believers a solid basis for the assurance of God's favor.

Predestination in the Theology of Heinrich Bullinger

Unlike John Calvin, who is commonly regarded as the leading theologian of the Reformed churches in the sixteenth century, Heinrich Bullinger is viewed as a 'Reformer in the wings'.[42] Bullinger, who

---

41. ibid., 3.24.5. Calvin's emphasis on the comfort of the doctrine of predestination is a common theme among the Reformed theologians of the period. Predestination, in a manner similar to the doctrine of justification by faith alone, is a teaching that simultaneously honors God's initiative of grace in salvation and undergirds the believer's confidence in that grace. By contrast, the Roman Catholic Church at the Council of Trent rejected the possibility of such assurance for believers unless by way of exception one is given a 'special revelation' of God's electing grace: 'No one, moreover, so long as he is in this mortal life, ought so far to presume as regards the secret mystery of divine predestination, as to determine for certain that he is assuredly in the number of the predestinate; as if it were true, that he that is justified, either can not sin any more, or, if he do sin, that he ought to promise himself an assured repentance; for except by special revelation, it can not be known whom God hath chosen unto himself' (in Schaff, *Creeds of Christendom*, 2:103).

42. This language derives from David C. Steinmetz's *Reformers in the Wings* (Philadelphia: Fortress, 1971). For a useful introduction to Bullinger's reformatory work and thought, see Bruce Gordon and Emidio Campi, eds., *Architect of Reformation: An*

succeeded Zwingli as the leading pastor of the Reformed churches in Zurich, is nonetheless a fitting figure to include in this survey of the doctrine of predestination in Reformation theology. Next to Calvin, no Reformed theologian was more influential during the sixteenth century. And on the doctrine of predestination, Bullinger offers a more moderately stated version of classic Augustinianism than that of Calvin.

In studies of Reformation theology, Bullinger's doctrine of predestination has elicited considerable controversy.[43] Since Bullinger expressed reservations about Calvin's formulations and declined to come strongly to Calvin's defense in the Bolsec controversy,[44] interpreters of Bullinger have debated whether he differed substantially from Calvin on the doctrine of predestination. Some have even argued that Bullinger privileged the doctrine of the covenant over that of election and was the 'fountainhead' of an alternative theological tradition to that stemming from Calvin.[45] While I do not believe there are substantial, or insuperable, differences between Bullinger and Calvin, there is no doubt that Bullinger expressed himself more reservedly on this doctrine.

Introduction to Heinrich Bullinger, 1504–1575, Texts and Studies in Reformation and Post-Reformation Thought (Grand Rapids: Baker Academic, 2004).

43. For general studies of Bullinger's doctrine of predestination, which provide an account of the debate regarding the compatibility of his view with that of Calvin, see Cornelis P. Venema, *Heinrich Bullinger and the Doctrine of Predestination: Author of 'the Other Reformed Tradition'?*, Texts and Studies in Reformation and Post-Reformation Thought (Grand Rapids: Baker Academic, 2002); Muller, *CD*, 39–47; and Peter Walser, *Die Prädestination bei Heinrich Bullinger im Zussamenhang mit seiner Gotteslehre* (Zurich: Zwingli Verlag, 1957).

44. The controversy over the doctrine of predestination in Geneva commenced when Jerome Bolsec, an ex-Carmelite monk and physician, publicly attacked Calvin's doctrine of predestination on October 16, 1551. For original source materials and treatments of the controversy, see Philip E. Hughes, *The Register of the Company of the Pastors of Geneva in the Time of Calvin* (Grand Rapids: Eerdmans, 1966), 133–86; Philip C. Holtrop, *The Bolsec Controversy on Predestination, From 1551–1555: The Statements of Jerome Bolsec, and the Response of John Calvin, Theodore Beza, and Other Reformed Theologians*, vol. 1, bks. 1 and 2, Theological Currents, the Setting and Mood, and the Trial Itself (Lewiston: Edwin Mellen, 1993); and Venema, *Heinrich Bullinger*, 58–63.

45. J. Wayne Baker, *Heinrich Bullinger and the Covenant: The Other Reformed Tradition* (Athens: Ohio University Press, 1980). My study *Heinrich Bullinger and the Doctrine of Predestination* offers an extensive and critical assessment of the claim that Bullinger authored another Reformed tradition that privileged the doctrine of covenant over that of election.

The best source for ascertaining Bullinger's mature teaching on the doctrine of predestination and election is the Second Helvetic Confession (*Confessio helvetica posterior*). Although Bullinger wrote on the topic of predestination on several occasions throughout his life, the Second Helvetic Confession sets forth themes that Bullinger consistently emphasized when treating this doctrine. This confession, which Bullinger probably began to write in 1561,[46] contains a comprehensive summary of Bullinger's understanding of the Reformed faith. Bullinger wrote the Second Helvetic Confession not only as a statement of his personal confession but also as a summary and defense of the 'catholic' faith of the Reformed churches. When he first penned this confession, Bullinger intended that it be affixed to his will as a kind of bequest to the Reformed churches that he had served as pastor. Little could he have anticipated the extent to which the Confession would be received and embraced among the Reformed churches on the Continent.[47]

In the sequence of topics treated in his confession, Bullinger took up the doctrine of predestination in a separate chapter, which follows chapters on the doctrines of providence, the fall into sin, and the freedom of the will, and which precedes a chapter on the person and work of Christ. Thus, the doctrine of predestination is framed between the topics of human sinfulness and God's gracious purpose to save His people in Christ. Predestination and election belong not to the doctrine of theology proper but to the doctrines of soteriology and Christology. By virtue of this arrangement of topics, Bullinger's presentation of the doctrine of predestination is infralapsarian in form. God's gracious election answers the need of fallen sinners, who

---

46. Ernst Koch, 'Die Textüberlieferung Der Confessio Helvetica Posterior Und Ihre Vorgeschichte,' in *Glauben und Bekennen: Vierhundert Jahre Confessio Helvetica Posterior*, ed. Joachim Staedtke (Zurich: Zwingli Verlag, 1966), 17.

47. The Second Helvetic Confession was translated into fifteen languages and published in more than 115 editions. It is arguably the most widely disseminated of the Reformed symbols of the sixteenth century. The English translations in what follows are taken from *The Book of Confessions* (2nd ed.; Office of the General Assembly of the United Presbyterian Church in the United States of America, 1970). In the following, I will cite the confession by chapter. The Latin text of the Second Helvetic Confession can be found in Wilhelm Niesel, *Bekenntnisschriften und Kirchenordnungen der nach Gottes Wort reformierten Kirche* (Zurich: A. G. Zollikon, 1938), 219–75.

are incapable of restoring themselves to favor with God or taking the initiative in response to the gospel's call to faith.[48]

God's work of redemption finds its ultimate source in God's election to save His people in Christ. Only the monergism of sovereign electing grace can redress the situation of fallen human beings, whose wills, though free from any external compulsion to evil, have no capacity to perform what is good. Predestination is defined as God's election to save His people in Christ and is not treated within the context of the divine decree as an aspect of the doctrine of God. Breaking from the traditional order of theological topics followed by Thomas Aquinas and earlier scholasticism, Bullinger viewed predestination not simply as a special providence (*providentia specialis*) but as the fountainhead of God's saving work in Christ. For Bullinger, predestination answered the question, How can fallen sinners, who have no free will or capability of responding in faith to the gospel on their own, be saved through faith in Christ?[49] The only explanation for the salvation of those who embrace the gospel promise in Christ is that God has freely chosen to grant them salvation and faith through the Holy Spirit's work with the gospel.

Although the doctrine of predestination includes, at least formally, the two elements of election and reprobation, Bullinger particularly emphasized the positive expression of God's decree, the election of some to salvation in Christ: 'From eternity God has freely, and of

---

48. Second Helvetic Confession, chap. 9: 'For the evangelical and apostolic Scripture requires regeneration of whoever among us wishes to be saved. Hence our first birth from Adam contributes nothing to our salvation.... Wherefore, man not yet regenerate has no free will for good, no strength to perform what is good.'

49. As Muller states, 'Juxtaposition of predestination with sin and the problem of the will represents a powerful affirmation of soteriological monergism: human inability answered directly by the electing will of God' (*CD*, 44). Of special importance in the Confession's treatment of anthropology is Bullinger's comment on 'curious questions' (*curiosae quaestiones*) that arise in considering Adam's fall into sin: 'Other questions, such as whether God willed Adam to fall, and similar questions we reckon among curious questions (unless perchance the wickedness of heretics, or of other churlish men compels us also to explain them out of the Word of God, as the godly teachers of the Church have frequently done), knowing that the Lord forbade man to eat of the forbidden fruit and punished his transgression.' Second Helvetic Confession, chap. 8. In this statement, Bullinger obliquely criticizes Calvin's inclusion of the fall within God's decree and echoes an argument that he had previously advanced in his correspondence with Calvin during the controversy with Bolsec.

his mere grace, without any respect to men, predestined or elected the saints whom he wills to save in Christ.'[50] Elaborating on this definition of predestination, which focuses on God's gracious purpose to save the elect in Christ, Bullinger closely associated election with the person and work of Christ. Christ is not only the Mediator who provides for the salvation of the elect but He is also the ground and source of God's electing grace. According to Bullinger, those whom God predestines are elect, 'not directly, but in Christ, and on account of Christ, in order that those who are now ingrafted into Christ by faith might also be elected.'[51] With this language, Bullinger did not intend to suggest that God's gracious election is on the ground of faith. Even though there is a close correlation between election and the believer's union with Christ by faith, faith itself is God's gift to the elect that enables them to have fellowship with Christ.[52] Consistent with his emphasis on the positive expression of God's predestination of the elect unto salvation, Bullinger offered only one observation about reprobation, namely, describing the reprobate as those who are 'outside of Christ'.[53] Though it might be possible to infer from God's election of some to salvation that this logically entails the nonelection of others, Bullinger was content to note simply that they are reprobate on account of their not having fellowship with Christ.

After defining the doctrine of predestination as God's free election of His people in and on account of Christ, Bullinger turned to pastoral questions that often surface in respect to God's purpose of election. With respect to the question concerning the scope of election, Bullinger emphasized that 'we must hope well of all and not rashly judge any man to be a reprobate'.[54] Rather than speculating about the relative number of the elect, whether they be few or many, we should encourage everyone to 'strive to enter by the narrow door' (Luke 13:24). Although Bullinger did not use the expression in the Second Helvetic Confession, his insistence both that no one be rashly considered reprobate and that

---

50. Second Helvetic Confession, chap. 10.

51. ibid.

52. ibid.

53. ibid. The Latin reads, 'Reprobi vero, qui sunt extra Christum.'

54. ibid.

believers hold out hope for all reflects his frequent claim that God is a 'lover of man' (*philanthrōpos*) who bears malice toward no one. And although he did not explicitly speak of the universal promises of God, he did speak of God's promises 'which apply to all the faithful' and ought to be the occasion for the believer's confidence before God.[55]

Bullinger concluded his consideration of election by addressing the important question of the believer's assurance of election. Consistent with the intimate conjunction of election with Christ, Bullinger noted that the believer's relationship with Christ is the basis for any assurance of election. We may not ask whether or not we are elect from eternity 'outside of Christ' (*extra Christum*).[56] Rather, we are called to believe through the preaching of the gospel promise in Christ. For 'it is to be held as beyond doubt that if you believe and are in Christ, you are elected.'[57] For Bullinger, 'being elect' and 'being in Christ' were correlated, just as 'being rejected' and 'being outside of Christ' through unbelief were correlated. Employing imagery used by Calvin to answer the question of having assurance of election, Bullinger asserted, 'Let Christ, therefore, be the looking glass [*speculum*], in whom we may contemplate our predestination. We shall have a sufficient and clear testimony that we are inscribed in the Book of life if we have fellowship with Christ, and he is ours and we are his in true faith.'[58] It is in this sense of our election being joined to our fellowship with Christ that admonitions are not in vain. As Augustine has shown, 'both the grace of free election and predestination, and also salutary admonitions and doctrines, are to be preached.'[59] Consequently, Bullinger concluded his discussion of predestination and election with the apostle Paul's admonition to work out our salvation with fear and trembling.

---

55. ibid.

56. ibid.

57. ibid.

58. ibid. The Latin reads, 'Christus itaque sit speculum, in quo praedestinationem nostram contemplemur. Satis perspicuum et firmum habebimus testimonium, nos in libro vitae inscriptos esse, si communicaverimus cum Christo, et is in vera fide noster sit, nos eius simus.' Cf. Calvin, *Institutes*, 3.24.5.

59. Second Helvetic Confession, chap. 10. As in his other writings on the subject of predestination, Bullinger's references to Augustine's writings show that he stands in the Augustinian exegetical and theological tradition.

Though Bullinger demonstrated greater reserve in the Second Helvetic Confession than in some prior instances of his consideration of the subject of reprobation – his definition of predestination there speaks only of election, not reprobation – his reluctance to draw a direct connection between God's will and the condemnation of those who are outside Christ certainly follows a pattern evident in his other writings. The pastoral quality of Bullinger's handling of the doctrine is also evident in the way the Second Helvetic Confession stresses such themes as the good hope believers should have for the salvation of all sinners, not rashly judging anyone a reprobate; the erroneous assumption that the number of the elect is only few; the importance of the means God uses in the accomplishment of His saving purposes; and the assurance of election through fellowship with Christ. Though these themes were by no means unique to Bullinger's formulation of the doctrine of predestination among the Reformed theologians of the mid-sixteenth century, including Calvin, the pastoral and homiletical manner in which Bullinger treated the doctrine of predestination in the Second Helvetic Confession bears many telltale traces of his distinctive view.[60]

Predestination in the Theology of Huldrych Zwingli and Peter Martyr Vermigli

In addition to Calvin and Bullinger, a number of other influential Reformed figures addressed the doctrine of predestination in their

---

60. For a discussion of how two of Calvin's contemporaries, Wolfgang Musculus (1497–1563) and Peter Martyr Vermigli (1499–1562), treat the doctrine of predestination, see Muller, *CD*, 39–75. While Muller finds these theologians employing a more 'scholastic form' in their handling of the doctrine, he rejects the claim that this form materially affects their understanding of predestination or represents a movement away from Calvin's close association of the doctrine with Christology and soteriology. As in Calvin's and Bullinger's theology, 'predestination and Christology both serve to focus and to ground the soteriological structure and themselves both develop out of the context of an overarching concern to delineate the pattern of divine working in the economy of salvation' (*CD*, 68). For Musculus' doctrine of predestination, see Wolfgang Musculus, *Common Places of Christian Religion* (London: R. Wolfe, 1563, 1578); Musculus, *Loci communes sacrae theologiae* (Basel: Johannes Hervagius, 1560, 1568, 1573). For Vermigli's doctrine, see *The Common Places of D. Peter Martyr Vermigli* (London: Denham, 1583); Vermigli, *Loci Communes D. Petri Martyris Vermigli* (London, 1576; rev. ed. 1583); Frank A. James III, *Peter Martyr Vermigli and Predestination: The Augustinian Inheritance of an Italian Reformer*, Oxford Theological Monographs (Oxford: Clarendon, 1998).

writings. Two of these theologians, Huldrych Zwingli and Peter Martyr Vermigli, deserve brief attention.

Zwingli's treatment of predestination is located within the framework of the doctrine of God's providence. In his most important treatment of the doctrine, Zwingli began with a general definition of providence: 'Providence is the enduring and unchangeable rule over and direction of all things in the universe.'[61] God is the good, wise, and just Ruler and Sustainer of all things, so that nothing takes place in the course of history that lies outside His providential care and rule. According to Zwingli, 'God is all-knowing, all-powerful, and good. Hence nothing escapes His notice, nothing evades His orders and His sway, nothing which He does is anything but good.'[62] Predestination is the aspect of God's providence that pertains to God's good and gracious will to grant salvation to the elect. In the strictest sense, predestination focuses especially on God's gracious election, which displays His undeserved mercy toward those whom He is pleased to save from the fallen human race, and not on His determination to leave others in their lost condition. Whereas gracious election especially displays God's mercy, God's determination not to save the nonelect displays His justice. Consequently, Zwingli defined election as 'the free disposition of the divine will in regard to those that are to be blessed.'[63] Though God's gracious election has as a corollary the nonelection of those whom God righteously condemns by leaving them in their sins, Zwingli clearly distinguished this feature of God's providence from His merciful and good election of some unto salvation. In spite of Zwingli's reluctance to treat God's determination not to save some as parallel to God's determination to save the elect, his decision to formulate the doctrine of election within the context of God's providential determination of all things troubled his successor, Bullinger.[64] Because Zwingli located

---

61. Huldrych Zwingli, *On Providence and Other Essays*, ed. William John Hinke (reprint; Durham, NC: Labyrinth, 1983 [1922]), 136. For a survey of Zwingli's doctrine of predestination, see Gottfried W. Locher, *Zwingli's Thought: New Perspectives*, *Studies in the History of Christian Thought 25* (Leiden: Brill, 1981), 121–41.

62. Zwingli, *On Providence*, 180.

63. ibid., 184.

64. Bullinger expressed his concern regarding Zwingli's doctrine of providence in his correspondence with Calvin regarding the controversy over Jerome Bolsec's doctrine of predestination in Geneva. When Bolsec criticized Calvin's teaching, he argued

his treatment of predestination in the context of his emphasis on God's all-inclusive providence, Bullinger feared that his doctrine did not sufficiently emphasize God's goodness and grace in the election of His people in Christ.

Peter Martyr Vermigli's doctrine of predestination is also worthy of notice.[65] Vermigli was one of a number of Italian theologians (including his good friend Jerome Zanchi) who influenced the early development of the Reformed theological tradition.[66] The most important statement of Vermigli's doctrine of predestination is provided in his *Loci Communes*, a collection of his lectures, treatises, and disputations posthumously published by Robert Masson in 1576.[67] Vermigli's treatment of the doctrine of predestination followed a far more 'scholastic' and rationalistic pattern than the one in Calvin and Bullinger's writings.[68] He began with an introductory discussion of two matters: the suitability of the doctrine of predestination for preaching and teaching, and the 'logician's question' of whether or not there is a divine predestination.[69]

that his view of predestination was similar to that of Zwingli. In his correspondence with Calvin, Bullinger expressed dissatisfaction with Calvin and Zwingli's incautious statements on the subject of predestination and providence. For a review of this correspondence, see Venema, *Heinrich Bullinger*, 58–63.

65. The most comprehensive treatment of Vermigli's life and writings remains C. Schmidt, *Peter Martyr Vermigli, Leben und ausgewählte Schriften* (Elberfeld: R. L. Friderichs, 1858). For a brief sketch of his life, see David C. Steinmetz, 'Peter Martyr Vermigli,' in *Reformers in the Wings*, 151–61. For a summary of his correspondence with Bullinger, see Marvin W. Anderson, 'Peter Martyr, Reformed Theologian (1542–1562): His Letters to Heinrich Bullinger and John Calvin,' *SCJ* 4, no. 1 (1973): 41–64.

66. For more recent treatments of Vermigli's doctrine of predestination, particularly within the framework of his Aristotelian scholasticism, see John Patrick Donnelly, *Calvinism and Scholasticism in Vermigli's Doctrine of Man and Grace, Studies in Medieval and Reformation Thought 18* (Leiden: Brill, 1976), esp. 3–41, 116–49; Muller, *CD*, 57–75; J. C. McClelland, 'The Reformed Doctrine of Predestination: According to Peter Martyr,' *SJT* 8, no. 3 (1955): 255–71; James, *Vermigli and Predestination*; Frank A. James III, 'Peter Martyr Vermigli: At the Crossroads of Late Medieval Scholasticism, Christian Humanism and Resurgent Augustinianism,' in Trueman and Clark, *Protestant Scholasticism*, 62–78.

67. Vermigli, *Loci communes*. References to Vermigli's treatise on predestination in the following notes are from the revised edition of 1583.

68. Donnelly and James document the influence on Vermigli's thought of Aquinas and Scotus among the scholastics and of the more explicitly developed doctrine in Gregory of Rimini and Martin Bucer among the Reformers. Donnelly, *Calvinism and Scholasticism*, 125–29; James, 'Peter Martyr Vermigli,' 52–78.

69. Vermigli, *Loci communes*, 3.1.1.

Only after addressing these matters and offering a defense against the objection that predestination leads to a doctrine of 'fatal necessity' (*necessitatem quidem fatalem*)[70] did Vermigli take up the subject of predestination. In doing so, he began with a broad and general statement of predestination and then spoke of a positive will of God in election and a negative or permissive will of God in reprobation.

In his initial definition of predestination, Vermigli maintained that God in His divine counsel (*consilium*) appointed all things to their particular end.[71] Though the divine counsel includes the election of some and the reprobation of others, Vermigli proceeded to link divine predestination most especially with election and formulated the doctrine of reprobation with the use of the scholastic doctrine of God's 'permissive' or 'passive' will. In his formal definition of predestination, Vermigli emphasized God's counsel to exhibit His love toward His own in Christ:

> I say, therefore, that predestination is the most wise counsel (*propositum*) of God by which he has decreed firmly from before all eternity to call those whom he has loved in Christ to the adoption of sons, to be justified by faith; and subsequently to glorify through good works, those who shall be conformed to the image of the Son of God, that in them the glory and mercy of the Creator might be declared.[72]

By contrast, Vermigli's definition of reprobation maintained that, though it had its source in the divine will from eternity, it was a passive act of God in which He withheld His love from the nonelect. He accordingly denied a direct or efficient will of God in reprobation. Those whom God chose not to save are fallen sinners whom He passed by in the divine decree. Vermigli defined reprobation as God's decree in eternity 'not to have mercy on those whom he has not loved'.[73]

This sketch of Vermigli's doctrine of predestination illustrates some differences between his doctrine and Bullinger's. Unlike Bullinger, Vermigli cast the doctrine of predestination in a far more scholastic form, exhibiting considerable dependence on a Thomist

---

70. ibid., 3.1.5.

71. ibid., 3.1.5.

72. ibid., 3.1.11. Translation by James, 'Peter Martyr Vermigli,' 75.

73. ibid., 3.1.5.

construction of the divine counsel with its distinction between God's 'efficient' and 'permissive' will. Vermigli's careful and extended exposition of the divine will insisted that all things fall within the scope of the divine counsel, whether by way of direct and positive willing or by way of indirect or permissive willing. He also developed more explicitly the decree of reprobation, linking it with God's passive will and acknowledging that it parallels in some, though not all, respects God's decree of election. In these emphases, he exhibited a willingness to explore rather fully, in the manner of the scholastic tradition, the diverse aspects of the divine counsel. In so doing, he distinguished himself from the more cautious and restrained handling of the doctrine by Bullinger.

However, it should also be noted that Vermigli's doctrine approximated Bullinger's in some respects more than that of Calvin. For example, he shared Bullinger's basically infralapsarian presentation of predestination: God's election to save some assumes the fall of all men into sin (*homo creatus et lapsus*). Also, by linking predestination positively with election and only passively with reprobation, he shared Bullinger's resistance to positing any direct connection between God's will and the nonsalvation of the reprobate. The fact that some are not saved cannot be ascribed to God's efficient will; they are merely left in their fallen condition, for which God bears no ultimate responsibility. God's will in relation to the reprobate is merely passive, not active.[74] Similarly with Bullinger, Vermigli resisted any attempt to draw a positive connection between God's predestination and the fall of Adam into sin.

Predestination in the Reformed Confessions

Undoubtedly, the most important sources for ascertaining the Reformed doctrine of predestination in the sixteenth century are the official confessions that were adopted by the Reformed churches. In addition to the Second Helvetic Confession, discussed above with

---

74. As Muller states, 'Reprobation remains a negative will, a decision to withhold mediation and to leave some men to a fate of their own making. Clearly, the scholastic foundation of Vermigli's argument is not the cause of a more rigid formulation of predestination but of a less overtly deterministic conception of the decrees' (*CD*, 66). Muller correctly makes this point against the claim of John Patrick Donnelly that Vermigli's doctrine of predestination was stricter than that of Calvin. See Donnelly, 'Calvinist Thomism,' *Viator 7* (1976): 445, 448.

reference to Bullinger, the following confessions offer insight into the Reformed understanding of the doctrine toward the close of the first, and most formative, period of the Reformation: the Gallican (French) Confession of 1559, the Scots Confession of 1560, the Heidelberg Catechism of 1563, and the Belgic Confession of 1567. In each of these confessions, the doctrine of predestination is set forth in order to underscore the doctrinal themes of human inability, salvation by grace alone through the work of Christ, the eternal purpose that underlies God's gracious provision for salvation in Christ, and the comfort that this teaching affords the believer. I will cite the most important statements of the doctrine in these confessions and then offer a synthesis of their common teaching.[75]

The Gallican Confession: 'We believe that from this corruption and general condemnation in which all men are plunged, God, according to his eternal and immutable counsel, calleth those whom he hath chosen by his goodness and mercy alone in our Lord Jesus Christ, without consideration of their works, to display in them the riches of his mercy; leaving the rest in this same corruption and condemnation to show in them his justice.'[76]

The Scots Confession: 'The same eternal God and Father, who by grace alone chose us in his Son Christ Jesus before the foundation of the world was laid, appointed him to be our head, our brother, our pastor, and the great bishop of our souls.'[77]

The Heidelberg Catechism: 'What do you believe concerning the holy catholic church? That the Son of God, out of the whole human race, from the beginning to the end of the world, gathers, defends, and preserves for Himself, by His Spirit and Word, in the unity of

---

75. For a more complete exposition of the Reformed confessions on the doctrine of predestination, see Jan Rohls, *Reformed Confessions: Theology from Zurich to Barmen*, trans. John Hoffmeyer, Columbia Series in Reformed Theology (Louisville: Westminster John Knox, 1998), 148–66.

76. 'The Gallican Confession,' art. 12, in Schaff, *The Creeds of Christendom*, 3:366–7.

77. 'The Scots Confession,' 3.08, in *Book of Confessions*. Though the doctrine of predestination in the Scots Confession is stated moderately and focuses only on God's gracious election of believers in Christ, it is noteworthy that John Knox, one of its principal authors, wrote a lengthy, strong defense of predestination: *An answer to a great number of blasphemous cauillations written by an Anabaptist, and aduersarie to Gods eternal predestination* (Geneva: Crespin, 1560).

the true faith, a Church chosen to everlasting life; and that I am, and forever shall remain, a living member thereof.'[78]

The Belgic Confession: 'We believe that, all the posterity of Adam being thus fallen into perdition and ruin by the sin of our first parents, God then did manifest Himself such as He is; that is to say, merciful and just: merciful, since He delivers and preserves from this perdition all whom He in His eternal and unchangeable counsel of mere goodness has elected in Christ Jesus our Lord, without any respect to their works; just, in leaving others in the fall and perdition wherein they have involved themselves.'[79]

These confessional statements share several common themes. All of them view the person and work of Christ, not only in the provision of salvation but also in its communication to believers by the work of His Spirit, to be rooted in God's eternal purpose of election. They also start from the conviction that all human beings are fallen in Adam and are unwilling and incapable of turning toward God in faith and repentance, unless God draws them according to His mercy and grace. The doctrine of predestination focuses primarily on God's merciful election to save His people. Although the doctrine includes both a decree of election and reprobation (*gemina praedestinatio*), there is an asymmetry between these two aspects of God's counsel. Election involves God's positive and merciful decision in and for the sake of Christ to save His people. Reprobation involves God's just decision to 'leave' others in their sins, and to condemn them for their own sinfulness. Without broaching the more speculative question of the relative order of the elements within God's decree, these confessions represent the doctrine of predestination in a decidedly 'infralapsarian' manner: the decree contemplates the human race in its fallen condition so that the proper occasion and cause for the condemnation of the reprobate is their own sin and unworthiness. Furthermore, the two primary themes that the doctrine of predestination accentuates are the glory of God, who alone authors the salvation of believers, and the comfort of believers, who may confidently rest in the assurance of God's grace and mercy as they are revealed in the gospel.

---

78. 'The Heidelberg Catechism,' in *The Good Confession: Ecumenical Creeds and Reformed Confessions* (Dyer, IN: Mid-America Reformed Seminary, 2013), 103.

79. 'The Belgic Confession,' art. 16, in *Good Confession*, 41.

Predestination in Early Reformed Orthodoxy

After the mid-sixteenth century's initial codification of the doctrine of predestination in the Reformed confessions, several important theologians further articulated the doctrine in the early period of early Reformed orthodoxy during the late sixteenth century. Though these theologians continued the earlier period's diversity of formulation, they generally reflected a more developed and 'scholastic' approach of the doctrine of predestination and the decrees of God.[80] In doing so, they set the stage for the early seventeenth-century controversies among the Reformed churches, which were addressed at the Synod of Dort in 1618–1619 and the Westminster Assembly in 1643–1645.[81] Since the confessions produced by these early seventeenth-century assemblies of the Reformed churches take us beyond the sixteenth century, I will merely identify three important topics that emerged during this period.

First, the precise order of the elements of God's decree became a topic for theological discussion, especially in the writings of Theodore Beza and William Perkins, two theologians who vigorously defended the Reformed doctrine of predestination.[82] While Reformed theologians exhibited no significant difference of opinion on the order

---

80. In addition to Musculus and Vermigli, two contemporaries of Calvin who treated the doctrine of predestination in a more 'scholastic' fashion, another important transitional figure in the development of early Reformed orthodoxy was Jerome Zanchius. For treatments of Zanchius' doctrine of predestination, see Muller, *CD*, 110–25; Venema, *Heinrich Bullinger*, 79–86.

81. For a survey of this period and the debates regarding the doctrine of predestination, see Rouwendal, 'Predestination in Reformed Orthodoxy,' 568–89.

82. For Beza's doctrine of predestination, see Theodore Beza, *Tabula Praedestinationis* (Geneva, 1555); John S. Bray, *Theodore Beza's Doctrine of Predestination, Bibliotheca Humanistica & Reformatorica 12* (Nieuwkoop: De Graaf, 1975); Muller, *CD*, 79–96; idem., 'Use and Abuse of a Document,' 33–61. For Perkins's doctrine of predestination, see William Perkins, *The Workes of ... Mr. William Perkins, vol. 2, A Golden Chaine, or the Description of Theologie, and A Treatise of the Manner and Order of Predestination* (Cambridge, 1612–1619); Muller, *CD*, 149–71; idem, 'Perkins' A Golden Chaine: Predestinarian System or Schematized Ordo Salutis?' *SCJ* 9, no. 1 (1978): 69–81. Perkins' *A Golden Chaine* was written as an elaboration of Beza's *Tabula Praedestinationis*. In his assessment of Perkins' scholastic elaboration of the doctrine of predestination, Muller concludes that 'though the statement of the doctrine of predestination has become more elaborate in a scholastic sense and, indeed, more speculative in terms of its statement of logical priorities, it has not become more deterministic than that of Calvin, nor has it become any less christologically oriented' (*CD*, 170).

in which God's purpose was executed in history, the distinction between infralapsarianism and supralapsarianism reflected two different views of the order of the distinct elements that are included within God's eternal decree.[83] Whereas infralapsarianism views God's decree to elect or not elect to salvation as 'below' (*infra*) or logically subsequent to His decree to permit the fall into sin (*lapsus*), supralapsarianism views God's decree of predestination as 'above' (*supra*) or logically prior to His decree regarding the fall. In the infralapsarian position, the objects of God's decree are created and fallen sinners (*homo creatus et lapsus*); in the supralapsarian position, the objects of God's decree are uncreated and unfallen sinners (*homo creabilis et labilis*). The order of the elements in God's decree in the infralapsarian scheme is as follows:

1. The decree to glorify Himself in the creation of the human race
2. The decree to permit the fall
3. The decree to elect some of the fallen human race to salvation and to pass by others and condemn them for their sins
4. The decree to provide salvation for the elect through Jesus Christ.

The order of the elements in God's decree in the supralapsarian scheme is as follows:

1. The decree to glorify Himself through the election of some and the nonelection of others
2. The decree to create the elect and the reprobate
3. The decree to permit the fall
4. The decree to provide salvation for the elect through Jesus Christ.

While the difference between the infralapsarian and supralapsarian views became an occasion for theological discussion in the period

---

83. For studies on the debates regarding infra- and supralapsarianism in the Reformed tradition, see Fesko, *Diversity Within the Reformed Tradition*; and Joel R. Beeke, *Debated Issues in Sovereign Predestination: Early Lutheran Predestination, Calvinian Reprobation, and Variations in Genevan Lapsarianism* (Göttingen: Vandenhoeck & Ruprecht, 2017).

of early Reformed orthodoxy, it is significant that the seventeenth-century confessions that offer the final and most comprehensive codification of the Reformed view – the Canons of Dort and the Westminster Standards – do not grant confessional status to either view. These confessions tend to express the doctrine of predestination in an infralapsarian manner, viewing election as a positive expression of God's will to save some out of the fallen human race and reprobation as a negative expression of God's will to 'pass by' others and to condemn them for their sins. The debate regarding the order of the elements within God's decree evidences a more scholastic, even speculative, approach to the doctrine of predestination in the period of early Reformed orthodoxy. However, it did not produce any substantial change in the Reformed tradition's confessional consensus regarding the doctrine.

Second, another topic that emerged in this period was associated with the theology of Theodore Beza (1519–1605), who sought to defend Calvin's doctrine against his critics. In addition to several important works on the doctrine of predestination, Beza was a transitional figure in later Reformed discussions of the relation between God's purpose of election and the extent of Christ's work of atonement. During the course of his conflict with the Lutheran theologian, Jacob Andreae, Beza criticized the traditional formula that Christ's death was 'sufficient for all, but efficient only for the elect.'[84] In Beza's estimation, this formula was ambiguously stated, since the preposition 'for' in the statement could be variously interpreted. To remove any ambiguity, Beza insisted that Christ's death was intended to provide only for the salvation of the elect. While Beza acknowledged the sufficiency and perfection of the work of Christ, he was among the first to explicitly teach the doctrine of definite or particular atonement. Since Calvin did not explicitly address the question of the extent of Christ's atonement,[85] at least not

---

84. For an account of the conflict, see Theodore Beza, *Ad Acta Colloqui Montisbelgardensis Tubingae edita, Theodori Bezae responsio* (Geneva: Joannes le Preux, 1588); Jill Raitt, *The Colloquy of Montbéliard: Religion and Politics in the Sixteenth Century* (New York: Oxford University Press, 1993). In his defense of Beza's doctrine of predestination, William Perkins also emphasized the divine intention in providing and applying Christ's work of redemption to the elect. See Muller, *CD*, 168.

85. Though Calvin was familiar with the expression, 'sufficient for all, efficient for the elect' (*pro omnibus … sufficientiam; sed pro electis … ad efficaciam*), which was

in the fashion in which Beza did during this controversy, some students of the history of Reformed theology have raised the question whether the later Reformed doctrine of definite atonement, which was codified in the second head of doctrine of the Canons of Dort, is consistent with the teaching of Calvin and the earlier Reformed tradition. In studies of the development of Reformed theology in this period, the question of the continuity or discontinuity of doctrine between Calvin and later Reformed orthodoxy has been cast as a question of 'Calvin and the Calvinists'.[86] Some interpreters argue that Beza and theologians of

found in Peter Lombard's *Sentences*, he did not find it an adequate formulation. See Calvin's comments on 1 John 2:2 in *CC* 22:173. For treatments of the extent or design of the atonement in Calvin and later Calvinism, see W. Robert Godfrey, 'Reformed Thought on the Extent of the Atonement to 1618,' *WTJ* 37, no. 2 (1975): 133–71; Peter L. Rouwendal, 'Calvin's Forgotten Classical Position on the Extent of the Atonement: About Efficiency, Sufficiency, and Anachronism,' *WTJ* 70, no. 2 (2008): 317–35; G. Michael Thomas, *The Extent of the Atonement: A Dilemma for Reformed Theology from Calvin to the Consensus* (1536–1675), Paternoster Biblical and Theological Monographs (Carlisle: Paternoster, 1997); Brian G. Armstrong, *Calvinism and the Amyraut Heresy: Protestant Scholasticism and Humanism in Seventeenth-Century France* (Madison: University of Wisconsin Press, 1969); Muller, *CD*, 33–35; Roger Nicole, *Moyse Amyraut (1596–1664) and the Controversy on Universal Grace: First Phase (1634–1637)* (PhD diss., Harvard University, 1966). In my judgment, Muller's comments on the implications of Calvin's view of particular election and the priestly intercession of Christ are especially appropriate: 'It is superfluous to speak of a hypothetical extent of the efficacy of Christ's work [in Calvin's theology] beyond its actual application. As shown in the doctrine of election, salvation is not bestowed generally but on individuals. The Gospel appeal is universal but Christ's intercession, like the divine election, is personal, individual, particular' (*CD*, 35). Though Calvin did not explicitly address the extent of the atonement in the manner of later writers, it seems evident that his doctrine of predestination and of Christ's work of atonement pointed in this direction.

86. For interpretations of the Reformed tradition that seek to contrast Calvin with later Calvinism, see R. T. Kendall, *Calvin and English Calvinism to 1649* (Oxford: Oxford University Press, 1979); Basil Hall, 'Calvin against the Calvinists,' in *John Calvin: A Collection of Distinguished Essays*, ed. G. E. Duffield, trans. G. S. R. Cox and P. G. Rix, Courtenay Studies in Reformation Theology 1 (Grand Rapids: Eerdmans, 1966), 19–37; Armstrong, *Calvinism and the Amyraut Heresy*. For a compelling refutation of this approach, see Richard A. Muller, 'Calvin and the "Calvinists": Assessing Continuities and Discontinuities between the Reformation and Orthodoxy,' Part 1, *CTJ* 30, no. 2 (1995): 345–75, and Part 2, *CTJ* 31, no. 1 (1996): 125–60; idem., *The Unaccommodated Calvin: Studies in the Foundation of a Theological Tradition*, Oxford Studies in Historical Theology (New York: Oxford University Press, 2000), 3–8; idem., *CD*, esp. 175–82; Paul Helm, *Calvin and the Calvinists* (Edinburgh: Banner of Truth, 1982); Carl R. Trueman, 'Calvin and Calvinism,' in *The Cambridge Companion to John Calvin*, ed. Donald K. McKim (Cambridge: Cambridge University Press, 2004), 225–44.

the orthodox period diverged from Calvin's more Christocentric view of predestination. However, the claims of these interpreters who pit Calvin against the later Calvinists have been ably refuted in recent years. While the theologians of the orthodox period cast Calvin's doctrine in a more scholastic form, they did not abandon Calvin's emphasis on election in Christ. There are also intimations of the later doctrine of definite atonement in Calvin's writings.[87]

And third, the debate regarding the degree of continuity or discontinuity between Calvin's view of predestination and that of Reformed orthodoxy has highlighted a long-standing question regarding the Reformed tradition's doctrine of predestination: Does the doctrine of predestination, especially in the period of orthodoxy, increasingly take on the character of a 'central dogma'? As noted in the introduction to this chapter, several nineteenth- and early twentieth-century interpreters of Reformation theology advanced the thesis that Calvin and the Reformed tradition set forth a predestinarian theology that differed significantly from the Lutheran tradition's focus on the doctrine of justification.[88] According to these interpreters, the Reformed tradition articulated a theology that began from the starting point of God's sovereign predestinating will. All the elements of the Reformed system of theology were then logically derived from this point of departure. The doctrine of the decree of God was transmuted into a 'decretalism' that subordinated Christology, the study of the person and work of Christ, and pneumatology, the study of the Holy Spirit's communication of the benefits of Christ's work to believers, to the doctrine of God.[89]

Among recent interpreters of the Reformed doctrine of predestination, Richard Muller has offered an extensive and compelling case against the 'central dogma' thesis. According to Muller, significant antecedents to the Reformed view existed in the patristic and medieval periods, and considerable differences of accent flourished among Reformed theologians throughout the sixteenth and seventeenth centuries. While continuities and discontinuities

---

87. See Muller, *CD*, 35, 175–82.

88. See note 26 above.

89. See Muller, 'The Myth of "Decretal Theology",' 159–67.

of formulation were present throughout this period, the difference between the early formulation of the doctrine in Calvin and his contemporaries and the later formulation of the orthodox period was largely a matter of casting similar doctrinal positions in a more 'scholastic' form. However, the scholastic method and form of the orthodox period did not produce a fundamentally different theological position on the doctrine of predestination. Compared to Calvin's formulation of the doctrine, the later orthodox formulation was no more reflective of a decretalism or predestinarian metaphysic. Like Calvin and earlier Reformed theologians, later theologians linked the doctrine of predestination with typical Reformation emphases on salvation by grace alone through the work of Christ alone. Since fallen human sinners are incapable of saving themselves, and since the faith required to benefit from Christ's saving work is a gracious gift of God, they formulated the doctrine of predestination in order to provide a theological account of the divine provision of Christ as Mediator and the efficacy of His saving work for His people.

Summary and Concluding Observations

This broad overview of the doctrinal formulations related to predestination in the sixteenth-century Reformation provides a basis for a few concluding observations.

In the first place, the Reformation doctrine of predestination and election was founded on an engagement with the teaching of Scripture and represents a continuation of a long-standing Augustinian legacy. Contrary to the teaching of Pelagianism and semi-Pelagianism, which grant a measure of human autonomy and free will in the believer's response to the gospel call to faith and repentance, the doctrine of predestination emphasizes the themes of salvation by grace alone and the divine initiative in providing salvation through the work of Christ alone. Rather than deflecting from the doctrine of justification through faith alone, the doctrine of predestination articulates the Reformation's primary concern for rooting the doctrines of Christology and ecclesiology in God's determination to grant salvation to fallen sinners in Christ, none of whom are capable of taking the initiative in turning toward God or responding favorably to the call of the gospel. Though the Reformed theologians of the sixteenth century were more apt to articulate the doctrine in a fulsome manner than other streams of Reformation theology, the doctrine of predestination was not unique to the Reformed tradition but was expressed as well by Luther and Lutheranism especially in the early part of the sixteenth century.

Furthermore, despite the diverse ways that sixteenth-century Reformed theologians formulated the doctrine of predestination, several common themes are evident, which were codified in the principal Reformed confessions of the period. The doctrine of predestination found common acceptance among the leading theologians of the period despite never being a 'central dogma' or organizing principle of Reformed theology. Even though more scholastic features of the doctrine surfaced only late in the sixteenth century – such as the question of the relative order of the elements within God's eternal counsel or the question of the design underlying Christ's work of atonement – several features of the doctrine were commonly embraced. While some theologians formulated the doctrine of double predestination more rigorously than others, the leading theologians of the Reformed tradition affirmed both God's merciful election of some and His just nonelection of others. On the one hand, they insisted that salvation and the work of Christ in providing salvation were rooted in God's gracious choice in and for Christ to save some fallen sinners and to grant them the gift of faith whereby to embrace the gospel promise. And on the other hand, they affirmed God's just determination to leave others in their lost estate and to condemn them on account of their sins and willful disobedience. In this respect, the Reformed theologians of the period commonly recognized the asymmetry between God's gracious choice to save some and His just choice not to save others.

Finally, the doctrine of predestination and election was closely linked with two emphases that also belong to the doctrine of justification. The first was the honor of God as the sole Savior of His people. The doctrine of predestination militates against any view of salvation that grants to fallen sinners any part in contributing to their own salvation. In Calvin's treatment of the doctrine, for example, predestination expresses most clearly that the salvation of God's people is born from God's undeserved generosity in Christ alone.[90]

---

90. See Calvin, *Institutes*, 3.21.1.

The second of these emphases was the comfort that derives from the doctrine of election. Far from undermining the believer's assurance of salvation, the doctrine of predestination and election affords believers a solid basis of comfort. When the knowledge of God's grace toward us in Christ is viewed as the only proper 'mirror' of election, then what follows is an assurance of God's mercy that hangs not on the thin thread of our choice and perseverance but on the unbreakable chain of God's sovereign grace and mercy. If God loves His people in Christ from all eternity, then nothing will be able to sever them from His love or frustrate the realization of His good purpose to save them.

CHAPTER 6

The Arminian Doctrine of Conditional Election and *The Canons of Dort*

IN the previous chapter, I observed that the Reformation's doctrine of salvation by grace alone through faith was buttressed by a recovery of the Augustinian doctrine of election. While the sixteenth-century Reformers offered diverse formulations regarding the doctrine of election, they shared a general conviction that the salvation of fallen human beings finds its deepest ground within God's eternal purpose of election in Christ. Augustine's formulation guided subsequent theologians and corresponded to their convictions regarding human inability and the prevenient, effectual grace of God in the salvation of His people.

The completion of this broad overview of the treatment of the doctrine in theological history requires turning to what was arguably the most important development in the post-Reformation period of Reformed orthodoxy. Arminianism arose as a dissenting position on the doctrine of election within the orbit of Reformed theology. Jacob Arminius, a Dutch Reformed minister and professor at the University of Leiden, argued for a substantially different view of predestination than the prevailing one among the Reformed during the sixteenth century. His revision provoked considerable controversy within the Dutch Reformed churches, as well as other Reformed churches throughout Europe, that led to the convening of an international synod in Dordrecht, the Netherlands, during 1618 and 1619. In many respects, the Arminian controversy and the codification in confessional form of the consensus view at the Synod of Dort have established the parameters of modern discussions regarding the doctrine of election within evangelical and Reformed churches. Speaking of the significance of the Arminian controversy, Richard A. Muller notes that

> The Arminian controversy of the first two decades of the seventeenth century marked a major turning point in the history of Protestant teaching. The great Reformers of the sixteenth century, whether Luther, Bucer, Zwingli, Calvin, Bullinger, Vermigli, or their various contemporaries, had taught a doctrine of justification by grace alone through faith and had anchored faith itself in the grace of God. All held one or another of the views of predestination found in the Augustinian exegesis of Paul and elaborated in the Augustinian tradition of the Middle Ages.[1]

Even though modern treatments of the doctrine of election have often attempted to move beyond the divide between Augustinian and Arminian formulations, these two positions have dominated the discussion. For this reason, a consideration of Arminius' doctrine provides a necessary background to understanding more recent formulations. To set the stage for consideration of the modern period, therefore, this chapter will treat the controversy regarding Arminius' doctrine in three respects. I will begin with a summary of Arminius' formulation of the doctrine of predestination. Then I will offer an evaluation of Arminius' view, and I will conclude with a summary of the Reformed response offered by the Synod of Dort.

Arminius' Doctrine of Predestination and Election[2]

While modern discussions of Arminius frequently view him as an opponent of Reformed theology, it is important to recognize that

---

1. 'Grace, Election, and Contingent Choice: Arminius' Gambit and the Reformed Response,' in *GGBW,* 2:251-2. As will be evident from my frequent citation of this essay throughout this chapter, I believe it is an especially incisive treatment of Arminius' teaching on predestination and election.

2. For summaries of Arminius' doctrine of predestination and election, including the history of the Arminian controversy, see Carl Bangs, *Arminius: A Study in the Dutch Reformation* (Nashville: Abingdon, 1971); Gerald McCulloh, ed., *Man's Faith and Freedom: The Theological Influence of Jacobus Arminius* (Nashville: Abingdon, 1962); A. W. Harrison, *Arminianism* (London: Duckworth, 1937); Peter Y. De Jong,

Arminius was a Reformed theologian whose theology embraced a wide range of topics, including the doctrine of predestination. Arminius studied Reformed theology at the Universities of Leiden and Geneva, and at the latter institution was a student of Calvin's successor, Theodore Beza. While a young student, Arminius learned the variety of predestination views represented in Reformed theology. These views included a moderate, infralapsarian statement like that found in *The Harmony of Reformed Confessions* or the Second Helvetic Confession, which was authored by Bullinger. He also encountered stricter statements associated with Calvin and especially Beza, who articulated the doctrine in a more supralapsarian form. Little evidence suggests that the young Arminius reacted to a 'rigidly supralapsarian' formulation of the doctrine, as he felt compelled to do later as professor of theology in Leiden.[3]

Arminius' polemical engagement with the Reformed view of predestination began in the last decade of the sixteenth century. During this period, he served as a pastor in Amsterdam and preached a series of sermons from Paul's epistle to the Romans. In the course of this series, he adopted several views at odds with the traditional Augustinian interpretation of key passages. This raised some suspicion among his Reformed colleagues regarding his orthodoxy. For example, in his treatment of the seventh chapter, Arminius argued that the apostle's struggle to live in obedience to the law's commandments characterized Paul prior to his conversion.[4] Since this interpretation

---

ed., *Crisis in the Reformed Churches: Essays in Commemoration of the Great Synod of Dort, 1618-1619* (2nd ed.; Grandville, MI: Reformed Fellowship, Inc., 2008 [1968]); Aza Goudriaan & Fred van Lieburg, eds., *Revisiting the Synod of Dort (1618-1619)* (Leiden/Boston: Brill, 2011); Keith D. Stanglin and Thomas H. McCall, *Jacob Arminius: Theologian of Grace* (Oxford: Oxford University Press, 2012); Keith D. Stanglin, *Arminius on the Assurance of Salvation: The Context, Roots, and Shape of the Leiden Debate, 1603-1609* (Leiden/Boston: Brill, 2007), esp. 73-114; Donald Sinnema, Christian Moser, & J. Selderhuis, eds., *Acta et Documenta Synodi Nationalis Dordrechtanae (1618-1619)*, vol. 1: *Acta of the Synod of Dort* (Göttingen: Vandenhoeck & Ruprecht, 2015); Richard A. Muller, *God, Creation, and Providence in the Thought of Jacob Arminius: Sources and Directions of Scholastic Protestantism in the Era of Early Reformed Orthodoxy* (Grand Rapids: Baker, 1991); and idem, GECC in *GGBW*, 2:251-78.

3. Muller, GECC, 254.

4. Jacob Arminius, *Dissertation on the True and Genuine Sense of the Seventh Chapter of the Epistle to the Romans,* in *The Works of James Arminius,* trans. James

assumed that Paul was willing to do what the law required even prior to his regeneration, it seemed to some sympathetic to the Pelagian teaching that human beings can desire to do good even apart from the work of God's grace. Perhaps more importantly, in his interpretation of chapter nine of Romans, Arminius maintained that Paul's reference to Isaac and Ishmael, as well as to Jacob and Esau, was a reference to them, not as individual persons, but as types or categories of persons.[5] This seemed to deny that Paul's reference to them was a basis for the doctrine of the predestination of specific individuals to salvation. Arminius' growing dissatisfaction with the traditional Reformed view of predestination was further fueled by his reading of William Perkin's *On the Mode and Order of Predestination.*[6] Since Perkins formulated the doctrine of predestination in an overtly supralapsarian fashion, placing God's decree of election logically before His decree to create and to permit the fall into sin, Arminius judged it to regard God's purposes in creation and the fall as merely subordinate means required to fulfill God's ultimate end. For Arminius, this threatened to make God the author of sin and to impugn His goodness toward His creatures.[7]

After the period of his labor as a pastor in Amsterdam, Arminius was appointed to succeed Junius as professor of theology in Leiden. This appointment was not without controversy, since Gomarus, who was at the time a professor of theology in Leiden, strongly opposed it. Once at Leiden, Arminius openly opposed the traditional Reformed understanding of predestination. The ensuing controversy was to preoccupy Arminius for the remainder of his life. He wrote a number of works thoroughly stating his view. These writings include his *Public Disputations,* which argued his case against early Reformed

---

Nichols and William Nichols, 3 vols. (London, 1825, 1828, 1875; reprint Grand Rapids: Baker, 1986), 2:491-2, 497-8, 541-4. Hereafter referred to as *WJA.*

5. *A Brief Analysis of the Ninth Chapter of St. Paul's Epistle to the Romans,* in *WJA,* 3:490-9. For a brief summary of Arminius' interpretation of Romans 9, see Stanglin and McCall, *Jacob Arminius,* 132-4.

6. Jacob Arminius, *Modest Examination of a Pamphlet, which that Learned Divine, Dr. William Perkins, published ... On the Mode and Order of Predestination,* in *WJA,* 3:276-98.

7. For a detailed account of this early period in Arminius' formulation of the doctrine of predestination, see Bangs, *Arminius,* 138-231.

orthodoxy, and the *Declaration of Sentiments* he offered to the States of Holland at The Hague in 1608.[8] Since the latter provides a comprehensive and mature statement of Arminius' doctrine of predestination, my consideration of Arminius' position will primarily appeal to his argument in this work.

Conditional Predestination

In his *Declaration of Sentiments,* Arminius opens with an extended critique of both supralapsarian and infralapsarian formulations of the predestination doctrine among his Reformed contemporaries. Most of his critique consists of objections to the supralapsarian formulation, which was vigorously espoused by his colleague Gomarus.[9] Though he spends less time in evaluating the infralapsarian view, he judges it liable to the same objections he raised against the supralapsarian view.[10] The principal complaint Arminius brings against the Reformed view is that God's decree is viewed as a single and absolute decree whose various aspects (creation, the fall into sin, the election of some, the non-election of others, etc.), whether ordered in a supralapsarian or infralapsarian manner, must necessarily come to pass. In Arminius' estimation, this view of God's decree makes God the author of Adam's fall into sin and also necessitates the sins of all those whom He does not elect to save. Accordingly, the Reformed insistence that God's decree of election is unconditional inevitably imperils the biblical doctrine of God's perfect goodness and justice. After setting forth his objections to the traditional Reformed view, Arminius proceeds to offer his own, alternative sentiments regarding the doctrine of predestination.

---

8. *Public Disputations,* in *WJA,* 2:80-312; and *Declaration of Sentiments of Arminius, delivered before the States of Holland,* in *WJA,* 1:580-732.

9. Stanglin and McCall, *Jacob Arminius,* 140, note that Arminius never uses the words 'predestine,' 'elect,' or 'reprobate' in his description of God's decrees in his *Declaration of Sentiments.* In their representation of Arminius' 'order of God's decrees' (*ordo decretorum Dei*), the order is as follows: (1) to create; (2) to permit the fall; (3) to appoint Christ as the foundation of election to redeem; (4) to save, in Christ, (the class of) penitent believers, and condemn unbelievers; (5) to provide means (grace) for repentance and faith; and (5) to save or condemn single, specific individuals foreknown to believe or not believe.

10. For a summary of these objections, see Stanglin and McCall, *Jacob Arminius,* 111-32.

Rather than viewing God's decree as a single, absolute decree with several logically distinguishable components, Arminius distinguishes four decrees within God's eternal mind and counsel. Arminius calls the first two of these decrees 'absolute,' because both of them are antecedent to, and independent of, anything that transpires within the order of creation in general and the acts of human creatures in particular. These two decrees express God's eternal mind and will respecting the salvation of all those who believe in Jesus Christ, whom God appointed as Mediator and Savior. While the third and fourth of these decrees are antecedent expressions of God's eternal mind and will respecting the salvation of fallen sinners, Arminius does not call them 'absolute' because they depend for their efficacy upon the free response of fallen sinners to the gospel offer of salvation in Jesus Christ. These decrees, though antecedent in the mind and will of God, are dependent upon, and effectual only in consequence of, what God eternally foreknew fallen sinners would freely do in response to the gospel offer. The efficacy of these decrees in respect to the salvation of fallen human beings ultimately depends upon what they freely will to do (or not do) in response to God's good will toward them.

In his definition of the first of God's decrees, Arminius clearly states that it expresses God's general and gracious intention to grant salvation to 'sinful man' and to appoint His Son as the Savior.

> The first absolute decree of God concerning the salvation of sinful man, is that by which he decreed to appoint his Son Jesus Christ for a Mediator, Redeemer, Saviour, Priest and King, who might destroy sin by his own death, might by his obedience obtain the salvation which had been lost, and might communicate it by his own virtue.[11]

Several observations can be made about this first absolute decree of God. It assumes the creation of the human race and the introduction of sin through the fall of Adam, which occurred by God's permission. In this respect, Arminius shares the opinion of his infralapsarian colleagues that God's decree of election contemplates human beings in their fallen condition. God chooses to save fallen human beings and to provide for their salvation by means of the person and work of

---

11. *Declaration of Sentiments,* in *WJA,* 1:653.

Christ, whom He appoints as Mediator.[12] In sharp contrast with the Reformed view, however, Arminius defines this decree in such a way that it expresses a 'general will' of God to provide for the salvation of 'sinful man'. For Arminius, God's absolute will to make salvation available in Christ does not contemplate any specific persons whom God determines to save, but rather the whole of the fallen human race. By itself, this first and absolute decree, which concerns God's gracious will and intention to save 'sinful man' in and through the work of Christ, does not address what needs to occur in order for any particular person to be saved.

The second absolute decree of God focuses upon how sinful human beings can come to be saved upon the basis of Christ's work as Mediator. According to Arminius,

> The second precise and absolute decree of God, is that in which he decreed to receive into favour those who repent and believe, and, in Christ, for his sake and through him, to effect the salvation of such penitents and believers as persevered to the end; but to leave in sin and under wrath all impenitent persons and unbelievers, and to damn them as aliens from Christ.[13]

Although Arminius calls this second feature of God's mind and will an 'absolute decree', it is not so much a decree as an expression of God's antecedent determination to receive with favor all who repent and believe in Jesus Christ. Consistent with the first absolute decree of God, this second decree affirms that salvation depends upon the work of Christ. However, this decree adds that the efficacy of Christ's saving work depends upon the persevering faith and repentance with which some respond to God's general offer of salvation in Christ. Like the first decree, the second does not convey God's particular

---

12. Muller, GECC, 257. Muller points out that, in his formulation of this first, absolute decree of God, Arminius 'quite distinct from the Reformed ... tends to subordinate the Son to the decree of the Father. In his Christology, in a parallel fashion, he emphasizes the subordination of the Son in the order of the Persons. The result is that the second person of the Trinity is, in the Arminian system, subordinate to the decree and not, as the Reformed insist, at the same time electing God and elected or anointed Mediator' (257-8). For a more extensive treatment of this issue, see Richard A. Muller, 'The Christological Problem in the Thought of Jacobus Arminius,' *Nederlands Archief voor Kerkgeschiedenis* 68, no. 1 (1988): 145-63.

13. *Declaration of Sentiments,* in *WJA,* 1:653.

intention to save some sinners and not to save others. Though it is not expressly stated by Arminius, the implication of this decree is that God wills to save those whom He foreknows will respond properly to the gracious offer of the gospel. Because those who are saved or not saved are defined in general terms – 'such penitents and believers as persevered ... all impenitent persons and unbelievers' – this decree seems to grant a certain priority to the human will in deciding to embrace the gospel offer.[14]

In his statement of God's third decree, Arminius continues to speak of God's antecedent mind and will in respect to fallen human beings in general. However, he now identifies God's will to employ particular means to communicate His grace and favor to those who are saved through repentance and faith in Christ.

> The third divine decree is that by which God decreed to administer in a sufficient and efficacious manner the means which were necessary for repentance and faith; and to have such administration instituted (1) according to the Divine Wisdom, by which God knows what is proper and becoming both to his mercy and his severity, and (2) according to Divine Justice, by which he is prepared to adopt whatever his wisdom may prescribe and to put it in execution.[15]

The language Arminius uses to describe this decree is rather abstract and general, though his point is not difficult to ascertain. If God's absolute decrees are to become effectual for the salvation of 'sinful man', He must appoint the means necessary to this end. For this reason, God's third decree is preoccupied with His appointment of specific means of grace (principally, the church's preaching of the gospel and the administration of the sacraments) which afford fallen human beings the opportunity to meet the 'conditions' required for their salvation in Christ. In order for sinners to be saved, they must believe in Christ and repent. And in order for sinners to believe in Christ and repent, they must hear the gospel offer of salvation with its call to faith and repentance. Since faith and repentance are the

---

14. Cf. Muller, GECC, 258: 'From a Reformed point of view, such teaching has a decidedly Pelagian tendency inasmuch as it raises in eternity the issue of the priority of human choice.'

15. *Declaration of Sentiments,* in *WJA,* 1:653

conditions for participating in the saving benefits of Christ's work as Mediator, God must appoint means that are sufficient for them.

While the first three decrees that Arminius identifies present God's mind and will respecting salvation in general terms, the fourth decree addresses the mind and will of God regarding those particular persons who believe and repent in response to the gospel offer of salvation in Christ.

> To these succeeds the fourth decree, by which God decreed to save and damn certain particular persons. This decree has its foundation in the foreknowledge of God, by which he knew from all eternity those individuals who would, through his preventing grace, believe, and, – according to the before-described administration of those means which are suitable and proper for conversion and faith; and, by which foreknowledge, he likewise knew those who would not believe and persevere.[16]

Arminius' fourth decree clearly draws the implications for the doctrine of predestination from the preceding three decrees. Though God wills absolutely and antecedently to save 'sinful man' in general, He wills relatively and consequently to save those particular persons whom He foreknew would believe and to damn those whom He foreknew would not believe.[17] The basis for God's decree to save and damn 'certain particular persons' is His foreknowledge of the way these persons would respond. Since this decree is based upon God's foreknowledge of those persons who would meet the 'conditions' (faith and repentance) required for actual salvation, Arminius' doctrine of predestination may properly be called a doctrine of 'conditional' predestination. Though Arminius insists that the faith and perseverance of those whom God decrees to save are the fruit of God's 'preventing [prevenient] grace', he does not explain at this point how God's grace proves effectual for those who believe and ineffectual for those who do not. To put the matter differently, the language Arminius uses to describe God's fourth decree unavoidably

---

16. *Declaration of Sentiments,* in *WJA*, 1:653-54.

17. Muller, GECC, 259: 'The antecedent will to save is juxtaposed with a consequent will to save particular human beings, and the effective will of God, therefore, rests on the foreknowledge of a future contingency.'

raises questions regarding his understanding of the relation between God's grace and the freedom of fallen human beings.

God's Grace and the Freedom of the Will

In his *Declaration of Sentiments* and other writings, Arminius does comprehensively address issues regarding God's grace, the nature of human freedom in relation to the gospel offer, and God's foreknowledge of those who would respond to the gospel with a persevering faith. Immediately after his summary of the doctrine of predestination in terms of the four decrees, Arminius turns to the topics of God's providence, the free-will of man, the perseverance of the saints, and the certainty of salvation.[18] Since these topics possess a 'close affinity' to the doctrine of predestination, Arminius presents them as an integral part of his comprehensive view on the subject.

Arminius shares the traditional view that predestination is that 'part of providence' (*pars providentiae Dei*) concerning God's decree to save some persons in Christ. Whereas predestination focuses upon God's purposes in salvation, providence more broadly refers to God's comprehensive preservation and governance of all that He has created.

> [Providence is] a solicitous, continued, and universally present supervision of God over the whole world in general, and all creatures in particular, without any exception, in order to preserve and direct them in their own essence, qualities, actions, and passions, such as befits him and is suitable to them, to the praise of his name and the salvation of believers.[19]

By His providence, God 'preserves, regulates, governs, and directs all things,' so that 'nothing in the world happens fortuitously or by chance'.[20] Creation is God's work whereby He called all things into existence out of nothing (*ex nihilo*). Providence is God's continuing work whereby He conserves the created order and governs it to accomplish His good purposes. In His work of providence, God respects the creatures He has called into existence, preserving and

---

18. For extensive treatments of Arminius' doctrine of providence, see Muller, *GCP,* 211-68; and Stanglin & McCall, *Jacob Arminius,* 94-140.

19. *Declaration of Sentiments,* in *WJA,* 1:657.

20. ibid.

directing them, as Arminius expresses it, 'in their own essence, qualities, actions, passions, such as befits him and is suitable to them.'[21]

Of particular importance to God's providence is the way He directs the actions of His rational creatures whom He endows with the power of free will. According to Arminius, 'both the free-will and even the actions of a rational creature' are directed by God so that 'nothing can be done without the will of God, not even any of those things which are done in opposition to it.'[22] To uphold God's goodness and justice, however, Arminius adds that a clear distinction must be made between God's will in respect to what is good and what is evil. Regarding good actions, we may affirm that God both 'wills and performs' them. But regarding evil actions, we may only affirm that God 'freely permits' them.[23] In the former, God moves, assists, and concurs with them. But in the latter, God only 'permits' them. His concurrence does not cause them to occur, but merely concurs in them as to their effect or consequence. God's concurrence in such evil actions is not to be understood as though God were the author of the evil act itself. As Muller summarizes it, for Arminius 'the divine *concursus* is, thus, necessary not only to the existence of the cause and of the effect but also to the existence of the causal activity, but the divine involvement is such that the secondary cause is determinative of its own action and, therefore, free.'[24]

Within the framework of this general view of God's providence, including the distinct ways in which God's will relates to the free actions of His rational creatures, Arminius takes up directly the topic of the 'free will of man'.

> In his primitive condition as he came out of the hands of his Creator, man was endowed with such a portion of knowledge, holiness, and power, as enabled him to understand, esteem, consider, will, and to perform the true good, according to the commandment delivered to him: Yet

---

21. ibid.

22. ibid., 1:658.

23. ibid.

24. *GCP,* 255. Cf. Jacob Arminius, *Certain Articles Diligently to be Examined and Weighed,* Art. 8.3, in *WJA,* 2:714: 'Divine providence does not determine a free will to one part of a contradiction or contrariety, that is, by a determination preceding the actual volition itself.'

none of these acts could he do, except through the assistance of Divine Grace. —But in his lapsed and sinful state, man is not capable, of and by himself, either to think, to will, or to do that which is really good; but it is necessary for him to be regenerated and renewed in his intellect, affections or will, and in all his powers, by God in Christ through the Holy Spirit, that he may be qualified rightly to understand, esteem, and perform whatever is truly good.[25]

In this statement Arminius clearly distinguishes his understanding of free will from a full-blown Pelagian view, which affirms that all human beings retain the power, ability, and will to choose to obey God's commandments *without God's prevenient grace*. Even before Adam's fall into sin, Arminius maintains that Adam could not perform the true good 'except through the assistance of the Divine Grace'. Moreover, now that human beings are fallen in Adam, they require the grace of God to know and to will what is good. Fallen human beings require the regeneration and renewal of their intellects, affections, and wills in order to be qualified for the performance of anything that is truly good. Remarkably, Arminius's definition of free will in his *Declaration of Sentiments* appears not only to distinguish his position from the Pelagian view, but also from semi-Pelagian formulations that deny the necessity of God's prevenient grace. By itself, his definition seems to be crafted in such a way that his Reformed adversaries would not be able to charge him with a Pelagian or semi-Pelagian doctrine of free will.

It would be too hasty at this point, however, to view this statement as an adequate representation of Arminius' sentiments on the issue of free will. In order to understand more fully what distinguished his view from his Reformed contemporaries, we need to note what

---

25. *Declaration of Sentiments,* in *WJA*, 1:659-60. Muller, 'Grace, Election, and Contingent Choice,' 260, observes that Arminius consistently places the intellect prior to the will and affections, unlike Calvin, who grants to the human will a 'distinct priority' in matters of sin and salvation. Though Arminius does not openly express himself in a synergistic fashion, the priority of the intellect in relation to the affections and will does open the door to a view that ascribes the movement of the will toward God as an act motivated by the intellect rather than by God's effectual grace. On this topic, see Richard A. Muller, 'Fides and Cognitio in Relation to the Problem of Intellect and Will in the Theology of John Calvin,' *CTJ* 25, no 2 (1990): 207-24; and idem, 'The Priority of the Intellect in the Soteriology of Jacob Arminius,' *WTJ* 55, no. 1 (1993): 55-72.

Arminius taught regarding the 'resistibility' of God's grace, the nature of human freedom as the power to choose the contrary, and the nature of God's foreknowledge of those who choose to believe and repent in response to the gospel call. When these issues are considered, it will become evident that Arminius offers a view of human freedom that is semi-Pelagian and synergistic.

Arminius clearly affirms that God's prevenient grace is necessary to enable fallen human beings to do what is required of them. In his formal definition of the work of God's prevenient grace in the *Declaration of Sentiments,* Arminius affirms that God's grace precedes, perpetually assists, and enables those who receive the gospel to respond in faith and repentance. However, even though Arminius affirms the necessity of God's prevenient grace in order for human beings to know, desire, and will to do what is good, he does not view God's grace as sufficient and effectual to ensure that those who hear the gospel call will actually believe and be saved. Rather, he uses language at the end of his definition of grace that introduces a 'synergism' between God's gracious will and the will of sinners who answer the gospel offer. God's grace *enables* the response of faith, but it falls short of *effecting* such faith. As Arminius puts it, 'God may then will and work *together with* man, that man may perform whatever he wills' (emphasis mine).[26] In the final analysis, God's gracious will, which is general and common toward all whom He graciously summons to faith, can be rendered ineffectual by any of its recipients.

For this reason, after insisting that he does not ascribe too much power to free will, Arminius expressly rejects the idea that God's grace is truly effectual. On this subject, Arminius is emphatic: 'I believe … that many persons resist the Holy Spirit and reject the grace that is offered.'[27] However, there is an element of studied ambiguity at this point in Arminius' position. None of his Reformed adversaries denied that fallen sinners can and do resist the Holy Spirit and reject the grace offered to them in the gospel. Indeed, they all acknowledged that the universal response of all fallen sinners to the gospel call would be

---

26. *Declaration of Sentiments,* in *WJA,* 1:664.
27. ibid.

one of resistance to the Holy Spirit and rejecting of the gospel offer, *unless and until the Spirit effectually works with the gospel to bring those whom God elects to salvation through faith in Christ.* By his insistence that all recipients of the gospel retain the freedom to believe or not to believe the gospel promise, however, Arminius reiterates the point made in what he earlier termed the 'fourth decree' of election: God elects to save those who choose to believe, and to damn those who choose not to believe. God's election of some to salvation is ultimately consequent upon their free decision to co-operate with His grace and believe.

Consistent with his emphasis upon the freedom of the human will in respect to the gracious offer of the gospel, Arminius nowhere affirms the common view of his Reformed contemporaries that the gospel call is 'effectual' in the case of the elect. For Arminius, the gospel call is a 'conditional offer' that invites all to believe, but it does not produce such faith in a way that wholly depends upon God's gracious work by the Spirit. The call of the gospel requires faith, but does not give to anyone what it requires. The gospel call must be accepted by faith 'by which a man believes that, if he complies with the requisition, he will enjoy the promise; but that if he does not comply with it, he will not be put in possession of the things promised, nay, that the contrary evils will be inflicted upon him, according to the nature of the divine covenant, in which there is no promise without a punishment opposed to it.'[28] Commenting on this view of the gospel call, Muller notes that it denies the efficacy of God's grace to save those who hear the gospel call:

> As in his doctrine of election, so too in his concept of calling, Arminius places the emphasis on the rejectability of the call and on the choice of the individual. Nor does Arminius broach the distinction raised by the Reformed between effectual and ineffectual calling. The 'efficacy' of calling, according to Arminius, results from the concurrence of the external calling of the preached Word with the internal calling of the Spirit, but this is an efficacy that may be rejected by the hearer of the Word who may resist the divine counsel and the work of the Spirit.[29]

---

28. Jacob Arminius, *Private Disputations*, 43.2, in *WJA*, 2:398.

29. Muller, GECC, 261.

The reason Arminius does not affirm effectual calling is clear. In Arminius' view, the Reformed view of effectual calling does not grant to the will of fallen sinners the power to choose to believe or not to believe. However, Arminius' doctrine of free will requires that those who respond to the gospel call have the power to choose to do or not to do what this call requires. Stated abstractly or formally, Arminius' doctrine of human freedom amounts to what is often termed today a doctrine of 'libertarian freedom'. According to Arminius, 'Divine providence does not determine a free will to one part of a contradiction or contrariety, that is, by a determination preceding the actual volition itself.'[30] As Stanglin and McCall observe,

> Arminius makes obvious what he means by human freedom: it is the choice to do some action A or to refrain from doing A.... In other words, when Arminius speaks of 'freedom,' he means what is now sometimes termed *libertarian freedom.* Freedom, according to this view, is a real choice between genuine alternatives, unconstrained by necessity, and therefore strictly incompatible with determinism. God is able to determine human wills, but doing so would remove free choice and would violate the kind of relationship that God desires to have with creation.[31]

Arminius believes that God's providence only concurs with the free decisions of human beings in respect to their 'effects' or actual decisions that are made. In Arminius' doctrine of providence, God's

---

30. 'Private Disputations,' 8.3, in *WJA*, 2:714.

31. *Jacob Arminius*, 101. For treatments of the way Arminius' doctrine of creation undergirds his view of human freedom in relation to God, see Stanglin and McCall, *Jacob Arminius*, 47-93; Muller, *GCP*, 211-85; idem, 'God, Predestination, and the Integrity of the Created Order: A Note on Patterns in Arminius' Theology,' in *Later Calvinism: International Perspectives*, ed. W. Fred Graham, vol. 22: *Sixteenth Century Essays & Studies* (Kirksville, MO: Sixteenth Century Journal Publishers, 1994), 431-46; and Oliver D. Crisp, 'Jacob Arminius and Jonathan Edwards on the Doctrine of Creation,' in *Reconsidering Arminius: Beyond the Reformed and Wesleyan Divide*, ed. Keith D. Stanglin, Mark G. Bilby and Mark H. Mann (Nashville: Abingdon, 2014), 91-112. All of these interpreters share the conviction that Arminius' doctrine of creation, though sharing many aspects of classical orthodoxy, involves a form of divine 'self-limitation' in which God grants His human creatures considerable freedom to thwart God's gracious will in respect to salvation. Arminius' use of the idea of God's 'middle knowledge' allows him, nonetheless, to retain the doctrine of God's comprehensive foreknowledge, even of choices that take place independently of God's will.

grace may be an 'assisting' or 'co-operating' grace, but it does not, strictly speaking, move or cause the human will to believe and repent. God may concur with the free decisions that fallen sinners make in response to the gospel call, but this concurrence is consequent upon the actual decisions that they choose to make. Such concurrence lies within the sphere of God's relative or consequent willing. Or, to put the matter more directly, God wills to *ratify* the free decisions of those who respond to the gospel call. God does not author or effect such decisions by virtue of a prior purpose of election; He merely acquiesces to the indeterminate and self-authored choices of the creature.

God's Foreknowledge and 'Middle Knowledge'

In order to complete our summary of Arminius' view of the relation between God's prevenient grace and the free decisions of those who respond to His grace in the way of faith, we need to consider how he understands God's foreknowledge of how all fallen sinners will freely respond to the gospel call. How does Arminius account for God's foreknowledge of human acts, particularly decisions to believe or not to believe, that do not actually occur because God wills them to occur? If God's will relates to such choices only *in consequence of* the free choices of rational creatures, how does He know these choices in advance of their occurrence? The problem that Arminius needs to address at this point is clearly set forth by Muller:

> Granting his emphasis on human choice in the work of salvation and on an antecedent and consequent divine will distinguished by the intervening choice to believe, what remained for Arminius was the definition or redefinition of divine knowing in such a way as to rest the consequent will of God on foreknown human action while at the same time relieving that action of dependence on the divine will.[32]

Before taking up Arminius' solution to this problem – how can God foreknow genuinely free actions that He has not willed antecedently and absolutely? – it needs to be observed that Arminius shared with his Reformed contemporaries a distinction between two broad categories of divine knowledge. In traditional medieval and Reformed

---

32. Muller, GECC, 263.

orthodox theology, it was common to distinguish God's 'necessary knowledge' (*scientia necessaria*) and His 'free knowledge' (*scientia libera*). God's necessary knowledge refers to His knowledge of all things that He must know, for example, His knowledge of Himself and all possibilities. Since God's necessary knowledge logically precedes, and therefore does not depend upon, an act of His will, it was often termed God's 'knowledge of simple intelligence' or His 'natural and indefinite knowledge' (*scientia simplicis intelligentiae seu naturalis et indefinita*). In distinction from such knowledge, God's 'free knowledge' refers to His knowledge of all that He wills to become actual. From out of all possibilities, God freely wills that some things become actual, and His knowledge of such actualities is, accordingly, a free knowledge. Since God's free knowledge is His knowledge of the actualities that He wills to exist, it was often termed God's 'visionary or definite knowledge' (*scientia visionis et definita*), or His 'voluntary knowledge' (*scientia voluntaria*).[33] Arminius embraces this distinction, and utilizes it in a manner that was common among his Reformed contemporaries. God's knowledge involves His knowledge of distinct categories of things, including their distinct modes of existence. He knows both those things that are necessary and those things that are contingent, namely, those things that need not be but become actual by virtue of God's will that they be so.[34]

However, in addition to these two categories of God's knowledge, Arminius departs from his Reformed contemporaries by embracing

---

33. Muller, *Dictionary of Latin and Greek Theological Terms,* 324-25, offers the following, helpful definition of these two categories of God's knowledge: 'The first category [necessary knowledge] ... is the uncompounded, unqualified, absolute, indefinite, or unbounded knowledge that God has necessarily according to his nature and by which God perfectly knows himself and the whole range of possibility.... This is an antecedent knowledge that logically precedes the eternal decrees and thus also precedes the free exercise of the divine will *ad extra*.... By way of contrast, the *scientia visionis* [knowledge of vision] ... is a consequent knowledge resting upon the divine will, a definite knowledge (*scientia definita* ...) or voluntary or free knowledge (*scientia voluntaria sive libera* ...) of actual things that are brought into existence by the divine will operating within the range of possibility perfectly known to God.'

34. Muller, 'Grace, Election, and Contingent Choice,' 264: 'Arminius points out that God's knowledge of things does not invariably impose necessity: God not only knows all things, he knows also the mode of a thing, whether necessary or contingent.... In none of these definitions did Arminius contradict the teaching of his Reformed contemporaries and colleagues.' See Arminius, *Private Disputations*, 17.7, in *WJA*, 2:342.

a third category. This category of knowledge, which Arminius likely learned from the writings of two medieval Jesuit theologians, Suárez and his student Molina, is commonly termed 'middle knowledge' (*scientia media*) because it refers to a knowledge of things intermediate between God's necessary and free knowledge.[35] In addition to God's necessary knowledge of all possibilities and His free knowledge of all actualities that He wills, God also knows those things that 'depend on the liberty of created choice or pleasure'.[36] Whereas God's free knowledge contemplates those things that He knows by virtue of His having freely willed them to be, God's middle knowledge concerns those acts of free creatures that occur wholly by virtue of their own independent choices. Since Arminius bases God's decree to elect some to salvation solely upon His foreknowledge of their faith and repentance in response to the gospel, he introduces the idea of middle knowledge to explain how God can foreknow the actual choices of creatures who have the power to believe or, to the contrary, disbelieve. As Muller describes Arminius' view, 'According to his *scientia media*, God knows how individuals will accept or resist the assistance of his grace and can destine them either to glory or to reprobation on the grounds of their free choice.'[37]

Arminius affirms the idea of God's middle knowledge, therefore, to explain the way God can know how recipients of the universal offer of the gospel will actually choose to respond, whether in faith or in unbelief, in a radically contingent circumstance. Since the

---

35. Muller, *GCP*, 161: 'Arminius nowhere cites Driedo, Molina, Suárez, or Origen and nowhere notes the contemporary Roman Catholic debate over middle knowledge. His only citation of Aquinas stands in no direct relation to the question of *scientia media,* but it is hard to rule out the influence of Molina and Suárez on his doctrine.' For a similar conclusion, see Eef Dekker, 'Was Arminius a Molinist?,' *SCJ* 27, no. 2 (1996): 337-52. For this reason, it is ironic that William Lane Craig ('Middle Knowledge: A Calvinist-Arminian Rapprochement?,' in *GGWM*, 141-64) has argued that the idea of God's 'middle knowledge' might serve to bridge the divide between Calvinist and Arminian views. Far from bridging the divide, the idea of 'middle knowledge' is contradictory to the fundamental concern of the Calvinist view, namely, that God's grace effectually calls those whom He has chosen to save and to grant faith and repentance. I will return to the Molinist idea of God's middle knowledge in chapter 8, which treats the neo-Arminian doctrine of election in what is known as 'open' or 'free-will' theism.

36. *Private Disputations,* 17.12, in *WJA*, 2:342.

37. *GCP*, 161.

actual choices of those who respond to the gospel offer do not occur because God willed them, God's middle knowledge is His ability to know human choices that are, in the strictest sense, not subject to His will or causality. In other words, the doctrine of God's middle knowledge provides a framework for Arminius' teaching that God wills absolutely and antecedently that all who believe in Jesus Christ be saved, and at the same time wills relatively and consequently that those specific persons whom He foreknows will actually believe be granted salvation.[38]

A Critical Evaluation of Arminius' Doctrine of Conditional Election

Before providing a brief summary of the resolution of the Arminian controversy in the Reformed churches of the Netherlands early in the seventeenth century, I want to offer a critical evaluation of Arminius' doctrine of conditional election. In my judgment, there are three significant problems in Arminius' teaching, each of which provides sufficient reason to reject his formulation of the doctrine of election.

Arminius' Mishandling of Romans 9

The first problem with Arminius' formulation is its incompatibility with Scripture, especially Paul's teaching in Romans 9 and other passages. Since I have provided a summary of the Scripture's witness in the first part of this study, I will only illustrate the lack of scriptural warrant for Arminius' view by evaluating his treatment of Romans 9.

In Arminius' interpretation of Paul's argument in Romans 9, the key issue in the chapter is whether the gospel promises salvation to those who obey the law or to those who receive Christ by faith. The apostle in this chapter is opposing the view of many of his Jewish contemporaries that salvation is granted upon the basis of works of the law rather than through faith in Christ and the righteousness of God revealed in Him. As Arminius expresses it, 'the gospel, not the law, is the power of God to salvation, not to the one who works, but to the one who believes; because in the gospel is made manifest

---

38. Cf. Muller, *GCP,* 164.

the righteousness of God, by which salvation is obtained through faith apprehended in Christ.'[39] According to Arminius, Paul's answer to the question whether the Word of God has failed in respect to his unbelieving kinsmen is to insist that evangelical faith alone, apart from works, is the condition whereby some obtain salvation. 'God, by his very word and expression of promise, signified that he would reckon as his sons those only of the Jews who would pursue righteousness and salvation from faith; but that he would hold as foreign those who would pursue the same from the law.'[40] The point of Paul's appeal to the examples of Isaac and Ishmael, and especially of Jacob and Esau, is to illustrate this fundamental truth. Jacob and Esau are not presented by the apostle 'in themselves, but as types.'[41] On the one hand, Jacob (also Isaac) is a type of that class of persons who find salvation through faith in Christ. On the other hand, Esau (also Ishmael) is a type of that class of persons who seek to obtain salvation through the law. What ultimately distinguishes those who are saved from those who are not is that some believe the gospel promise in Christ whereas others do not. The typology of Jacob and Esau is a 'sign' that God's purpose of election 'does not depend on works, but on him who calls; that is, that God loves those who seek righteousness and salvation by faith in Christ but hates those who seek for the same from the works of the law.'[42]

The problem with Arminius' interpretation of Romans 9 is not that he emphasizes the role of faith as a necessary instrument to embrace the gospel promise of salvation. Nor is Arminius to be faulted for his focus upon how Paul insists that salvation comes only through faith in Christ, apart from works performed in obedience to the law. This emphasis is certainly a major part of Paul's argument throughout Romans, including chapters 9 and 10. The problem lies with Arminius' claim that God's purpose of election ultimately is based upon an act of faith in response to the gospel's call, and that Jacob and Esau serve typologically to illustrate how this is the case.

---

39. 'Analysis of Romans 9,' in *WJA*, 3:485-6.

40. ibid., 3:488.

41. ibid., 3:490.

42. ibid., 3:489-95.

The insuperable difficulty with Arminius' interpretation is that it expressly contradicts the point Paul makes throughout Romans 9 regarding God's purpose of election, and especially in his appeal to the example of Jacob and Esau. When Paul adduces the example of Jacob and Esau, he does so in order to demonstrate what is already clear from the Old Testament's account of the birth of these twin sons of Isaac and Rebekah. Before their birth, God announced His intention to show mercy to the younger son, Jacob, and not to the older, Esau. As Paul puts it, 'though they were not yet born and had done nothing either good or bad – in order that God's purpose of election might continue, not because of works but because of him who calls – she [Rebekah] was told, "The older will serve the younger." As it is written, "Jacob I loved, but Esau I hated"' (Rom. 9:11-13). By his appeal to God's choice of Jacob rather than Esau, Paul removes altogether the possibility that the election of Jacob was based upon any work on his part that distinguished him as the proper recipient of God's mercy. Because Jacob was not yet born, and had accordingly done nothing either good or bad, God's purpose of election to show him mercy was *unconditional* in the strictest sense of the term. For this reason, Paul follows his appeal to God's choice of Jacob by noting that God will have mercy on those whom He will, and His mercy does not depend upon 'human will or exertion' (Rom. 9:16). Precisely because the election of Jacob was based solely upon God's will to show him mercy, Paul anticipates that someone might object that this is an act of injustice on God's part (Rom. 9:14). He likewise anticipates someone might further object that this removes any ground for God justly finding fault with those who resist His will through unbelief (Rom. 9:19). These objections make sense only upon the assumption that what distinguishes Jacob and Esau was God's will to show mercy to one rather than the other. If God's election depended upon something Jacob did (or could do) to distinguish himself from Esau, there would be no reason to question the justice of His choice, or to ask how God could fault anyone who resists His will.

Arminius' interpretation of Romans 9, however, affirms exactly what the apostle Paul denies. According to Arminius, Jacob is chosen to be the recipient of God's mercy upon the basis of his faith. Arminius' interpretation makes evangelical faith a kind of *work* that some sinners, who belong to the class represented by Jacob, perform in order to be saved according to God's purpose of election. As Augustine observed in his controversy with Pelagius, Paul's argument in Romans 9 excludes altogether the teaching that God's election depends upon any human act, even the indispensable act of responding to the gospel call through faith. In doing so, Augustine rightly insisted that God's purpose of election is the ultimate source from which faith itself results, when God effectually calls His elect through the gospel. However, on Arminius' interpretation of Romans 9, what distinguishes Jacob and all those whom he represents as the proper objects of God's purpose of election is the good work of faith that God foreknows Jacob will perform. In this way, Arminius answers the question of what makes Jacob differ from Esau with an appeal to Jacob's righteous act of responding appropriately to the gospel call rather than to God's merciful election. To borrow language used by the apostle Paul in 1 Corinthians 4:7, Jacob could then justly declare that his election and salvation, which distinguish him from Esau, were on account of something he did and in which he could boast! He certainly could not say that he had nothing except what he received by God's grace in Christ.

In addition to this fundamental fault in Arminius' interpretation of Romans 9, it should be noted that he also makes God's purpose of election indefinite and ineffectual. God merely elects to save a class of persons, and those who belong to this class are those who persist in the way of faith. God's purpose of election does not contemplate any particular persons, but only a type of person who fulfills the required condition. For Paul's argument in Romans 9 to be persuasive, however, the distinction between those who belong to true Israel as 'children of the promise' and those who do not must illustrate the power and effectiveness of the Word of God, which does not fail in respect to those whom God has chosen. The burden of Paul's argument in Romans 9 is that those who belong to the true Israel do so because of God's purpose of election. This purpose, far from being indefinite and non-specific, contemplates particular persons whom God identifies in the course of His dealings with Israel as a people. God elects specific persons who have particular names, and whose salvation wholly rests upon God's sovereign and merciful election of them.

Arminius' interpretation of Romans 9 also begs the question whether faith itself is graciously granted by God to those whom He saves. In the historic Reformed understanding, God's merciful election of His people in Christ includes the appointment of Christ as Mediator, and the appointment of the gracious means necessary to save those whom God has chosen. To use the language of Romans 8:29-30, those whom God predestines to be conformed to the image of His Son, He also calls to Himself through the gospel, granting them the faith and repentance needed to benefit from Christ's saving work. In Arminius' view, however, there is a sense in which faith precedes God's merciful election and subsequent calling. Believers are not brought to faith by virtue of their election, but they are elect by virtue of their (foreseen) faith. God does not make some to be elect by His merciful choice of them. God only finds through His foreknowledge of faith those who are elect. Though Romans 9 does not expressly speak of faith as God's gift, which corresponds to and is in consequence of God's purpose of election, there are clear instances in the apostle Paul's epistles where this is taught (see, e.g., Eph. 2:8-10; Phil. 1:29). The call of the gospel does require the response of faith on the part of its recipients. But faith is only possible by virtue of God's effectual grace. When the Spirit accompanies the gospel call, regenerating and renewing the heart, will, and affections of those to whom the call is extended, the response of faith is both God's gift and the believer's act (John 1:12-13; 3:3-8). However, on Arminius' interpretation of Romans 9, the class of persons whom Jacob represents consists of those who choose to believe, not by virtue of their election or a prior efficacious working of the Spirt, but as a human work in respect to which God is a passive bystander.

God's 'Consequent Will' of Election and the Specter of Semi-Pelagianism

The second problem with Arminius' formulation of the doctrine of election relates to his distinction between God's *absolute, antecedent* will to save all fallen sinners through the work of Christ and the means of grace that He has appointed, and God's *relative, consequent* will to save only those sinners whom He knows will respond to the gospel call with a persisting faith. By this distinction between

God's absolute and consequent will, Arminius posits a remarkable contradiction between specific aspects of God's eternal will regarding the salvation and non-salvation of fallen human beings. On the one hand, God's absolute will expresses His gracious will to save all on the basis of Christ's work as Mediator. On the other hand, God's consequent will expresses His will to save those specific persons whom He foreknows will respond appropriately to the gospel call. Though God wills absolutely to save all human beings in Christ, He also wills consequently to save only those specific persons who choose to respond to the gospel in faith. Thus, Arminius is left with a view of God's will in which there is a profound tension between what God *truly* wills to occur and what He *consequently* (and actually) wills to occur. While God in His goodness wills salvation for all, in His will respecting what will actually occur in history, He wills that some specific persons be saved and not others. Furthermore, despite God's will to save all, His consequent will renders certain only the salvation of some and therefore expresses a divergent outcome than the one He really desires. Within the depths of God's eternal willing, there is a conflict between what God truly desires and what He wills to occur in consequence of the choice fallen sinners make either to believe or not to believe.[43]

In addition to the introduction of a conflict between God's will in its absolute and consequent aspects, Arminius' position also requires the conclusion that God's absolute and antecedent will to save all is profoundly ineffectual. God's antecedent, absolute will ensures the salvation of no one, since it depends for its fruition upon the

---

43. Muller, GECC, 274: 'According to this doctrine, God genuinely wills that which he knows will never happen, indeed, what he wills not to bring about!' Muller notes that Reformed theologians acknowledge distinctions within the divine will, including a distinction between God's 'will of decree' (what God eternally and absolutely wills to occur) and His 'will of precept' (what God declares to be pleasing to Him, even though it may be disobeyed by His creatures). Regarding this distinction, Muller aptly observes that 'when Reformed theologians approached the concept of an antecedent and a consequent divine will, they understood that the former referred to the absolute or decretive will and the latter to the preceptive will of God. Thus, the former "was determined by God from eternity before any created things existed" while the latter rests on the eternal decree without contradicting it: the divine precepts fully concur with the righteousness of the eternal decree, are consequent upon it, and may be ignored or disobeyed by sinful human beings' (GECC, 273).

willingness of fallen sinners to meet the condition of faith. Unless those whom God truly wills to save choose to co-operate with His grace, God's will can always be resisted. Accordingly, though Arminius affirms the universal extent of God's will to save all and to provide for their salvation through the work of Christ, he is compelled to deny the universal efficacy of God's gracious will. Even though the work of Christ provides an atonement sufficient to save all who believe, Christ's work of atonement depends for its efficacy upon the willingness of those who are called to embrace the gospel promise. God's gracious will and Christ's work of atonement make salvation available to all who are addressed through the gospel call, but *neither God's will nor Christ's work ensures the actual salvation of anyone.* In the final analysis, God's gracious will to save all sinners, and to provide for their salvation though Christ's works as Mediator, leaves Him, so far as His consequent will is concerned, in the position of a hapless spectator. God can only wait upon those whom He addresses with the gospel, impotent in His desire to save them. God wills what He knows will not take place, and He does so in a way that can only entail a sort of divine disappointment with the failure of many to do what is required of them and to render His gracious purpose fruitful. In Arminius' scheme, God is ultimately the student who must learn (through His eternal foreknowledge) what will transpire in history, not the invincible Savior who effectively achieves what He wills.

Lest my assessment of Arminius' position be deemed too severe, it must be noted that the root of these problems lies in what might be termed the 'synergism' or 'semi-Pelagianism' of Arminius' view of human freedom. In the final analysis, the will that counts so far as the actual salvation of human beings is concerned is not God's, but the sinner's. It is no accident that, when Arminius finally gets to the will of God regarding the actual salvation of specific sinners, he makes God's will depend upon His foreknowledge of human choices. For all of Arminius' emphasis upon God's prevenient and sufficient grace that enables believers to embrace the gospel promise, he never affirms that the actual choice of some to believe comes about by virtue of the working of God's grace alone. He ascribes belief and unbelief as within the power of those who are summoned to faith through the gospel. God's grace can always be resisted or frustrated. God does not ultimately move sinners to believe, since His will depends upon, and is in consequence of, what He foreknows *they will choose to do.* As I noted in my exposition of Arminius' position, God 'concurs' with the choice some make to believe *only in respect to the 'effect' of the choice made.* This means that God's will regarding those whom He foreknows will believe is a 'passive' will, which only registers or 'learns' those who are numbered among the elect from the choices He foresees they will make. As Arminius puts it, God's consequent will to save or not to save 'does not lead [human beings] to life or to death, except after certain precedent actions of theirs.'[44]

Consequently, even though it would be unfair to describe Arminius' position as Pelagian, it certainly represents a reintroduction of a form of semi-Pelagianism that was popular throughout the medieval period.[45] Since Arminius maintains that all sinners remain free to resist God's grace in Christ and to frustrate God's saving will, his position amounts to a 'synergism' in which the human will acts in a way that does not depend upon God's grace at the most crucial point, namely, in choosing to believe or not believe.[46]

The Problem of God's 'Middle Knowledge'

The last problem that needs to be addressed is Arminius' use of the idea of God's 'middle knowledge'.

The first observation necessary to make is that his use of this notion clearly confirms the serious problems already identified regarding his position. It is consistent with his view that God's electing will is 'consequent' upon the decision of some persons to believe. The idea of God's middle knowledge fits comfortably with the 'synergism' and 'semi-Pelagianism' that characterize Arminius' position. Since God's will to elect certain persons to salvation depends upon their free decision to believe and not resist His grace, Arminius is obliged

---

44. 'Examination of Gomarus,' in *WJA,* 3:560.

45. Muller, GECC, 262: 'From the Reformed perspective, … this understanding of predestination was a synergism inimical not only to the Reformed, Augustinian, and Pauline doctrine of predestination but also the fundamental teaching of the Reformation that salvation is by grace alone.'

46. Cf. Francis Turretin, *Institutes of Elenctic Theology,* trans. George Musgrave Giger, ed. James T. Dennison, Jr. (Phillipsburg, NJ: Presbyterian & Reformed, 1992), 1:355.

to account for God's knowledge of a future contingency (the choice to believe) that does not become actual by virtue of His willing it to occur. Arminius' use of the idea of middle knowledge, therefore, is born out of desire to preserve not only God's omniscience (with respect to all future actualities) but *especially to preserve the freedom of human creatures, apart from any dependence upon God and His will, to believe or not to believe.* It confirms further that, in the matter of election and salvation, the key actor is not God but the human respondent to God's grace. The efficacy of God's saving will in Christ ultimately is determined by what fallen sinners choose to do when summoned to faith through the gospel call.[47] If there were any doubt regarding Arminius' teaching that God's election of some persons to salvation in Christ ultimately depends upon what these persons do *in and of themselves*, Arminius' appeal to the idea of middle knowledge confirms it.[48]

Though the reason Arminius appeals to the idea of God's middle knowledge is clear, it is not so evident that this idea is compatible with the biblical understanding of God's works of creation and providence. In the biblical view of God, the being and existence of the created order, indeed of all things, depends wholly upon God's free determination to create the world that exists. Only God is self-existent, absolute, and independent in His being, works, and eternal will. The creation – the being and existence of all creatures, together with their actions in time – depend wholly upon God's free decision to grant them existence. Out of all the possibilities that God necessarily knows by His 'simple intelligence,' God wills to create a world that actualizes some of these potentialities. Furthermore, when God creates the actual world that He wills, He does not give the world or any of His creatures the kind of absolute independence of existence that

---

47. Cf. Muller, GECC, 266: 'if the salvation of human beings rests on divine foreknowledge, the human being is clearly regarded as the first and effective agent in salvation, and God is understood simply as the one who responds to an independent human action.' Bavinck, *RD*, 2:221, makes a similar point: 'In the theory of middle knowledge, that is precisely the case with God. God looks on, while humans decide. It is not God who makes distinctions among people, but people distinguish themselves. Grace is dispensed, according to merit; predestination depends on good works.'

48. Cf. Turretin, *Institutes of Elenctic Theology,* 1:216.

belong alone to Him.[49] To do so would require Him to cease to be the God He is, since the created order would include creatures no longer dependent upon Him. In Arminius' view, the freedom God grants to human beings is tantamount to making them 'little gods', namely, creatures whose existence and choices are independent of God's being and will. However, in the biblical view of God's providence, God continues to preserve the created order and governs all things in a way that accords with His will for them. While God's providential preservation and governance of creation differ in respect to the kinds of creatures, He nonetheless preserves and governs all things so that nothing takes place in radical independence of His sovereign will.[50]

While this brief summary of the biblical view of creation and providence may seem rather abstract, it has significant implications for the way Arminius construes God's middle knowledge. In Arminius' understanding of the relation between God's will and the creature's will, God's will does not concur with the creature's will in its origin or moving cause. God's concurrence with such choices takes place only in respect to their 'effect', not to their origination. In a manner of speaking, God's relation to the choices human beings make in response to the gospel amounts to a sort of eternal 'after the fact' (*ex post facto*) endorsement of what was determined in absolute independence from Him. When it concerns the choice to believe or not to believe, human beings enjoy a godlike form of self-existence and freedom undetermined by anything or anyone, including God Himself. In Arminius' view, there are contingent beings and effects in the created order that exist in some measure outside of God's will and in strict independence of His concurring will. Muller calls this view an 'ontological absurdity', namely, the idea that a finite creature could exist and exercise his will in a way that mimics God's incommunicable attribute of self-existence and absolute independence upon anything outside of Himself.[51]

Consistent with the biblical view of God's creation and providential governance, Christian theologians have generally insisted that human

49. Muller, GECC, 266.

50. Cf. WCF 3.1, 5.2.

51. Muller. GECC, 267.

choices in response to the gospel call do not take place apart from God's will.[52] Although it may be impossible for us to fully comprehend, these choices (for which we are responsible and which are genuinely ours) do not occur in a way that is radically independent of God's concurring will. In order for human beings to make contingent choices, God must not only create them with this capacity but also sustain them and concur with their choices, not simply in their effect but in the act of choosing itself.[53]

If these problems with the idea of God's middle knowledge were not serious enough, there is another question that must be pressed: How can God possibly know in advance the free decisions of human beings that are truly indeterminate? If these decisions are genuinely made outside of God's will, and upon no other basis than the power of human beings to believe or to not believe, there is no basis upon which even God could foreknow what will be decided. Were we to grant that such a thing as God's middle knowledge exists, we would be obliged to conclude that God's knowledge of human free decisions renders these decisions *certain*. But if these free, indeterminate decisions will certainly become actual (otherwise, God's knowledge of them would not be a true knowledge), they cease to be decisions of finite agents with freedom to do the contrary. As Turretin observes:

> middle knowledge can have no certainty because it is occupied about an uncertain and contingent object (viz, the indifference [*adiaphoron*] of the will). I ask, therefore, whence can God certainly know what will or will not take place? ... If it [the divine foreknowledge] foresees it [the decision to believe or not believe] as certain, how could the foresight of an uncertain and indifferent thing be itself certain?[54]

When human agents are granted a godlike independence in respect to their decisions to believe or not to believe, even God must remain uncertain as to what they will decide to make actual. The future actions of an undetermined will with the power of contrary choice,

---

52. I intentionally use the language, 'Christian theologians,' since this is the prevalent position among Augustinian, Thomist, and Reformed theologians throughout the history of theology.

53. Muller, GECC, 268.

54. Turretin, *Institutes of Elenctic Theology,* 1:215.

cannot be known by God because, for God to know such actions truly and certainly, these actions would no longer be taken by agents who could do otherwise than what God knows they will do. How could God know something whose actuality depends solely upon a future contingency that does not yet exist, does not become actual by His will, and is the product of an indifferent, arbitrary will? As Herman Bavinck expresses this problem:

> If God infallibly knows in advance what a person will do in a given case, he can foreknow this only if the person's motives determine his or her will in one specific direction, and his will therefore does not consist in indifference. Conversely, *if* that will were indifferent, foreknowledge would be impossible, and only post-factum knowledge would exist. God's foreknowledge and the will conceived as arbitrariness are mutually exclusive. For, as Cicero already phrased it, 'if he knows it, it will certainly take place, but if it is bound to take place, no such thing as chance exists.'[55]

The difficulty that Turretin and Bavinck are identifying with respect to the idea of God's middle knowledge was already recognized by Thomas Aquinas. The choices of an undetermined will are not predictable, and even God is left with at best a 'conjectural' knowledge of what will become actual through such choices.[56]

The Resolution of the Arminian Controversy at the Synod of Dort

Because Arminius departed from some basic features of the Reformed doctrine of election, it is not surprising that his teaching became the eye in a storm of controversy among the Reformed churches in the Netherlands. Two parties emerged during the late sixteenth and early seventeenth centuries, one favoring Arminius and the other opposing him. Two important events also occurred, preparing the way for the calling of an international synod in Dordrecht in 1618.

---

55. Bavinck, *RD*, 2:202. Bavinck puts his finger on a key issue regarding human freedom: if the choices human beings make, especially in respect to the gospel summons to faith, are indeterminate, they are also radically arbitrary, unmotivated by anything in the person's character, affections, and dispositions that would incline them to make the particular choice they do.

56. Aquinas, *Summa Theologica,* I, Q. 14, Art. 13.

After Arminius' death in 1609, the Arminian party in the Dutch Reformed churches prepared a summary statement of their position. On January 14, 1610, more than forty representatives who championed Arminius' views gathered in Gouda. These representatives drew up a *Remonstrance* or petition in which their case was set forth and defended. After complaining that their cause had been misrepresented by their opponents, the Remonstrants presented the Arminian position in a series of five articles.[57] They hoped the civil authorities would approve this statement, thereby answering the charge that their doctrine conflicted with Scripture and the Reformed confessions.

Shortly after this *Remonstrance* was prepared, the States of Holland made arrangements for a meeting between representatives of the Arminian or Remonstrant and the anti-Arminian parties. This meeting took place from March 10 until May 20, 1611, and occasioned the preparation of a reply to the five points of the Arminians. The response of the Reformed opponents to Arminianism was termed the *Counter Remonstrance of 1611*.[58] Its main features anticipated the later and more expansive statement of the *Canons of Dort*. When the debate between the Arminian/Remonstrant and anti-Arminian/Counter-Remonstrant parties showed no signs of abating in the Netherlands,

---

57. Hence this *Remonstrance* is often termed the 'Five Arminian Articles' (Latin: *Articuli Arminiani sive Remonstrantia*). For an English translation of this *Remonstrance*, see Peter De Jong, ed., *Crisis*, 243-5. These five articles became the organizing pattern for the discussions and debates which ensued, including the five 'heads of doctrine' of the *Canons of Dort*. Hence the 'five points of Calvinism', commonly so-called, are really five 'counter-points' to the errors of the Arminians or Remonstrants. Today, they are often known in English-speaking circles by the acronym, 'TULIP' (Total depravity, Unconditional election, Limited atonement, Irresistible grace, and the Perseverance of the saints). Unfortunately, this acronym is of recent vintage, changes the order of the five points, and also employs terminology (especially in the case of 'total depravity', 'irresistible grace', and 'limited atonement') that does not adequately express the Reformed view. For critical assessments of the value of this acronym, see Richard Muller, *Calvin and the Reformed Tradition: On the Work of Christ and the Order of Salvation* (Grand Rapids: Baker Academic, 2012), 58-62; Kenneth J. Stewart, *Ten Myths About Calvinism: Recovering the Breadth of the Reformed Tradition* (Wheaton, IL: IVP Academic, 2011), 75-96; and Timothy F. George, *Amazing Grace: God's Initiative—Our Response* (Nashville: LifeWay, 2002). George suggests an alternative acronym, 'ROSES' (Radical depravity, Overcoming grace, Sovereign election, Eternal life, and Singular redemption).

58. For an English translation of this *Counter Remonstrance*, see De Jong, *Crisis*, 247-50.

the States-General of the Republic of the Netherlands finally called a national synod to settle the dispute. The express purpose of this synod, to be held in 1618 in Dordrecht, was to judge whether the position of the Remonstrants was in harmony with the Word of God and the Reformed Confessions, particularly Article 16 of the Belgic Confession.[59] Though officially a synod of the Reformed churches of the Netherlands, the synod had twenty-six delegates from eight foreign countries.[60]

On the basis of its deliberations, the Synod of Dort judged the five articles of the Remonstrants to be contrary to the Word of God and the confession of the Reformed churches. Against the Arminian teachings of divine election based on foreseen faith, resistible or ineffectual grace, and the possibility of a lapse from grace, the Canons set forth the Reformed teachings of unconditional election, definite atonement, pervasive depravity, effectual grace, and the perseverance of the saints. In form, the Canons were structured to answer the five points of the Remonstrants. On each major head of doctrine, the Canons first present a positive statement of the scriptural teaching and then conclude with a rejection of the corresponding Arminian error. In order to provide an account of the resolution of the Arminian controversy at the Synod of Dort, I will offer a brief statement of the five main points of doctrine adopted by the Synod of Dort.[61]

---

59. Article 16 of the Belgic Confession reads as follows: 'We believe that, all the posterity of Adam being thus fallen into perdition and ruin by the sin of our first parents, God then did manifest Himself such as He is; that is to say, merciful and just: merciful, since He delivers and preserves from this perdition all whom He in His eternal and unchangeable counsel of mere goodness has elected in Christ Jesus our Lord, without any respect to their works; just, in leaving others in the fall and perdition wherein they have involved themselves.'

60. For a list of the delegates to the Synod, see De Jong, *Crisis,* 253-58.

61. For a treatment of the recognition of the Canons as a confessional standard, see Donald Sinnema, 'The Canons of Dordt: From Judgment on Arminianism to Confessional Standard,' in *Revisiting the Synod of Dordt (1618-1619),* ed. Aza Goudriaan & Fred van Lieburg, 313-33. For a comprehensive treatment of the scriptural basis for the Canons' teaching, see David N. Steele and Curtis C. Thomas, eds., *The Five Points of Calvinism: Defined, Defended, Documented* (New Jersey: Presbyterian & Reformed Publishing Co., 1963), 30-38. For popular treatments of the Canons, see Cornelis P. Venema, *But for the Grace of God: An Exposition of the Canons of Dort* (Grand Rapids: Reformed Fellowship Inc., 1994, 2011); James Montgomery Boice and Philip Graham Ryken, *The Doctrines of Grace* (Wheaton, IL: Crossway, 2002); and Timothy F. George, *Amazing Grace.*

The First Main Point of Doctrine: Unconditional Election. In the first main head of doctrine, the authors of the Canons affirm that God's gracious election of His people in Christ is unconditional. Contrary to the position of Arminius, which bases God's election of some persons to salvation upon the basis of His foreknowledge of their faith, the Canons insist that faith itself is God's gift to those toward whom He eternally wills to show mercy.

> The fact that some receive from God the gift of faith within time, and that others do not, stems from [God's] eternal decision. For *all his works are known to God from eternity* (Acts 15:18; Eph. 1:11). In accordance with this decision he graciously softens the hearts, however hard, of his chosen ones and inclines them to believe, but by his just judgment he leaves in their wickedness and hardness of heart those who have not been chosen. And in this especially is disclosed to us his act – unfathomable, and as merciful as it is just – of distinguishing between people equally lost. (Art. 6)

> Election is God's unchangeable purpose by which he did the following: Before the foundation of the world, by sheer grace, according to the good pleasure of his will, he chose in Christ to salvation a definite number of particular people out of the entire human race, which had fallen by its own fault from its original innocence into sin and ruin. Those chosen were neither better nor more deserving than the others, but lay with them in the common misery. He did this in Christ, whom he also appointed from eternity to be the mediator, the head of all those chosen, and the foundation of their salvation. (Art. 7)

After articulating the scriptural teaching of unconditional election, the Canons further affirm that this sovereign and gracious election of a particular number of persons unto salvation means that some sinners have been 'passed by' and 'left' in their sins.

> Moreover, Holy Scripture especially highlights this eternal and undeserved grace of our election and brings it out more clearly for us, in that it further bears witness that not all people have been chosen but that some have not been chosen or have been passed by in God's eternal election—those, that is, concerning whom God, on the basis of the entirely free, most just, irreproachable, and unchangeable good pleasure, made the following decision: to leave them in the common misery into which, by their own fault, they have plunged themselves;

not to grant them saving faith and the grace of conversion; but finally to condemn and eternally punish them (having been left in their own ways and under his just judgment), not only for their unbelief but also for all their other sins, in order to display his justice. And this is the decision of reprobation, which does not at all make God the author of sin (a blasphemous thought!) but rather its fearful, irreproachable, just judge and avenger. (Art. 15)[62]

The formulation of this article is expressly 'infralapsarian'. Those whom God does not elect to save in Christ belong to the company of all fallen sinners who 'by their own fault' have willfully plunged themselves into a 'common misery'. Whatever parallel may exist between God's merciful election and just reprobation, they remain profoundly asymmetrical. In the case of the elect, God mercifully and graciously elects to grant them salvation in and through the work of Christ. In the case of the reprobate, God demonstrates His justice by choosing to withhold His grace and to condemn them for their sins and unbelief.[63]

The Second Main Point of Doctrine: Definite Atonement or Particular Redemption. After describing the necessity of Christ's atoning work, the Canons' second main point affirms the infinite value and worth of Christ's satisfaction. His atoning sacrifice 'is the only and entirely complete sacrifice and satisfaction for sins', and 'is of infinite value and worth, more than sufficient to atone for the sins of the whole world.'[64] Therefore, the church must 'indiscriminately'

---

62. For an extensive treatment of the Synod of Dort's treatment of reprobation, see Donald W. Sinnema, 'The Issue of Reprobation at the Synod of Dort (1618-19) in Light of the History of this Doctrine' (Ph.D. diss., University of St. Michael's College, Toronto School of Theology, 1985).

63. Cf. Herman Bavinck, *RD*, 2:396.

64. The Canons employ language at this point that was often used throughout the Middle Ages and into the Reformation period, namely, that Christ's work of atonement was 'sufficient' for all but 'efficient' for the elect alone. This language was first used by Peter Lombard, and was liable to a variety of interpretations as to its implications for an understanding of the extent and efficacy of Christ's atoning work. For an extensive treatment of this issue, including the debates before and during the convening of the Synod of Dort, see William Robert Godfrey, 'Tensions Within International Calvinism: The Debate on the Atonement at the Synod of Dort, 1618-1619' (Ph.D. diss., Stanford University, 1974); and Muller, *Calvin and the Reformed Tradition*, 70-106.

proclaim the gospel of salvation through Christ to 'all nations and peoples, to whom God in his good pleasure sends the gospel.' However, the atoning work of Christ was by God's design and intention provided for the elect in particular:

> For it was the entirely free plan and very gracious will and intention of God the Father that the enlivening and saving effectiveness of his Son's costly death should work itself out in all his chosen ones, in order that he might grant justifying faith to them only and thereby lead them without fail to salvation. In other words, it was God's will that Christ through the blood of the cross (by which he confirmed the new covenant) should effectively redeem from every people, tribe, nation, and language all those and only those who were chosen from eternity to salvation and given to him by the Father; that he should grant them faith (which, like the Holy Spirit's other saving gifts, he acquired for them by his death); that he should cleanse them by his blood from all their sins, both original and actual. (Art. 8)

There is a perfect harmony in God's counsel and redemptive work between His sovereign good pleasure to save His people and His gracious provision through Christ of the satisfaction required to redeem them. The Father wills to give to the Son those whom He purposed to save and the Son redeemed with His precious blood.[65]

The Third and Fourth Main Points of Doctrine: Human Depravity and Effectual Grace. The Canons of Dort treat together the third and fourth main points of doctrine, human depravity and effectual grace, because the real point of divergence between the Reformed and Arminian views emerges most clearly at the fourth point.[66]

---

65. This is a good place to note the position of Moïse Amyraut, a French Reformed theologian of the seventeenth century, who attempted to find a mediating position on the atonement between Reformed and Arminian views. Known as 'Amyraldianism' or the doctrine of 'hypothetical universalism', this position distinguished a twofold decree of God: one, to send Christ into the world to save *all* by His atoning death on the condition of faith; and two, to give to the elect a special grace enabling them to believe and secure their redemption through Christ. This view seeks to combine an 'unlimited atonement' with a doctrine of 'particular redemption'. However, it does so at the price of sacrificing the effectiveness of Christ's atoning work on behalf of all for whom He made atonement. It also posits a conflict between the Son's *universal work* of atonement and the Father's *particular purpose* of election. For secondary sources on Amyraut's view, see chapter 5 of this volume, fn85; and Muller, *Calvin and the Reformed Tradition*, 107-25.

66. It should be noted that, in the history of controversy in the Netherlands between the Remonstrants (Arminians) and the contra-Remonstrants, there was an apparent

The position of the Canons on the plight of sinful man is starkly portrayed in the first five articles of this section of the confession. In the first and third articles, a sharp contrast is drawn between man's original state of integrity, as he was created by God, and his sinful state after the fall.

> Man was originally created in the image of God and was furnished in his mind with a true and salutary knowledge of his Creator and things spiritual, in his will and heart with righteousness, and in all his emotions with purity; indeed, the whole man was holy. However, rebelling against God at the devil's instigation and by his own free will, he deprived himself of these outstanding gifts. Rather, in their place he brought upon himself blindness, terrible darkness, futility, and distortion of judgment in his mind; perversity, defiance, and hardness in his heart and will; and finally impurity in all his emotions. (Art. 1)

> Therefore, all people are conceived in sin and are born children of wrath, unfit for any saving good, inclined to evil, dead in their sins, and slaves to sin; without the grace of the regenerating Holy Spirit they are neither willing nor able to return to God, to reform their distorted nature, or even to dispose themselves to such reform. (Art. 3)

Due to the pervasive effects of sin, the Canons maintain that fallen sinners are unable to respond to the gracious call of the gospel, unless God's Spirit grants the faith and repentance this call requires. Through the gospel, which is to be preached to all nations, God 'seriously and genuinely' makes known what is 'pleasing to him: that those who are called should come to him. Seriously he also promises rest for their souls and eternal life to all who come to him and believe' (Art. 8).[67] However, unless God by His Spirit efficaciously grants to sinners what the gospel call requires, they are unable and unwilling to respond to

---

agreement on this third main point of doctrine. The contra-Remonstrants did not object to the third article of the Remonstrance of 1610, dealing with the subject of the extent of sinful man's depravity and need for the regenerating grace of God. This accounts in part for the treatment of the third and fourth main points of doctrine together in the Counter Remonstrance of 1611 and the Canons of Dort.

67. The language of the Canons, describing the serious and genuine call that God issues through the gospel to all, is virtually identical with that employed by the Remonstrants in their fourth opinion. However, the authors of the Canons refused to follow the logic of the Arminians, who drew the conclusion that all sinners must then be able of themselves to comply with the gospel's demands.

God's gracious call in the way of faith and repentance. Only those whom God has eternally chosen in Christ are effectually called and converted through the ministry of the gospel. What distinguishes those who resist the gospel call and those who embrace it by faith, is God's effectual calling of the elect.

> The fact that others who are called through the ministry of the gospel do come and are brought to conversion must not be credited to man, as though one distinguishes himself by free choice from others who are furnished with equal or sufficient grace for faith and conversion (as the proud heresy of Pelagius maintains). No, it must be credited to God: just as from eternity he chose his own in Christ, so within time he effectively calls them, grants them faith and repentance, and, having rescued them from the dominion of darkness, brings them into the kingdom of his Son, in order that they may declare the wonderful deeds of him who called them out of darkness into this marvelous light, and may boast not in themselves, but in the Lord, as apostolic words frequently testify in Scripture. (Art. 10)

The Fifth Main Point of Doctrine: The Perseverance of the Saints. Within the setting of this biblically realistic view of the believer's daily struggle with sin, the Canons conclude by affirming God's gracious preservation of those whom He elects to save. Were believers left to their own resources, they 'could not remain standing in this grace' for a moment (Art. 3). Only as God, being faithful and merciful, strengthens and enables them, are believers able to continue in fellowship with Christ.

> For God, who is rich in mercy, according to his unchangeable purpose of election does not take his Holy Spirit from his own completely, even when they fall grievously. Neither does he let them fall down so far that they forfeit the grace of adoption and the state of justification, or commit the sin which leads to death (the sin against the Holy Spirit), and plunge themselves, entirely forsaken by him, into eternal ruin. (Art. 6)

With this affirmation of the perseverance of the saints, the Canons return to a theme that runs throughout the five main points of doctrine. Because God alone is the author of the salvation of the elect in Christ, we may have every confidence that the work He has begun will be brought to completion (Phil. 1:6). In this way, the scriptural doctrine of election not only ascribes all praise to God for His saving grace but also affords believers great comfort in knowing that His grace will be sufficient to save them without fail.

Conclusion

Undoubtedly, the preparation of the Canons of Dort represents an especially important moment in the history of reflection upon the doctrine of election. In the modern period of theology after the Arminian controversy, no formulation of the doctrine of election may avoid direct engagement with the alternatives represented by the Augustinian/Calvinist statement of the Canons of Dort and the position of Arminius. If I may paraphrase a comment of Jaroslav Pelikan regarding Augustine, the history of theological reflection on the doctrine of election in the modern period reads often like a 'series of footnotes' to the controversy that arose between the Reformed and Arminian views in the period of Reformed orthodoxy.[68] In the same way western theology 'oscillated' between Augustinianism and Pelagianism from the time of the Synod of Orange in A.D. 529 until the sixteenth-century Reformation, so it has oscillated between Augustinianism and Arminian semi-Pelagianism from the time of the Synod of Dort in the early seventeenth century until the present.

At the most basic level, the principal difference between Augustinianism and Arminianism is not hard to discern. Whereas Augustinianism teaches a doctrine of unconditional election, Arminianism teaches a doctrine of conditional election. A doctrine of unconditional election is one that it is thoroughly and consistently monergistic: God alone, by virtue of His gracious choice to save His people in Christ, is the author and finisher of the faith and salvation of all believers (cf. Heb. 12:2). By contrast, a doctrine of conditional election is one that is unavoidably synergistic: God's grace makes it possible for any fallen sinner to be saved, but does not actually effect the faith and salvation of anyone. Fallen sinners – enabled, to be sure, by God's indispensable grace and help – are ultimately saved upon the

---

68. Pelikan, *The Christian Tradition,* 1:330. As I noted earlier in a chapter on Augustine (Chap. 4, fn2), Pelikan (paraphrasing Whitehead's epigram about Plato and the history of philosophy) observes that the history of western theology amounts in some ways to 'a series of footnotes' to Augustine.

condition of what they do in response to the gospel call to faith in Christ. According to the Canons of Dort, believers do not become elect persons because they choose to believe; rather, they believe because they are elected to salvation and effectually called by God. According to Arminius, believers become elect persons because they choose to believe and persist in believing. Between these alternatives – with their associated views of God's grace (effectual or ineffectual), the fallen condition of human beings, and human freedom – there does not appear to be any middle ground or mediating view that would bridge the divide. As my critical evaluation of Arminius' view should make clear, I am convinced that the Augustinian/Calvinistic consensus expressed in the Canons of Dort provides a more faithful statement of the Scripture's teaching. Only the Augustinian view can properly answer the apostolic question put in 1 Corinthians 4:7: 'What do you have that you have not received?' In the same way Augustine pressed this question against Pelagius and Pelagianism, so we must press it against the semi-Pelagianism of Arminius.

Nonetheless, it would be premature at this point to close the book on the history of the doctrine of election. Despite the formative nature of the controversy between Arminius and his Reformed contemporaries in the seventeenth century, the doctrine of election has continued to engage the attention of a number of influential authors. Of special importance is the way both the Augustinian/Calvinist and Arminian views have undergone revision by partisans, who are anxious to rescue their respective views from what they regard as problematic features in traditional formulations. Consequently, the last part of this study will focus upon two such revisionist views. The first of these revisionist views is associated with the name of Karl Barth, who offers a significantly modified version of the Augustinian/ Calvinistic view. The second of these revisionist views is associated with a number of evangelical and Arminian theologians, who offer what in their view is a more consequent form of the Arminian view. These two revisionist views are among the most important footnotes that modern theological reflection has contributed to the history of the doctrine of election. Each of them confirms the truth of Pelikan's observation that the names of Augustine and Pelagius have dominated theological engagement with the topic of election in the western church. Even the modern chapters of theological reflection on election have unavoidably joined the ongoing conversation and controversy about election that began in earnest with Pelagius and Augustine in the early church.

CHAPTER 7

Karl Barth's Revision of the Augustinian/Calvinist View of Election: God's Election to Be the God Who is For Us in Jesus Christ

SINCE the Arminian controversy regarding election in the early seventeenth century, modern discussions of the doctrine have largely focused upon the historic divergence between Augustinian/Calvinistic and Arminian formulations. Even theologians who seek to find a way out of the impasse have often found it difficult to avoid finally coming down on one side or the other. Either they embrace the Augustinian view that God unconditionally elects in Christ to save some persons out of the fallen human race, or they embrace some version of the Arminian view that God conditionally elects those He foreknows will respond appropriately to the gospel's call to faith and repentance.

The dominance of these formulations regarding election is attested by two remarkable developments in the modern period. On the one hand, Karl Barth, perhaps the most influential Reformed theologian of the twentieth century, articulated a revisionist doctrine of election in order to address certain problems he saw in Augustine's and Calvin's views. While Barth embraced the conviction that unconditional election belongs to the heart of the biblical gospel, he found certain features of the traditional Reformed view to be insufficiently governed by the conviction that our knowledge of God must be based wholly upon His revelation of Himself in the person and work of Christ. On the other hand, a number of evangelical theologians have sought to formulate the doctrine of election by revising certain features of traditional Arminianism. These theologians have argued that Arminius' doctrine of human freedom requires a more consistent formulation, which entails a denial of God's foreknowledge of those who will respond to the gospel's invitation in faith and repentance. While Arminius properly insisted upon the freedom of all human beings to render God's grace ineffectual, he failed to see the implications for God's ability to foreknow how specific human beings will respond. In the judgment of these theologians, Arminius' claim that God elects specific persons, whom He foreknows will respond to the gospel with a persevering faith, cannot be sustained.

Though the treatment of the doctrine of election in the modern period has many facets, my aim in this third part of our study is to provide an account of these two revisionist formulations. In this chapter, I will address Karl Barth's formulation of the doctrine of election. Though Barth intends to 'correct' some aspects of the traditional Reformed view, he believes his revisionist formulation is necessary to rescue the Reformed understanding of election from some objectionable features. For this reason, it is possible to describe Barth's revision as a sort of 'neo-Reformed' or 'neo-Calvinist' doctrine of election. In a subsequent chapter, I will take up the revision of Arminius' doctrine of election that might likewise be termed a 'neo-Arminian' reformulation of election. These revisionist views testify to a measure of dissatisfaction with the historic formulations of the doctrine of election. Ironically, they also confirm the extent to which the Augustinian/Calvinistic and Arminian viewpoints continue to shape modern formulations, even when they diverge from them.

Key Features of Barth's Doctrine of Election

No theologian in the modern period – and that includes not a few Reformed theologians of considerable ability – has written more extensively on the doctrine of election than Barth.[1] Nor has any theologian offered a more substantial revision of the contours of traditional Reformed teaching on predestination than Barth. In his *Church Dogmatics,* Barth locates the doctrine of election squarely within the context of the doctrine of God.[2] Consistent with the starting point of his Dogmatics in the doctrine of God's self-revelation in and through Jesus Christ, Barth insists that election lies at the heart of what God has revealed regarding Himself. God can only be known through God, and that knowledge is given to us exclusively in His acts in Jesus Christ, the eternal Word of God become incarnate. The doctrine of election reveals who God is in His eternal self-determination to be a God for us in Jesus Christ. For this reason, early in his treatment of election, Barth insists, 'The election of grace [is] ... the sum of the Gospel ... the whole of the Gospel, the Gospel *in nuce.*'[3] The good news that is revealed to us in the gospel is the good news that God has determined to be known by the name of Jesus Christ, that is, as the God who wills graciously to be for us in Him.

But it is not only that Barth places the doctrine of election at the core of his doctrine of God. He also intends to offer a revised doctrine of election that removes the difficulties allegedly associated with the traditional doctrine of Calvin. Already in the preface to volume II/2 of the *Church Dogmatics,* Barth notes that he found it necessary to depart from Calvin's theology at this juncture:

> The work has this peculiarity, that in it I have had to leave the framework of theological tradition to a far greater extent than in the first part on

---

1. For general summaries of Barth's doctrine of election, see Geoffrey W. Bromiley, *Introduction to the Theology of Karl Barth* (Grand Rapids: Eerdmans, 1979), 84-98; G. C. Berkouwer, *The Triumph of Grace in the Theology of Karl Barth* (London: The Paternoster Press, 1956), 262-96; Fred Klooster, *The Significance of Barth's Theology* (Grand Rapids: Baker, 1961), esp. 64-73; Graafland, *Van Calvijn Tot Barth*, 508-32; Suzanne McDonald, *Re-Imaging Election: Divine Election as Representing God to Others & Others to God* (Grand Rapids: Eerdmans, 2010), 59-86; Shao Kai Tseng, *Karl Barth's Infralapsarian Theology* (Downers Grove, IL: IVP Academic, 2016); David Gibson, *Reading the Decree: Exegesis, Election and Christology in Calvin and Barth* (London: T & T Clark, 2009); and Williams, *The Election of Grace,* 179-210. In addition to these summaries, I will cite a number of studies in what follows that address recent debates regarding Barth's doctrine of election.

2. Karl Barth, *Church Dogmatics,* vol. II/2: *The Doctrine of God*, ed. G. W. Bromiley and T. F. Torrance (Edinburgh: T & T Clark, 1957).

3. ibid., II/2:13-14.

the doctrine of God. I would have preferred to follow Calvin's doctrine of predestination much more closely, instead of departing from it so radically.... But I could not and cannot do so. As I let the Bible itself speak to me on these matters, as I meditated upon what I seemed to hear, I was driven irresistibly to reconstruction.[4]

In Barth's estimation, Calvin's doctrine of election burdens the Scripture's teaching with the notion of a secret, inscrutable, and non-gracious will of God. The note of God's triumphant grace in Jesus Christ is muted in Calvin's teaching, and placed alongside a contrary note, one which speaks of an unknown God, who opposes those toward whom He chooses not to be gracious.

The Starting Point for a Correct Doctrine of Election

Barth begins his treatment of the doctrine of election by reiterating the key features of the doctrine of God that he developed in the first part of volume 2 of his *Church Dogmatics*. The starting point for a correct doctrine of election, as is true for all the topics in *Church Dogmatics*, must be what we know of God as He reveals Himself in Jesus Christ, the Word become flesh. Any knowledge or speech about God that is not based upon God's free decision to enter into covenant with man in the person of Jesus Christ is an abstraction. God is who He is in Jesus Christ, and there is no other God than the God who determines to be for us in Him. As Barth puts it,

> If we would know what election is, what it is to be elected by God, then we must look away from all others, and excluding all side-glances or secondary thoughts we must look only upon the name of Jesus Christ and upon the actual existence and history of the people whose beginning and end are enclosed in the mystery of His name.[5]

For Barth, all knowledge of the true and living God must be derived from the way God acts in His free decision to elect humanity for communion with Himself in Christ. In this act, and in the history of Jesus Christ that flows from it, we find God Himself to be One who loves in freedom and who is free in His loving. When speaking of election, therefore, we must speak only in a manner

---

4. ibid., II/2:x.

5. ibid., II/2:58-9.

that corresponds to God's own choice to be, and to be known by us, as He is in Jesus Christ.

Consistent with this starting point and orientation to the doctrine of election, Barth insists that election lies at the core of Christian theology, particularly the doctrine of God. The first and primal decision of God is His decision to be One who loves in freedom, and who eternally wills to elect His people in Jesus Christ. God's election is His eternal self-determination to be God in the act of electing His Son or Word. In the eternal act of election, God determines His own being as the Word, full of grace and truth. In this eternal act of self-determination, God chooses to be and to be known only in this way: as the God who eternally wills to covenant with all men in Jesus Christ, and to give Himself wholly to the realization of this purpose through the reconciling work of Christ.

> In so far as God not only is love, but loves, in the act of love which determines His whole being God elects. And in so far as this act of love is an election, it is at the same time and as such the act of His freedom. There can be no subsequent knowledge of God, whether from His revelation or from His work as disclosed in that revelation, which is not as such knowledge of this election. There can be no Christian truth which does not from the very first contain within itself as its basis the fact that from and to all eternity God is the electing God.[6]

Upon the basis of these claims regarding our knowledge of God's act of election, Barth develops his revised view under three broad headings: first, God's election is 'the election of Jesus Christ';[7] second, God's election is the 'election of the community';[8] and third, God's election is 'the election of the individual'.[9]

The Election of Jesus Christ
The most important revision of the traditional doctrine of election occurs in Barth's treatment of the election of Jesus Christ. Contrary to the idea of an 'absolute decree' (*decretum absolutum*) in which God

---

6. ibid., II/2:76-77.

7. ibid., II/2:94ff.

8. ibid., II/2:195ff.

9. ibid., II/2:306ff.

secretly and sovereignly elects to save some and not others, Barth maintains that God's election is an eternal act in Jesus Christ, who is both electing God and elected man. The fatal error of the older doctrine of election is that it posits an unknown God who elects to save some and not others. Jesus Christ is not the beginning and the end of all of God's gracious purposes, but merely a means to an end. But if Jesus Christ is the eternal Word of God, as we read in the prologue of the Gospel of John ('in the beginning was the Word, and the Word was God'), then we may not speak or know anything *extra* about God in the doctrine of election than what we are given to know in Jesus Christ alone.

> Before Him and without Him and beside Him God does not, then, elect or will anything. And He is the election (and on that account the beginning and the decree and the Word) of the free grace of God. For it is God's free grace that in Him He elects to be man and to have dealings with man and to join Himself to man. He, Jesus Christ, is the free grace of God as not content simply to remain identical with the inward and eternal being of God, but operating *ad extra* in the ways and works of God.[10]

While Barth explicitly rejects the idea that God's election in Jesus Christ was 'necessary' for God to be who He is, he emphasizes that God's eternal election is an act whereby God determines to be gracious toward us, and to bear the name of Jesus Christ.[11] By virtue of this eternal act of self-determination, 'God has put Himself under an obligation to man, willing that that should be so which according to Jn. 1:1-2 actually is so. It is grace that it is so, and it is grace God willed it to be so.'[12] As the subject of election, Jesus Christ is not simply the instrument through whom God's purpose of election is realized. Jesus Christ is Himself the God who elects, and His will to do so is also the will of God to be the God who is for us in Him.

Barth bases his understanding of the election of Jesus Christ upon an unusual reading of John 1:1. According to Barth's reading, the language used about the Word who was 'with God in the beginning,'

---

10. ibid., II/2:94-5.

11. In the last section of this chapter, I will return to this issue, and address the controversy regarding the implications of this claim among interpreters of Barth.

12. CD II/2:101.

and 'who was God,' refers to God's eternal self-determination to be for us in Jesus Christ: 'The electing [of Jesus Christ, both as electing God and the elected man] consists in this Word and decree in the beginning.'[13] Traditionally, Christian theologians have read John 1:1 as though it taught the self-existence of the eternal Son of God, who is to be distinguished from the Father and the Son, and through whom all things were made. In the language of theology, this eternal Word is the *Logos asarkos* (the Word apart from His incarnation), the eternal Word who was and always is, prior to and independent of His incarnation as the *Logos ensarkos* (the Word become flesh, the incarnate Word). Interestingly, Barth recognizes that his use of this passage is unusual, but he argues that it provides the proper biblical context within which to present a revised doctrine of election. Contrary to the traditional view, which assumes the pre-existence of the eternal Word 'before' His self-determination to be electing God, Barth insists that God determines 'to be' and 'to be known' in no other act than as the electing God in Jesus Christ. For Barth, the interpretation of Romans 9 and other biblical passages that speak of God's purpose of election must be hermeneutically governed by what he understands to be the teaching of John 1:1.

But Jesus Christ is more than the subject of election – the God who freely and lovingly wills to elect man in Him. For Barth, Jesus Christ is also, and at the same time, the object of God's election of man. '[B]efore all created reality, before all being and becoming in time, before time itself, in the pre-temporal eternity of God, the eternal divine decision as such has as its object and content the existence of this one created being, the man Jesus of Nazareth, and the work of this man in His life and death, His humiliation and exaltation, His obedience and merit.'[14] The solution to the problem posed by the traditional doctrine of election, which distinguishes between God's election of some to salvation and His reprobation of others to condemnation, lies in the proper recognition that God's election is the election of the one man, Jesus Christ, and in Him the election of all. Once this is established, the truth embedded in the traditional 'supralapsarian' view of the order

13. ibid., II/2:100.

14. ibid., II/2:116.

of God's decrees becomes evident. God's election of Jesus Christ is indeed the first, primal act of God from which all that God does in time follows. The true 'object of election' (*obiectum praedestinationis*) must not be viewed either as a particular number of already created and already fallen human beings (the infralapsarian view) or as a particular number of not yet created and not yet fallen human beings (the supralapsarian view). Because the true object of election is the man Jesus Christ (and all human beings in Him), we may affirm the truth of supralapsarianism, namely, that the first act of God's self-determination is His gracious election or free decision to love all men in the one man whom He has elected, Jesus Christ.[15]

At this point in his exposition of the doctrine of election, Barth offers a remarkably novel interpretation of the legitimate sense in which we may speak of God's purpose of election and reprobation. In the older 'double predestination' view of Augustine and Calvin, God's purpose of election is twofold: first, to show mercy to those individuals whom He wills to save (election); and second, to show justice to those individuals whom He wills to pass by (preterition) and condemn for their sins. Barth believes that this understanding of double predestination removes any sure footing for an assurance of God's grace and favor toward us in Jesus Christ. Who is able to fathom the depths of God's 'secret will' so as to determine whether or not God's Word in Christ is a word in which God's grace triumphs? However, if the object of election is the man Jesus Christ, who is both the God who elects and the man whom He elects, then we have assurance that God's grace triumphs in God's act of election.

In Barth's view, God's election is double in two closely related, albeit different, senses. The first of these senses, we have already considered: on the one hand, the God who elects, or the active subject

---

15. Cf. Tseng, *Karl Barth's Infralapsarian Theology,* who offers an extensive case for the thesis that Barth's doctrine of election is more in line with the historic infralapsarians in the Reformed tradition rather than the supralapsarians. Tseng makes this claim on the basis of Barth's view that election in Christ contemplates the salvation of fallen human beings. In my estimation, Hunsinger, in the Foreword to Tseng's study, offers a more nuanced view: 'I think it would be better to agree with Barth that in the end he was a "purified supralapsarian," while still accepting the thesis, as advanced by Professor Tseng, that he has strong "infralapsarian" tendencies' (ibid., 9-10).

in election, is Jesus Christ Himself; and on the other hand, the man whom God elects, or the object of election, is Jesus Christ. Jesus Christ is both electing God and elected man. The second of the senses in which election is double, however, now needs to be explored further.

According to Barth, we must recognize that election means gracious election for the man Jesus Christ and reprobation for God. Election has a double consequence, grace and judgment, Yes and No, and this double consequence is assumed by God Himself in Jesus Christ. At one and the same time, Jesus Christ is the elected man and the reprobated God. By His free decision of election, God has chosen to bear the rejection, punishment, and condemnation that all human beings deserve. And at the same time, God has chosen to say 'Yes' to Jesus Christ as the man of His choosing, and in Him to say 'Yes' to all men. The following statement of Barth is representative of his view:

> If the teachers of predestination were right when they spoke always of a duality, of election and reprobation, of predestination to salvation or perdition, to life or death, then we may say already that in election of Jesus Christ which is the eternal will of God, God has ascribed to man the former, election, salvation and life; and to Himself He has ascribed the latter, reprobation, perdition and death.[16]

In Barth's understanding of election and reprobation, Jesus Christ, electing God and elected man, is the object of both God's grace and judgment. Furthermore, the 'Yes' of election and the 'No' of reprobation are not symmetrical or equally ultimate. Even the 'No' of reprobation, God's election to suffer that condemnation or judgment otherwise due man, serves the purpose of the 'Yes' of God's decision to covenant with man in Jesus Christ. For this reason, Barth observes that 'the will of God in election is indeed double ... but not dual.'[17] When we understand election as the act whereby God elects Himself to be the man, Jesus Christ, it is no longer possible to view election as equally directed toward the salvation of some human beings and the damnation of others. Such a view fails to recognize that God suffers the damnation that human beings deserve in order that they might be the recipients of His love and favor. It fails to confirm how

16. CD II/2:163.
17. ibid., II/2:171.

the doctrine of election is the best and most blessed Word that God
has spoken or speaks.

The Election of the Community: Israel
and the Church (Romans 9)

In addition to this primary emphasis upon Jesus Christ as electing
God and as elected/reprobated man, Barth develops his doctrine of
election under two further headings. The first of these is 'the election
of the community' in Jesus Christ.

By the election of the community, Barth refers to the way in which
God's act of election in Jesus Christ is 'simultaneously' the election
of one community, the people of God, through whose existence the
grace of God in Christ is attested to the whole world.[18] Contrary to
the tendency of the traditional doctrine of election, which quickly
speaks of God's election of specific individuals to salvation, Barth
insists that election does not 'immediately envisage the election of the
individual believer'.[19] Before we speak of the particular persons who
are elected in Christ, we must speak of the community of believers
whose existence is bound up with the person and work of Christ and
through whom all human beings are summoned to faith in Him. In
Barth's understanding, this community whom God elects in Jesus
Christ is comprised of two peoples, Israel and the church. Each of
these peoples is called to a 'peculiar service' in the realization of
God's electing purpose in Christ.[20] On the one hand, Israel is the
people whose unbelief and resistance to God's gracious election
testify to His judgment upon human sinfulness, which is borne by
Jesus Christ in His suffering and death upon the cross. And on the
other hand, the church is the people of God whose salvation testifies to
God's grace, and the triumph of His grace in the resurrection of Jesus
Christ from the dead. Through Israel's unbelief, the passing form of
the people of God is attested; and through the church's calling and
salvation, the coming form of the people of God is attested. However,
these two sides of the elect community of God are not ultimate, but

---

18. ibid., II/2:195.
19. ibid.
20. ibid., II/2:196.

penultimate. God's electing grace in Christ will ultimately triumph in the gathering of the one community, comprised of Israel and the church, which will include God's putting an end to Israel's unbelief.[21]

In the second part of his exposition of the election of the community, Barth extensively treats Romans 9–11. Consistent with this approach to the interpretation of Paul's argument, especially in Romans 9, Barth accents the respective roles of the two forms of the elect community, Israel and the church. Furthermore, he develops these respective roles in a way that corresponds closely to the Christological basis of his doctrine of election. Unlike the traditional reading of Roman 9, Barth focuses throughout upon the corporate identity of the people of God as it is represented in Israel and the church.

The novelty of Barth's exposition of Romans 9–11 can only be explained in terms of his fundamental revision of the traditional doctrine of election. God's self-determination in Christ to be electing God and elected man undergirds every aspect of Barth's exposition of Paul's argument. Since the history of redemption represents the realization in time of God's gracious election in Christ, the respective roles of Israel and the church in this history correspond to the two sides of the one act of God in election: judgment (reprobation) and blessing (election). And since the respective roles of Israel and the church work in tandem to realize God's ultimate intention to covenant with all human beings in Christ, these roles can never frustrate God's gracious purpose to gather one community.

In his treatment of Romans 9–11, which is set forth in a series of lengthy small-print expositions throughout his consideration of the election of the community, Barth distinguishes four topics: (1) Israel and the Church (Rom. 9:1-5); (2) The Judgment and the Mercy of God (Rom. 9:6-29); (3) The Promise of God Heard and Believed (Rom. 9:30–10:21); and (4) The Passing and the Coming Man (Rom. 11). Because the first two of these topics are most relevant to my summary of Barth's view, I will consider them in some detail. By comparison, my comments on the third and fourth topics will be quite limited, and only provided to illumine what is distinctive to Barth's reading of Romans 9.

---

21. ibid., II/2:259ff.

In Barth's understanding of the opening verses of Romans 9, the sorrow expressed by the apostle Paul testifies to his 'solidarity' with Israel. The unbelief of Paul's kinsmen, the Israelites, is the occasion for his sorrow, but it does not represent an irrevocable separation between Paul and Israel. 'Even in their unbelief they are and remain his "brethren." His faith, the Church's faith in Jesus Christ, unites him with them.'[22] When Paul witnesses the unbelief of his kinsmen, he does not express a sorrow born of despair that they may not be included within the scope of God's purpose of election and so will not be saved. Paul's sorrow flows from his awareness, as an apostle to the Gentiles and a prophet to Israel, that Israel's present unbelief separates her from the church. Such a separation, however, may not be regarded as final, since it is contrary to the ultimate unity that God intends for the community of faith. Paul's anguish, which he expresses poignantly in his willingness to be 'anathema' for Israel's sake, is fueled by his awareness of his calling as an apostle. Since Paul knows that Israel is God's elect people destined for unity with the church, he desires that Israel should come to know her place in God's electing purpose as one form of the community of God. For Barth, Paul is powerfully expressing his unwillingness to give up on Israel's destiny as a form of the one community God has elected to save in Jesus Christ.

The solidarity with Israel that Paul expresses in the opening verses of Romans 9 is further evidenced in the way he speaks of 'those who are kinsmen according to the flesh'. They remain 'Israelites', and as such members of the same elect community of which Paul considers himself a member. As Barth interprets this language, Paul identifies himself as 'a believer and therefore a true Israelite – he is still united and bound to them, so they for their part, in spite of their unbelief, continue to be for him the elected community of God which has received for its possession no less than everything on which the faith of the Church is based, from which it draws sustenance, which makes it possible, necessary and real.'[23] For this reason, Paul's enumeration of the various blessings that accompanied Israel's election to be the

---

22. ibid., II/2:202.
23. ibid., II/2:203.

first form of the community of God illustrates how Israel, despite its temporary unbelief, continues to possess everything given by God to the church. Even though the church has now come to receive what was first given to Israel, we must not regard this as though Israel's election has changed. What Israel has temporarily lost as the community of God's people is now continued in the new form of God's people, the church. However, the role of the church as the new form of the community of God does not entail the end of Israel's election. Rather, the church is called to 'confess the One who ... does not even, in view of this form of [Israel's] death, cease to be the living Head of the whole community and therefore the hope even of this dead.'[24]

Although this statement of the problem may seem a little vague, what Barth means by speaking of Israel and the church as the two forms of the community of God becomes clearer in his exposition of subsequent verses in Romans 9. For Barth, Israel and the church together typify what God wills in the election of Jesus Christ. Barth entitles the second part of his treatment of the election of the community, 'The Judgement and the Mercy of God,' in order to recall his Christocentric definition of election. The election of the community serves typologically to call attention to the two parts of election in Christ: the judgment Christ suffers, as well as the mercy He grants, for the sake of all who are elect in Him. The community of God 'is elected to serve the presentation (the self-presentation) of Jesus Christ and the act of God which took place in Him.'[25] In this way, the election of the community points to the one man, Jesus Christ, in whom God has elected Himself for judgment and mercy.

In the introduction to his treatment of the community of God, Barth provides a remarkable description of what this means for Israel and the church respectively. The peculiar service for which Israel is determined 'within the whole of the elected community is to reflect the judgment from which God has rescued man and which He wills to endure Himself in the person of Jesus of Nazareth.'[26] The peculiar service for which the church 'as the perfect form of the one elected

---

24. ibid., II/2:205.
25. ibid.
26. ibid., II/2:206.

community is determined, whether Israel obeys its election or not, consists always in the fact that it is the reflection of the mercy in which God turns His glory to man.'[27] The Christological basis for these distinctive services is even more clearly manifest in the parallel Barth draws between them and Christ's work of reconciliation: 'The Church form of the community stands in the same relation to its Israelite form as the resurrection of Jesus to His crucifixion, as God's mercy to God's judgment.'[28] In the course of God's dealings with Israel and the church, Christ's election to be both reprobate and elect man is represented in the forms of Israel's judgment for her unbelief and the church's blessing for her believing response to the gospel promise. Furthermore, just as the two sides of election in Christ, judgment and mercy, are not equally ultimate or symmetrical, so it is in the case of Israel and the church. God's gracious election is not 'Yes' and 'No' in equal measure; God's grace, His free decision to elect man in Christ, ultimately triumphs in the history of Israel and the church. In the final destiny of the elect community, both Israel and the church will be united in the one community of God and the truth of God's universal purpose of election will be realized.

Barth's overall interpretation of Paul's argument in Romans 9:6-29 is governed by this understanding of the respective roles of Israel and the church in the history of redemption. Rather than interpreting Paul's distinctions between Isaac and Ishmael, and between Jacob and Esau, as though they represented God's purpose of election in the salvation of some and the non-salvation of others, Barth interprets these distinctions in terms of the peculiar witness of the two forms of the community of God. When Paul responds to the unbelief of many of his fellow Israelites by noting that 'not all who descended from Israel belong to Israel' (Rom. 9:6), he means to declare that not 'all bearers of the name Israel, were appointed to become members of the Church. They were certainly appointed members of the one elected community of God.... But they were not appointed members of the Church hidden in Israel and revealed in Jesus Christ.'[29] The unbelief

---

27. ibid., II/2:210.
28. ibid., II/2:211.
29. ibid., II/2:214.

of Paul's Jewish contemporaries witnesses to the 'order' of God's election. Israel's unbelief, far from removing her from the reach of God's election, reminds us of Israel's unique service as the first and provisional form of the community of God. There remains 'no doubt that as such Abraham's seed is the elected people of God, determined in accordance with its election *to be the mirror of the divine judgment, which is, for its part, the veil of the divine mercy.* This is God's order in Israel just because Israel is the elected people.'[30]

In the distinction between Isaac and Ishmael, we have an illustration of the two sides of God's election of the community. Both Isaac and Ishmael are members of the community of Israel, but in different ways: Isaac testifies to Israel's election, and Ishmael testifies to Israel's rejection. The people of Israel are in this respect equally an 'elected' and 'rejected' people. But Isaac serves to prefigure the new form of the people of God, the church, while Ishmael serves to typify the old form of God's people in its provisional existence. Even more importantly, Isaac serves peculiarly as a 'prefiguration' of the 'Son of God and Man, the proclamation of the divine mercy, the children of Abraham in the sense of v. 7b, the bearers of the spiritual name of his seed.'[31] The election of Isaac, in distinction from the rejection of Israel, repeats and establishes the election of Abraham and the 'pre-existent church' that is built up in him. According to Barth, Isaac's election serves indirectly to witness to the election of all Israel. When Paul distinguishes between Isaac and Ishmael, therefore, he does so to show that the Word of God has not proven false but is established in and through the 'unbelieving Synagogue' of Israel.

In Barth's view, the same point is made by Paul in his appeal to the typological significance of God's choice of Jacob and not Esau. But in this instance, the insight of Paul into the significance of Israel's election in distinction from that of the church is even more 'acute'. Here too the distinction is not between two individuals, one whom God elects to save and another whom He elects not to save, but between two peoples, Israel and the Church. Though there is a real distinction between these two peoples that finds its ground in

30. ibid.
31. ibid., II/2:215.

God's election of the one and not the other, this is not a distinction that involves salvation and damnation. It is a distinction that serves God's election of Israel and the Church to peculiar vocations within the history of redemption.[32] Though God elects Jacob and Esau to different vocations within His purpose of election, He does not do so in order to exclude Esau finally from God's blessing or care.

> We must not lose sight of the fact that it is in this race that by God's free disposing the Church is founded and built up by the operation of this separation which repeatedly means exclusion. The very fact that the κατ' ἐκλογὴν πρόθεσις is continued in this race means that its honour and hope continuingly benefit all its members. Even its rejected members (just because of the separation which excludes them) are not forsaken, but after, as before, share in the special care and guidance of the electing God.[33]

For Barth, the distinction between Jacob and Esau is provisional and will finally serve the purpose of God to confirm His name as the One who shows mercy to whom He will.[34]

Though I will not provide an extensive summary of Barth's remaining treatment of Romans 9–11, he does so under the headings, 'the promise of God heard and believed' (Rom. 10) and 'the passing and the coming man' (Rom. 11). In his exposition of these topics, Barth continues to develop his Christological understanding of election in terms of the respective vocations of Israel and the church. Because the vocations of Israel and the church, as the two forms of the community of God, mirror the two sides of election, judgment and mercy, they finally serve to show forth the election and rejection of all in Christ. The twofold determination of election requires that the history of Jesus Christ be mirrored in the history of Israel and the church. When Paul describes the gathering of the believing church in Romans 10, he is describing the vocation of the church in its confirmation of God's electing grace in Christ. And when Paul describes the re-engrafting of Israel in Romans 11, he demonstrates that Israel's vocation, though it involves her provisional rejection in service to the gathering of the

---

32. ibid., II/2:217.
33. ibid.
34. ibid.

believing church, will not frustrate God's name in showing mercy to the fullness of the community of God inclusive of Israel and the church. The 'specific service' that Israel serves in the purpose of God is 'the praise of the mercy of God in the passing, the death, the setting aside of the old man, of the man who resists his election and therefore God.'[35] The conclusion of Paul's treatment of Israel in Romans 11 makes clear 'that the man [represented by Israel's unbelief and rejection] who resists God is in process of passing, that he must pass in order to receive incorruptible life in peace with God, and that for his salvation he will not be spared this passing – in and with the passing to which God has subjected Himself in His Son.'[36]

The Election of the Individual

In the last major section of Barth's treatment of the doctrine of election, the election of the individual, he addresses election in relation to the salvation of individual human beings. While Barth criticizes the tendency of traditional treatments of election to make this the primary topic of interest, he acknowledges that it has a legitimate place, provided it is treated in the broader framework of God's election of Jesus Christ and all human beings in Him. When viewed from the vantage point of his revised doctrine of election, Barth argues that it is the church's responsibility to testify to the objective election of all in Christ. In the proclamation of the gospel, the church is obliged to declare to all that they are elect in Christ, and that human rejection of fellowship with God has been rejected in the reprobation that God has assumed on their behalf.

---

35. ibid., II/2:260. Because Barth views the vocation of Israel to be a paradigm of divine judgment, it is not surprising that interpreters have raised the question whether this does not imply the presence, at least latently, of an anti-Semitic note in his view. For a treatment of this question, see M. F. Sulzbach, 'Karl Barth and the Jews,' *Religion in Life* 21. No. 4 (1952), 585-93; D. E. Demson, 'Israel as the Paradigm of Divine Judgment: An Examination of a Theme in the Theology of Karl Barth,' *JES* 26 (1981): 611-27; and David Gibson, *Reading the Decree,* 94-6. Gibson offers a helpful comment, speaking of both Calvin and Barth's reading of Romans 9–11: 'To charge both interpreters with forms of anti-Semitism here would be both a damning and an ironic verdict, given that both see clearly (in different ways) that the point of Paul's argument is actually to circumvent a form of Christian anti-semitism in his strong warnings against the boasting of Gentile Christians' (96).

36. CD II/2:260.

According to Barth, it is appropriate to speak of the election of the individual inasmuch as the election of Christ includes the election of the individual in Him. The problem with the traditional doctrine of election, however, is that it failed to see how the election of Christ precedes and is the basis for the election of all human beings. Contrary to the traditional doctrine, which spoke of the election of some persons and the reprobation of others, we must say that the election of Christ always included the 'election of the many (from whom none is excluded).'[37] Consistent with his understanding of Jesus Christ as electing God and elected man, as well as his insistence that in Jesus Christ God has assumed the reprobation that all deserve, Barth is very clear that the election of God is universal. No human being is to be viewed in any other way than in terms of their identity by virtue of their election in Jesus Christ. Christology, as in all aspects of Christian doctrine, must determine anthropology or the doctrine of humanity. Although Barth affirms the election of all in the election of Jesus Christ, he does acknowledge that not all persons live in a way that accords with their election. Some persons live as those who do not yet know of their election. Others no longer live as they once did when they acknowledged their election. Still others choose to live only in part or not at all as though they were elect in Christ. Barth speaks of these three categories of persons as the 'not yet', the 'no longer', and the only 'in part or never'.[38] Nonetheless, the church is called to witness to every person that 'he belongs eternally to Jesus Christ and therefore is not rejected, but elected by God in Jesus Christ; that the rejection which he deserves on account of his perverse choice, is borne and cancelled by Jesus Christ; and that he is appointed to eternal life with God on the basis of the righteous, divine decision.'[39]

At this point, one of the most striking and controversial aspects of Barth's doctrine of election emerges. Consistent with the main tenets of his revised doctrine of election, Barth maintains that God has rejected human unbelief and opposition to God in His act of election in Christ.

---

37. ibid., II/2:195. Cf. CD II/2:306.

38. ibid., II/2:321.

39. ibid., II/2:306.

The witness of the community of God to every individual man consists in this: that this choice of the godless man is void; that he belongs eternally to Jesus Christ and therefore is not rejected, but elected by God in Jesus Christ; that the rejection which he deserves on account of his perverse choice is borne and cancelled by Jesus Christ; and that he is appointed to eternal life with God on the basis of the righteous, divine decision.[40]

In the final analysis, failure on the part of some to acknowledge the objective truth of their election in Christ is a kind of 'impossible possibility' that attempts to do what is 'objectively impossible':

> By permitting the life of a rejected man to be the life of His own Son, God has made such a life objectively impossible for all others. The life of the uncalled, the godless, is a grasping back at this objective impossibility, an attempt to expose oneself again to the threat which has already been executed and consequently removed.[41]

The implications of Barth's position at this point seem clear: all human beings are elected to salvation in Jesus Christ, and therefore any attempt to deny this truth is ruled out altogether. For this reason, interpreters of Barth's doctrine of election have frequently raised the question whether or not he teaches a doctrine of 'universal salvation' (*apokatastasis pantōn*).[42] Undoubtedly, Barth teaches a doctrine of universal election and the reconciliation of all human beings in and through the work of Christ. He also declares human unbelief and rejection of God to have become 'void' or impossible by virtue of the truth of what God has determined for man in the election of Jesus Christ.[43] However, since Barth expressly disavows actual universalism, I will reserve further comment on this question to my critical assessment of his position.

---

40. ibid.

41. ibid., II/2:346.

42. For general treatments of the subject of universalism in Barth's doctrine of election, see Williams, *The Election of Grace*, 179-210; Berkouwer, *The Triumph of Grace*, 262-96; Klooster, *The Significance of Barth's Theology*, esp. 64-73; and McDonald, *Re-Imaging Election*, 59-86. Williams well summarizes the difficulty of interpreting Barth's position: 'after we think we have been soaked for several hundred pages in the claim that all humans are elect willy-nilly, Barth tells us this: "As he [man] measures himself against God he necessarily judges himself. Unless he accepts this question – however it is answered – he obviously cannot be elect" [CD II/2:511]' (182).

43. CD II/2:346.

A Critical Assessment of Barth's Doctrine of Election

Barth's revision of the traditional Augustinian/Calvinistic doctrine of election represents one of the most provocative chapters in the history of Christian theology. As Barth acknowledges in the preface to the volume in his *Church Dogmatics* that treats the doctrine of election, his revision of the doctrine of election does involve a 'radical departure' from the Augustinian/Calvinist view. Due to the breadth and depth of Barth's response to more traditional formulations of the doctrine, it is not surprising that assessments of his achievement vary among interpreters of his theology. In my critical assessment, I will especially focus upon three problematic features of Barth's revisionist view, each of which has been a subject of controversy among interpreters of Barth's doctrine of election: (1) the relation between the Trinity and the doctrine of election; (2) the question whether Barth's view is a form of universalism; and (3) Barth's exegesis of Romans 9–11 and the election of the individual.

Does the Election of God Presuppose the Trinity or Constitute God's Being Triune?

Perhaps the most important question that has emerged in recent assessments of Barth's doctrine of election has to do with the implications of Barth's claim that God's 'being' is constituted by His 'act' of electing to be the God who is for us in Jesus Christ. Does Barth's 'actualistic' doctrine of God's being, which argues that the history of Jesus Christ is the unfolding of God's self-determination to be this God, the God who is for us in the incarnation of the Logos, amount to a denial of any distinction between the immanent or ontological Trinity and the economic Trinity? Or does Barth stop short of identifying who God eternally and necessarily is in Himself as triune with who God freely wills to be in the economy of redemption? As one participant in the discussion about this question among students of Barth puts it: 'Is the Trinity [for Barth] complete in itself from all eternity and apart from God's determination to become incarnate in Jesus Christ, or is it constituted by the eternal decision of election?'[44]

---

44. Michael T. Dempsey, ed., *Trinity and Election in Contemporary Theology* (Grand Rapids: Eerdmans, 2011), 'Introduction,' 1. The essays in this volume, which were

The first beginnings of the debate about this question can be dated to some comments of Bruce McCormack at the close of his much-acclaimed study of Barth's theology, *Karl Barth's Critically Realistic Dialectical Theology*.[45] In these comments, McCormack argued that Barth's development of the doctrine of election led him to ground the triune being of God in His eternal will to be the God who is for us in Jesus Christ. The eternal decision of God to elect Jesus Christ, and in Him to elect all human beings, is a decision that constitutes God's being in His self-revelation as Father, Son, and Holy Spirit. In McCormack's words, Barth's doctrine of the election of God led him to the radical conclusion that 'the being of God is itself established in the act of revelation'.[46] Subsequent to the publication of his influential study of Barth's theology, McCormack authored a provocative article for *The Cambridge Companion to Karl Barth*.[47] In this article, McCormack maintained that Barth's doctrine of election represented a far more radical break with the traditional Reformed view than was previously acknowledged. According to McCormack,

---

written by some of the principal interpreters of Barth's view of the relation between Trinity and election, provide an excellent introduction to this debate and the extensive literature on the subject.

45. Bruce L. McCormack, *Karl Barth's Critically Realistic Dialectical Theology: Its Genesis and Development 1909-1936* (Oxford: Oxford University Press, 1995).

46. ibid., 460-1.

47. Bruce McCormack, 'Grace and Being: The Role of God's Gracious Election in Karl Barth's Theological Ontology,' in *The Cambridge Companion to Karl Barth,* ed. John Webster (Cambridge: Cambridge University Press, 2000), 92-110. A slightly revised version of this essay, which I will cite in what follows, is reprinted in Bruce McCormack, *Orthodox and Modern: Studies in the Theology of Karl Barth* (Grand Rapids: Baker Academic, 2008), 183-200. Among interpreters of Barth who are sympathetic to McCormack's position, see Matthias Gockel, *Barth and Schleiermacher on the Doctrine of Election: A Systematic-Theological Comparison* (Oxford: Oxford University Press, 2006), 164-97; Kevin W. Hector, 'God's Triunity and Self-Determination: A Conversation with Karl Barth, Bruce McCormack, and Paul Molnar,' in *TECT,* 29-46; Aaron T. Smith, 'God's Self-Specification: His Being is His Electing,' in *TECT,* 201-25; Paul Helm, 'Karl Barth and the Visibility of God,' in *Engaging with Barth: Contemporary Evangelical Critiques,* ed. David Gibson and Daniel Strange (Nottingham: Apollos, 2008), 273-99; and idem, 'John Calvin and the Hiddenness of God,' in *Engaging the Doctrine of God: Contemporary Protestant Perspectives,* ed. Bruce L. McCormack (Grand Rapids: Baker Academic, 2008), 67-82. Though Helm assumes McCormack's interpretation of Barth's view, he offers an unsympathetic assessment of the negative implications of this interpretation for Barth's position.

Barth's view is that 'election is the event in God's life in which he assigns to himself the being he will have for all eternity. It is an act of Self-determination by means of which God chooses in Jesus Christ love and mercy for the human race and judgment and reprobation for himself.'[48] By means of God's free decision to be the God who is for us in Christ, He chooses from eternity to be no other being than 'a being for this event'.[49] Barth's view involves, accordingly, a clean break with an 'essentialist ontology', including Calvin's, which knows a mode of God's being that is independent of, and prior to (the *Logos asarkos*, the Word apart from or before the incarnation), His being as the Redeemer in Christ (the *Logos ensarkos* or *incarnatus*, the Word incarnate or to be incarnate). Barth rejected the idea that the eternal Logos has any other mode of existence than that mode of existence that God determines in His election of Jesus Christ as the *Logos ensarkos*.

In his argument for this interpretation of Barth's doctrine of election, McCormack notes that Barth does affirm the 'essence' or 'being' of God, but that, in keeping with his actualistic ontology, this essence is 'given in the act of electing and is, in fact, constituted by that eternal act.' McCormack writes:

> It [God's essence or being] is not an independent 'something' that stands in back of all God's acts and relations. God's being, for Barth, is a being-in-act—first as a being-in-act in eternity and then, corresponding to that, as a being-in-act in time. Philosophically expressed, Barth's ontology is thus 'actualistic' (i.e., being is actualized in the decision for activity in time). It would be even more accurate, however, to express Barth's ontology *theologically* as a 'covenant ontology,' since it is not in 'relationality' in general that God's being is constituted but in a most concrete, particular relation.[50]

According to McCormack, the benefits of this ontology for Barth's doctrine of election cannot be overstated. Unlike the traditional doctrine, which speaks of a God who has another mode of being than God in the flesh, revealed in Jesus Christ, Barth's doctrine knows no

48. 'Grace and Being,' 189.
49. ibid.
50. ibid., 190.

other God than the One who has turned toward man in love and grace. Barth's doctrine allows us to say that 'God in himself *is* God "for us".'[51] Rather than an 'unknown' and 'unknowable' God, Barth's God is One whose 'essence is not hidden to human perception'. Barth's radical revision of the doctrine of election (and the doctrine of God) grants us full assurance and confidence that God is always and only the One who is for us in Jesus Christ. It resolves the ever-present problem in the traditional Augustinian/Calvinistic doctrine, namely, that God's 'absolute decree' of election remains secret and ultimately inscrutable. By contrast, Barth's doctrine provides a basis for trusting 'that the love and mercy towards the whole human race demonstrated in Jesus' subjection of himself to death on a cross is "essential" to God and that election is therefore universal in scope.'[52]

In the course of his argument for this interpretation of Barth's doctrine of election, McCormack acknowledges some inconsistency in Barth's writings. In his estimation, Barth offers a more radical actualistic ontology in volume II/2 of his *Church Dogmatics*, which treats the doctrine of election, than in volume II/1, which treats the doctrine of God proper. Furthermore, even in his later formulations, Barth continues to make statements about God's Trinitarian being that are inconsistent with the radical actualism that belongs to his formulation of the doctrine of the Trinity.[53] According to McCormack, Barth's inconsistent view of the relation between God's Trinitarian being and His eternal will in the election of Jesus Christ requires that we make a 'critical correction' in Barth's formulations, 'the goal of which will be to remove what I view as an inconsistency in Barth's thought.'[54] He suggests we reject those places in Barth's theology where he fails to think consistently about what it means to deny the eternal Logos has a mode of existence other than that of the incarnate Word:

---

51. ibid.

52. ibid.

53. ibid., 193. McCormack adduces the following statement from a late volume of Barth's *Church Dogmatics* as an illustration of this inconsistency: 'The second "person" of the Godhead in Himself and as such is not God the Reconciler. In Himself and as such He is not revealed to us. In Himself and as such He is not *Deus pro nobis,* either ontologically or epistemologically' (IV/1:52).

54. ibid.

The denial of the existence of a *Logos asarkos* in any other sense than the concrete one of a being of the Logos as *incarnandus*, the affirmation that Jesus Christ is the Second Person of the Trinity and the concomitant rejection of free-floating talk of the 'eternal Son' as a mythological abstraction—these commitments require that we see the triunity of God, logically, as a function of divine election. Expressed more exactly, the eternal act of Self-determination in which God is God 'a second time in a very different way' and a third time as well is *given in* the eternal act in which God elects himself for the human race. The *decision* for the covenant of grace is the ground of God's triunity and therefore of the eternal generation of the Son and the eternal procession of the Holy Spirit from Father and Son.[55]

According to McCormack, God's triunity in His being and actions depends upon His free and eternal decision to elect Jesus Christ to be the Word become flesh. On this reading of Barth, the 'immanent' Trinity (who God is as triune before and apart from His electing to save in Jesus Christ) is wholly identified with the 'economic' Trinity (who God is as triune by virtue of His free act of electing to save in Jesus Christ).[56]

Not surprisingly, McCormack's radical correction of Barth's alleged consistency on the question of the relation between the Trinity and the election of Jesus Christ has provoked considerable discussion. The most extensive criticism of McCormack's proposal has come from two pre-eminent students of Barth's theology, Paul D. Molnar and George Hunsinger.[57]

---

55. ibid., 193.

56. In response to the charge that his interpretation of Barth's view is 'revisionist', McCormack appeals to a similar reading of Barth among earlier, German authors. Among the authors he cites are: Eberhard Jüngel, *God's Being is in Becoming: The Trinitarian Being of God in the Theology of Karl Barth,* trans. John Webster (Edinburgh: T & T Clark, 2001); Wilfried Härle, *Sein und Genade: die Ontologie in Karl Barths Kirchlicher Dogmatik* (Berlin/New York: Walter de Gruyter, 1975); and Hans Theodor Goebel, 'Trinitätslehre und Erwählungslehre bei Karl Barth,' in *Wahrheit und Versöhnung: Theologische und Philosophische Beiträge zur Gotteslehre,* ed. Dietrich Korsch and Hartmut Ruddie (Gütersloh: Gütersloher Verlagshaus Gerd Mohn, 1989), 147-66.

57. For Molnar and Hunsinger's criticisms of McCormack's interpretation of Barth, see Paul D. Molnar, *Divine Freedom and the Doctrine of the Immanent Trinity: In Dialogue with Karl Barth and Contemporary Theology* (London: T & T Clark, 2002); 61-64; idem, *Faith, Freedom and the Spirit: The Economic Trinity in Barth, Torrance*

Molnar's initial criticism of McCormack's proposal can be found in his comprehensive study on the freedom of God and the immanent Trinity (God's eternal unity of being and trinity of Persons), *Divine Freedom and the Doctrine of the Immanent Trinity*. According to Molnar, if McCormack's claim that Barth identifies the immanent Trinity with the economic Trinity is correct, serious consequences follow for the doctrine of God's freedom and the sheer graciousness of God's election of Jesus Christ and all human beings in Him. On McCormack's interpretation of Barth, God becomes dependent upon the world, and His freedom in electing Jesus Christ to be for us is not a genuine freedom. If God's triunity depends upon a prior act of His will to elect Jesus Christ, then the world's existence and the salvation of human beings through the work of Christ become necessary prerequisites to God's being the Father, the Son, and the Holy Spirit. In Molnar's opinion,

> we turn ... His being God for us, into a necessary attribute. God's being is then essentially limited and conditioned as a being revealed, i.e., as a relation of God to man. Man is thus thought of as indispensable to God. But this destroys God's freedom in the act of revelation and reconciliation, i.e., it destroys the gracious character of this act.[58]

For his part, Hunsinger shares Molnar's concerns with McCormack's interpretation of Barth's doctrine of election. In Hunsinger's view, Barth understands God's election of Jesus Christ to be an eternal act of *self-determination* on the part of the triune God, not an eternal act of *self-origination*. Unless the Father, Son, and Holy Spirit necessarily exist prior to this eternal act of self-determination, we would have to conclude that the actual subject of this act is the Father alone, and that the Son's generation and the Spirit's procession find their

---

and Contemporary Theology (Downers Grove, IL: IVP Academic, 2015); idem, 'Can the Electing God Be God Without Us? Some Implications of Bruce McCormack's Understanding of Barth's Doctrine of Election for the Doctrine of the Trinity,' in *TETC*, 63-90; George Hunsinger, *Reading Barth with Charity: A Hermeneutical Proposal* (Grand Rapids: Baker Academic, 2015); and idem, 'Election and the Trinity: Twenty-Five Theses on the Theology of Karl Barth,' in *TECT, 91-114*. See also Edwin Chr. Van Driel, 'Karl Barth on the Eternal Existence of Jesus Christ,' *SJT* 60, no. 1 (2007): 45-61; and Bruce C. McCormack, 'Seek God Where He May Be Found: A Response to Edwin Chr. Van Driel', *SJT* 60, no. 1 (2007): 62-79.

58. Molnar, *Divine Freedom,* 62.

origin in this act. Like Molnar, Hunsinger believes that McCormack's interpretation of Barth would lead to the conclusion that God's Trinitarian being depends upon the being of the world. If we were to embrace McCormack's account of Barth's doctrine of election, 'Jesus Christ would not be the subject but merely the consenting object of the decision' of election.[59] Contrary to McCormack's interpretation, we must affirm that Barth consistently taught that the election of God was made by the Father, Son, and Holy Spirit, who eternally and necessarily exist in the perfection and fullness of their intra-trinitarian relations and mutual coinherence.[60]

This debate regarding the relation between Trinity and election in Barth's theology raises a number of serious questions regarding Barth's achievement.

The first, and most obvious, question is whether or not Barth's position can be defended upon the basis of the witness of Scripture. Or is Barth's claim that Jesus Christ is the acting Subject of the election of God, an ideologically-driven interpretation of the Scripture's testimony? In my judgment, Barth's claim on this point does not have an adequate scriptural basis, however attractive it may be. Ironically, in the course of arguing for his interpretation of Barth's view, McCormack acknowledges this:

> That Jesus Christ, the God-human in his divine-human unity, should be conceived of as the Subject of election is a claim which finds no *direct* confirmation in the New Testament. Barth defends it through a close exegesis of the prologue to John's Gospel, a passage which identifies the Logos who was 'in the beginning' with God and was in fact God as the One who also 'became flesh' (John 1:14) so that his 'glory' might even be observable to human eyewitnesses.[61]

Though McCormack hastens to add that Barth's claim in this respect is 'unimpeachable', I am unconvinced. Barth's interpretation of the prologue to John's Gospel is a novel one to say the least. The traditional view that John is speaking of the eternal Logos prior to, and in distinction from, His will to become the incarnate Logos

---

59. 'Election and the Trinity: Twenty-Five Theses,' 110.

60. ibid., 107.

61. ibid.

in time, might better be termed 'unimpeachable'. In this view, the eternal Logos is not simply identified with the incarnate Logos, but is represented in His pre-existent fellowship with the Father, as the One through whom all things were made. Though the acting Subject in the Gospel of John is the triune God (the Father who sends the Son, the Son who is sent, the Holy Spirit who proceeds from the Father and the Son), it is not true that Jesus Christ Himself (as *Logos incarnandus*, 'to be incarnate,' or as *Logos incarnatus,* 'incarnate') is that Subject. While John offers ample testimony that the Father, Son, and Holy Spirit concur in willing to grant salvation to those for whom Christ comes to lay down His life, there is no testimony that the Subject of this divine will is Jesus Christ, the incarnate Word.

In addition to the lack of support for the idea that Jesus Christ is the acting Subject in the election of God, Barth's claim that God's election in Jesus Christ embraces all human beings likewise lacks scriptural support. Ironically, the Gospel of John, which purportedly provides the clearest evidence for Barth's claim that Jesus Christ is the Subject of God's election, provides some of the most compelling testimony to the kind of particularism Barth rejects. Throughout this Gospel, both the Father and the Son are represented as the active Subjects of God's election, but they are also represented as electing particular persons.[62] Nowhere is this more evident than in the discourse in John 10 regarding Jesus Christ as the Good Shepherd who lays down His life for His sheep (John 10:1-26). In this discourse, there is a perfect coincidence of will and purpose between the Father and the Son. The Father gives to the Son those for whom He came to lay down His life. Those for whom Christ lays down His life are precisely those for whom He came. Christ 'knows' His sheep, and they respond accordingly to His voice.[63] Thus, Barth's claims that Jesus Christ is the electing Subject in the election of God, and that this election is

---

62. See John 6:35-45; 10:1-26; 15:14-19; 17:6-9.

63. Calvin's comments on this passage are instructive: 'As many as were at last incorporated into the body of Christ were God's sheep, as Christ Himself testifies (John 10:16), though formerly wandering sheep and outside the fold. Meantime, though they did not know it, the shepherd knew them, according to that eternal predestination by which He chose His own before the foundation of the world, as Augustine rightly declares' (*Concerning the Eternal Predestination of God* [1552], trans J. K. S. Reid [London: James Clarke, 1961], 150).

a universal election of all, do not find support in the witness of the Gospel of John.[64] Nor do they find support in the general testimony of the New Testament to the election of some, but not all persons, to salvation in Jesus Christ.[65]

The second question that Barth's doctrine of election raises, especially on McCormack's representation of it, is whether it is possible to carry through consistently the idea that God's being is strictly to be identified with His acts. When Barth's actualism is carried through in the manner that McCormack proposes, the consequences are quite serious as Molnar and Hunsinger have observed. The Trinitarian being of God is constituted by God's eternal will to be the God who is for us in Jesus Christ. By virtue of this primal act of God's will, God becomes triune and the existence of the world with its inhabitants likewise becomes necessary to His being the God He is. God would not be the God He is without this act of self-determination, which, according to McCormack's view, amounts to an act of self-origination. Furthermore, in this view, the eternal generation of the Son and the procession of the Holy Spirit are not, strictly speaking, necessary relations within the self-existent and self-sufficient Godhead. They are dependent upon God's free election to be the God whom He wills Himself to be. Each of these consequences is sufficiently weighty to warrant careful engagement with McCormack's interpretation of Barth's doctrine of election. Since Barth expressly rejects these consequences, the judgment of charity, as Hunsinger argues, ought to give pause before accepting McCormack's proposed correction of Barth's inconsistency in thinking through the implications of his doctrine regarding election.

In addition to these problems McCormack's proposal raises, there are further difficulties with McCormack's claim that Barth's doctrine

---

64. For a similar assessment of Barth's exegesis of these particularistic texts, see Williams, *The Election of Grace,* 179-210; and McDonald, *Re-Imaging Election,* 59-86. Regarding Barth's emphasis upon universal election, Williams correctly notes that '[e]lection, however we interpret its detailed theological content, is always discriminate in Scripture. Israel or the church or particular individuals are elected' (187).

65. For an extensive treatment of the witness of the New Testament to the election of particular persons in Christ, including a treatment of a number of key passages in the Gospel of John, see Chapter 2.

resolves the problems of God's 'hidden-ness' or uncertainty regarding His gracious purpose of election. In my judgment, this claim can be contested in at least two further respects.

In the first respect, McCormack's interpretation of Barth's doctrine of election aggravates rather than alleviates the problem of God's unknowability. Since Helm presents the problem with such clarity, I will start with his summary:

> The pressing question is, *Who* is this God who assigns himself a being (presumably a being of a certain character) that he will have to all eternity? Despite Barth's pains to eliminate every vestige of a hidden God, the idea here returns with a vengeance, at least by McCormack's understanding. Barth is positing a God who assigns himself a being, or a character (but not, apparently, a 'role'!). Barth's God freely gives himself the character of Redeemer together with all that is necessary for having such a character. But who is this God who so acts? It is no good saying, with McCormack, that '"essence" is given in the act of electing, and is, in fact, constituted by that eternal act' .... Actions necessarily have agents. The act of electing is the act of someone; it cannot be an act of no one which, upon its occurrence, constitutes a someone. That is incoherent. So Barth is hoisted by his own petard. The God of Karl Barth, who wills his essence in the act of electing, is by definition a hidden, undetermined God.[66]

Admittedly, Helm makes his point on the assumption that McCormack's interpretation of Barth's doctrine of election accurately reflects Barth's viewpoint. Nonetheless, Helm makes an important point. Even if we do not embrace McCormack's reading of Barth, the claim that Barth has eliminated every vestige of the idea of God's hidden-ness is not warranted. Indeed, we do not know anything about who God is as God (logically) prior to His election to become who He is in Jesus Christ. Nor do we know whether He might will to become otherwise than He has willed thus far. As Helm observes, McCormack's interpretation of Barth's doctrine of election implies that God's freedom allows Him to choose to be other than the God who is for us in Christ. Moreover, even if we assume that Molnar's and Hunsinger's interpretation of Barth's doctrine of election is correct, it remains unclear how Barth has

---

66. 'John Calvin and the Hiddenness of God,' 79.

successfully eliminated any element of hidden-ness respecting God's being 'before' His free determination to be for us in Jesus Christ. Though the triune being of God may be 'reiterated' in the economy of redemption, we are still left with the inescapable fact that God's being is not exhausted in His self-revelation, nor is it ever able to be comprehended fully by any creature. The doctrine of the *Logos asarkos* cannot be expunged from Christian theology altogether, lest we end up with the position that McCormack ascribes to Barth, namely, that God has no other being or existence than what He chooses to be in Jesus Christ.

In a second respect, McCormack's judgment that Barth's view redresses the problem of assurance in the traditional understanding of election seems at best an exaggeration, and at worst a serious misrepresentation of the traditional view. While I will return later to the question whether Barth has genuinely resolved the problem of assurance regarding God's electing favor toward us, at this point I wish to cite a characteristic passage from Calvin regarding this issue:

> If we have been chosen in him [Christ] we shall not find assurance of our election in ourselves; and not even in God the Father, if we conceive him as severed from his Son. Christ, then, is the mirror wherein we must, and without self-deception may, contemplate our own election. For since it is unto his body the Father has destined those to be engrafted whom he has willed from eternity to be his own, that he may hold as sons all whom he acknowledges to be among his members, we have a sufficiently clear and firm testimony that we have been inscribed in the book of life if we are in communion with Christ.[67]

What Calvin affirms in this passage about the assurance believers may have of their gracious election in Christ, is common among proponents of the traditional view of election. Contrary to Barth's frequent complaint that the traditional view leaves us with an unknowable will of God respecting our election, Calvin offers a robust doctrine of assurance in this passage and others. While Calvin acknowledges we do not have an exhaustive or perfect knowledge of God's being and will (we are, after all, creatures), he does insist that

---

67. *Institutes*, 3.24.5.

God has provided a sufficient revelation of Himself in the gospel of Jesus Christ to make assurance possible.

While Barth dismisses Calvin's claim that believers may be assured of their election in Christ as untenable,[68] it is not clear that Barth's doctrine of election provides a compelling resolution of the pastoral problem of assurance. Unless we adopt something of the older idea of a 'fixed and unchanging' decree, there seems no safeguard against positing God's freedom to choose to be otherwise than He is in Jesus Christ. How can we be sure that Barth's insistence that the Subject of election is a universalistic Christ has warrant? The Christ who is represented in the Scriptures seems patently to be a particularistic Christ, One who came to save those whom the Father wills to give to Him and for whom He lays down His life. If this is the case, how can we be confident that Barth's universalistic Christ is the real Christ? Though universalism seems to be a cardinal, non-negotiable feature of Barth's doctrine of election, it is not at all clear that it can be justified by a straightforward appeal to the biblical witness. Indeed, it is difficult to suppress the conviction that Barth's doctrine of universal election functions as a kind of hermeneutical rule trumping the actual testimony of many biblical passages. For Barth's view of election to provide the kind of unimpeachable assurance that he wishes to establish, it must be true. But how can we be sure that Barth's Christ is the true Christ, when the scriptural witness diverges from his view?

The Question Regarding Barth's Universalism

Though the controversy regarding Barth's view of the Trinity and election may seem elusive of a sure resolution, something similar could be said about the debate regarding Barth's universalism. Some interpreters of Barth's doctrine of election argue that it requires a universalistic conclusion, namely, that all human beings who are elect in Christ and reconciled by His work as Redeemer must and therefore will be saved. Despite Barth's explicit denials of this conclusion, these interpreters claim Barth's doctrine of election amounts to a form of universalism. In their view, no other conclusion yields a coherent and consistent understanding of Barth's

---

68. See, e.g., CD II/2:64.

teaching regarding election. Others, respecting Barth's express rejection of universalism, maintain that we must honor Barth's words and conclude that he was not a universalist. One proponent of this opinion has said, '[I]f some of Barth's critics refuse to take this divine freedom seriously with respect (especially) to Barth's doctrine of election and consequently suspect him of implicit universalism then that is their problem rather than his and probably says more about them than it says about him.'[69]

In order to address this question, I want to offer an argument for three theses: (1) Barth's own comments on this question are deliberately evasive, neither expressly denying nor affirming universalism; (2) Barth's doctrine of universal election and reconciliation warrant the conclusion that he does teach a form of universalism that is incoherent with his denial of an actual universalism; and (3) that the incoherence of Barth's denial of universalism by way of an appeal to God's freedom raises further questions regarding Barth's claim to have resolved the problem of the assurance of God's electing grace toward us in Christ.

In the first place, it must be acknowledged that Barth persistently refused to draw the conclusion that all human beings will be saved by virtue of God's universal election. According to Barth, such a conclusion amounts to a kind of formal and abstract 'historical metaphysics':

> We cannot venture the statement that it [actual salvation] must and will finally be coincident with the world of man as such (as in the doctrine of the so-called *apokatastasis*). No such right or necessity can legitimately be deduced. Just as the gracious God does not need to elect or call any single man, so He does not need to elect or call all mankind. His election and calling do not give rise to any historical metaphysics, but only to the necessity of attesting them on the ground that they have taken place in Jesus Christ and His community.[70]

Though this statement of Barth does not explicitly speak of God's freedom, it is evident that his refusal to affirm an actual universalism stems from a worry this would entail a deterministic view of history.

---

69. John Colwell, 'The Contemporaneity of the Divine Decision: Reflections on Barth's Denial of Universalism,' in *Universalism and the Doctrine of Hell,* ed. Nigel Cameron (Carlisle: Paternoster, 1992), 160.

70. CD II/2:417-18.

By a 'historical metaphysics', Barth seems to mean a view of history whose outcome is fixed by virtue of God's decree. Such a view inadequately protects the freedom of God as well as the freedom of human beings to persist in their refusal to embrace their election in Jesus Christ. To affirm the actual salvation of all human beings would, in a manner of speaking, place God's freedom within the straitjacket of a deduction we draw from God's election of all human beings in Christ. An unqualified affirmation of universal salvation would make God the prisoner of His own decree of election and deny to human beings the impossible possibility of rejecting their election in Christ.

Remarkably, Barth makes the same point regarding the alternative deduction, namely, the denial of universalism. Though some interpreters maintain that Barth rejected the idea of the salvation of all human beings, Barth takes an equally evasive attitude toward this conclusion.[71]

> But, again, in grateful recognition of the grace of the divine freedom we cannot venture the opposite statement that there cannot and will not be this final opening up and enlargement of the circle of election and calling.... We would be developing an opposing historical metaphysics if we were to try to attribute any limits—and therefore an end of these frontier-crossings—to the lovingkindness of God.[72]

If we take these denials of Barth at face value, it seems we can draw no other conclusion than that Barth neither affirms nor denies that all human beings will finally be saved. Barth clearly views the affirmation or denial of actual universalism to entail a deterministic conception of history. On the one hand, universalism fails to honor God's freedom not to save those who deny their reconciliation in Christ. It also fails to respect the way human beings may persist in choosing the impossible possibility of unbelief in the face of the church's witness

---

71. See Klooster, *The Significance of Barth's Theology*, 65. Klooster properly cites Berkouwer as an example of an interpreter of Barth who claims that Barth expressly rejected the idea of the salvation of all human beings. Cf. Berkouwer, *The Triumph of Grace*, 116: 'there is no alternative to concluding that Barth's refusal to accept the *apokatastatis* cannot be harmonized with the fundamental structure of his doctrine of election.'

72. CD II/2:418. For a citation of Barth's statements regarding universalism throughout his life, see Klooster, *The Significance of Barth's Theology*, 72-4.

to their election in Jesus Christ. On the other hand, particularism fails to hold open the hope that all human beings will ultimately find their true identity in Jesus Christ. Those who prematurely close the door to the salvation of all human beings in Christ impoverish the church's witness to the universal embrace of God's election of all in Jesus Christ. While Barth refuses to promote universalism, he reserves his most severe criticism for particularism. For Barth, the theologian who espouses particularism shows himself captive to a sort of 'morosely gloomy' skepticism, which places 'limits to the loving-kindness of God which has appeared in Jesus Christ'.[73]

Even though Barth neither affirms nor denies universalism in his express statements, the question regarding the coherence and consistency of his position still cannot be avoided. To use the language of one critic, it is certainly fair to ask whether Barth's position on universalism is 'muddled', though not 'disingenuous'.[74]

In order to see why Barth's view is incoherent, we need to rehearse his claims about the election and reconciliation of all human beings in Jesus Christ. Because Barth's starting point lies in the objective sphere of gospel truth about the identity of all human beings in Christ (Christology must define what it is to be human), he insists that the church's witness must always be to what is true regarding them in Christ. To use the traditional language of theology, the objective election and reconciliation of Christ determines what is true in the subjective sphere. The church does not witness to the mere *possibility* that all human beings are elect and reconciled in Christ. Rather, the church witnesses to the *actuality* that all human beings are elect and reconciled in Christ. Barth's doctrine of election shares the traditional Reformed emphases that God's will of election is unconditional, and that His consequent provision of reconciliation through the atoning work of Christ accomplishes what is necessary to the salvation of all those whom God elects. For Barth, God does not elect some persons whom He foreknows will respond in faith to the gospel call, as in

---

73. Karl Barth, *The Humanity of God,* trans. Thomas Wieser and John Newton Thomas (Richmond, VA: John Knox Press, 1968), 62.

74. Oliver D. Crisp, 'On Barth's Denial of Universalism,' *Themelios* 29, no. 1 (2003): 18-29. In his introduction, Crisp cites several authors to illustrate the diversity of opinion among Barth's interpreters on the subject of universalism.

traditional Arminianism. Nor does God merely make reconciliation available or possible for those who freely choose to become beneficiaries of Christ's work in the way of faith. In the electing and reconciling work of Jesus Christ, all human beings are objectively and actually given an identity as elect and reconciled persons. Because this is the case, Barth makes a number of striking assertions about the content of the church's witness to the world and all its inhabitants. According to Barth, the church must testify that all who endeavor to deny their election in Christ are engaged in a 'pointless' exercise: 'Their desire and their undertaking are pointless in so far as their only end can be to make them rejected. And this is the very goal which the godless cannot reach, because it has already been taken away by the eternally decreed offering of the Son of God to suffer in place of the godless, and cannot any longer be their goal.'[75] No one can deny or undo the truth of their reconciliation in Jesus Christ. Furthermore, Barth does not view the gospel witness as a call to faith as though such faith were a 'condition' for salvation. The gospel witness of the community is that all are elect and reconciled in Christ, and that faith is the human response of acknowledging the priority and actuality of what God has already decided and effected.[76] Accordingly, unbelief in response to this witness is a nullity, which cannot overture the truth in Jesus Christ.

> And because the divine election of grace, because Jesus Christ, is the beginning of all the ways and works of God, man chooses that which is in itself nothing when he returns to this satanic possibility, when he chooses isolation in relation to God. His choice itself and as such is, therefore, null. He chooses as and what he cannot choose. He chooses as if he were able to choose otherwise than in correspondence to his election. He chooses the possibility which God has excluded by his election.[77]

If we take Barth's words seriously at this point, it seems difficult to understand how he can opt for any other conclusion than that all

---

75. CD II/2:318.

76. Hunsinger, *How to Read Karl Barth: The Shape of His Theology* (Oxford: Oxford University Press, 1991), 130-1: 'since, in Barth's understanding, God has already freely included us [in salvation], it falls to us henceforth freely to receive our inclusion as the gift it is proclaimed to be.'

77. CD II/2:316.

are saved in Jesus Christ. Some persons may not know about their salvation in Christ. Others may choose to reject it. Still others may joyfully embrace their election. But no one is able to change the actuality of his or her election and salvation in Jesus Christ.[78]

Nevertheless, Barth leaves the option of particularism on the table, and he does so, as we have seen, by appealing to God's freedom and the freedom of human beings to refuse their election. Barth himself admits this has all the appearance of a theological inconsistency. However, we must live with this inconsistency in order to honor God's freedom in granting salvation and human freedom in the reception of it: 'Even though theological consistency might seem to lead our thoughts and utterances most clearly in this direction (that is, the direction of universalism), we must not arrogate to ourselves that which can be given and received only as a free gift.'[79] One of Barth's defenders puts his position in dramatic terms. 'Barth does not reject universalism because the future of the pagan is uncertain. He rejects universalism because the future of all men is uncertain.'[80]

Assuming these comments properly express the reason for Barth's refusal to affirm universalism opens the door to my third thesis regarding Barth's view, namely, that his position raises further questions regarding the assurance of election. Despite Barth's insistence that his doctrine of election alleviates the problems of an 'unknown' God whose 'secret will' may be other than what He reveals of Himself in Jesus Christ, his rejection of universalism re-introduces an 'unknown' God through the back door. Remarkably, after all the ink Barth spills in arguing that the traditional view of God's decree leaves us with an unknowable God, his ambivalence regarding the issue of universalism allows an unknown God to reappear. If the future, eschatological salvation of all human beings is not secure upon the basis of all Barth says about their election in Jesus Christ, then what remains of his claim that he has solved the problem of God's unknowability in the traditional doctrine of God's

78. Crisp, 'On Barth's Denial of Universalism,' 29.

79. CD IV/3:477.

80. Joseph D. Bettis, 'Is Karl Barth a Universalist?,' in *SJT* 20, no. 4 (1967): 433.

decree? Fred Klooster expresses well the dilemma Barth faces at this juncture:

> Barth's view of election really seems to involve something of an Unknown God. Although all men are elect in Christ, so that what Christ has done has been done for all men, Barth leaves open the question as to what the freedom of God might yet involve. Barth's leaving open the question of a possible universalism, and his refusal to affirm or deny this theory, seems to involve an unknown God. The frontier from election to rejection and vice versa can be repeatedly crossed and criss-crossed. In view of the freedom of God, Barth insists that we must leave open the possibility as to what will eventually happen. But this view of the freedom of God involves an Unknown God and is in conflict with Scripture.[81]

In addition to his reintroduction of the specter of an Unknown God, Barth's refusal to embrace universalism also seems to reflect a view of human freedom that likewise aggravates the problem of assurance. For Barth, just as universalism violates God's freedom by saying that all human beings will certainly be saved, so it violates human freedom by saying that it is impossible for anyone to oppose God's gracious will of election in Jesus Christ. One of the frequent complaints brought against Barth's doctrine of election is that it diminishes the urgency of gospel preaching.[82] The real decision regarding salvation takes place in the objective, not the subjective, sphere. Whether human beings know it or not, they are elect in Christ. God's being-for-us in Christ triumphs over the futility and nullity of human godlessness and unbelief. For this reason, Emil Brunner compares Barth's view of fallen human beings to 'people who seem perishing in a stormy sea. But in reality they are not in a sea where one can drown, but in shallow water, where it is impossible to drown. Only they do not know it.'[83] Perhaps Barth's

---

81. Klooster, *The Significance of Barth's Theology*, 70.

82. Cf. Klooster, *The Significance of Barth's Theology*, 71: 'His [Barth's] view simply calls for informing men who are universally involved in what Christ has done. Hence the urgency of preaching is gone, and the biblical significance of the call to repentance and faith loses its relevance.'

83. Emil Brunner, *Dogmatics*, vol. 1: *The Christian Doctrine of God* (Philadelphia: Westminster Press, 1950), 351. Though Brunner raises a legitimate concern regarding Barth's view, his own universalism might be subjected to the same criticism.

unwillingness to affirm universalism testifies to his sensitivity to this criticism and represents his way of staving off the complaint that the free response of human beings to the witness of the church lacks urgency on his view.

Whatever the precise rationale for Barth's denial of universalism, it is evident that Barth's doctrine of election does not include a work of the Spirit that ensures the election *and salvation* of all human beings. Even though Barth explicitly resists the Arminian view that God's act of election is based upon His foreknowledge of the human decision to believe in Jesus Christ, he seems to vacillate on the question whether the Spirit of God is able to overcome the incorrigible resistance of some human beings in their response to His work of testifying to their election. Because Barth appeals to human freedom as an explanation for this resistance, no less an interpreter of Barth's theology than McCormack speaks of a doctrine of the 'relative autonomy' of human beings in resisting the testimony of the Holy Spirit to their election in Christ.[84] Ironically, Barth's insistence upon the freedom of human beings to resist their election, including the witness of the Spirit with the Word, leaves him in a position that does seem similar to Arminianism. If it is possible for human beings to resist the truth of their election and reconciliation in Christ, it would seem to follow that the specific identity of the elect and the reprobate is ultimately determined by the free, indeterminate choice of some to believe and the free, indeterminate choice of others not to believe.

---

84. McCormack, 'The Actuality of God: Karl Barth in Conversation with Open Theism', in *Engaging the Doctrine of God,* 230-1. In support of his claim, McCormack cites two illustrative passages from Barth's *Church Dogmatics*: III/3:144 ('If the supremacy of this [God's] work is the supremacy of Word and Spirit, it does not prejudice the autonomy, the freedom, the responsibility, the individual being and life and activity of the creature, or the genuineness of its own activity, but confirms and indeed establishes them') and III/3:145 ('Even under this divine lordship the rights and honour and dignity and freedom of the creature are not suppressed and extinguished but vindicated and revealed'). While these statements could be construed in a different way than McCormack takes them, they certainly are open to a reading that grants human beings the ultimate freedom to frustrate God's will and successfully render His grace ineffectual. Considering the open theist view of human autonomy and freedom, which I will address extensively in the next chapter, McCormack's claim that Barth's view bears some similarities is remarkable.

However, Barth expressly rejects Arminianism at this juncture, and argues that the Spirit grants faith to those who believe the truth concerning their election in Christ. Barth also affirms that God withholds His Spirit from those who reject their election, and expresses this in the dialectical language of God's 'non-willing' in respect to them. Remarkably, Barth appears to end up with a view quite similar to the traditional view of Augustine and Calvin, namely, that the number of the elect is determined by God's election of them in Christ and His actual incorporation of them into Christ by the (objective) work of the Holy Spirit. By refusing to embrace universalism and insisting that the actual salvation of some (not necessarily all) human beings depends wholly upon the free decision and work of the triune God, Barth's position 'tacitly' includes elements of the older doctrine of individual double predestination. In the context of an extended treatment of Barth's doctrine of the Holy Spirit in relation to his doctrine of election, Suzanne McDonald describes well this implication of Barth's position:

> Barth's assertion that the rejected exist in the sphere of God's 'non-willing' must therefore be balanced against a pneumatology which dictates that this 'non-willing' of God is also the expression of God's decision to withhold the Spirit. While we may indeed continue to resist our participation in Christ's election, our only possibility of freely choosing to share in it lies in God's own decision to bestow the Spirit to this purpose. If God chooses to grant this gift efficaciously to some and not to others, and if a negative response contains the real threat of ultimate exclusion from the reality of participation in election in Christ, then for all Barth's rhetoric to the contrary, there are aspects of his mature doctrine of election that tacitly remain with the dynamics of individual double predestination.[85]

McDonald's point is the same one I wish to make: if Barth does not hold to an Arminian view of ineffectual grace in his understanding of the work of the Spirit, and if he simultaneously affirms that some may

---

85. McDonald, *Re-Imaging Election,* 75. McDonald appeals to the way Barth speaks of the 'rejection' of those who persistently refuse their election in Christ. This 'rejection' by God is a form of 'non-willing' on His part. See, e.g., CD II/2:27, 450, 458. Barth's use of this language bears some similarities to the use of the language of God's 'permissive will' in traditional Reformed orthodoxy.

not be saved because they persistently reject the Spirit's testimony to their election, his view seems fairly similar to the traditional Augustinian/Calvinistic doctrine of individual double predestination.

The problem with Barth's view at this point is the way he appeals to the freedom of God and the freedom of human beings in relation to God's election of all in Christ. On the one hand, Barth appeals to God's freedom as a reason for denying universalism. By doing so, he raises the specter once again of an Unknown God. On the other hand, Barth's view of human freedom further compounds the problem of the assurance of salvation. How can anyone be sure that God wills to grant them faith and actually does so by an effectual work of the Spirit with the Word? Since Barth acknowledges the possibility that some human beings may prove incorrigible in their unbelief, he leaves open the prospect that some of the elect will never enjoy the fruits of God's electing intention or the Spirit's testimony to their election.

Barth's Exposition of Romans 9–11 and the Election of the Individual

In my critical assessment of Barth's doctrine of election thus far, I have noted that Barth's emphasis upon the election of all human beings in Christ does not enjoy scriptural support. Barth's insistence upon this point seems to be ideologically driven rather than exegetically warranted. I would like to return to this subject by briefly commenting on Barth's exposition of Romans 9–11. Does Barth succeed in his argument that Romans 9–11 is exclusively about the salvation of two communities, the people of Israel and the community of the church?

My interpretation of Paul's argument in Romans 9–11 follows broadly the perspective of Augustine and Calvin, and I am not convinced that Barth's view can be sustained.[86] Undeniably, the occasion for Paul's treatment of election in this passage is the question of God's electing purpose with respect to the people of Israel in distinction from the Gentiles, as Barth argues. When Paul raises the question whether or not the Word of God has failed to effect the salvation of many of his kinsmen according to the flesh, however, he

---

86. For a more extended treatment of Romans 9–11 in respect to this question, see my treatment of this passage in Chapter 3.

is not merely asking whether or not Israel has lived up to its calling in the course of redemptive history. He is asking whether or not God's Word of promise, demonstrated in the person and work of Christ, has and will achieve God's gracious and merciful purpose of election in respect to them.

Paul's answer to this question in Romans 9 is that God's Word has certainly not failed by virtue of the unbelief of many among God's people. In God's redemptive dealings with Israel, His purpose of election was – and continues to be – achieved among an elect remnant toward whom God has chosen to show His mercy. The core of Paul's answer requires a distinction between Israel as an elect people and those among this people who are 'children of the promise' in terms of God's purpose of election. Paul's appeal to God's choice of Isaac rather than Ishmael, and of Jacob rather than Esau, constitutes an essential part of his argument. Since the corporate-election-of-Israel position cannot accommodate this distinction, which plays such a fundamental role in the way Paul makes his case in Romans 9, it glosses over one of the most decisive features of Paul's argument.

Even though Barth and other proponents of the corporate-election-of-Israel interpretation of Romans 9–11 properly emphasize the wide embrace of God's mercy in redemptive history, they are not warranted in their claim that Paul's argument includes no reference to God's just severity in choosing not to show mercy to all. The corporate-election-of-Israel reading of this passage is finally unable to give a plausible explanation for Paul's question in Romans 9:14: 'What shall we say then? Is there injustice on God's part?' This question is occasioned by Paul's appeal to God's merciful choice of some, but not all, of the children of Israel according to the flesh. It finds its basis in the fact that God distinguishes, according to His purpose of election, between Isaac and Ishmael, and between Jacob and Esau. Within the framework of Barth's corporate-election-of-Israel reading, this question loses the urgency it transparently has for Paul. For in the corporate election view, this distinction is always a penultimate one, which has to do only with Israel's role in the history of redemption.[87]

---

87. In the historic interpretation of this passage in Reformed theology, which follows the lead set forth by the influential church father, Augustine, Romans 9 is understood to teach the unconditional election of a particular number of persons unto salvation.

In my estimation, Calvin's comments on Paul's argument, especially in Romans 9, capture more accurately Paul's answer to the question whether or not the Word of God has failed with respect to Israel. Calvin rightly notes that the apostle's answer starts with an important distinction that must be drawn between God's 'general election of the people of Israel' and His 'choosing for Himself by His secret counsel those whom He pleases'.[88] When Paul declares in verse 6, 'But it is not as though the word of God has failed,' he does so because 'not all who are descended from Israel belong to Israel, and not all are children of Abraham because they are his offspring.' Commenting on these words, Calvin notes that 'Paul's proposition is that the promise was given to Abraham and to his seed, but in such a way that his inheritance does not relate to all of his descendants without distinction.'[89] For Calvin, the point of Paul's proposition in verse 6 is that a distinction must be drawn between the historic election of Israel as a people and the 'true election' of some from among her number unto salvation.

> We may, if it is preferred, put it in a different way: 'The general election of the people of Israel does not prevent God from choosing for Himself by His secret counsel those whom He pleases.' God's condescension in making a covenant of life with a single nation is indeed a remarkable illustration of undeserved mercy, but His hidden grace is more evident in the second election (*secunda electione*), which is restricted to a part of the nation only.[90]

Among the Reformed churches, this understanding is codified confessionally in the Canons of Dort I/10, which appeals expressly to Romans 9:11-13 to confirm that God's purpose of election involves His free and gracious decision to adopt 'certain particular persons' for salvation: 'But the cause of this undeserved election is exclusively the good pleasure of God. This does not involve his choosing certain human qualities or actions from among all those possible as a condition of salvation, but rather involves his adopting certain particular persons from among the common mass of sinners as his own possession. As Scripture says, *When the children were not yet born, and had done nothing either good or bad ..., she* (Rebecca) *was told, "The older will serve the younger." As it is written, "Jacob I loved, but Esau I hated"* (Rom. 9:11-13). Also, *All who were appointed for eternal life believed* (Acts 13:48).'

88. *Comm. Rom.* 9:6, *CNTC* 8.197 (CO 49:175).

89. *Comm. Rom.* 9:6, *CNTC* 8.197 (CO 49:175).

90. *Comm. Rom.* 9:6, *CNTC* 8.197-98 (CO 49:175): 'But now he [i.e., Paul] plainly refers the whole cause to the unmerited election of God, which in no way depends on men. Cf. Calvin, *Institutes*, 3.21.6, where Calvin distinguishes the general election

When this distinction between 'all the descendants' of Abraham and those among them who are 'true sons' is acknowledged, the problem of the unbelief expressed by many of Abraham's descendants can be resolved. The unbelief of many among the descendants of Abraham confirms that they do not truly belong to Israel. As Calvin summarizes Paul's argument,

> [i]n the salvation of the godly we are to look for no higher cause than the goodness of God, and no higher cause in the destruction of the reprobate than His just severity. Paul's first proposition, therefore, is as follows: 'As the blessing of the covenant separates the people of Israel from all other nations, so also the election of God makes a distinction between men in that nation, while He predestinates some to salvation, and others to eternal condemnation.' The second proposition is, 'There is no other basis for this election than the goodness of God alone, and also His mercy since the fall of Adam, which embraces those whom He pleases, without any regard whatever to their works.' The third is, 'The Lord in His unmerited election is free and exempt from the necessity of bestowing equally the same grace on all. Rather, He passes by those whom He will, and chooses whom He wills.'[91]

While there is more that could be said regarding Paul's argument in Romans 9, this brief overview is sufficient for my purpose here. With Augustine and Calvin, I believe Paul's appeal to the cases of Isaac and Ishmael, of Jacob and Esau, provides evidence that God elects to show mercy to some among the people of Israel. God's merciful election distinguishes between those who are truly children of the promise and those who are not. In my judgment, Augustine and Calvin's interpretation of Paul remains more persuasive than that offered by Barth.

Conclusion

It should be evident from my critical evaluation that I am not convinced Barth's revision of the Augustinian/Calvinistic view truly resolves the problems he alleges against it. Barth's revision not only fails to do

---

of the people of Israel from what he calls 'a second, more limited degree (*secundus gradus restrictior*) of election, or one in which God's more special grace was evident, that is, when from the same race of Abraham God rejected some but showed that he kept others among his sons by cherishing them in the church.'

91. *Comm. Rom.* 9:11, *CNTC* 8.199-200 (CO 49:177).

justice to the particularism that belongs to the scriptural testimony regarding God's election of His people in Christ, but it also exhibits several features that are particularly troublesome. In my reflection upon Barth's doctrine of election, I have identified three such features: (1) an ambivalence regarding the relation between God's Trinitarian being and His election to be the God who *is* for us in Jesus Christ; (2) the incoherence of Barth's emphasis upon universal election and reconciliation in Christ, and his unwillingness to affirm or deny universalism by appealing to God's freedom to leave some who are incorrigibly unbelieving in their lost condition; and (3) the failure of Barth to do justice to the biblical witness to God's election in Christ of particular persons toward whom He chooses to be merciful. For all that Barth wishes to affirm about the universal election of all in Christ, and the assurance that such election affords us, he still leaves us with a God whose electing will can be nullified either by an act of His own freedom or by the refusal of some fallen human beings to embrace their election. Each of these features of Barth's view is sufficient to raise serious objections to it. However, when taken together, they conspire to form a compelling case against Barth's doctrine of election.

CHAPTER 8

Neo-Arminianism: Free-will or Open Theism – God Neither Elects Nor Foreknows Those Whom He Will Save

IN recent discussions of predestination and election, a number of evangelical authors in North America have advanced what they commonly call 'free will' or 'open theism'.[1] Although the extent to which open theism corresponds to or diverges from classic Arminianism is disputed, the proponents of this view are clearly more in line with an Arminian than an Augustinian/Calvinistic position. With traditional Arminians, they affirm that election is conditional. Only those who freely respond to the gospel by faith will be saved, and

---

1. The term 'open theism' was popularized by the book, *The Openness of God: A Biblical Challenge to the Traditional Understanding of God* (Downers Grove, IL: InterVarsity, 1994). The authors of this volume, Clark Pinnock, Richard Rice, John Sanders, William Hasker, and David Basinger, are the leading contemporary proponents of this view. The following sources are among the most important defenses of open theism: John Sanders, *The God Who Risks: A Theology of Providence* (Downers Grove, IL: InterVarsity, 1998); Gregory A. Boyd, *God of the Possible: A Biblical Introduction to the Open View of God* (Grand Rapids: Baker Books, 2000); Clark Pinnock, *Most Moved Mover: A Theology of God's Openness* (Grand Rapids: Baker Academic, 2001); and David Basinger, *The Case for Freewill Theism: A Philosophical Assessment* (Downers Grove, IL: InterVarsity, 1996).

this response lies within the capacity of all human beings to whom the gospel call is extended. As the term 'free will theism' suggests, these writers assume that all human beings have the freedom to accept or reject the gospel promise of salvation in Christ. On this assumption, they generally agree with historic Arminianism.

What distinguishes the open theist view from more traditional forms of Arminianism is the rigor with which its proponents work out the implications of the Arminian doctrine of the freedom of the will.[2] Whereas Arminius held to key features of an orthodox understanding of God's omniscience, open theists advocate an understanding of God's omniscience that diminishes His ability to foreknow all things, particularly the free response of human beings to the gospel call. For open theism, such actions are simply unknowable even to God prior to their occurrence in time. Since God Himself cannot know in advance how free human beings will respond to the call to faith, He cannot elect them to salvation upon the basis of His foreknowledge. Arminius taught that God elected to save those whom He foreknows will believe in Christ, but open theists teach that God only knows in a general way that His intention to save all who believe in Christ will issue in the salvation of some who freely choose to believe.

This chapter will focus primarily upon the significance of open theism for an understanding of the doctrine of election. Since a number of excellent, critical studies of open theism have already been written, I will not offer a general, wide-ranging evaluation.[3] Rather,

---

2. Cf. Clark Pinnock, *Most Moved Mover,* xii: 'The open view of God continues the much older debate between theological determinists, like Calvin, and free will theists, like Wesley, but also adds something new. It makes the choices even sharper and clearer, being itself *a more coherent alternative to Calvinism than Arminians presented before.'*

3. For critical assessments of open theism, see John Frame, *No Other God: A Response to Open Theism* (Phillipsburg, NJ: Presbyterian and Reformed, 2001); Bruce Ware, *God's Lesser Glory: The Diminished God of Open Theism* (Wheaton, IL: Crossway Books, 2000); idem, *God's Greater Glory: The Exalted God of Scripture and the Christian Faith* (Wheaton, IL: Crossway Books, 2004); idem., *Their God is Too Small: Open Theism and the Undermining of Confidence in God* (Wheaton, IL: Crossway Books, 2003); John Piper, Justin Taylor, Paul Kjoss Helseth, eds., *Beyond the Bounds: Open Theism and the Undermining of Biblical Christianity* (Wheaton, IL: Crossway Books, 2003); Norman Geisler, *Chosen But Free: A Balanced View of Divine Election* (2nd ed.; Minneapolis, MN: Bethany House Publishers, 2001), esp. 104-18; and Gary L.W. Johnson and R. Fowler White, *Whatever Happened to the Reformation?* (Phillipsburg, NJ: Presbyterian and Reformed Publishing, 2001).

I will consider only those features with a direct bearing upon the formulation of God's purpose of election. My approach will consist of two primary steps: first, I will summarize the principal components or tenets of open theism, especially as they bear upon the formulation of the doctrine of election; and second, I will assess critically these tenets and their consequences for an understanding of divine election. My conclusion will note the serious implications of the open theist view of election for the confidence of believers regarding the gracious promises of God in Christ.

Open Theism's Principal Tenets and the Doctrine of Election

Proponents of open theism commonly employ the terms 'free will' and 'open' to describe their understanding of God and His relationship with the world. Both terms capture the way this view moves beyond historic Arminian teaching. According to open theists, if God has created human beings with the free will Arminianism affirms, then we must reckon with the far-reaching consequences such freedom has for God's control of what will transpire in time. In an important volume, which offers a comprehensive summary and defense of open theism by a number of different authors, Clark Pinnock offers a succinct statement of these consequences:

> Our understanding of the Scriptures leads us to depict God, the sovereign Creator, as voluntarily bringing into existence a world with significantly free personal agents in it, agents who can respond positively to God or reject his plans for them. In line with the decision to make this kind of world, God rules in such a way as to uphold the created structures and, because he gives liberty to his creatures, is happy to accept the future as open, not closed, and a relationship with the world that is dynamic, not static.[4]

Creation as an Act of Divine Self-Limitation

The place to begin a summary of open theism is to consider its view of creation as an act of divine self-limitation. Open theists affirm that God freely determined to create all things 'out of nothing' (*ex nihilo*). God was under no external constraint to call the world into

---

4. Pinnock, 'Systematic Theology,' in *The Openness of God*, 103-4.

existence. Nor was God under any obligation to create the actual world He decided to create rather than other possible worlds known to Him. In these respects, open theists eagerly distinguish their position from what is known as 'process theology'. Unlike process theism, which denies the reality of creation out of nothing and teaches the necessary interdependence of God and the world, open theism shares with orthodox Christian theology the conviction that God did not need to create the world.[5] Since God exists eternally in three Persons, the Father, the Son, and the Holy Spirit, He did not have to create the world in order to enjoy fellowship. Love always characterizes the intra-Trinitarian relations between these Persons.[6]

Although open theists affirm God's freedom to create the world, they also maintain that God's decision to create the world necessarily limits His power. The actual world God created includes free agents (angels or human beings who bear God's image) to whom God grants the freedom to act independently. As John Sanders expresses it, 'Not only does God choose to share existence, the fact that God delegates responsibility implies that he is willing to share power with humans. God sovereignly decides that not everything will be up to God. Some important things are left in the hands of humanity as God's cocreators such that we are to collaborate with God in the achievement of the divine

---

5. For an introduction to process theology by two of its leading proponents, see John B. Cobb, Jr. and David Ray Griffin, *Process Theology: An Introductory Exposition* (Philadelphia: The Westminster Press, 1976). For a brief summary of the similarities and differences between process theology and open theism, see William Hasker, 'A Philosophical Perspective,' in *The Openness of God*, 138-41. Cf. John W. Cooper, *Panentheism: The Other God of the Philosophers* (Grand Rapids: Baker Academic, 2006), esp. 165-93. Cooper describes open theism as a form of 'voluntary panentheism', since it views God's act of creation to limit God in a way that is materially similar to process theism's limitation of God. Interestingly, Cooper's volume offers considerable historical evidence for the thesis that the 'god of the philosophers' (including ancient Greek philosophy) is one-and-the-same with the god of process and open theism alike. This belies the oft-repeated argument of open theists that their view is more biblical and less 'Greek' than the view of classic Christian theism.

6. Sanders, *The God Who Risks*, 161. Due to the comprehensiveness and thoroughness of Sanders' argument for open theism, I will cite his book extensively in what follows. There are differences between open theist authors on the extent of God's providential control over what takes place in history, but these are intramural in nature and do not substantively diverge from Sanders' basic point. See, e.g., Basinger, *The Case for Freewill Theism*, 83-92, where he maintains that Sanders ascribes too much control to God.

project.'[7] Contrary to the Calvinist view of God's decree to foreordain whatsoever comes to pass, open theism regards the act of creation itself as introducing other independent actors onto history's stage.

When open theists argue that God's act of creation entails self-limitation, they recognize this has significant implications for the doctrine of God's attributes. The classic doctrine of God's perfections includes the attributes of eternality (God is supratemporal, transcending the limitations of time as temporal duration), immutability (God is unchanging in His being, counsel, and will), omniscience (God knows Himself perfectly and necessarily, as well as all possibilities and those actualities that result from His will to effect them, whether past, present, or future), and omnipotence (God sovereignly sustains, governs and superintends all that takes place). In contrast, open theism teaches that creation requires God to limit Himself in respect to these attributes. For example, God's decision to enter into meaningful relations with His creatures is incompatible with the idea that God absolutely transcends time. God only needs to transcend time in the sense that He has no temporal beginning or ending. Open theists believe the scriptural teaching that God acts in the course of history obliges us to think of God as subject to the temporal sequence of past, present, and future. We should acknowledge that God is changed by His inter-relations with His creatures in time. While God remains unchanging in His character as One who is ever-loving, ever-truthful, ever-wise, and the like, He undergoes innumerable changes in the course of His actions in time and space.[8]

God's General, Non-Meticulous, Providence
Consistent with the divine self-limitation that belongs to God's decision to create a world with genuinely free creatures, open

7. Sanders, *The God Who Risks,* 44.

8. For treatments of God's attributes that largely defend the classical understanding against the claims of open theists, see Millard Erickson, *God the Father Almighty: A Contemporary Exploration of the Divine Attributes* (Grand Rapids: Baker Books, 1998); Ronald H. Nash, *The Concept of God: An Exploration of Contemporary Difficulties with the Attributes of God* (Grand Rapids: Zondervan Publishing House, 1993); John M. Frame, *The Doctrine of God,* 21-118, 387-618; Paul Helm, *Eternal God: A Study of God without Time* (New York: Oxford University Press, 1988); and idem, *The Providence of God, Contours of Christian Theology* (Downers Grove, IL: InterVarsity, 1994), 39-50.

theism argues for a view of God's providence that does not involve His comprehensive control over all that occurs. What takes place throughout history is partly governed by God and partly governed by the undetermined decisions of free creatures. God is the principal Actor in the course of history, but He is not the only actor. The future course of events is not entirely within God's control. Much of what takes place is the result of free actions of creatures.

For this reason, John Sanders entitles his book on the open theist view of God's providence, *The God Who Risks*. Sanders argues that God cannot avoid the risk that belongs to the creation of 'significant others who are ontologically distinct from himself and upon whom he showers his caring love in the expectation that they will respond in love. God grants humans genuine freedom to participate in this project, as he does not force them to comply.'[9] In the world God created, there is an inevitable 'contingency in God's relation with creation'.[10] Since God has chosen to enter into a give-and-take relationship with human beings, there is an unavoidable indeterminateness in how this relationship will unfold or be developed through time. 'God is free to sovereignly decide,' says Sanders, 'not to determine everything that happens in history. He does not have to because God is supremely wise, endlessly resourceful, amazingly creative and omnicompetent in seeking to fulfill his project.'[11] The only alternative to such a risk view of God's providence is to affirm a form of 'theological determinism or exhaustive sovereignty'.[12] The problem with theological determinism, however, is that it does not provide a basis for the cultivation of a true relationship between God and human beings. When one partner in the relationship has all the power and control, the mutual love essential to true communion is missing.[13]

---

9. ibid.

10. ibid.

11. ibid.

12. ibid., 171.

13. Open theists commonly claim that their view provides a solution to the problem of evil. Because the sinful and evil actions of free creatures lie outside of God's control, He bears no responsibility for them. See, e.g., Sanders, *The God Who Risks*, 253-67; Pinnock, *Most Moved Mover*, 176-7; Boyd, *God of the Possible*, 135-6; David Basinger, *The Case for Freewill Theism*, 83-104; and idem, 'Practical Implications,' in *The Openness of God*, 168-71. There are two vulnerabilities, however, to this open

Libertarian Human Freedom

The assumption behind the open theist view of creation and providence is a certain understanding of human freedom.[14] Though the open theist view of human freedom is most commonly termed 'libertarian,' this terminology is not especially helpful. Because the term 'libertarian' derives from the Latin word for freedom, the expression 'libertarian freedom' is redundant and unhelpful. For this reason, alternative expressions are sometimes used, such as the 'freedom of contrary choice' or a 'freedom of equipoise'. These alternative expressions are more useful, since they capture the essential claim of this view, namely, that free human beings have the power to choose or not to choose to act in certain ways, especially when these choices involve moral (to do what is good or evil) or religious matters (to love or not to love God). Unless human beings are able to choose equally between different options in moral and religious matters, they cannot be said to be genuinely free.[15] Furthermore, since the libertarian view of human freedom assumes that such freedom is incompatible with God's sovereign foreordination of what occurs in history, it is often termed an 'incompatibilist' understanding of human freedom. For many proponents of open theism, the libertarian view of human freedom

theist claim: first, God's decision to create free human beings who could sin and bring evil into the world hardly exonerates Him from any responsibility for what they might do in virtue of His unleashing them upon the world; and second, God is unable to work in such a way as to achieve His good purposes through the evil He permits.

14. Frame, *No Other God*, 119.

15. Here and throughout this study I am deliberately limiting my focus to human freedom as it relates to moral, ethical, and religious choices. I am not interested in the more general discussion of human freedom in respect to non-moral or non-religious choices. Even among Reformed theologians, who commonly reject the idea of libertarian freedom, there is an ongoing debate about the nature of human freedom, the adequacy of the terminology of 'compatibilism', and the exercise of human freedom in mundane matters that are unrelated to moral and religious choices. For an introduction to this debate, see Willem J. van Asselt, J. Martin Bac, and Roelf T. te Velde, eds., *Reformed Thought on Freedom: The Concept of Free Choice in the History of Early Modern Reformed Theology* (Grand Rapids: Baker Academic, 2010); *Journal of Reformed Theology (Special Issue: Reformed Accounts of Free Will* 8/3 [2014]); and Richard A. Muller, *Divine Will and Human Choice: Freedom, Contingency, and Necessity in Early Modern Reformed Thought* (Grand Rapids: Baker Academic, 2017).

scarcely requires any argument for its cogency. In their estimation, this is the only view that corresponds with the common 'human experience' of what it means to make choices and opt for one course of action rather than another.[16]

Among contemporary defenders of open theism, William Hasker has provided one of the more precise definitions of libertarian freedom:

> On the libertarian (or 'incompatibilist') understanding of free will, *an agent is free with respect to a given action at a given time if at that time it is within the agent's power to perform the action and also in the agent's power to refrain from the action.* To say that the action is 'within one's power' means that nothing whatever exists that would make it impossible for the power in question to be exercised. If I am free in this sense, then whether or not the action is performed depends on me; by deciding to perform the action I bring it about that things happen in a certain way, quite different from some other, equally possible, way things might have happened had I refrained from the action.[17]

Libertarian freedom means that human beings ordinarily have the power in any circumstance to do the contrary. There are no factors extraneous to this power of choice that pre-determine the choice a truly free person makes. In order for the agent freely to decide to act or to refrain from acting, the agent 'must have it in her power without qualification to perform the action and also have the power to refrain from performing it.'[18]

The Nature of God's Omniscience and Foreknowledge

The last tenet of open theism we consider is God's omniscience, especially His foreknowledge of future contingencies. If the world is populated with human beings who enjoy libertarian freedom, the question of the extent of God's knowledge, especially as it concerns future events, becomes pressing. From the perspective of open

---

16. Cf. Clark Pinnock, *Most Moved Mover*, 41: 'Scripture, like human experience itself, assumes libertarian freedom, i.e. the freedom to perform an action or refrain from it. With such freedom, people usually have alternatives in any situation. It is a gift that makes loving relationships that imply free response possible.'

17. Hasker, 'A Philosophical Perspective,' 137 (emphasis his).

18. ibid.

theism, traditional views of God's exhaustive foreknowledge are not compatible with human freedom.

The first view excluded by open theism is that God has an exhaustive knowledge of all actualities in history, past, present, and future, because He wills them to occur. In this view, which has a long pedigree in the history of Christian theology, God's knowledge of all things is a necessary consequence of His foreordination of all things: God eternally knows what He has eternally determined to take place. However, open theism also rejects the historic Arminian view of God's omniscience. While historic Arminianism assumes a similar libertarian human freedom as open theism, open theists maintain that such freedom is incompatible with the traditional Arminian understanding of God's foreknowledge. Once the existence of genuinely free creatures is acknowledged, it is no longer possible to retain the view that God has an exhaustive knowledge of all future events in history. On this subject, open theism aims to be more consequent than historic Arminianism by revising the doctrine of God's omniscience.

To understand this open theist objection to the historic Arminian view, we need to return to the Molinist doctrine of God's 'middle knowledge' considered in an earlier chapter on Arminius' teaching. To defend a doctrine of God's omniscience, including His exhaustive knowledge of all free choices of human beings who enjoy libertarian freedom, Molina developed the idea of God's middle knowledge or a knowledge intermediate between God's *necessary* knowledge and God's *free* knowledge.[19]

As we noted previously, Molina's doctrine of middle knowledge is based upon a distinction between God's 'necessary', 'free', and 'middle' knowledge, each of which refers to God's knowledge of

---

19. For Molina's view of God's foreknowledge, see Luis de Molina, *On Divine Foreknowledge (Part IV of the Concordia),* trans., with an Introduction and Notes, by Alfred J. Freddoso (Ithaca, NY: Cornell University Press, 1988); Richard A. Muller, *Post-Reformation Reformed Dogmatics,* vol. 3: *The Divine Essence and Attributes* (Grand Rapids: Baker Academic, 2003), 417-32; and Kirk R. MacGregor, *Luis de Molina: The Life and Theology of the Founder of Middle Knowledge* (Grand Rapids: Zondervan, 2015), 79-105. For critical assessments by open theists of Molina's doctrine of middle knowledge, see Sanders, *The God Who Risks,* 196-98; and Hasker, 'A Philosophical Perspective,' 143-7.

different sorts of truths. God's *necessary knowledge* consists of all that God knows about Himself, necessary truths (such as the laws of logic or arithmetic), and all scenarios in every possible world. When God knows Himself, necessary truths, and all possibilities, He knows truths that are logically antecedent to His will. For example, regarding Himself, God knows necessarily that He exists eternally in three Persons, that the Son is begotten of the Father, and that He is perfectly holy. God also has exhaustive knowledge of all possibilities, that is, of all possible things and events that do not exist, have not existed, and will not exist. Because God's necessary knowledge does not depend upon His decree, but derives from who He is by nature, scholastic theologians, including Aquinas, described it as a 'knowledge of simple intelligence'.[20] Simply by virtue of who He is, God necessarily and perfectly knows Himself, as well as all scenarios, all concatenations of possibilities, in every possible world.

In distinction from His necessary knowledge, God's *free knowledge* refers to His knowledge of all things that are actual (or exist) by virtue of His will. God's exhaustive knowledge of creation and history, past, present, and future, is a knowledge that depends upon His free decision to create or actualize this world. In a way analogous to our knowing what we have done by the performance of a specific action, God eternally knows what is true about the actual world by willing it.[21] For example, God eternally foreknows that the Declaration of Independence will be written in 1776, but this knowledge of an actual event depends upon His free will to make it actual.[22] Because God's free knowledge is a perfect knowledge of His own all-comprehensive and unchangeable will, Aquinas and later

---

20. Aquinas, *Summa Theologica*, 1.14.10 and 12.

21. I use the language 'analogous' to distinguish the way in which God eternally knows what is actual by virtue of His will to make it so from the way we *come to know* what we have done after the deed is performed. Our knowledge is derived from our acquaintance with the act already performed. God's foreknowledge of the actual world is derived from His eternally willing it to be so.

22. For this reason, even though God's free knowledge means that what He wills is certain to happen, such knowledge does not undermine the contingency of creation and its subsequent history. For any actual thing or event to be contingent or not necessary, it must wholly depend upon God's will alone to make it actual. Though God's foreknowledge of any future contingency makes it certain to be or to occur, such foreknowledge does not make it any less contingent.

theologians termed God's exhaustive knowledge of the actual world a 'knowledge of vision'.

Molina introduced the idea of God's *middle* knowledge in order to account for God's knowledge of truths that are neither necessary (God cannot but know them as such) nor free by virtue of God's will to make them actual. According to Molina, God's middle knowledge is His knowledge of events that He has not willed to take place, but that take place wholly through the creature's exercise of libertarian freedom. Through His middle knowledge, God is able to foreknow the free choices of creatures in all circumstances, even though these choices were not willed by God and none of these circumstances determine the choices such creatures will make. Unlike God's necessary knowledge, which is *absolute* or antecedent to anything that He wills to be, God's middle knowledge is *dependent* or consequent upon God's ability to foresee by a kind of special intuition what free creatures will do in any circumstance. One way to understand Molina's point is to view God's middle knowledge as a kind of rehearsal in God's mind of how an agent with libertarian freedom would choose to act in all possible circumstances in the actual world. In his definition of God's middle knowledge, Molina argues that middle knowledge explains how God could will to create an actual world with genuinely free agents who retain the power to do the opposite of what they choose to do:[23]

> Finally, the third type is *middle* knowledge, by which, in virtue of the most profound and inscrutable comprehension of each free will, He saw in His own essence what each such will would do with its innate freedom were it to be placed in this or in that or, indeed, infinitely many orders of things—even though it would really be able, if it so willed, to do the opposite.[24]

According to open theists, the Molinist doctrine of God's exhaustive foreknowledge of all future events, which Arminius utilized to

---

23. A common way of expressing this is to say that God's middle knowledge includes an exhaustive knowledge of 'counter-factuals of freedom', that is, those actions that free creatures could freely choose to do but would not under circumstances known to God.

24. Luis de Molina, *On Divine Foreknowledge*, disputation 52, par. 9. Cf. Richard A. Muller, *Dictionary of Latin and Greek Theological Terms*, 325, for a concise definition of 'middle knowledge' and its importance to historic Arminian formulations of the doctrine of election.

preserve libertarian freedom, must be rejected as untenable. However subtle Molina's doctrine of middle knowledge may appear, it fails to stand up to scrutiny. If free agents possess genuine libertarian freedom, even God cannot know how they will choose to act in future circumstances and conditions. According to Hasker,

> There are serious questions concerning the logical compatibility of comprehensive divine foreknowledge and libertarian free will. The idea, roughly, is this: If God knows already what will happen in the future, then God's knowing this is part of the past and is now fixed, impossible to change. And since God is infallible, it is completely impossible that things will turn out differently than God expects them to. But this means that the future event God knows is also fixed and unalterable, and it cannot be true of any human beings that they are both able to perform a certain action and able not to perform that action. If God knows that a person is going to perform it, then it is impossible that the person fail to perform it.[25]

Open theist authors claim, therefore, that we have to redefine God's omniscience as a knowledge of all things and events *so far as it is logically possible for God to know them.* God's knowledge in respect to past and present events is perfect and exhaustive. Indeed, as one open theist remarks, God is 'the first to know' such events.[26] But it is logically impossible that God should have foreknowledge of future events that depend upon genuinely free agents.

Gracious Election: God's General Goal to Save All Persons

The foregoing summary of the open theism's principal tenets provides a framework for considering its doctrine of election. The claims of open theists imply that the two major views which have dominated theological discussion since the early seventeenth century, the

---

25. Hasker, 'A Philosophical Perspective,' 147. Cf. Helm, *The Providence of God,* 59: 'The universe cannot, given the strong view of freedom endorsed by the Molinists, have a shadow form; a form of a purely conditional kind which is the mirror-image of how the universe will be when it is actual. For how it will be when it is actual is, at least in part, up to the free actions of the agents who are actualized, once God decided to actualize that universe.' It is noteworthy that open theists agree at this point with the traditional Reformed objection to middle knowledge, namely, that even God cannot foreknow a future contingency that is indeterminate in the most radical sense.
26. ibid., 148.

Augustinian-Calvinistic and its Arminian alternative, are not viable in their classical forms. In the writings of open theism's leading advocates, it is remarkable how little consideration is actually given to the interpretation of scriptural passages that speak of God's predestination or election of some persons to salvation in Christ.[27] However, when open theist authors do treat passages like Romans 8:28-30, Romans 9–11, and Ephesians 1:3-11, it becomes clear how their position requires a radical revision of more traditional formulations of election, including even the Arminian view.

Open theist authors typically regard these passages as descriptions of God's *general* and *non-particular* love for all human beings whom He wills to save but whose salvation depends upon their meeting freely the conditions for anyone to be saved. For example, Richard Rice, in his article, 'Biblical Support for a New Perspective,' treats these passages with the prior assumption of the open view of God. Rice declares that they must be interpreted in the light of many scriptural passages that speak of God's plans being frustrated or thwarted. In particular, we should remember how many biblical passages describe God's will or intention that all human beings come to salvation, and yet God's will 'does not guarantee the outcome that he desires'.[28] Since we know that unbelief and disobedience often thwart God's gracious will to save all human beings, we must understand these passages to describe God's universal intention to save all who respond to the gospel call in the way of faith. Furthermore, Rice maintains that these passages should not be interpreted to refer to God's election and calling of particular individuals. Rather, these passages refer to a 'corporate call to service' or a 'corporate body' rather than the specific persons who compose the number of those who will be saved.[29] Since the calling of the gospel is conditional,

---

27. See, e.g., Roger Nicole, 'A Review Article: God of the Possible,' *R&R* 10, no. 1 (2001): 170-1, who observes that Gregory Boyd's book, *God of the Possible,* 'contains no reference to any of the 26 passages in which the words "elect" or "election" are found, except Rom. 8:33, 9:11, and 11:28.' Nicole also notes that Boyd refers only to four of the nine passages that deal with God's purpose before creation, and only five of the eighty-nine passages 'in which God is presented as the one who chooses those on whom he will bestow his blessing'.

28. Rice, 'Biblical Support for a New Perspective,' 55.

29. ibid., 56-7. Cf. Boyd, *God of the Possible,* 139-44.

God's election is His general and inclusive 'goal' that all human beings should be saved.

John Sanders takes a similar approach in his treatment of Romans 9–11. Sanders argues that the burden of Paul's argument in Romans 9–11 is not the 'pancausality' of God's sovereign predestinating will in respect to the salvation of specific persons whom God elects.[30] Paul's aim throughout these chapters is to defend God's faithfulness to His promises, and to demonstrate the breadth of God's mercy extended to Jews and Gentiles alike. Throughout the course of history, God works relentlessly to show mercy toward and save all human beings without exception. Though God's gracious purpose is often thwarted through unbelief, we may be confident that God will faithfully pursue His good intentions toward all. Since God has assumed the risk entailed by the creation of genuinely free human beings, He cannot always expect to get His way or avoid failure in His endeavor to save everyone.

A Critical Assessment of the Open Theist View of Election

Upon the basis of my summary of the most important tenets of open theism, especially as they bear upon the doctrine of election, I want to offer a critical assessment of the open theist view. Does this view provide a more satisfactory account of scriptural teaching than the alternatives of the Augustinian/Calvinist tradition or historic Arminianism, as its advocates claim? Does it provide a coherent account of how God's act of creation, including the creation of free human beings, must limit His power to ensure that His goal to save fallen sinners through Jesus Christ will be successful? Are open theists correct, when they argue that the Arminian notion of libertarian human freedom is incompatible with the traditional doctrine of God's exhaustive foreknowledge of future human choices?

---

30. Sanders, *The God Who Risks*, 122. For a critical assessment of the claim by modern interpreters of Romans 9–11 that Paul is only speaking of the election of corporate peoples rather than individuals, see Cornelis P. Venema, '"Jacob I Loved, But Esau I Hated": Corporate or Individual Election in Paul's Argument in Romans 9?', 7-58.

Does Creation Require God to Limit Himself?

While open theists claim to hold to a traditional understanding of God's act of creating the world out of nothing, they wrongly insist that God's free decision to create the world was an act of self-limitation. There are at least two weighty objections against this claim and the arguments for it.[31]

First, open theists mistakenly argue that God's decision to limit His power by creating the world is similar to other ways in which theologians have acknowledged divine limitations. In his argument for this claim, Sanders confuses two distinct senses in which we may speak of limitations with respect to God. As one perceptive critic of the open theist view of divine self-limitation puts it, Sanders 'fails to distinguish between negative language that *imposes* a limit and negative language that *removes* a limit'.[32] When classic Christian theology says that God cannot lie, it does not impose a limit upon God but expresses in negative form the fact that God's truthfulness is unlimited. Far from limiting God, this language distinguishes God as One who is perfectly, surpassingly, and incomprehensibly great in His truthfulness. Such language is no more than an abstract way of saying what the apostle James declares in a more elegant way, when he says that 'Every good and perfect gift is from above, coming down from the Father of lights with whom there is no variation or shadow due to change' (James 1:17). Or, to put it in the more prosaic language of Hebrews 6:18, 'it is impossible for God to lie.' No limit is placed upon God by this language. Rather, God's truthfulness is magnified.

The same holds true for the historic conviction of Christian theology that God does not limit His power by His act of creation. Christian theologians traditionally rejected the idea of creation as a form of self-limitation because they believed it was inconsistent with God's self-existence or independence. Whereas God exists from Himself, all created things exist only by God's free decision to give them existence and thereafter to conserve their existence.

---

31. See Ron Highfield, 'The Function of Divine Self-Limitation in Open Theism: Great Wall or Picket Fence?,' *JETS* 45, no. 2 (2002): 279-99. In my assessment of the open theist idea of divine self-limitation, I make grateful use of Highfield's essay.

32. ibid., 287.

What distinguishes God as Creator from all created things is that He never depends upon any creature He has called into existence. What distinguishes all creatures is that they 'live and move and have their being' in God alone as their Creator (Acts 17:28). However, the open theist doctrine of God's self-limitation is set forth precisely in order to affirm that some creatures have a limited form of self-existence. For open theists, God's decision to create free creatures whom He cannot move to act in one way or another, entails a limitation upon His independence. By virtue of this act of self-limitation, God must cease in some respects to be independent in His being, power and works. God's power is now circumscribed by the existence of creatures who possess unlimited power within a domain that belongs to them alone.[33] As Ron Highfield expresses it,

> Sanders does not appear to recognize, however, that a being that is uncontrollable by God (or independent of God) could be considered a sort of second God. Sanders's argument, then, begs the question of the ontological status of an 'uncontrollable' being. One need not be a hidebound traditionalist to suspect that uncontrollability (or independence) in any strict sense is an attribute of God alone. Attributing to God the 'ability' to create a second independent being actually calls God's unique deity into question. Conversely, the (traditional) statement, 'God cannot create an independent being,' really removes a limit from God and affirms his unique deity.[34]

Second, the open theist view of creation as an act of divine self-limitation also entails that the world's existence enriches God. Once God decides to create the world, the world adds something to reality that would be lacking were God the only being with existence. God's self-limitation entails that He make space and time for another form of (created) being whose existence reduces His omnipresence and omnipotence. By creating the world, God placed insurmountable boundaries upon what He can now do. The net effect of God's work

---

33. Although open theists frequently allege that the traditional doctrine of God's providence owes more to the influence of Greek philosophy than scriptural teaching, it is remarkable how similar the open theist view is to ancient Greek philosophy, which affirmed a plurality of independent beings and advocated a libertarian view of human freedom. For a concise treatment of this point, see Frame, *No Other God,* 27-32.

34. Highfield, 'The Function of Divine Self-Limitation,' 288-9.

of creation is that reality now consists of two kinds of being, a sort of 'metaphysical dualism', wherein the being of God is less than the being of God and the world.[35] However, if God truly created the world 'out of nothing', it is not possible to say that God 'needs' the world or that God-plus-the-world is more than God alone (cf. Acts 17:25). The doctrine of creation out of nothing obliges us to acknowledge that there is nothing in the world that was not first in God, or that does not serve to reveal His inexhaustible goodness and wisdom. The doctrine of creation means that 'No good, power, being, or beauty resides in the world that was not already in God.'[36]

The reason open theists view creation as an act of divine self-limitation is not hard to discern: God is obliged to limit His power in order to provide room for free creatures with libertarian freedom. There are two difficulties with this claim. In the first place, it assumes that human freedom must be defined in terms of libertarian freedom, apart from which there is no genuine reciprocity in the relationship between God and human beings. I use the term 'assumes' deliberately, since open theists offer little or no argument for their claim that a truly loving relationship between God and human beings requires the kind of 'give-and-take' (perhaps better: 'take it or leave it') reciprocity that they assume as a given.[37] And in the second place, the open theist argument for God's 'choice' to create a world with libertarian freedom is governed by a pre-established set of possibilities over which God Himself has no control. In each of these respects, open theism is based upon unexamined assumptions regarding human freedom and divine independence that do not stand up to scrutiny.

---

35. ibid., 291.

36. ibid. Highfield observes that 'for all its criticisms of classical theology's use of "pagan" philosophy, open theism reasons about God's relationship to the world on presuppositions that resemble metaphysical dualism more than they resemble the Christian doctrine of creation. It assumes that God's relation to the world is now (even if it was not eternally) constitutive of God' (291-2).

37. I cannot help noting that the ideal marriage (either in a relationship between a man and a woman or in the relationship between God and His people) is an 'unbreakable bond' between the two parties. Why, then, should we assume that a true love relationship always requires that one or both of the parties remain free to do the contrary, that is, break or dissolve the relationship?

The Incoherence of Libertarian Human Freedom

The most important unexamined assumption of open theism is its view of libertarian human freedom. All of the principal tenets of open theism are based upon this assumption, which functions as a kind of basic presupposition for its proponents. What is most remarkable about the idea of libertarian human freedom is that it abstracts the way human beings make choices from who such human beings concretely are, what kind of choices they are called upon to make, and under what circumstances this may occur. Hasker's definition of libertarian freedom is illustrative: 'An agent is free with respect to a given action at a given time if at that time it is within the agent's power to perform the action and also in the agent's power to refrain from the action.'[38] With this definition, Hasker ascribes to human freedom a godlike independence, such that the choice to act or to do the contrary is ultimately determined by nothing other than the free person's naked power to make (arbitrary) choices. For this reason, open theists have no option but to limit God's power in respect to such choices. God must limit His power in order to create human beings whose choices are uncontrolled and uncontrollable. No one, not even God, could foreknow how such creatures will choose to act in circumstances of genuine responsibility and accountability. Accordingly, free will theists are obliged to say that such libertarian freedom is 'incompatible' with a strong view of divine providence or divine foreknowledge of future contingencies.

Before I proceed to offer a critical evaluation of libertarian human freedom, it is necessary to offer a few comments regarding a very different conception of human freedom. Among theologians who affirm a strong view of God's providential rule over all things and His foreknowledge of the future, human freedom is defined as a freedom of *self-determination*. In this understanding of human freedom, human beings are free when they not constrained by some kind of external

---

38. Hasker, 'A Philosophical Perspective,' 136-7. Cf. R. K. McGregor Wright, *No Place for Sovereignty: What's Wrong with Freewill Theism* (Downers Grove, IL: InterVarsity Press, 1996), 43-4, who defines libertarian human freedom as follows: '[T]he belief that the human will has an inherent power to choose with equal ease between alternatives. ... Ultimately, the will is free from any necessary causation. In other words, it is autonomous from outside determination.'

compulsion to do what they do, but are moved to act according to what they judge to be desirable or good. In the words of Millard Erickson, a proponent of this understanding of human freedom,

> Freedom ... is freedom from constraint or external compulsion. It is freedom from unwilling action. This is freedom to act consistently with who one is. It is freedom to act as one chooses, and choose as one wishes. But it does not necessarily mean pure spontaneity, nor does it mean freedom to choose contrary to one's nature or character. Just as ... God is not truly free to act contrary to his nature, to lie, be cruel, or break his covenant word, so humans are not necessarily free either to act in ways that presuppose that they are someone other than themselves. We may be free to do as we please, but we are not necessarily free to please as we please.[39]

In this understanding of human freedom, the power of human beings to choose responsibly and be accountable for their choices is fully acknowledged. But the choices that human beings make are not made in a vacuum. They do not float freely, as if they could be detached from the persons who make them. Rather, they are choices that are informed by what a person knows to be desirable.[40] They are shaped,

---

39. Erickson, *God the Father Almighty,* 206-7. Cf. Francis Turretin, *Institutes of Elenctic Theology,* 1:675: 'In vain is it said that man can do this or that if he will, since it is evident that he is not able to will; not because he is destitute of natural power to will (because thus he differs from brutes), but because he is without the disposition to will what is good (concerning which alone we are speaking in this question.' Turretin's point is the same as Erickson's: the exercise of human freedom does not occur in a vacuum, but takes place in the context of human discernment, dispositions, affections, etc.

40. For older and more recent elaborations of this view of freedom as a freedom of self-determination, see Turretin, *Institutes of Elenctic Theology,* 1:665-82; Jonathan Edwards, *Freedom of the Will* (New Haven: Yale University Press, 1973); D. A. Carson, *How Long, O Lord? Reflections on Suffering and Evil* (Grand Rapids: Baker, 2006), chapters 11 & 12; John S. Feinberg, *No One Like Him,* Foundations of Evangelical Theology (Wheaton, IL; Crossway, 2001), chapters 13-16; and Mark R. Talbot, 'True Freedom: The Liberty That Scripture Portrays as Worth Having,' in *Beyond the Bounds,* 77-109. For a recent popular defense of this view, see Scott Christensen, *What About Free Will? Reconciling Our Choices with God's Sovereignty* (Phillipsburg, NJ: Presbyterian and Reformed, 2016). For an extensive, academic discussion of the understanding of human freedom in the period of Reformed orthodoxy, see Muller, *Divine Will and Human Choice.* Muller's study delves deeply into the question of human freedom in Reformed theology in order to argue that the common distinction in contemporary debates between 'compatibilism' and 'incompatibilism' does not adequately represent the orthodox Reformed view. Muller argues that orthodox

and can therefore be explained, only in terms of the kind of person who makes them. Just as a good tree bears good fruit, and an evil tree bears evil fruit (Matt. 7:17), so the character of human persons influences and directs them in the choices they make.[41] Human beings are highly complex, and their choices and actions reflect this complexity. When free human beings make moral and religious choices particularly, they do so in a way that reflects the state of their hearts, out of which are the issues of life (Prov. 4:23; cf. Luke 6:45). They make such choices in accordance with their dispositions, inclinations, values, sentiments, and the like, and these together provide an explanation for the choices that are made.[42]

If we define human freedom as a freedom of self-determination, it is possible to have some inkling as to how God could foreordain and foreknow the choices that human beings will make in the actual world that He wills to exist. In this understanding of human freedom, God's foreordination and foreknowledge of what will occur is compatible with the non-coerced actions of responsible human beings. Since God knows all possible human beings whom He could bring into existence, and He also knows how they will be pleased to act in every possible circumstance, He can determine to create a world in which what He has foreordained and foreknown will come to passage with certainty.

Reformed theology affirmed a more robust understanding of human freedom than is often assumed, especially in respect to human choices regarding mundane matters not directly related to salvation. According to Muller, the use of language like 'compatibilism' or 'soft determinism' in the modern period is symptomatic of a 'loss of fluency in the scholastic language of the early modern Reformed, particularly in the distinctions used to reconcile the divine willing of all things, the sovereignty of grace, and overarching divine providence with contingency and freedom, not merely epistemically but ontically understood as the possibility for things and effects to be otherwise' (22).

41. Highfield, 'The Function of Divine Self-Limitation,' 295: 'Hasker's "agent" then appears to be a transcendental (pure) will hovering above the entire causal nexus, above itself as a concrete entity or even beyond itself as an essence.'

42. I have often used the following, relatively trivial, illustration of this truth. I have a friend who loathes pizza and who was once given, as a gag gift, a package of frozen pizzas. What he did with these pizzas was easily predictable: although he was perfectly free to eat them, he chose instead to trash them. Because he had no 'taste' or 'appetite' for them, he did what his friends assumed he would do. So it is with human beings who make choices, especially in moral and religious matters, to do what they find palatable.

God can ensure what will happen, but not in a way that diminishes the freedom of any human to do what he or she is pleased to do. In a manner of speaking, God so orchestrates the course of events that His will is always done, but in no way diminishes the freedom of human beings to act as they are pleased to act. Millard Erickson summarizes well these implications of a compatibilist doctrine of human freedom:

> God works in numerous ways to bring about his will by rendering it certain that I and each other individual will freely choose what he foreordained. He does this through placing circumstances such that I will want to act in a certain way. ... He has control over all sorts of circumstances that most humans could not control or even influence. And out of this, he does not coerce but renders his will certain. There may be various ways in which he brings this about in different situations. In some cases, he provides the means or the strength to accomplish something. In others, he simply refrains from intervening to prevent a particular action.[43]

I will return in the next section to the implications of a compatibilist view of creaturely freedom for an understanding of God's providential governance and exhaustive foreknowledge of all things. At this point, however, I want to offer several observations that demonstrate the incoherence of the idea of libertarian human freedom.

First, in the scriptural representations of the responsibility of human beings to obey God and submit to His will, we do not find any hint of an incompatibility between such accountability and God's foreordination and foreknowledge of the actual choices human beings make in their responses to Him. For example, the narrative of Joseph's betrayal by his brothers concludes with Joseph saying to his brothers, 'As for you, you meant evil against me, but God meant it for good, to bring it about that many people should be kept alive, as they are today' (Gen. 50:20). Joseph's brothers are held fully responsible for what they did against Joseph, even though their actions fulfilled God's will to bring about His good purposes. Similarly, in the well-known words of Peter in his Pentecost sermon, the crucifixion of Jesus, which was brought about through the culpable actions of 'lawless men', occurred in accordance with 'the definite plan and foreknowledge of God'

---

43. Erickson, *God the Father Almighty*, 207.

(Acts 2:23). These passages are not exceptional in the Scriptures, but illustrate a common pattern: human choices occur in accordance with God's will, even when they involve disobedience to His revealed rule of conduct. Nonetheless, the human actor in these choices remains fully responsible for them.[44] Although the Scriptures do not provide a technical, theological account of the nature of human freedom, their descriptions of the responsible acts of human beings make clear that the freedom of such acts does not require that they take place *independent* of God's will.

Second, the libertarian view of human freedom does not account for the motivations that underlie human choices. One of the most common questions we may pose regarding any human choice is what *moved* or *inclined* a human being to act in a particular way. In the prosecution, for example, of a person who commits a crime, one of the most important pieces of evidence is the determination of the perpetrator's motive. However, in the libertarian understanding of human freedom in response to the gospel call, there can ultimately be no satisfactory answer to this question. The best you can say is something like, 'though I was equally free to do otherwise, I exercised my indeterminate will to do what I did.' A libertarian will is one that always retains the inherent power to do the contrary, especially in respect to the gospel's call to faith. Perhaps another way to make this point is to observe that a truly free action in the libertarian sense springs from 'nothing'. Such an act is analogous to God's creating the world 'out of nothing'. For this reason, the libertarian view of human freedom in salvation is aptly called a 'freedom of equipoise'. In the circumstances that obtain when a truly free act is performed, the actor is in the same place as a high wire or trapeze artist finds himself. So long as such a high wire artist maintains perfect equipoise, balanced

---

44. For additional examples of this compatibility in Scripture, see Frame, *No Other God,* 57-88; and Ware, *God's Greater Glory,* 35-160. My use of the language, 'rule of conduct,' is related to a traditional distinction in Reformed theology between God's 'will of decree' and God's 'will of precept'. God's 'will of decree' is His will whereby He foreordains whatsoever will come to pass, which is never frustrated. God's 'will of precept' is the rule of life that God has revealed for the conduct of His moral creatures, which is often disobeyed. For a brief treatment of this distinction, see Berkhof, *Systematic Theology,* 77. For a treatment of this distinction and its relevance for a critical assessment of open theism, see Frame, *No Other God,* 105-18.

by the equal weight of a pole so as to preserve his balance and keep him from falling to the left or to the right, he will keep balance. There is literally nothing that would cause him to fall in one direction or another. Such a state of equipoise is perfectly equivalent to a form of paralysis. Or, to change the analogy, such a person's freedom is not unlike Alice in Wonderland, when she comes to a fork in the road. When Alice asks the Cheshire cat what way she should go, the cat asks where she is going. To this question Alice replies by saying, 'I don't know.' To which the Cheshire cat responds, 'Then it doesn't matter.' In a similar way, the libertarian view of human freedom amounts to saying that the free choices that we make arise out of nothing, and are not made for any reason other than that we made them.[45]

Third, the libertarian view of human freedom raises questions regarding the nature of God's freedom and the freedom of human beings who bear His image. Christian theologians commonly affirm that the three Persons of the Trinity, the Father, the Son, and the Holy Spirit, enjoy an eternal and perfect communion of love. There is an eternal communion and reciprocal relationship between the three Persons of the Godhead. In their relations, the three Persons act in perfect freedom, even though they cannot do otherwise! The three Persons necessarily exist and inter-relate in loving fellowship, which theologians call the 'perichoresis' or mutual indwelling of their Persons (see, e.g., John 14:10-20; 17:20-6). Just as God cannot lie, being perfectly truthful, so the Persons of the Trinity cannot fail to love each other perfectly. God's freedom to be loving is not incompatible with saying that He necessarily is loving and could not be otherwise than loving. God's freedom is radically dissimilar to the libertarian view of freedom in respect to human beings, which according to open theists must always permit them to do the contrary. In a similar way, in order to affirm that God is morally responsible and free in all of His actions in relation to the world, we do not need to

---

45. I cannot help being reminded of a similar illustration. Yogi Berra, the legendary player for the New York Yankees and well-known for his amusing way of putting things, was once asked which way a person should go when coming to a fork in the road. Yogi's answer, 'Take it,' sounds suspiciously like the libertarian view of the abstract, inexplicable, and irrational choices that human beings make in circumstances of genuine freedom. It is no wonder that neither God nor the person who makes the choice has a reasonable basis to predict what choice will ensue.

affirm that He was free to do the contrary in every choice He makes. Though God is free to create a different world than the one He chose to create, He is not free to act in any possible world in a way that conflicts with who He is. One way in which this comes to expression in theology is to say that God is 'impeccable'. God, though free to act or not to act, is never free or able to sin in any of His actions.[46] God must 'do all his holy will', and therefore He cannot do anything contrary to His holiness.[47]

If it is true that God's freedom is perfectly compatible with His inability to do anything in conflict with His character, there does not seem to be any reason that human beings, who were created in God's image, must have libertarian freedom in order to be morally or religiously responsible. If there is an analogy between God's freedom and the freedom of creatures who bear His image, creatures who act in accordance with their character are no less free on that account. The open theist insistence that a truly reciprocal and loving relationship between God and human beings requires libertarian human freedom cannot be sustained. Why could the divine-human relationship, which enjoys some analogy to the relationship between the three Persons of the Trinity, not be genuinely free and reciprocal, and at the same time immutable and unbreakable?

Fourth, a consistently incompatibilist view of human freedom is unable to account for the final state of those whom God redeems. In the biblical understanding of the believer's glorification in union with Christ, God's work of salvation ultimately brings the believer to a state of perfect, consummate holiness. Since God aims in salvation to 'conform' those whom He elects to the image of His Son (Rom. 8:29), the sanctifying work of God's Spirit is not finished in believers until they become 'impeccable' or no longer able to sin. This seems to be the clear implication of the scriptural language of 'perfection' or 'maturity', when the goal of God's redemptive work in believers is reached (1 Cor. 13:9-12; cf. Eph. 4:13). In the language of the author

---

46. Cf. Sanders, *The God Who Risks,* 328fn47. Remarkably, Sanders suggests that 'impeccability', even if it were affirmed of God, is an 'incommunicable' attribute that cannot be shared by human beings who bear His image.

47. The phrase 'do all his holy will' is taken from an answer to the question in a children's version of the Westminster Shorter Catechism, 'Can God do all things?'

of Hebrews, believers will be joined in irrevocable union with Christ and the 'spirits of just men made perfect' (Heb. 12:23). For this reason, the same author describes Christ as the 'founder and perfecter' of the faith of believers (Heb. 12:2). Or, as the apostle John says, believers will be 'like' Christ at His appearing, for they 'will see him as he is' (1 John 3:2).

The implications of these passages for our understanding of true human freedom are compelling. True freedom is not the freedom to act or not act in conformity with God's will. True freedom is the glorious liberty that belongs to the children of God, when they are brought to a condition where they are not able, because always unwilling, to sin. Because the believer's condition in glorification is that of someone who is sanctified through and through (1 Thess. 5:23), it is impossible for a believer in glory to be or do anything but what is holy, righteous, and good. Upon the assumptions of open theism, however, no such liberty seems possible, now or in the future. But if human freedom in the highest state of glorification precludes libertarian freedom, the assumption of open theism that libertarian freedom is an ultimate value to be prized above God's independence, omnipotence, and omniscience, is exposed as fallacious. What open theism prizes, libertarian freedom, is contrary to the perfection God aims to provide believers through the work of Christ and His indwelling Spirit.

And fifth, the open theist doctrine of libertarian free will is based upon the same premise that drove Pelagius to deny that believers are saved by grace alone on the basis of the work of Christ alone. The premise assumed is that humans are not responsible for their actions unless they are able to perform these actions by their will and power alone. Human freedom can only flourish within a circumstance in which the obligation God stipulates is within the capacity of the person to whom the obligation is given. Although this premise has some plausibility and application in certain respects, it fails to recognize that it is possible for those who are unable to do what God requires to be responsible for having lost this ability. The biblical doctrine of original sin teaches that human beings were created with the ability to do what God required of them, but through the willful disobedience and sin of Adam this ability has been lost. The only way a fallen sinner can do what God requires is by a powerful intervention of

God's grace that ensures that this requirement is meant. To paraphrase the church father, Augustine, God's grace allows Him to command what He will and give to us the ability to do what He commands.

God's Providence is Not Mere 'Conservation'

Before I take up directly the open theist view of divine election, I need yet to consider the open theist claim that God's providence is a general, non-meticulous providence that leaves room for human beings with libertarian freedom.

In the history of theology, a common distinction is drawn between three aspects of God's providence: (1) God's 'conservation' (*conservatio*) or 'sustenance' (*sustenatio*) of creation and all created beings throughout history subsequent to the initial act of creation out of nothing; (2) God's 'concurrence' (*concursus*) with the free actions of creatures who in a non-coercive way act in conformity to His will; and (3) God's 'governance' (*gubernatio*) or rule over all created beings throughout history by which He unfailingly realizes His good purposes. The identification of these three components of God's providence belongs not to Reformed theology alone, but was a 'commonplace' (in the technical sense of the term) among scholastic theologians since at least the end of the sixteenth century and thereafter. Roman Catholic (Aquinas), Lutheran, Arminian, and orthodox Reformed theologians utilized these terms to articulate the nature of God's comprehensive providence.[48] While each of these dimensions of God's providence needs to be distinguished for the purpose of clarity, none of them can properly be affirmed and understood apart from the other. They are like three strands that are woven together in the comprehensive, rich tapestry, which is God's providential handiwork.

---

48. See, e.g., Aquinas, *Summa Theologica,* 1.21; Turretin, *Institutes of Elenctic Theology,* 1:501-15; and Bavinck, *RD,* 2:604-19. For an exposition of Arminius' view of God's providence, which distinguishes it from the view of open theism, see John Mark Hicks, 'Was Arminius an Open Theist? Meticulous Providence in the Theology of Jacob Arminius,' in *Reconsidering Arminius: Beyond the Reformed and Wesleyan Divide,* eds. Keith Stanglin, Mark G. Gilby, and Mark H. Mann (Nashville, TN: Abingdon Press, 2014), 137-60. Hicks shows that Arminius' doctrine of providence included each of the aspects of conservation, concurrence, and governance.

The first component of God's providence, conservation, refers to the way God, after having called all creatures into existence (sometimes called 'first creation', *creatio prima*), acts to conserve or preserve their existence (sometimes called 'continued creation', *continuata creatio*). Because God alone is absolutely independent, deriving His existence and being from Himself, all creatures to whom God first granted existence and endowed with unique properties and powers, can continue to exist as God conserves them.[49] For this reason, Louis Berkhof defines conservation as 'that continuous work of God by which He maintains the things which He created, together with all the properties and powers with which He endowed them.'[50] Contrary to pantheism, which teaches that all that is and occurs represents a necessary overflow of God's being (like a great waterfall that endlessly cascades downward), the biblical doctrine of providence insists that God distinctly and willfully acts, subsequent to creation, in a way that sustains all things in being and action.

The second component of God's providence, concurrence, focuses on the way God acts in and with the actions of His creatures to whom He grants real power to act in ways commensurate with their natures and properties. The special interest of the doctrine of concurrence is to provide an explanation (to the extent this is possible) of the inter-relation between God's will and the creature's will. By means of His concurring providence, God accomplishes His good purposes through the willful actions of creatures who are themselves fully engaged and responsible for all that they do. Louis Berkhof offers the following helpful summary of God's concursus:

> It should be noted at the outset that this doctrine implies two things: (1) That the powers of nature do not work by themselves, that is, simply by their inherent power, but that God is immediately operative in every act of the creature. This must be maintained in opposition to the deist position. (2) That second causes are real, and not to be regarded simply as the operative power of God. It is only on condition that second causes are real, that we can properly speak of a concurrence or co-operation of the

---

49. Berkhof, *Systematic Theology,* 169-70. Among the Scripture passages that Berkhof adduces for the idea of conservation, the following are illustrative: Deut. 33:12, 25-8; Ps. 107:9; Matt. 10:29; Acts 17:28; Col. 1:17; Heb. 1:3.

50. *Systematic Theology,* 170.

First cause with secondary causes. This should be stressed over against the pantheistic idea that God is the only agent working in the world.[51]

In the Westminster Confession of Faith's treatment of God's providence, the idea of concursus is expressed clearly: 'Although, in relation to the foreknowledge and decree of God, the first Cause, all things come to pass immutably, and infallibly; yet, by the same providence, he orders them to fall out, *according to the nature of second causes*, either necessarily, *freely, or contingently*' (WCF 5.2, emphasis mine). The point of this language is to affirm that, in the case of responsible or free creatures, God concurs with their actions in such a way as to effect His will, but not in such a way as to diminish the real engagement of the creature's will in the act performed. Furthermore, concursus involves the *simultaneous* working of God and the creature, but not the *co-ordinate* or *partitive* working of God and the creature.[52] God's will remains prior and determinative. The creature's will always depends upon and is governed by God's will. While the creature's will and action are real and operative, the creature never wills and acts independently of the divine concursus in a manner that makes the action partly God's act and partly the creature's act.[53]

---

51. *Systematic Theology,* 171-2. Among the scriptural passages that Berkhof adduces in support of concursus, the following are illustrative: Gen. 45:5; 50:19-20; Exod. 10:1, 20; Acts 2:23; 1 Cor. 12:6; Eph. 1:11; Phil. 2:12-13; Acts 17:28. Philippians 2:13 is a classic example: '... work out your own salvation with fear and trembling, for it is God who works in you, both to will and to work for his good pleasure.'

52. In a helpful essay on the failure of open theists to recognize the 'analogical' nature of all biblical and theological language about God, Michael Horton ('Hellenistic or Hebrew? Open Theism and Reformed Theological Method,' in *Beyond the Bounds*) makes an important observation about the way God's providential concursus does not exclude genuine human agency: 'Methodologically, theological proposals must do more than offer an alternative to a dominant position that nobody actually holds. For Pinnock, it is either "libertarian freedom" or despotic "omnicausality," not even recognizing that Reformed theology (like other traditions) affirms a fairly well-developed and well-known account of double agency.' The point Horton is making is that God's will and the human will may not be viewed univocally, as though we were speaking of two equivalent actors on the same stage, not recognizing the difference between God as Creator and human beings as creatures.

53. For this reason, Benjamin B. Warfield chose to speak of the 'mode of revelation' known as 'inspiration' as an instance of God's 'concursive operation'. Although the common language today is that of 'organic inspiration', the idea is that God is the primary author of Scripture, but He concursively works through human authors who are fully engaged and responsible for what they chose to write. See Benjamin B. Warfield,

The third component of God's providence, governance, refers to the way God rules all things, directing them to the end He has ordained for them. When God's providence is viewed from the vantage point of the telos or end God wills to accomplish, the idea of God's rule over all that takes place comes to the foreground. God's conservation of, and concurrence with, all that occurs in the course of history require the acknowledgment of His governance of all things. Likewise, God's governance of all things presupposes His conservation and concurrence in all things.[54]

When God's providence is defined in terms of these three components, it becomes clearer how God can foreknow all the acts, past, present, and future, of creatures who have genuine freedom. God's foreknowledge of these acts corresponds to His foreordination and providential work to make them occur. God knows all that He wills to do in conserving, concurring, and governing the free, contingent acts of His creatures in the course of history. Without His providential conservation, concurrence in, and government of what transpires, no free creature would have existence or be endowed with the powers required to make decisions or act in a particular way. Furthermore, by His concurrence in the free acts of His creatures, God works to accomplish His will, but He does so in a way that fully respects the real decisions such creatures make. Although it may be impossible to understand fully how this can be, God's providence is exhaustive, even 'meticulous', to use the term open theists employ when they argue for their alternative view of a general, non-controlling and non-exhaustive providence. But God's providence does not coerce any free creature to act contrary to what the creature is pleased to do or not do. Nor does God's providence diminish the responsibility of free creatures whose choices accord with what they judge to be pleasing or valuable.

The problem with the open theist view of God's providence is that God's conservation of all things, including the free actions of some

---

The Inspiration and Authority of the Bible, ed. Samuel G. Craig (Philadelphia: The Presbyterian and Reformed Publishing Co., 1948), 94-6.

54. Berkhof, Systematic Theology, expresses the intimate interplay and inseparability of conservation, concurrence, and governance, by noting that each of them is not simply a 'part' of God's providence but the 'whole of it' viewed from a different vantage point (175). For a comprehensive treatment of these aspects of God's providence in relation to the claims of open theism, see Ware, God's Greater Glory, 35-160.

creatures, is affirmed, but His concurrence with and governance of such actions are denied. Open theists acknowledge that the doctrine of creation out of nothing requires God's providential conservation of human beings who enjoy libertarian freedom. For example, in his treatment of God's providence, Hasker distinguishes open theism from process theology by noting that the 'persistence of any entity in existence depends wholly on the divine activity—which is just what is affirmed by the doctrine of divine conservation.'[55] Hasker also observes elsewhere, 'All created things depend on God for their existence from moment to moment; this is the divine "conservation" of created reality.'[56] However, it is not at all clear that open theists can retain a robust affirmation of God's conservation, when at the same time they deny God's concurrence and governance in the case of the free actions of human beings. In the open theist understanding of libertarian human freedom, free human beings have a God-like power to act independently of any reliance upon God. This means that free human decisions spring forth *ex nihilo* by virtue of the indeterminate power of libertarian freedom.[57] Such decisions have no other source than the independent power of free human beings to act and not to act in various circumstances.

The point of these remarks is that 'mere conservationism' represents an untenable view of God's providence.[58] This was already acknowledged in the scholastic theological discussions of the doctrine of providence in the late sixteenth and early seventeenth centuries. For example, the sixteenth-century Spanish Jesuit theologians, Luis de Molina and Francisco Suarez, argued that it was impossible to affirm

---

55. Hasker, 'An Adequate God,' in *Searching for An Adequate God: A Dialogue Between Process and Free Will Theists*, eds. John B. Cobb, Jr. and Clark H. Pinnock (Grand Rapids: Eerdmans, 2000), 225.

56. ibid., 219.

57. Cf. Hasker, 'God as Personal,' in *GGWM*, 176: 'Our Response is, in a real sense, *ex nihilo*, since it originates within us and not merely the effect of divine causation.' This statement might be clarified by removing the qualifier 'merely'.

58. Alfred J. Freddoso, 'God's General Concurrence with Secondary Causes: Why Conservation is Not Enough,' *Philosophical Perspectives* 5 (1991), 554: 'According to mere conservationism, God contributes to the ordinary course of nature solely by creating and conserving natural substances and their accidents, including their active and passive powers.'

God's conservation of human beings in their free choices without also affirming His concurrence and governance of these choices. Even though Suarez and Molina differed in their understanding of God's middle knowledge, they nonetheless concurred (no pun intended) on the inseparability of God's conservation, concurrence and governance of the free actions of human beings. According to Molina,

> No effect at all can exist in nature unless God ... immediately conserves it ... But since that which is necessary for the conservation of a thing is *a fortiori* necessary for the first production of the thing, it surely follows that nothing at all can be produced by secondary causes unless at the same time the immediate and actual influence of the First Cause intervenes.[59]

Similarly, Suarez argued that

> If God does not have an immediate influence on every action of a creature, then a created action itself does not of itself require God's influence essentially in order to exist, even though it, too, is a participation in being; therefore, there is no reason why the form that comes to exist through such an action should require for its conservation an actual influence of the First Cause.[60]

In these incisive comments, Molina and Suarez identify the critical problem with any view of providence that involves no more than God's conservation of a free creature's existence and power of choice. In the same way that a creature has no existence or power of choice except through God's act of conservation, so no creature can exist and exercise this power in a particular way except through God's concurrence and governance.

The Eclipse of God's Eternal and Merciful Election

Upon the basis of my critical evaluation of the open theist view, I want to conclude with a few comments on the implications of what I have argued regarding the open theist doctrine of election. The burden of my argument in the foregoing is that *open theism has no*

---

59. *Concordia,* II. 25, 14 (as quoted in Alfred J. Freddoso, 'God's General Concurrence with Secondary Causes,' *Philosophical Perspectives* 5 [1991], 554).

60. *Disputationes Metaphysicae* 22, I, 9 (as quoted in Freddoso, 'God's General Concurrence with Secondary Causes', 571).

true doctrine of election. The claims of open theists amount to the 'eclipse' of the scriptural understanding of God's merciful election of His people in Christ from before the foundation of the world. They also confirm that the Arminian view of conditional election is vulnerable to a more radical formulation that diverges significantly from the biblical view.

There are several key features of the scriptural teaching on election that are undeniably absent from, or contradicted by, the open theist position.

First, in several important scriptural passages, God's election or predestination of His people in Christ is described as belonging to His eternal counsel and purpose. In these passages, God's gracious intention to save those whom He elects is not viewed as a response in time to an unanticipated turn of events, namely, the fall and disobedience of human beings whom God discovers are now in need of redemption. Election is certainly not represented as a wise strategy that God adopts to try to save sinners whom He could not have known would choose to disobey Him. Rather, God's purpose of election in Christ belongs to His eternal counsel to magnify His mercy in the salvation of a great number of fallen sinners whom He created after His image and permitted to fall into sin. Perhaps the most striking example of this emphasis upon God's pre-temporal purpose of election is found in Ephesians 1:3-4, where Paul blesses 'the God and Father of our Lord Jesus Christ, who has blessed us in Christ with every spiritual blessing in the heavenly places, even as he chose us in him before the foundation of the world.' In this passage, Paul also declares that believers were predestined for salvation by God 'who works all things according to counsel of his will' (Eph. 1:11).[61] This passage is consistent with Scripture's general teaching that God knows Himself and all His works from eternity (Acts 15:18; Col. 1:15-20). It is also corroborated by passages that speak of Christ's work of atonement upon the cross as a work that God purposed from eternity (Acts 2:23; Heb. 13:20; Rev. 13:8; 1 Pet. 1:20). These passages clearly teach that the saving work of Christ in time was planned by God within His eternal counsel,

---

61. See also 2 Tim. 1:8-10; 1 Pet. 1:1-2; Rom. 8:28-30; and Rom. 9:6-13.

and that this work is effectual to draw those whom God chooses to Himself.[62]

Second, the open theist denial of God's foreknowledge of those whom He elects in Christ contradicts the scriptural teaching that God elects particular persons to salvation, and the explicit teaching of Romans 8:28-30. In the open theist view, God's gracious purpose of election does not concern any particular human beings whom God elects to save. God's election is His indefinite, gracious will and intention to save all human beings, provided they choose freely to believe and not to disbelieve. If we may speak of 'elect persons', we are speaking only of those whom God does not know or love in any distinctive way until they choose to believe and no longer frustrate His good intentions for them. Furthermore, within the framework of the tenets of open theism, there is no way for God to know that a human being with libertarian freedom will not at some future point choose to become unbelieving and forfeit through such unbelief the salvation they possessed only for a time. The salutary feature of open theism is the way it exposes the vulnerability of the traditional Arminian understanding of libertarian human freedom. If human beings always have the power of contrary choice, then it does seem impossible to claim that God could foreknow those who are elect and who will certainly be saved.

If there is a common thread shared by Augustinian/Calvinistic and Arminian theologies, it is that the apostle Paul's language in Romans 8:28-30 settles the question whether or not God knows beforehand those whom He predestines to save. In verses 29-30 of this passage, Paul declares, 'For those whom he foreknew he also predestined to be conformed to the image of his Son, in order that he might be the firstborn among many brothers. And those whom he predestined he also called, and those whom he called he also justified, and those whom he justified he also glorified.' While the meaning of the language 'foreknew' is disputed between Augustinian/Calvinistic and Arminian interpreters, I have argued it means that God distinguished

---

62. This is evident in several passages in the Gospel of John: 6:35-65; 10:1-18, 29; 13:18; 15:16; 17:2, 6, 9, 24; 18:9. For a treatment of the Gospel of John's representation of God's sovereignty in relation to human responsibility, see D. A. Carson, *DSHR*, 184-98.

beforehand those who were the distinct objects of His saving grace and mercy.[63] Those whom God foreknew are not a faceless crowd of persons out of which some will emerge because they choose to believe and not disbelieve (and persist in believing). They are a definite number of persons, known to and loved by God from beforehand, whom God will call, justify, and finally glorify. None of those who belong to this number will fail to enjoy these and all other spiritual blessings that are theirs in Christ. On a straightforward reading of this passage, there is no escaping the conclusion that God foreknows perfectly those whom He has purposed to save, and He knows them in the most intimate way.

Third, the open theist view of libertarian human freedom is incompatible with the scriptural portrait of the plight of all human beings who have sinned in Adam (original sin), who are now captive to the dominion of sin (actual sin), and who have become incapable of performing any saving good. The biblical teaching regarding God's sovereign and merciful election of His people in Christ corresponds to its teaching that fallen human beings are not able to save themselves from their bondage to sin and enmity toward God. Though they remain responsible before God and liable to the consequences of their willful disobedience, they are not able to respond to the gospel call to faith and repentance, unless God Himself draws them by the Spirit and Word of Christ.

Accordingly, it is not difficult to adduce scriptural passages that describe the plight of fallen human beings in a way that fits better with a compatibilist than an incompatibilist view of human freedom. Without diminishing human responsibility in relation to God, the Scriptures clearly teach the inability of fallen sinners to restore themselves to favor with God. Even though the gracious summons of the gospel calls all sinners to believe in Jesus Christ for salvation, they are unable to respond properly to this summons without the initiative, provision, and enablement of God's electing grace. The inability of fallen sinners to save themselves is entirely of their own making, and corresponds to the deepest inclinations of their hearts. Contrary to the

---

63. For the exegetical argument that supports this interpretation, see S. M. Baugh, 'The Meaning of Foreknowledge,' in *GGBW*, 183-200, as well as my treatment of this passage in Chapter 3.

open theist insinuation that God's electing will is directly responsible for the failure of fallen sinners to respond favorably to the gospel's invitation, fallen sinners, when left to themselves, have no desire to seek God or embrace His truth (Rom. 3:11). The real-life predicament of sinners when they hear the gospel call, is captured well in the saying, 'there is none so blind as he who will not see, none so deaf as he who will not hear.' Any number of scriptural characterizations of the condition of fallen humans beings bear this out: they are not able to see or enter the kingdom of God without being given new birth by the Holy Spirit (John 3:3-8); they are spiritually dead in their trespasses and sins (Eph. 2:1); they are blind to the truth of God, which they suppress in unrighteousness (Rom. 1:18); they have minds that are blinded by the 'god of this world' (2 Cor. 4:4); they are willfully subject to the dominion and power of sin and unrighteousness (Rom. 6:15-23); and their minds are 'hostile' against God so that they cannot submit to His will (Rom. 8:7). While fallen sinners may be free to do what pleases them, they are not free to be pleased to do what pleases God.

Fourth, in the biblical understanding of God's gracious purpose of election, there is an important link between God's electing will and the gracious and powerful means that God is pleased to use to accomplish what He wills. In the writings of open theists, the Augustinian/Calvinistic view of God's election is frequently described as 'deterministic' or 'fatalistic'. According to open theists, the Augustinian/Calvinistic view reduces human beings to mere puppets in the hands of God, robotic figures who play out their pre-programmed roles. On the one hand, those whom God elects not to save are denied any genuine freedom to respond to God's desire to save them. And on the other hand, those whom God elects to save are so controlled as to be coercively compelled to respond to the gospel in faith.

Though open theists believe that their quarrel is with Augustine and Calvin, their real quarrel is with the way the Scriptures represent God's saving work through the Word of the gospel and the Spirit who accompanies this Word. In the scriptural representation of the work of God's grace in the hearts and lives of His people, we see that God accomplishes His purpose of election in a way that magnifies His sheer grace while at the same time underscoring the responsibility of believers to respond to His call to faith in Christ. In the 'extraordinary providence' of God's saving work in time, believers discover that God alone is able to grant them the new birth requisite to their response to the gospel summons (John 3:1-8). They find that God alone is able to rescue them from all the tyranny of devil, the inclinations of their sinful flesh, and the pressures to be conformed to worldly standards. They also find that their spiritual blindness is removed by God's re-creative act whereby He causes the light of the gospel that shines in the face of Jesus Christ to shine in their hearts (2 Cor. 4:6).[64] God works through His Spirit and Word in a way that honors the believer's responsibility to believe and to repent, but ascribes to His conserving, concurring, and sovereign grace the power to grant this response (cf. Acts 16:14; Eph. 2:8-10). At no point do believers find God's gracious work as a kind of divine act of 'strong-arming' them into the kingdom. And at no point does God act in a way diminishing the responsibility of the individual to believe in Jesus Christ and embrace Him with all His promises.

Though it may be difficult, if not impossible, to grasp fully how God achieves His good purpose to save His people in Christ, He achieves it, not at the expense of the believer's full and hearty engagement, but by granting the very response that He requires.[65] Believing in Jesus Christ, embracing the gospel promises, turning from sin and toward God, discerning the things of the Spirit, being

---

64. For this reason, believers sing, 'Amazing grace, how sweet the sound, that saved a wretch like me! I once was lost, but now am found, was blind but now I see. 'Twas grace that taught my heart to fear, and grace my fears relieved.'

65. One of the finest statements of this truth is found in the Canons of Dort: 'Moreover, when God carries out this good pleasure in his chosen ones, or works true conversion in them, he not only sees to it that the gospel is proclaimed to them outwardly, and enlightens their minds powerfully by the Holy Spirit so that they may rightly understand and discern the things of the Spirit of God, but, by the effective operation of the same regenerating Spirit, he also penetrates into the inmost being of man, opens the closed heart, softens the hard heart, and circumcises the heart that is uncircumcised. He infuses new qualities into the will, making the dead will alive, the evil one good, the unwilling one willing, and the stubborn one compliant; he activates and strengthens the will so that, like a good tree, it may be enabled to produce the fruits of good deeds. ... For this reason, man himself, by that grace which he has received, is also rightly said to believe and to repent' (Canons of Dort 3/4.11-12.)

heartily ready and willing to do what God requires – these are all responses that believers themselves freely and gladly make in response to God's summons.

Summary

The true test of any formulation of the doctrine of election consists of two questions: (1) is the triune God – the Father, the Son, and the Holy Spirit – glorified as the sovereign and gracious Savior of His people?; and (2) are the elect, who are saved by God's grace alone in Christ, genuinely comforted?

When the open theist view of election is measured by these questions, it cannot but be regarded as unsatisfying. In the final analysis, the open theist view amounts to saying that human beings have it within their power to save themselves. All they need do is to make the right choice to believe and persist in believing. Though God intends that all human beings be saved, His good intentions are not enough to save anyone. Indeed, God's best intentions can always be, now and in the future, frustrated. God is powerless to do what He wills, and must remain passively behind the wall of human freedom that He created but over which He has no lordship. When all is said and done, the God of open theism makes no promises in Christ that He can ensure will bear fruit in the lives of those to whom these promises are made. Rather than saying to those who are saved, 'what do you have that you have not received?' (1 Cor. 4:7), the open theist is obliged to ask, 'what do you have that you have not obtained by your powerful will alone?' God is diminished and human beings are magnified in the imaginary world of open theism.

As to the second question, open theism fares no better. By magnifying libertarian human freedom and diminishing God's purpose of election, open theism leaves believers with precious little comfort. There is no room in the open theist world for a God who is able to work all things for good in the lives of those whom He elects to save. Nor is there any basis for the confidence of which the apostle Paul speaks in Romans 8, that nothing can separate God's elect from His love for them in Christ.

One of the most beautiful expressions of the comfort that believers derive from God's powerful work of grace in the lives of His elect people is found in the opening question and answer of the Heidelberg Catechism:

> *Q.* What is your only comfort in life and in death?
>
> *A.* That I, with body and soul, both in life and death, am not my own, but belong unto my faithful Savior Jesus Christ; who with His precious blood has fully satisfied for all my sins, and delivered me from all the power of the devil; and so preserves me that without the will of my heavenly Father not a hair can fall from my head; yea, that all things must be subservient to my salvation, wherefore by His Holy Spirit He also assures me of eternal life, and makes me heartily willing and ready, henceforth, to live unto Him.

Interestingly, this question and answer does not explicitly speak of God's gracious election to save His people in Christ. However, no one could speak in the language of Lord's Day 1, unless they knew the God of the Scriptures, who sets His love upon His people from all eternity, who sends His Son in the fullness of time to accomplish what was needed for their redemption, and who makes His people, by His indwelling Spirit, members of Christ, heartily willing and ready henceforth to live for Him. This God is the God of 'all comfort' (2 Cor. 1:3) whose grace toward His people in Christ is invincible.

CHAPTER 9

Concluding Theological and Pastoral Reflections

THE primary goal of this study of the doctrine of election is to provide a broad overview of the biblical, historical, and theological dimensions of the topic. However, in this concluding chapter, I wish to address several recurring objections that often arise when the subject of election is addressed. I do not pretend to be able to answer these questions in a way that removes all the difficulties that the doctrine of election poses; however, these questions are unavoidable, and need to be addressed in a clear, concise and biblical manner. Although it will not be my purpose in what follows to summarize what has already been argued in previous chapters, I do aim to apply what we have found to several questions that recur in discussions of the doctrine of election.

Doesn't Election Unduly Complicate the Simplicity of the Gospel?

Due to the controversy that often swirls around the doctrine of election, it is sometimes suggested that this doctrine unduly complicates the simplicity of the gospel of salvation through faith in Jesus Christ. Since the theme of election so often raises a number of difficult theological questions, some argue that it would be better to avoid the topic altogether or perhaps restrict the discussion of it to the narrow precincts of the Christian academy. Why encumber the gospel with a discussion of God's eternal purpose of election, which can only prove to be a kind of labyrinth from which there is no escape?

Remarkably, John Calvin, whose name is inextricably linked in popular imagination with an allegedly exaggerated attention to the topic of predestination, directly addresses this question in his *Institutes*. Before offering his exposition of the biblical teaching regarding predestination, Calvin notes that there are two kinds of persons who fail to do justice to this theme. On the one hand, there are those whose unbridled curiosity lands them in a labyrinth of their own making from which there is no escape. Rather than remain within the boundaries of what Scripture teaches us, they 'unrestrainedly ... search out things that the Lord has willed to be hid in himself.'[1] Against this temptation, Calvin wisely counsels us to only seek to know what God in His wisdom has decided to reveal for our benefit. When we do so, we will humbly admit that our knowledge is limited, even in some respects a 'certain learned ignorance', as Calvin describes it. On the other hand, there are those who, fearful of rash presumption and arrogance in the handling of the doctrine of election, avoid the subject altogether. Such persons think it best to avoid this topic in the same way sailors carefully avoid a reef at sea. In Calvin's estimation, this timidity in handling the doctrine of election amounts to a kind of 'anxious silence' that questions the wisdom of the Holy Spirit whose school is the Holy Scriptures in which 'as nothing is omitted that is both necessary and useful to know, so nothing is taught but what is expedient to know.'[2] While we must be careful not to go beyond what is made known to us in Scripture, we must also be willing to go as far as the Holy Spirit teaches us in the Scriptures. Since the Holy Spirit teaches us about God's gracious election, we would be remiss not to consider the necessity and usefulness of this teaching.

In my summary of the Bible's teaching about election, we witnessed the truth of Calvin's comments regarding the unavoidable need to treat this subject. If we take our cue from the testimony of Scripture, we can hardly avoid an engagement with the doctrine of election. The story of redemption recounted in Scripture is, from its beginning to its consummation, all about the relentless work of the triune God who grants salvation in and through Christ to those whom He has elected to

---

1. *Institutes*, 3.21.2.
2. ibid, 3.21.4.

save. The only way to make biblical sense of the story of redemption is to recognize it as a story of the unfolding of God's eternal purpose to elect His people in Christ. Though the telling of this story begins with the election of Israel, it ultimately finds its fulfillment in the election of Christ as God's chosen servant through whom all the families of the earth will enjoy the blessing of salvation. God's purpose of election entails not only the salvation of those whom He calls from among the people of Israel, but also those from among the Gentile peoples whom He effectually calls through the gospel. To state the matter differently, the theme of God's gracious election of His people in Christ does not lie on the periphery of the history of redemption. God's election of His people in Christ from before the foundation of the world constitutes the ultimate source for His redemptive works in time. Without God's free and gracious decision to save His people in and through Christ, the biblical story of redemption would be unintelligible in the same way a novel would be senseless without a plot-line. God's redemptive work throughout history, culminating in the coming of Christ, would amount to nothing but a series of ad hoc, discrete and unrelated acts. It would not be the story of God's gracious purpose to save His people in and through the work of Christ as Mediator.

But it is not only the pervasiveness of the theme of election in Scripture that demands our attention. It is also the striking way in which God's merciful election actually underlines the simplicity of the gospel of salvation by grace alone through faith in Christ alone. The doctrine of God's gracious election to show mercy and save His people for Christ's sake is a necessary corollary of the biblical teaching that our acceptance before God depends alone upon His gracious granting and imputing to us the perfect righteousness of Jesus Christ. Our salvation is not based upon our worthiness or meritorious works. It rests completely upon the free gift of God's grace in Jesus Christ. For this reason, Augustine was compelled again and again throughout his writings against Pelagius and Pelagianism to have recourse to the apostle Paul's questions in 1 Corinthians 4:7: 'What do you have that you did not receive? If then you received it, why do you boast as if you did not receive it?' These questions are the rock that shatters any view of election and salvation that bases God's gracious choice upon the worthiness of those whom God elects. For if we deny the truth of unconditional election, then we must ultimately say that the reason some are saved is due to a quality that distinguishes them from others. However this distinguishing quality is defined – foreseen faith, the humility to trust in Christ, the wisdom to accept the truth of God's Word, a virtuous life, and so on – the specter of Pelagianism rears its ugly head. For this reason, the biblical teaching of election is the only fence that provides an insuperable obstacle to every form of boasting in the matter of salvation in the presence of God. Far from unduly complicating the simple gospel, God's purpose of election in Christ expresses the truth of the gospel of salvation by grace alone, and not upon the basis of human merit, with unmatched clarity.

Is God Unjust or Unfair in Electing Some and not Others?

One of the most common questions that the doctrine of election provokes is whether or not God acts justly or fairly in choosing to save some but not others. In the apostle Paul's well-known exposition of God's merciful election of some to salvation in Romans 9, he expressly anticipates the objection that God's purpose of election does not accord with justice. Throughout the extended history of theological engagement with the doctrine of election, this objection has repeatedly surfaced. In the course of the controversy with Pelagianism in the early church, and later in the context of the Arminian controversy in the Netherlands, this objection was frequently raised against the teaching that God graciously elects to save some sinners but not others. Doesn't such a teaching represent God acting in a way that is unfair? How can it be just for God to choose to grant salvation to some persons on the basis of the work of Christ, but not to others?

There are several observations that may be made in reply to this objection.

First, it is important to distinguish carefully between God's justice and His mercy. Though God's justice, like all of His divine attributes, is not fully comprehensible to us, it includes the aspect of what is sometimes called 'retributive' justice or the administration of penalties that are commensurate with the offence committed or the debt owed. God's justice, even as is true in human relations, ordinarily entails that human beings be treated according to what is due or properly owed them. When human beings act properly and comply with the law, they have a right to be regarded as innocent and be treated accordingly. When human beings act improperly and do not comply with the law, they can expect to suffer the just punishment due to them. While they may, so to speak, throw themselves upon the mercy of the court, their appeal for mercy is clearly distinct from an appeal for justice. Since all human beings are fallen in Adam, and since all are worthy of condemnation and death on account of their original and actual sins, no one may claim that justice requires God to save them. As the apostle Paul says in Romans 6:23, 'the wages of sin are death, but the free gift of God is eternal life.' When God requires that the wages of sin be paid, He acts justly. But when God freely and graciously grants the gift of eternal life, He acts mercifully. As Augustine observed in his writings against Pelagius, even in human society it is acknowledged that a creditor has the right to exact from a debtor what is owed to him. Likewise, God in His justice has the right to exact payment from fallen sinners who are in no position to repay Him for the debts of their sins. As Augustine put it, 'No one can be charged with unrighteousness who exacts what is owing to him. Nor certainly can he be charged with unrighteousness who is prepared to give up what is owing to him. This decision does not lie with those who are debtors but with the creditor.'[3] Though God may mercifully choose to show mercy to a fallen sinner, He is under no obligation of justice to do so.

Second, one of the best arguments often adduced for an 'infralapsarian' view of the order of God's decrees is that it underscores more clearly than the supralapsarian view the justice of God's decision to leave some sinners in their lost condition. Though there may be room for some diversity of opinion regarding the order of God's decrees, the Scriptures commonly speak in a non-technical and broadly infralapsarian manner, when they describe God's gracious election to save His people in Christ. Divine election is an election unto salvation, which assumes that those whom God elects are fallen sinners who need to be saved. For example, when the apostle Paul speaks of the election of believers 'in Christ' from

---

3. *To Simplician,* 2.16.

before the foundation of the world (Eph. 1:4), he affirms that God's election includes the provision of Christ whose work as Mediator will provide for the salvation of the elect. In this way, the infralapsarian view highlights the *asymmetry* between God's *gracious* election of some to salvation and His *just* decision to leave others in their sinful condition and deserved condemnation. Whereas God's gracious election is unconditional, expressing His positive will to grant His unmerited favor to the elect, His non-election or reprobation of others leaves them in their lost estate and justly condemns them for their sins.[4] For this reason, Turretin, who devotes careful attention to the order of God's decrees, finds the infralapsarian view more satisfying than the supralapsarian, which 'falsely' supposes that God 'exercises an act of mercy and justice towards his creatures in the destination to salvation and destruction who are neither miserable nor guilty; yea, who are not even conceived of as yet existing.'[5]

Third, when we recognize the difference between God's justice and mercy, God's gracious election to save His people in Christ does not so much raise questions about His justice as it does about the marvel of His mercy and grace. Since God could have justly left all fallen sinners in their sin and misery, His gracious choice to save many represents an amazing and unexpected display of undeserved mercy. Even though we may not know precisely why God chooses to save those whom He elects, we certainly know that He did not do so because they were more deserving than others (cf. 1 Cor. 4:7). Perhaps the clearest (albeit partial and incomplete) explanation for God's choice of those whom He wills to save is to be found in a passage like 1 Corinthians 1:27-29, which echoes themes found in the Old Testament's account of God's election of Israel. In this passage, we are told that 'God chose what is foolish in the world to shame the wise; God chose what is weak in the world to shame the strong; God chose what is low and despised in the world, even things that are not, to bring to nothing things that are, so that no human being might boast

---

4. Cf. Bavinck, *RD*, 2:396. Also cf. Berkhof, *Systematic Theology*, 117.

5. Turretin, *Institutes of Elenctic Theology*, 1:418. Though Turretin sides with the infralapsarian view, he also acknowledges that the theological ordering of God's decrees is 'with respect to our manner of conception' and involves 'various inadequate conceptions that we cannot compass in one single conception' (1:430).

in the presence of God.' While it is often alleged that the doctrine of election encourages a kind of smug sense of superiority on the part of believers, nothing could be farther from the truth, at least the biblical truth that lies at the heart of the theme of gracious election. Believers may be 'chosen' people, but they are decidedly not 'choice' people.[6] As the apostle Paul's language reminds us, God has chosen those who are weak, lowly, and despised, in order to shame the strong, the wise, and the great. When believers consider their election in biblical perspective, they can only stand amazed at God's choice of the most unlikely of sinners. And at the same time, they are reminded that the doctrine of election is no less scandalous than the gospel of Christ, who was crucified in weakness in order to save His people from their sins. Just as the cross is foolishness and weakness to those who are wise and strong, so God's electing choice represents a scandal to those who would base salvation ultimately upon human merit or worthiness.

And fourth, the final word on the question of God's justice must be the one spoken by Augustine in his polemics with Pelagius. Although we may not be able to plumb the depths of the wisdom, knowledge, and justice of God, we must remain steadfast in our conviction that God has His reasons, even though not wholly known or comprehensible to us, for graciously choosing to save those whom He will. Though God's ways may be to us inscrutable and incomprehensible, they remain altogether just even as He is just.

Are the Elect Few in Number?

Even though it seems evident that God does not act unjustly when He elects to save some fallen sinners and not others, the question can still be pressed in another direction: Why doesn't God choose to show mercy to all fallen sinners? Though it may be true that God is not obligated to save everyone, what accounts for the fact that He chooses not to show mercy toward all? In the history of theology, this question has occasionally led some to embrace universalism, that is, the view that in the end all fallen human beings will be saved by God on the basis of the work of Christ. Like the attractiveness of a human story that ends happily for everyone, universalism often is born out

---

6. The language is Tim Keller's (*Romans 8–16 For You* [The Good Book Company, 2015], 214).

of the all-but-irresistible desire to see God's grace in Christ triumph in the salvation of all sinners.[7] Such universalism aims to magnify the reach of God's mercy, while at the same time mitigating the apparent arbitrariness of God's decision not to save some who are no more or less deserving of His favor than those toward whom He chooses to be merciful.

While I believe there are ample biblical reasons to reject universalism, I am also persuaded that some defenders of the biblical doctrine of election have unnecessarily burdened the biblical teaching with the presumption that, in the final analysis, the number of the elect will be relatively few. In the history of Christian theology, beginning with Augustine and into the late medieval period, a common view was that the number of the elect was limited to the number of fallen angels. As we observed in considering Augustine's teaching, he was also compelled to limit the reach of God's purpose of election to those who receive the grace of baptismal regeneration and, subsequent to baptism, are preserved by God's electing grace in a state of grace. For Augustine, as well as for many theologians in the history of theology, the sacrament of baptism is indispensable to the salvation of any fallen sinner born and conceived in sin. Consequently, it was difficult to affirm that God's purpose of election might include persons, such as infants, who die without receiving the sacrament.

But it was not only the necessity of baptism that led Augustine and others to limit the number of the elect. They also appealed to biblical passages that seem to support this view. For example, the language of a 'remnant' is used to refer to those whom God elects from among the greater company of His corporate people, Israel (e.g.,

---

7. I use the language 'born out of,' since universalism goes beyond the mere desire that all be saved and actually affirms that this is the case. As I shall argue later in this chapter, there is a sense in which God Himself does not desire the death of the wicked, even though He may not choose (for reasons not entirely known to us) to save all. If this is the case, then there seems no reason to deny the legitimacy of this desire, so long as it does not give birth to the unbiblical tenet that God will finally save all sinners. Cf. Oliver Crisp, *Saving Calvinism: Expanding the Reformed Tradition* (Downers Grove: IVP Academic, 2016), 96: 'I do not think it is appropriate to desire the death of the wicked if God does not (Ezek. 33:11). Since Scripture clearly teaches that God desires the salvation of all humans, we should do likewise.' Calvin makes a similar point, appealing to the opinion of Augustine that 'we ought to be so minded as to wish that all men be saved' (*Institutes,* 3.23.14).

1 Kings 19:10; Rom. 11:1-6). The Gospel of Luke records Christ's sobering exhortation, which was prompted by the question, 'Lord, will those who are saved be few?': 'Strive to enter through the narrow door. For many, I tell you, will seek to enter and will not be able' (Luke 13:23-24). This language seems to imply that a limited number will enter through the narrow door. It is also reminiscent of similar sayings of Christ, such as Matthew 22:14 where He says at the end of a parable regarding the invitation to the wedding banquet, 'many are called, but few are chosen.' Similarly, Christ addresses His disciples as a 'little flock' in Luke 12:32, and prophesies that as the end draws near, the 'love of many will grow cold' (Matt. 24:12; cf. Luke 18:8; Rev. 20:7-10). When these passages are brought together, they seem to amount to a strand of evidence for the limited scope of God's purpose of election.

While the presence of these kinds of passages in Scripture needs to be acknowledged, I do not believe that they warrant any speculative or unwarranted conclusions regarding the relative number of the elect. The testimony of Scripture on the number of those whom God promises to save is diverse, and also includes passages that emphasize the broad scope of God's saving mercy. In the Old Testament, God's promises to Israel include the promise to Abraham that in his seed 'all the families of the earth' will be blessed (Gen. 22:18; cf. Gen. 12:3). God promises Abraham that his offspring will be as innumerable as the dust of the earth (Gen. 13:16) and the stars of the heavens (Gen. 15:5; cf. Gen. 17:5-6; Num. 23:10). Throughout the Old Testament Psalter (e.g., Pss. 2; 22; 45; 67; 72; 110), as well as in the Messianic prophecies of Isaiah (e.g., Isa. 2:2-4; 9:6-7; 11:6, 9-10; 40:4-5; 49:6), the promise of the coming Savior includes the assurance that He will reign in the midst of history, overcoming His enemies and subjecting all nations under His feet. In the New Testament, Christ is represented as the One through whom these promises are fulfilled and to whom the nations will be given as His rightful inheritance (Matt. 28:16-20; cf. 1 Cor. 15:25; Eph. 1:3-23). When the apostle Paul treats the topic of God's purpose of election, he not only speaks of an elect remnant, but also of the extraordinary reach of God's saving mercy. Within the counsel and purpose of God, Paul emphasizes that God's mercy will ultimately embrace the 'fullness' of the Gentiles and 'all Israel'

(Rom. 11:11-32). Furthermore, in the book of Revelation, John's vision of those who are redeemed by the blood of the Lamb is of 'a great multitude that no one could number, from every nation, from all tribes and peoples and languages, standing before the throne and before the Lamb' (Rev. 7:8; cf. Rev. 5:9-10). The presence of these passages should caution us against drawing a settled conclusion regarding the relative number of the elect. At the least, they should caution against leaving the impression that the reach of God's electing mercy is narrow, not wide and embracing.[8]

In this connection, I believe it is significant that the Reformed churches historically have affirmed that God's purpose of election includes the salvation of some persons who are in no position to respond appropriately to the call of the gospel through the ordinary means of the Word and sacraments. The Canons of Dort affirm that godly parents 'ought not to doubt the election and salvation of their children whom God calls out of this life in infancy'.[9] The Westminster Confession of Faith goes further, when it affirms that 'Elect infants, dying in infancy, are regenerated, and saved by Christ, through the Spirit, who worketh when, and where, and how he pleaseth; so also are all other elect persons who are incapable of being outwardly called by the ministry of the Word.'[10] The Second Helvetic Confession likewise notes that, in addition to those who are called through the ordinary means of grace, 'we recognize that God can illuminate whom and when he will, even without the external ministry, for that is in his

---

8. See Jewett, *Election and Predestination*, 121-8, for a helpful treatment of the question of the relative number of the elect. Jewett inclines toward a view that limits the elect to a minority, although in doing so he seems to violate his own stricture that 'we should not speculate about how many are elect' (125).

9. Canons of Dort, I/17. For an extended treatment of this topic, see Venema, *Christ and Covenant Theology*, 214-55.

10. For an extensive treatment of the topic of the salvation of infants in the history of Christian theology, see Benjamin B. Warfield, 'The Development of the Doctrine of Infant Salvation,' in *The Works of Benjamin B. Warfield*, vol. 9: *Studies in Theology* (reprint; Baker Book House, 1981), 411-44. Warfield leans toward the view that all infants, whether of unbelieving parents or not, are elect. Like his predecessor at Princeton, Charles Hodge, Warfield believed the number of the elect was far greater than the number of the non-elect. Cf. Charles Hodge, *Systematic Theology* (reprint; Grand Rapids: Eerdmans, 1952 [1871]), 3:880. According to Hodge, the number of the lost 'will prove very inconsiderable as compared with the whole number of the saved'.

power.'[11] In these confessional statements, the Reformed churches leave to God's freedom the merciful election of many, especially infants, to salvation, even though they may not have the opportunity to respond in faith and repentance to the gospel call. Though there may be room to debate whether all infants, including those of unbelieving parents, are included within the embrace of God's merciful election, there is no biblical reason to argue that such may not be the case. No less reputable a Reformed theologian than Voetius offers a sage comment on this possibility: 'I would not wish to deny, nor am I able to affirm' (*nolim negare, affirmare non possum*).[12] Although Voetius does not presume to affirm this as a settled conclusion based upon the express teaching of Scripture, he leaves open the possibility of a wider reach of God's electing mercy toward those who die in infancy. Indeed, it seems a fitting possibility, congruent with what we know of God's rich mercy and overflowing goodness.

Though the teaching of Scripture may not permit us a firm judgment on the question of the exact scope or wideness of God's electing mercy, it should be noted further that Reformed theology suffers no disadvantage on this point, when compared to other theologies, including Arminian and semi-Pelagian views. As Bavinck notes,

It is a fact that in Reformed theology the number of elect need not, for any reason or in any respect, be deemed smaller than in any other theology. In fact, at bottom the Reformed confessions are more magnanimous and broader in outlook than any other Christian confession. It locates the ultimate and most profound source of salvation solely in God's good pleasure, in his eternal compassion, in his unfathomable mercy, in the unsearchable riches of his grace that is both omnipotent and free. Aside from it where could we find a firmer and broader foundation for the salvation of a sinful and lost human race? However troubling it may be that many fall away, still in Christ the believing community, the human race, the world, is saved.[13]

---

11. The Second Helvetic Confession, chap. 1.

12. G. Voetius, *Select. dispu.,* II:413 (as quoted by Bavinck, *RD*, 4:725). Bavinck also notes that Junius, another esteemed and influential Reformed theologian, 'would rather surmise out of love that they [children of non-believing parents who die in infancy] were saved than that they were lost' (*RD*, 4:725).

13. Bavinck, *RD*, 4:727.

While we do not need to embrace an unbiblical universalism in order to 'save Calvinism', neither are we obliged to embrace an unduly parsimonious view of the wideness of God's mercy.[14] Though God's grace is granted according to His sovereign good pleasure, it is nonetheless lavish and rich (cf. Eph. 1:8; 2:4). In the final analysis, perhaps the best answer to the question of the scope of God's election remains the one given in the Second Helvetic Confession:

> And although God knows who are his, and here and there mention is made of the small number of elect, yet we must hope well of all, and not rashly judge any man to be a reprobate. For Paul says to the Philippians, 'I thank my God for you all' (now he speaks of the whole Church in Philippi), 'because of your fellowship in the Gospel, being persuaded that he who began a good work in you will bring it to completion at the day of Jesus Christ. It is also right that I have this opinion of you all' (Phil. 1:3 ff.). ... And when the Lord was asked whether there were few that should be saved, he does not answer and tell them that few or many should be saved or damned, but rather he exhorts every man to 'strive to enter by the narrow door' (Luke 13:24): as if he should say, It is not for you curiously to inquire about these matters, but rather to endeavor that you may enter into heaven by the straight way.[15]

Doesn't Election Diminish the Urgency of Evangelism?

Among evangelical believers who oppose the teaching that God has graciously and unconditionally elected some sinners to salvation, a practical and pastoral objection is often raised: Why pray or engage in the work of evangelism? If God's purpose of election cannot be frustrated, all whom He elects will certainly be saved whether or

---

14. Cf. Crisp, *Saving Calvinism,* esp. 87-107. Crisp argues for what he calls an 'optimistic particularism', which he thinks best accords with the Scriptures' encouragements to 'be hopeful about the scope of salvation in Christ' (106). While Crisp seems to overstep Voetius' caution regarding the Scripture's teaching (dare we affirm what is not clearly taught in Scripture?), his position is not outside the boundaries of what may be regarded as possible (why would we wish to deny?). We must recognize the difference between holding an opinion on the question of the relative number of the elect and insisting that this opinion is a good and *necessary* consequence of the Scriptures' express teaching.

15. Second Helvetic Confession, chap. 10.

not the church actively engages in the work of evangelism. And in the case of those whom God has not elected to save, no amount of evangelistic fervor will bring them to faith and repentance. Accordingly, many evangelical Christians fear that the doctrine of election will significantly hinder the church's resolution to carry out the Great Commission of Matthew 28:16-20.

Before responding directly to this question, it must be acknowledged that there are some who may be vulnerable to this objection. For example, J. I. Packer cites the case of William Carey who, upon announcing his intention to begin a missionary society, was told by an older pastor, 'Sit down, young man! When God is pleased to convert the heathen, he will do it without your aid, or mine.'[16] I recall a member of a congregation I served who complained that too much emphasis was being placed upon the need to evangelize and disciple those who were not believers and members of the church. According to this church member, the church had no special responsibility to reach out with the gospel. As he rather bluntly put it, 'The doors of the church were not locked,' and there was nothing to prevent those whom God elects from coming through them. Though the number of people with such a perspective is happily few, it cannot be denied they exist or they suffer from the mistaken notion that God's purpose of election diminishes the urgency of pursuing the church's evangelistic calling.

However, such passivity in pursuing the task of calling sinners to faith and salvation does not properly reflect the biblical understanding regarding how God wills to grant salvation to those whom He elects to save. If we distinguish, without separating, between God's purpose of election and *the means that He appoints to realize this purpose*, it will be evident that the doctrine of election is not an impediment to the work of evangelism. Fallen sinners are not saved simply because God has elected to save them. Though God's gracious purpose is the ultimate reason believers are saved, this purpose is ordinarily effected through the ministry of the gospel. There is a difference between God's purpose to save, and the way He is pleased to realize this purpose. Those whom God elects, He also effectually calls through

---

16. J. I. Packer, *Evangelism and the Sovereignty of God* (Downers Grove, IL: InterVarsity, 1961), 33.

the gospel of Jesus Christ and the work of the Holy Spirit. Though fallen sinners are not saved on account of their faith, they also are not ordinarily saved without responding in faith to the gracious invitation of the gospel.

Therefore, while it is true that God unconditionally elects to save His people in Christ, the actual realization of this purpose in time is accomplished through the ordinary means of grace, that is, the church's preaching and teaching of the gospel together with the administration of the sacraments. According to the Great Commission, these are the means the church is commanded to employ in order to make disciples of all nations. When the apostle Paul describes his ministry of the gospel, he explains how his labor on behalf of the lost was motivated by his desire to see the elect obtain salvation: 'Remember Jesus Christ, risen from the dead, the offspring of David, as preached in my gospel, for which I am suffering, bound with chains as a criminal. But the word of God is not bound! Therefore, I endure everything for the sake of the elect' (2 Tim. 2:8-10). Paul's preaching (and the preaching of the church until the present day) is born out of the conviction that 'faith comes from hearing, and hearing through the Word of Christ' (Rom. 10:17). Similarly, in the discourse on the Good Shepherd in John 10:14-16, Christ identifies those who belong to His flock as those who hear His voice and respond properly to the call of the gospel. When it comes to the urgency of the work of evangelism, accordingly, there is nothing in the biblical doctrine of election that diminishes in the least the responsibility of the church to call sinners everywhere to faith in Jesus Christ. Though believers do not become elect through an act of faith, their election requires that they be effectually called to faith through the gospel. And this is the task which Christ has given to the church and its ministry.

Moreover, the biblical view of election also has positive implications for the manner in which the work of evangelism is undertaken. On the one hand, the truth of God's purpose of election encourages confidence that God will effectively use the means He has appointed to produce faith and repentance in many who hear the gospel message. Though one person may sow the seed of the Word and another water, God, who is the true missionary agent in evangelism, will undoubtedly give the increase as He wills (cf. 1 Cor. 3:5-9). To be fruitful in this work, the church does not need to attenuate the message of the gospel or to smooth over its sharp edges to make it palatable to contemporary tastes. Those who minister the Word are not obliged to indulge in evangelistic schemes belying the truth that God is pleased to save His chosen people through the foolishness of the preaching of the cross of Christ. Nor should we expect immediate results, quickly losing heart when the response is limited. Rather, with great patience and boldness (cf. Acts 13:46; 2 Tim. 4:2), we may herald the gospel message of the kingdom to all peoples and nations, confident that God will add His blessing to the church's evangelistic work when it is performed in obedience to His commission.

On the other hand, the ministry of the Word will always be accompanied by fervent prayer for God's blessing upon the spreading of the gospel and the calling of many to conversion. As Packer well describes it,

> Prayer ... is a confessing of impotence and need, an acknowledging of helplessness and dependence, and an invoking of the mighty power of God to do for us what we cannot do for ourselves. In evangelism ... we are impotent; we depend wholly upon God to make our witness effective; only because He is able to give men new hearts can we hope that through our preaching of the gospel sinners will be born again. These facts ought to drive us to prayer.[17]

Interestingly, in Augustine's writings on the topic of election and predestination, the prayers of the church were often cited as compelling proof that salvation is ultimately of the Lord and not by virtue of any human initiative. For Augustine, these prayers prove the catholicity of the church's conviction that salvation is a work of God's unmerited grace from beginning to end. Virtually all petitions of the Lord's Prayer testify to our need for God's grace, not only to believe but to persevere in believing, especially in the face of temptation and the evil one's schemes. When Christians pray, they offer the most profound testimony to the conviction that God, and God alone, is able to save and to preserve in salvation those whom He elects to save in Christ. Far from diminishing the need to evangelize and pray,

---

17. ibid., 122.

election compels us to accompany the ministry of the gospel with constant prayer.

What About the Well-meant Gospel Offer?

In the historical discussion regarding election, one of the more controversial issues is that of the so-called free or well-meant offer of the gospel. During the dispute between the Arminians and the Calvinists in the Netherlands in the early seventeenth century, the Arminians complained that the Calvinist doctrine of election nullified the genuineness of the gospel offer of salvation. In their opinion, if God has unconditionally elected to save a certain number of persons, then the gospel-call could not *seriously* or *genuinely* summon all persons to faith. Because some of these persons are not elect, and since God has no intention of bringing them to salvation, the call of the gospel, when extended to the non-elect, is disingenuous. Neither God nor those who speak for Him can sincerely call all sinners through the gospel to salvation, expressing a genuine desire that they would believe in Christ and be saved. In the estimation of Arminius and his followers, the doctrine of unconditional election calls into question what the Bible teaches about God's goodness and love toward all fallen sinners. They judged the doctrine of unconditional election as contrary to the Bible's teaching that God desires for all to be saved, taking no delight in the death of any fallen sinner.

While it may be difficult, even impossible, for us to comprehend, the only biblical answer to this question is that God's will regarding the salvation of fallen human beings must be distinguished into two aspects.[18] On the one hand, God's purpose of election expresses *His gracious will and intention to save* those toward whom He chooses to be merciful. The biblical doctrine of election means God *uniquely and particularly wills* to save some sinners in and through the work of Christ. On the other hand, God also reveals through the gracious call of the gospel how He nonetheless *genuinely wills* that all fallen

---

18. For a more extensive treatment of this topic, see John Piper, 'Are There Two Wills in God? Divine Election and God's Desire for All to Be Saved,' in *GGBW*, 1:107-32. For a historical treatment of the way this topic was handled by Calvin and others in the Reformed tradition, see Muller, *Calvin and the Reformed Tradition,* 107-25.

sinners should respond in faith and so be saved. When fallen sinners are urgently, seriously, and sincerely summoned through the gospel to come to Christ in faith in order to be saved, this summons expresses God's desire for them to do so. The call of the gospel is born out of God's mercy, and expressly reveals God's good will toward all fallen sinners. For this reason, the Canons of Dort affirm that 'all who are called through the gospel are called seriously. For seriously and most genuinely God makes known in his Word what is pleasing to him: that those who are called should come to him. Seriously he also promises rest for their souls and eternal life to all who come to him and believe' (I/8).[19]

Despite the difficulty of explaining how these two distinct aspects of God's will are compatible, both are clearly taught in Scripture. Indeed, there are several ways in which the Scriptures attest God's gracious will that all fallen human beings turn from their sin and find salvation through faith in Christ.[20] For example, several biblical passages in the Old Testament represent God to desire the salvation of all to whom He reveals His mercy (e.g., Deut. 5:29; 32:29; Ps. 81:13; Isa. 48:18). In these passages, God expresses His desire for the salvation of those who do not fear Him or keep His commandments. In a similar way, a number of biblical passages reveal how God takes no pleasure in the death of the wicked, but earnestly calls them to turn from their sinful ways and be saved (e.g., Ezek. 18:23; 33:11; Matt. 23:37-39; Luke 13:34-36). In the gospel accounts of Jesus' lament over the unbelief of many inhabitants of Jerusalem ('O Jerusalem, Jerusalem, the city that kills the prophets and stones those sent to it! How often I would have gathered your children together as a hen gathers her brood under her wings, and you would not!'; Luke 13:34),

---

19. John Murray, 'The Free Offer of the Gospel,' in *Collected Writings of John Murray* (Carlisle, PA: Banner of Truth, 1982), 4:113-114: 'The question then is: what is implicit in, or lies back of, the full and free offer of the gospel to all without distinction? The word "desire" has come to be used in the debate, not because it is *necessarily* the most accurate or felicitous word but because it serves to set forth quite sharply a certain implication of the full and free offer of the gospel to all. This implication is that the free offer expresses not simply the bare preceptive will of God but also the disposition of loving-kindness on the part of God pointing to the salvation gained through compliance with the overtures of gospel grace.'

20. For an extensive treatment of the biblical basis for the free offer of the gospel, see Murray, 'The Free Offer of the Gospel,' 114-31.

Jesus expresses His deep anguish at the unwillingness of many of Jerusalem's inhabitants to believe. When this is interpreted in the light of the context, which speaks of their failure to enter into the kingdom of God, it is evident Jesus is lamenting their unwillingness to be saved.

Another, often overlooked, biblical argument regarding the well-meant offer is the apostle Paul's poignant expression of his heart's desire and prayer to God for the salvation of his 'kinsmen according to the flesh' (Rom. 9:1-5; 10:1). In the face of the unbelief of many of his contemporaries among the people of Israel, the apostle declares his own personal desire that they should come to faith in Christ. Strikingly, in the same passage in which the apostle teaches particular election, he also expresses his desire for the salvation of all his unbelieving kinsmen. In a similar way, there are other passages in the New Testament speaking of God's desire for the salvation of all to whom the gospel is preached (cf. 1 Tim. 2:3-4; 2 Pet. 3:9).

Admittedly, it is difficult to comprehend the consistency or coherence of these distinct aspects of God's will. To affirm simultaneously the teachings of unconditional, particular election and the well-meant gospel offer seems to violate ordinary canons of logic. How can God sovereignly decree not to save a lost sinner, and yet nonetheless desire his or her salvation? This seems tantamount to saying that God has two contrary impulses: to save and not to save, to love and to hate. It appears to introduce, so far as God's will with respect to the salvation of lost sinners is concerned, a kind of duality into God's purposes. Though it is not possible to comprehend fully the harmony within God's will in this respect, some observations can help alleviate the difficulty.

First, the wisest course at this point is to insist that, though the tension here is *apparent,* it is ultimately not *real.* Though the mystery of the full harmony of God's will may finally lie beyond our grasp, we must be content to follow the teaching of Scripture wherever it leads. If the Scriptures teach unconditional election, we should affirm this teaching. If the Scriptures teach the well-meant gospel offer, we should affirm this teaching as well. That we are unable to see through the consistency of these things says something about the limits of our understanding. But it is conceit on our part to insist that, because we cannot fully comprehend it, it is not true. As is often the case, Calvin offers wise counsel in this area:

> Although, therefore, God's will is simple, yet great variety is involved in it, as far as our senses are concerned. Besides, it is not surprising that our eyes should be blinded by intense light, so that we cannot certainly judge how God wishes all to be saved, and yet has devoted all the reprobate to eternal destruction, and wishes them to perish. While we look now through a glass darkly, we should be content with the measure of our own intelligence. (1 Cor. 13:12). When we shall be like God, and see him face to face, then what is now obscure will then become plain.[21]

Second, we must remember that the well-meant offer has to do with the *revelation of God's will in the preaching of the gospel.* When we speak of the well-meant gospel offer, we are in the orbit of what Reformed theology calls God's *revealed will*, not His *decretive will*. Though this distinction may only seem to paper over the apparent contradiction between the free offer of the gospel and God's decree of election, it does remind us that the divine desire and good will expressed in the gospel offer do not exactly coincide with God's sovereign purposes of election. Therefore, it is an unfortunate confusion when the language of God's 'will' to save the lost, as it relates to the free offer of the gospel, is regarded to have the same meaning as the language of God's 'will' to save the lost, as it relates to His decree of election.

Third, it is at least conceivable to imagine a circumstance in which God might desire something that He has not simultaneously determined to effect. Robert Lewis Dabney addresses this point in his essay, 'God's Indiscriminate Proposals of Mercy, As Related to His Power, Wisdom, and Sincerity.'[22] In this essay, which is an extraordinarily complex handling of our question, Dabney maintains that we can imagine circumstances in which a person might harbor a strong desire or 'propension' to show mercy but at the same time, for reasons sometimes unknown to us, determine to effect something quite different. He mentions, for example, General Washington's

---

21. Comm. Ezek. 18:23, *Calvin's Commentaries* (Grand Rapids: Baker Book House, 1979 [1843-55]), 12:247-8.

22. *Discussions of Robert Lewis Dabney* (Carlisle, PA: The Banner of Truth Trust, 1982 [1891]), 1:282-313.

decision to sign a death-warrant during the Revolutionary War for Major André. Though Washington felt deep and genuine compassion for Major André, he resolutely fulfilled his obligation in bringing him to justice for his treason during war-time. While admitting that this and other analogies drawn from human experience are inadequate to account for the harmonious, yet complex, ways of God in dealing with lost sinners, Dabney maintained that it might help us see how God could be simultaneously and sincerely compassionate toward lost sinners while, for reasons known alone to Him, be resolute in His sovereign determination not to save them. Though God's complex will toward lost sinners would not involve the kind of tension and disharmony that often accompanies human motives and purposes, His will with respect to lost sinners is undoubtedly an infinitely complex one, which could accommodate at the same time a propensity to show mercy to lost sinners while sovereignly determining not to save them. Only an 'overweening logic', Dabney argued, would insist that God could not simultaneously reveal a sincere desire to show mercy to lost sinners and yet harbor in His sovereign designs a purpose to save some and not others.

Although Reformed theology recognizes the difficulty of harmonizing the scriptural teachings of a sovereign decree of election and a well-meant gospel offer, it seeks to affirm both, to insist upon their ultimate harmony, and to admit that the 'ways of God' in this and other respects lie beyond our capacity fully to comprehend. In doing so, it witnesses to the truth that God's work of election is a work in which He takes great delight, whereas His work of withholding His saving mercy from some is a reluctant work.[23]

What About Human Freedom and Responsibility?

On several occasions throughout this study, I addressed the difficult question of human freedom and responsibility in relation to the call of the gospel. In both the controversy between Pelagius and Augustine in the early church, and between Arminius and Reformed theology in the seventeenth century, a principal point of contention was the nature and extent of human freedom and responsibility in relation

---

23. Cf. Bavinck, *RD*, 2:398.

to God. According to Pelagius, human freedom regarding the gospel call must involve the plenary ability of its recipients to do what is required of them. The 'ought' of the gospel call implies 'can' on the part of its recipient. Unless sinners retain the ability to do what God requires of them, they cannot be held accountable or responsible for what they choose to do. Though Arminius ascribed a great deal more to the enablement of God's grace than did Pelagius, he also insisted upon the independent power of sinners to resist or to embrace the gracious invitation of the gospel. Neither for Pelagius nor for Arminius is the prevenient grace of God alone effectual to grant the believing response that the gospel call requires. In the final analysis, the ability and willingness to believe or not to believe lie with those who are called through the gospel to faith. On the assumptions of Pelagius and Arminius, the doctrines of unconditional election and its corollary, effectual calling, are incompatible with this understanding of human freedom, which always entails the independent ability to do or not to do what the gospel call requires.

There are several observations that need to be made in reply to this claim.

First, it is most important to remember that this question focuses particularly upon the freedom and responsibility of fallen human beings regarding the gospel call to faith and repentance. Though the broader question of the nature of human freedom in respect to non-moral or non-religious choices may be an important one, it is not directly germane to the question here.

Second, it must be acknowledged that the gospel call to faith in Christ necessarily places all those whom it addresses under an obligation to respond appropriately. When God addresses fallen sinners through the gospel, summoning them to *respond* to the gospel's invitation, He not only respects but also heightens the *responsibility,* in the basic sense of this term, of all whom He summons to faith. A responsible person is someone who is obliged to do what is required of him or her, and in the case of the gospel call, what is most urgently required is that a fallen sinner should believe the gospel promise and turn in repentance to God. Although critics of the Augustinian/ Calvinistic view of election are fond of representing it as a species of fatalism or determinism, there is nothing in this view that diminishes the responsibility of lost sinners to answer the gospel summons to faith in Jesus Christ in order to be saved. With the exception of a few hyper-Calvinists, who hesitate to call indiscriminately all lost sinners to faith unless they have reason to believe that they are elect, no responsible advocate of the doctrine of unconditional election denies the accountability and responsibility of fallen sinners to answer the gospel call in the way of faith.

Third, in the biblical understanding of the fallen condition of the human race, it is evident that no fallen sinners will ever respond properly to the gospel call, unless God effectually calls them by His Spirit and Word. Though the gospel call provides all of its recipients with an opportunity to believe, without a mighty, life-bestowing work of God's Spirit in regeneration and renewal, the response of all sinners to this call will be to do *as they please*. Without constraint or coercion, fallen sinners will always act in a way that expresses their deepest inclinations and desires. According to the scriptural portrait, lost sinners have no desire to seek God or understand Him (Rom. 3:11); are blind to the truth of the gospel (2 Cor. 4:4); are hostile to God and unwilling to please Him (Rom. 8:6-8); are dead in trespasses and sins (Eph. 2:1); are enslaved to sin and unrighteousness (Rom. 6:17); and are darkened in their understanding (Eph. 4:18). When lost sinners are summoned to faith and repentance, they are responsible for the way they answer this summons. However, they will inevitably respond in a way that spontaneously and properly expresses what they find most desirable. Left to themselves, they will freely and emphatically say 'no' to the overtures of God's grace in the gospel. On the other hand, when believers respond in faith to the gospel call, they do so by virtue of God's effectual calling. They respond as they ought because God graciously gives them the eyes to see the glory of Christ (2 Cor. 4:6); the heart to receive Him (Acts 16:14); and the faith to embrace the gospel promise (1 Cor. 1:26-31; Eph. 2:8-9).

Fourth, the only position on human freedom that is compatible with the biblical doctrine of unconditional election and effectual calling is the view known commonly as 'compatibilism'. According to this view, human beings are always free to do as they please in their response to the call of the gospel. When left to themselves, they will invariably resist the gracious summons of the gospel. The number of fallen sinners who desire to see and enter the kingdom of God without being moved to do so by God's grace is nil. But when God effectually calls fallen sinners to faith and repentance, He acts in such a way as to produce a spontaneous, willful, and heartfelt desire on the part of those who gladly embrace the gospel promise of salvation in Christ. By virtue of effectual calling, believers who otherwise would refuse the overtures of the gospel are moved to willingly embrace these overtures. Though God's grace alone moves believers to faith and repentance, believers are not moved against their wills or, in a manner of speaking, 'strong-armed' into the kingdom of God. Rather, the concursus between God's gracious working and the believer's heartfelt response involves a perfect coincidence and harmony between God's choice to grant faith and the believer's decision to respond in faith. When believers respond as they are called to, they do so freely and delightedly, not by any compulsion, constraint, or coercion. They enjoy a new-found freedom in believing the gospel promise and embracing Christ by faith.

And fifth, the view of human freedom associated with Pelagianism and Arminianism has insuperable problems. On the one hand, it ascribes to lost sinners the capacity and obligation to make an indeterminate choice in response to the gospel call. Because the choice to believe or not to believe is entirely and exclusively within the sinner's power, salvation is not by God's grace but by a human work or act. For this reason, Bavinck observes that Pelagianism (and semi-Pelagianism) has 'no pity'.[24] According to this view, there is only hope for those who make the right choices and persist in them. Correspondingly, there is no hope for those who, left to their own devices, would refuse God's overtures of mercy. On the other hand, this view of human freedom renders inexplicable the actual choices that human beings make in response to the gospel. What accounts for the fact that one person believes and another does not? If human freedom requires a radical 'indifference' or 'equipoise' regarding the

---

24. Bavinck, *RD*, 2:404: 'If it [election] were based on justice and merit, all would be lost. But now that election operates according to grace, there is hope even for the most wretched. If work and reward were the standard of admission into the kingdom of heaven, its gates would be opened for no one. Or if Pelagius's doctrine were the standard, and the virtuous were chosen because of their virtue, and Pharisees because of their righteousness, wretched publicans would be shut out. Pelagianism has no pity.'

choice to believe or not to believe, the actual choices made become as inexplicable to God as they are to us. Unless we make choices in respect to the gospel that reflect our true inclinations, affections, and dispositions, these choices are born out of nothing. And while it may not be true for God, it is certainly true for human beings as creatures that 'out of nothing, nothing comes.' Only God has the power to give life to the dead and 'call into existence the things that do not exist' (Rom. 4:17).

How Can We Be Assured of Election and Salvation?

In the history of reflection on the biblical doctrine of election, the question of the assurance of salvation has often arisen. In Augustine's doctrine of election, little emphasis is placed upon the confidence that believers may have regarding their election. Since Augustine taught that some true believers may fall out of a state of grace after their baptism, he rejected the idea that believers may ordinarily be assured of their election. Only those who persevere in faith until death, especially those who suffer martyrdom, can be assured that they truly are elect. However, during the sixteenth century, the leading Reformers emphasized the pastoral comfort of the doctrine of election. Because the doctrine of election militates against the notion that believers are saved by their works, it provides the same assurance of God's gracious favor as the Reformers found in the doctrine of free justification by grace alone. In the twentieth century, a great deal of Barth's motivation for revising the traditional Augustinian/ Calvinist view of election was his desire to provide an even more sure footing for the assurance of election. According to Barth, Calvin's doctrine of double predestination, and his language regarding God's 'secret' and unknown will, failed to anchor the believer's assurance in the person and work of Jesus Christ, who is both electing God and elected man. From the perspective of Arminius and his followers, the Augustinian/Calvinist view aggravates the problem of assurance by limiting the objects of the electing love and mercy of God in the work of Jesus Christ as Mediator. For Arminius, any limit upon God's gracious disposition toward all sinners casts a shadow over the gospel summons to faith.

Before addressing the question of the assurance of election directly, it should be noted that the problem of the assurance of salvation is not unique to Reformed theology. Nor is it a problem that is left unanswered in the confessions of the Reformed churches. Whereas a good part of the Christian church throughout its history actively discouraged the assurance of salvation, the churches of the Reformation (both Lutheran and Reformed) strongly affirmed that such assurance belongs to true faith. In his great work, *The Bondage of the Will,* Luther argues that the gospel and its promises depend upon the truth of God's foreknowledge and foreordination of all things. Unless we 'know that God does not lie, but does all things immutably, and that his will can neither be resisted nor changed nor hindered,' the consolation that is ours in the gospel of Jesus Christ would be undermined.[25] In reply to the opinions of the Remonstrants, the Canons of Dort vigorously affirm the assurance believers may have of their election and preservation in the faith. Since God's plan 'cannot be changed, his promise cannot fail, the calling according to his purpose cannot be revoked, the merit of Christ as well as his interceding and preserving cannot be nullified, and the sealing of the Holy Spirit can neither be invalidated nor wiped out,' believers may have certainty regarding their election and salvation.[26] The Westminster Confession likewise speaks of an 'infallible assurance' that believers may have of their salvation in Christ.[27] In contrast to these affirmations of the assurance of election and salvation, it is remarkable that the Council of Trent expressly rejected the idea that believers may ordinarily possess such assurance: 'no one can know with a certainty of faith, which cannot be subject to error, that he has obtained the grace of God.'[28] According to the Council of Trent, believers can only be assured of their election by an extraordinary revelation of God.

The best resolution of the question of the assurance of election is to focus upon the gracious promises in Christ that are revealed through

---

25. LW, 33:43.

26. Canons of Dort, V/8.

27. WCF, chap. 18.

28. Canons and Decrees of the Council of Trent, session 6, chap. 9 (Schaff, *The Creeds of Christendom,* 3:99).

the gospel. The warrant for the assurance of election is the same as the warrant for the assurance of salvation.[29] The gospel promise is simply that God will save to the uttermost those who come to Him through Christ (Heb. 7:25). The gracious invitation of the gospel is that we should come to Christ in faith, trusting that His saving work is altogether adequate to the need of any sinner (Acts 16:31; cf. John 3:16). The language of the gospel summons is nowhere more wonderfully put than in Jesus' words: 'Come to me, all who labor and are heavy laden, and I will give you rest' (Matt. 11:28). We do not make judgments regarding our election and salvation by curiously inquiring into the secret things of God, but by listening to what He reveals to us regarding His grace and mercy in Jesus Christ (Deut. 29:29). For this reason, as the following statements of Calvin and the Second Helvetic Confession illustrate, the 'mirror' of the believer's election is to be found in the clear testimony of the gospel to God's grace in Jesus Christ:

> Accordingly, those whom God has adopted as his sons are said to have been chosen not in themselves but in his Christ, for unless he could love them in him, he could not honor them with the inheritance of his Kingdom if they had not previously become partakers of him. But if we have been chosen in him, we shall not find assurance of our election in ourselves; and not even in God the Father, if we conceive him as severed from his Son. Christ, then, is the mirror wherein we must, and without self-deception may, contemplate our own election. ... [W]e have a sufficiently clear and firm testimony that we have been inscribed in the book of life if we are in communion with Christ.[30]

> We therefore find fault with those who outside of Christ ask whether they are elected. And what has God decreed concerning them before all eternity? For the preaching of the Gospel is to be heard, and it is to be believed; and it is to be held as beyond doubt that if you believe and are

---

29. For a helpful discussion of the warrant for the believer's assurance of election and salvation, see Sinclair B. Ferguson, 'Blessed Assurance, Jesus is Mine: Definite Atonement and the Cure of Souls,' in *From Heaven He Came and Sought Her: Definite Atonement in Historical, Biblical, Theological, and Pastoral Perspective,* eds. David Gibson and Jonathan Gibson (Wheaton, IL: Crossway, 2013), 607-31; and idem, *The Whole Christ: Legalism, Antinomianism, and Gospel Assurance—Why the Marrow Controversy Still Matters* (Wheaton, IL: Crossway, 2016), 177-229.

30. Calvin, *Institutes,* 3.24.5.

in Christ, you are elected. For the Father has revealed unto us in Christ the eternal purpose of his predestination, as I have just now shown from the apostle in II Tim. 1:9-10. This is therefore above all to be taught and considered, what great love of the Father toward us is revealed to us in Christ. We must hear what the Lord himself daily preaches to us in the Gospel, how he calls and says: 'Come to me all who labor and are heavy-laden, and I will give you rest' (Matt. 11:28). 'God so loved the world, that he gave his only Son, that whoever believes in him should not perish, but have eternal life' (John 3:16). Also, 'It is not the will of my Father that one of these little ones should perish' (Matt. 18:14). Let Christ, therefore be the looking glass, in whom we may contemplate our predestination. We shall have a sufficiently clear and sure testimony that we are inscribed in the Book of Life if we have fellowship with Christ, and he is ours and we are his in true faith.[31]

The believer's assurance of election and salvation comes through faith in Jesus Christ, as He is revealed to us in the gospel. Such assurance does not depend upon an inappropriate and curious speculation regarding who is elect, but upon the ordinary means of grace, the preaching of the gospel and the administration of the sacraments.[32]

This answer to the question of assurance compares favorably to that offered within the framework of an Arminian view of election. Upon the basis of the Arminian view, the assurance of election rests upon little more than the hope that believers will decide to persevere in the way of faith until the end. This view affords no confidence that the good work God has begun in His people will be brought to completion (Phil. 1:6). It offers no reassurance that the call to work out my salvation with fear and trembling comes with the promise of God

---

31. Second Helvetic Confession, chap. 10.

32. In reply to those who might fear that they are not elect, but those from whom God wills to with-hold His mercy, Bavinck offers a helpful comment: 'The purpose of election is not—as it is so often proclaimed—to turn off the many but to invite all to participate in the riches of God's grace in Christ. No one has *a right* to believe that he or she is a reprobate, for everyone is sincerely and urgently called to believe in Christ with a view to salvation. No one *can* actually believe it, for one's own life and all that makes it enjoyable is proof that God takes no delight in his death. No one *really* believes it, for that would be hell on earth. But election is a source of comfort and strength, of submissiveness and humility, of confidence and resolution. The salvation of human beings is firmly established in the gracious and omnipotent good pleasure of God' (*RD*, 2:402).

as the One who is 'at work in me, both to will and work for his good pleasure' (Phil. 2:13). Though the Arminian view aims to magnify the saving love and mercy of God in Christ toward all sinners, it does so at the price of denying the invincibility of God's love toward His people in Jesus Christ, a love from which they cannot be separated (Rom. 8:31-9). For Arminius, the love of God embraces everyone, but it does not have the power to save anyone to the uttermost. The only assurance believers may have within the Arminian scheme is that they will never choose to let loose their grip upon God, not that nothing can snatch them out of God's fatherly hand (John 10:29). In the nature of the case, an 'infallible assurance' of election and salvation cannot be built upon the quicksand of a fallen sinner's uncertain perseverance in choosing to believe.

A Concluding Note on Election and the Glory of God

In contrast to the controversy and divisiveness that the topic of election has so often elicited in the history of the church, the key note sounded in the Scriptures in response to God's gracious election is one of praise and doxology. For this reason, I wish to conclude this study, not with another difficult question that the doctrine of election poses, but with a comment on the relation between God's gracious election of His people in Christ and the doxology that it must always provoke.

When the apostle Paul treats the theme of God's purpose of election, he begins and ends with doxological outbursts of praise and thanksgiving to God for His undeserved grace toward us in Jesus Christ. In chapter 1 of the book of Ephesians, the apostle's teaching regarding God's election of His people in Christ before the foundation of the world is couched within an extended doxology that blesses God for all of the spiritual blessings that are ours in Christ Jesus. When he enumerates some of these blessings flowing from God's gracious election, Paul observes how these are given so that we might praise God for 'his glorious grace, with which he has blessed us in the Beloved' (Eph. 1:6). Throughout the extended doxology in Ephesians 1:3-14, the note of exuberant praise to God for what He has freely lavished upon His people in Christ predominates. In arguably the most extensive passage on the doctrine of election in the Scriptures, Romans 9–11, the apostle Paul concludes his exposition of the reach of God's electing and saving mercy in Christ with one of the most well-known and powerful doxologies in the Bible. Similarly, in a passage to which Augustine turned often in his writings against Pelagius and Pelagianism, Paul reminds us how we should respond to God's free and unmerited favor toward us in Christ. Since whatever we have in Christ is freely given to us, not by virtue of our deserving or meriting, we should respond by boasting only in the Lord (1 Cor. 4:7). Indeed, God's purpose in choosing those who are 'low and despised in the world' was to ensure that their boasting would be in Him and His grace in Christ, not in themselves or in anything that they have done (1 Cor. 1:26-31).

The truest and best response to what the Bible teaches about God's gracious purpose of election remains one that follows the pattern of the apostle Paul's great doxology at the end of Romans 9–11. While we may have questions for which there seem to be no satisfying answers, at some point these questions must be put aside, and what remains is only thankful praise:

> Oh, the depth of the riches and wisdom and knowledge of God! How unsearchable are his judgments and how inscrutable his ways! 'For who has known the mind of the Lord, or who has been his counselor?' 'Or who has given a gift to him that he might be repaid?' For from him and through him and to him are all things. To him be the glory forever. Amen. (Rom. 11:33-36)

Recommended Resources

CHAPTER 1

Surveys of the doctrine of election in the Old Testament:

D. A. Carson, *Divine Sovereignty and Human Responsibility: Biblical Perspectives in Tension* (Grand Rapids: Baker Book House, 1994 [1981]), 9-40.

Joel S. Kaminsky, *Yet I Loved Jacob: Reclaiming the Biblical Concept of Election* (Eugene, OR: Wipf & Stock, 2007).

William W. Klein, *The New Chosen People: A Corporate View of Election* (Grand Rapids: Zondervan, 1990), 25-41.

Robert A. Peterson, *Election and Free Will: God's Gracious Choice and Our Responsibility* (Phillipsburg, NJ: Presbyterian & Reformed, 2007), 37-52.

Horst Dietrich Preuss, *Old Testament Theology,* vol. 1, trans. Leo G. Perdue (Louisville, KY: Westminster John Knox Press, 1995).

H. H. Rowley, *The Biblical Doctrine of Election* (London: James Clarke and Co., 1950).

Th. C. Vriezen, *Die Erwählung Israels nach dem Alten Testament* (Zürich, 1953).

Stephen N. Williams, *The Election of Grace: A Riddle without a Resolution?* (Grand Rapids: Eerdmans, 2015), 13-58.

CHAPTER 2

Surveys of the doctrine of election in the New Testament:

William W. Klein, *The New Chosen People: A Corporate View of Election* (Grand Rapids: Zondervan, 1990), 63-256.

Steven J. Lawson, *Foundations of Grace,* vol. 1: *A Long Line of Godly Men* (Lake Mary, FL: Reformation Trust, 2006), 241-440.

Robert A. Peterson, *Election and Free Will: God's Gracious Choice and Our Responsibility* (Phillipsburg, NJ: Presbyterian & Reformed, 2007), 53-124.

Thomas R. Schreiner and Bruce A. Ware, eds. *The Grace of God, the Bondage of the Will* (Grand Rapids: Baker Books, 1995), 47-200.

B. B. Warfield, *The Works of Benjamin B. Warfield,* vol. 2: *Biblical Doctrines* (reprint; Grand Rapids: Baker Book House, 1981), 32-67.

Stephen N. Williams, *The Election of Grace: A Riddle without a Resolution?* (Grand Rapids: Eerdmans, 2015), 59-102.

CHAPTER 3

For Arminian approaches to God's foreknowledge:

J. Kenneth Grider, *A Wesleyan-Holiness Theology* (Kansas City: Beacon Hill Press, 1994), 249-51.

Grant R. Osborne, 'Exegetical Notes on Calvinist Texts,' in *Grace Unlimited,* ed. Clark H. Pinnock (Eugene, OR: Wipf & Stock, 1999).

Jerry L. Walls and Joseph R. Dongell, *Why I Am Not a Calvinist* (Downers Grove, IL: InterVarsity Press, 2004).

For an extensive treatment of the corporate people of Israel and the Gentiles in Romans 9:

Cornelis P. Venema, ' "Jacob I Loved, But Esau I Hated": Corporate or Individual Election in Paul's Argument in Romans 9?' *MAJT* 26 (2015): 7-58.

For the 'corporate election' interpretation of Romans 9:

Brian J. Abasciano, *Paul's Use of the Old Testament in Romans 9.10-18* (London: T & T Clark, 2005).

idem, 'Corporate Election in Romans 9: A Reply to Thomas Schreiner,' *JETS* 49, no. 2 (2006): 351-71.

Paul J. Achtemeier, *Romans,* Interpretation (Atlanta: John Knox Press, 1985), 153-63.

Matthew W. Bates, *Salvation by Allegiance Alone: Rethinking Faith, Works, and the Gospel of Jesus the King* (Grand Rapids: Baker Academic), 170-75.

C. E. B. Cranfield, *A Critical and Exegetical Commentary on the Epistle to the Romans,* 2 vols., ICC (Edinburgh: T & T Clark, 1979), 444-79.

William W. Klein, *The New Chosen People: A Corporate View of Election* (Grand Rapids: Zondervan, 1990), 158-212.

Herman Ridderbos, *Paul: An Outline of His Theology,* trans. John R. de Witt (Grand Rapids: Eerdmans, 1959), 203-31.

A. Chadwick Thornhill, *The Chosen People: Election, Paul and Second Temple Judaism* (Downers Grove, IL: IVP Academic, 2015), 229-53.

N. T. Wright, *Paul and the Faithfulness of God,* Parts 2 & 3 (Minneapolis, MN: Fortress, 2013), 774-1042.

For an extensive treatment of the debate regarding the meaning of Romans 11:26:

> Cornelis P. Venema, '"In this Way All Israel Will Be Saved": A Study of Romans 11:26,' *MAJT* 22 (2011): 19-40.

For a good summary of the primary interpretations of the phrase, 'and in this way all Israel will be saved':

> J. A. Fitzmyer, *Romans: A New Translation with Introduction and Commentary,* Anchor Bible, vol. 33 (New York, Doubleday, 1993), 619-20.

For a presentation and defense of the dispensational view of 'all Israel' as the conversion of Israel in the future millennium:

> J. Dwight Pentecost, *Things to Come* (Findlay, OH: Dunham, 1958), 504-7.

> Michael G. Vanlaningham, 'Romans 11:25-27 and the Future of Israel in Paul's Thought,' *MSJ* 3. no. 3 (Fall 1992), 141-74.

> John F. Walvoord, *The Millennial Kingdom* (Findlay, OH: Dunham, 1959), 167-92.

For a presentation and defense of the premillennialist view of 'all Israel' as a future conversion of Israel prior to the future millennium:

> Oscar Cullmann, *Christ and Time: The Primitive Christian Conception of Time and History,* trans. Floyd V. Filson (Philadelphia: Westminster, 1960), 78.

> George E. Ladd, *A Theology of the New Testament* (Grand Rapids: Eerdmans, 1974), 561-63.

For a presentation and defense of the view of 'all Israel' as a large company of those among the Jewish people who will be gathered into the church:

> S. Greijdanus, *De Brief Van Den Apostel Paulus Aan De Gemeente Te Rome,* vol. 2 (Amsterdam: H. A. Van Bottenburg, 1933), 515-17.

> Charles Hodge, *A Commentary on the Epistle to the Romans* (Philadelphia: Alfred Martien, 1873), *ad loc.*

> Keith A. Mathison, *Postmillennialism: An Eschatology of Hope* (Phillipsburg, NJ: Presbyterian & Reformed, 1999), 121-30.

> Douglas J. Moo, *The Epistle to the Romans,* The New International Commentary on the New Testament (Grand Rapids: Eerdmans, 1996), *ad loc.*

John Murray, *The Epistle to the Romans*, vol. 2., The New International Commentary on the New Testament (reprint. Grand Rapids: Eerdmans, 1975), 91-103.

Thomas Schreiner, *Romans,* Baker Exegetical Commentary on the New Testament (Grand Rapids: Baker Academic, 1998), 612-23.

Geerhardus Vos, *The Pauline Eschatology* (Princeton: University Press, 1930), 89.

For a presentation and defense of the view of 'all Israel' as referring to the sum total of the remnant of elect Jews whom God has gathered, is gathering, and will yet gather throughout redemptive history until Christ's second coming:

Herman Bavinck, *Reformed Dogmatics,* vol. 4: *Holy Spirit, Church, and New Creation* (Grand Rapids: Baker Academic, 2008), 668-72.

Louis Berkhof, *Systematic Theology* (Grand Rapids: Eerdmans, 1939, 1941), 698-700.

William Hendriksen, *Israel in Prophecy* (Grand Rapids: Baker, 1974), 39-52.

idem, *New Testament Commentary: Exposition of Paul's Epistle to the Romans* (Grand Rapids: Baker, 1980, 1981), 379-82.

Anthony Hoekema, *The Bible and the Future* (Grand Rapids: Eerdmans, 1994), 139-47.

Herman Ridderbos, *Paul: An Outline of His Theology*, trans. John R. de Witt (Grand Rapids: Eerdmans, 1959), 354-61.

O. Palmer Robertson, 'Is There a Distinctive Future for Ethnic Israel in Romans 11?' in *Perspectives on Evangelical Theology*, ed. K.S. Kantzer and S.N. Gundry (Grand Rapids: Baker, 1979), 209-27.

Robert B. Strimple, 'Amillennialism,' in *Three Views of the Millennium and Beyond,* ed. Darrell L. Bock (Grand Rapids: Zondervan, 1999), 112-18.

CHAPTER 4

For a summary of Pelagius' views and the history of Augustine's engagement with Pelagianism:

Gerald Bonner, *St Augustine of Hippo: Life and Controversies* (Philadelphia: The Westminster Press, 1963), 312-93.

idem, *Freedom and Necessity: St. Augustine's Teaching on Divine Power and Human Freedom* (Washington, D.C.: The Catholic University of America Press, 2007).

J. B. Mozley, *A Treatise on the Augustinian Doctrine of Predestination* (3rd ed.; London: John Murray, 1883), esp. 46-99, 126-232.

'Pelagius, Pelagianism,' in *The New Schaff-Herzog Encyclopedia of Religious Knowledge,* ed. Samuel M. Jackson, vol. 8 (Grand Rapids: Baker Book House, 1950), 438-444.

B. B. Warfield, 'Augustine and the Pelagian Controversy,' in *The Works of Benjamin B. Warfield,* vol. 4: *Studies in Tertullian and Augustine* (reprint; Grand Rapids: Baker Book House, 1981 [1930]), 289-412.

For general treatments of Augustine's doctrine of election:

Gerald Bonner, *St Augustine of Hippo: Life and Controversies* (Philadelphia: The Westminster Press, 1963), 352-93.

idem, *Freedom and Necessity: St. Augustine's Teaching on Divine Power and Human Freedom* (Washington, D.C.: The Catholic University of America Press, 2007).

Peter Brown, *Augustine of Hippo* (Los Angeles: University of California Press, 1967).

J. N. D. Kelly, *Early Christian Doctrines* (2nd ed.; New York: Harper & Row, 1960), 361-8.

Matthew Levering, *Predestination: Biblical and Theological Paths* (Oxford: Oxford University Press, 2011), 44-54.

idem, 'On the Predestination of the Saints,' in *The Theology of Augustine: An Introductory Guide to His Most Important Works* (Grand Rapids: Baker Academic, 2013), 71-88.

J. B. Mozley, *A Treatise on the Augustinian Doctrine of Predestination* (3rd ed.; London: J. Murray, 1883).

A. D. R. Polman, *De Praedestinatieleer van Augustinus, Thomas van Aquino en Calvijn: Een Dogmahistorische Studie* (Franeker: T. Wever, 1936), 27-186.

B. B. Warfield, 'Augustine and the Pelagian Controversy,' in *The Works of Benjamin B. Warfield,* vol. 4: *Studies in Tertullian and Augustine* (reprint; Grand Rapids: Baker Book House, 1981 [1930]), 289-412.

For interpreters who argue that Augustine does not generally view the non-elect as the direct objects of God's predestinating will:

Karl Barth, *Church Dogmatics,* vol. 1, pt. 2, eds. G. W. Bromiley and T. F. Torrance, trans. G. W. Bromiley *et al.* (Edinburgh: T & T Clark, 1957), 16.

Emil Brunner, *Dogmatics,* vol. 1: *The Christian Doctrine of God,* trans. Olive Wyon (Philadelpha: The Westminster Press, 1949), 341.

J. V. Fesko, *Diversity Within the Reformed Tradition: Supra- and Infralapsarianism in Calvin, Dort, and Westminster* (Greenville, SC: Reformed Academic Press, 2001), 19.

Adolph von Harnack, *The History of Dogma,* ed. T. K. Cheyne and A. B. Bruce, vol. 5 (3rd ed.; London: Williams & Norgate, 1898), 216.

Charles Hodge, *Systematic Theology,* vol. 2 (Grand Rapids: Eerdmans, 1993), 316.

For more extended treatments of the legacy of Augustinianism in medieval theology:

Harry Buis, *Historic Protestantism and Predestination* (Philadelphia: Presbyterian and Reformed, 1958), 14-27.

J. V. Fesko, *Diversity Within the Reformed Tradition: Supra- and Infralapsarianism in Calvin, Dort, and Westminster* (Greenville, SC: Reformed Academic Press, 2001), 21-56.

Matthew Levering, *Predestination: Biblical and Theological Paths* (Oxford: Oxford University Press, 2011), 68-97.

J. B. Mozley, *A Treatise on the Augustinian Doctrine of Predestination* (3rd ed; London: J. Murray, 1883), 259-93.

For discussions of the development of embrace and defense of Augustine by Thomas Bradwardine and Gregory of Rimini:

Gordon Leff, *Bradwardine and the Pelagians: A Study of His 'De Causa Dei' and Its Opponents* (Cambridge: Cambridge University Press, 1957).

Heiko A. Oberman, *Archbishop Thomas Bradwardine, a Fourteenth-Century Augustinian: A Study of His Theology in Its Historical Context* (Utrecht: Kemink & Zoon, 1958).

P. Vigneaux, *Justification et predestination au XIVe siècle: Duns Scot, Pierre d'Auriole, Guillaume d'Occam, Gregoire de Rimini* (Paris: Librairie Philosophique J. Vrin, 1981).

CHAPTER 5

For an extensive treatment of Luther's work, including a history of its reception in the developing Lutheran tradition:

Robert Kolb, *Bound Choice, Election, and Wittenberg Theological Method: From Martin Luther to the Formula of Concord,* Lutheran Quarterly Books (Grand Rapids: Eerdmans, 2005).

For recent studies of the exchange between Erasmus and Luther, written by respected Lutheran theologians:

Gerhard O. Forde, *The Captivation of the Will: Luther vs. Erasmus on Freedom and Bondage*, ed. Steven D. Paulson, Lutheran Quarterly Books (Grand Rapids: Eerdmans, 2005).

Robert Kolb, *Bound Choice, Election, and Wittenberg Theological Method: From Martin Luther to the Formula of Concord*, Lutheran Quarterly Books (Grand Rapids: Eerdmans, 2005), 11–28.

For a treatment of Melanchthon's relationship with Luther:

Timothy J. Wengert, 'Melanchthon and Luther / Luther and Melanchthon,' *Lutherjahrbuch* 66 (1999): 55–88.

idem, 'Philip Melanchthon's Contribution to Luther's Debate with Erasmus over the Bondage of the Will,' in *By Faith Alone: Essays on Justification in Honor of Gerhard O. Forde*, ed. Joseph A. Burgess and Marc Kolden (Grand Rapids: Eerdmans, 2004), 110–24.

For a treatment of Melanchthon's early comments on predestination in Romans 9:

Robert Kolb, 'Melanchthon's Influence on the Exegesis of his Students,' in *Philip Melanchthon (1497–1560) and the Commentary*, ed. Timothy J. Wengert and M. Patrick Graham (Sheffield, England: Sheffield Academic Press, 1997), 194–215.

For assessments of the distinction between God's 'hidden' and 'revealed' will in Luther's theology:

Paul Althaus, *The Theology of Martin Luther*, trans. Robert C. Schultz (Philadelphia: Fortress, 1966), 274–86.

David C. Steinmetz, *Luther in Context* (2nd ed.; Grand Rapids: Baker Academic, 2002), 23–31.

For general surveys of the doctrine of predestination in Reformed theology:

Harry Buis, *Historic Protestantism and Predestination* (Philadelphia: Presbyterian and Reformed, 1958).

Richard A. Muller, *Christ and the Decree: Christology and Predestination in Reformed Theology from Calvin to Perkins*, Studies in Historical Theology 2 (reprint; Grand Rapids: Baker, 1988 [1986]).

Cornelis Graafland, *Van Calvijn tot Barth: Oorsprong en ontwikkeling van de leer der verkiezing in het Gereformeerd Protestantisme* ('From Calvin to Barth: The Origin and Development of the Doctrine of Election in Reformed Protestantism') ('s-Gravenhage, The Netherlands: Uitgeverij Boekencentrum, 1987).

Pieter Rouwendal, 'The Doctrine of Predestination in Reformed Orthodoxy,' in *A Companion to Reformed Orthodoxy*, ed. Herman J.

Selderhuis, Brill's Companions to the Christian Tradition 40 (Leiden: Brill, 2013), 553–89.

Among the many sources on Calvin's doctrine of predestination, the following are especially valuable:

R. Scott Clark, 'Election and Predestination: The Sovereign Expressions of God (3.21–24),' in *A Theological Guide to Calvin's Institutes: Essays and Analysis*, ed. David W. Hall and Peter A. Lillback, Calvin 500 Series (Phillipsburg, NJ: Presbyterian & Reformed, 2008), 90–122.

Paul Jacobs, *Prädestination und Verantwortlichkeit bei Calvin* (Kasel: Oncken, 1937).

Fred H. Klooster, *Calvin's Doctrine of Predestination* (Grand Rapids: Baker, 1977).

Richard A. Muller, *Christ and the Decree: Christology and Predestination in Reformed Theology from Calvin to Perkins*, Studies in Historical Theology 2 (reprint; Grand Rapids: Baker Academic, 1988), 17–38.

Carl R. Trueman, 'Election: Calvin's Theology of Election and Its Early Reception,' in *Calvin's Theology and Its Reception: Disputes, Developments, and New Possibilities*, ed. J. Todd Billings and I. John Hesselink (Louisville: Westminster John Knox, 2012), 97–120.

François Wendel, *Calvin: The Origins and Development of His Religious Thought* (New York: Harper & Row, 1963), 263–83.

For representative presentations of the thesis that predestination is a 'central dogma' in Calvin's theology and in later Calvinism:

Cornelis Graafland, *Van Calvijn tot Barth: Oorsprong en ontwikkeling van de leer der verkiezing in het Gereformeerd Protestantisme* ('From Calvin to Barth: The Origin and Development of the Doctrine of Election in Reformed Protestantism') ('s-Gravenhage, The Netherlands: Uitgeverij Boekencentrum, 1987).

Ernst Bizer, *Frühorthodoxie und Rationalismus* (Zurich: EVZ Verlag, 1963).

Alexander Schweizer, *Die Protestantischen Centraldogmen in ihrer Entwicklung innerhalb der reformierten Kirche*, 2 vols. (Zurich: Orell, Füssli, 1854-1856).

Hans Emil Weber, *Reformation, Orthodoxie Und Rationalismus*, vol. 1, pt. 1, *Von Der Reformation Zur Orthodoxie* (Gütersloh: Gerd Mohn, 1937).

For critical, persuasive refutations of the thesis that predestination is a 'central dogma' in Calvin's theology and in later Calvinism:

Willem J. van Asselt and Eef Dekker, 'Introduction,' in *Reformation and Scholasticism: An Ecumenical Enterprise*, ed. Willem J. van Asselt and

Eef Dekker, Texts and Studies in Reformation and Post-Reformation Thought (Grand Rapids: Baker Academic, 2001), 11–43.

Richard A. Muller, *Christ and the Decree: Christology and Predestination in Reformed Theology from Calvin to Perkins*. Studies in Historical Theology 2 (reprint; Grand Rapids: Baker Academic, 1988), esp. 1–13, 177–82.

idem, 'The Use and Abuse of a Document: Beza's *Tabula Praedestinationis*, the Bolsec Controversy, and the Origins of Reformed Orthodoxy,' in *Protestant Scholasticism: Essays in Reassessment*, ed. Carl R. Trueman and R. Scott Clark (Carlisle: Paternoster, 1999), 33–61.

For helpful analyses of the significance of where Calvin placed the doctrine of predestination in the *Institutes:*

Paul Helm, 'Calvin, the "Two Issues," and the Structure of the *Institutes*,' *CTJ* 42, no. 2 (2007): 341–48.

Richard A. Muller, 'The Placement of Predestination in Reformed Theology: Issue or Non-Issue?' *CTJ* 40, no. 2 (2005): 184–210.

In addition to Calvin's treatment of predestination in the *Institutes*, the following sources offer an extensive presentation of his view:

John Calvin, *Concerning the Eternal Predestination of God*, trans. J. K. S. Reid (Louisville: Westminster John Knox, 1997).

idem, *The Bondage and Liberation of the Will: A Defence of the Orthodox Doctrine of Human Choice against Pighius*, ed. A. N. S. Lane, trans. G. I. Davies, Texts and Studies in Reformation and Post-Reformation Thought 2 (Grand Rapids: Baker, 1996).

For general studies of Bullinger's doctrine of predestination, which provide an account of the debate regarding the compatibility of his view with that of Calvin:

Richard A. Muller, *Christ and the Decree: Christology and Predestination in Reformed Theology from Calvin to Perkins*. Studies in Historical Theology 2 (reprint; Grand Rapids: Baker Academic, 1988), 39–47.

Cornelis P. Venema, *Heinrich Bullinger and the Doctrine of Predestination: Author of 'the Other Reformed Tradition'?*, Texts and Studies in Reformation and Post-Reformation Thought (Grand Rapids: Baker Academic, 2002).

Peter Walser, *Die Prädestination bei Heinrich Bullinger im Zussamenhang mit seiner Gotteslehre* (Zurich: Zwingli Verlag, 1957).

For a useful introduction to Bullinger's reformatory work and thought:

Bruce Gordon and Emidio Campi, eds., *Architect of Reformation: An Introduction to Heinrich Bullinger, 1504–1575*, Texts and Studies in Reformation and Post-Reformation Thought (Grand Rapids: Baker Academic, 2004).

For original source materials and treatments of the Bolsec Controversy on predestination:

Philip C. Holtrop, *The Bolsec Controversy on Predestination, From 1551–1555: The Statements of Jerome Bolsec, and the Response of John Calvin, Theodore Beza, and Other Reformed Theologians*, vol. 1, bks. 1 and 2, *Theological Currents, the Setting and Mood, and the Trial Itself* (Lewiston: Edwin Mellen, 1993).

Philip E. Hughes, *The Register of the Company of the Pastors of Geneva in the Time of Calvin* (Grand Rapids: Eerdmans, 1966), 133–86.

Cornelis P. Venema, *Heinrich Bullinger and the Doctrine of Predestination: Author of 'the Other Reformed Tradition'?*, Texts and Studies in Reformation and Post-Reformation Thought (Grand Rapids: Baker Academic, 2002), 58–63.

For Musculus's doctrine of predestination:

Wolfgang Musculus, *Common Places of Christian Religion* (London: R. Wolfe, 1563, 1578).

idem, *Loci communes sacrae theologiae* (Basel: Johannes Hervagius, 1560, 1568, 1573).

For Vermigli's doctrine of predestination:

Frank A. James III, *Peter Martyr Vermigli and Predestination: The Augustinian Inheritance of an Italian Reformer*, Oxford Theological Monographs (Oxford: Clarendon, 1998).

Vermigli, *The Common Places of D. Peter Martyr Vermigli* (London: Denham, 1583).

idem, *Loci Communes D. Petri Martyris Vermigli* (London, 1576; rev. ed. 1583).

For Zwingli's doctrine of predestination:

Gottfried W. Locher, *Zwingli's Thought: New Perspectives*, Studies in the History of Christian Thought 25 (Leiden: Brill, 1981), 121–41.

For more on Vermigli's life and writings:

C. Schmidt, *Peter Martyr Vermigli, Leben und ausgewählte Schriften* (Elberfeld: R. L. Friderichs, 1858).

David C. Steinmetz, 'Peter Martyr Vermigli,' in *Reformers in the Wings* (Philadelphia: Fortress Press, 1971), 151–61.

For a summary of Vermigli's correspondence with Bullinger:

Marvin W. Anderson, 'Peter Martyr, Reformed Theologian (1542–1562): His Letters to Heinrich Bullinger and John Calvin,' *SCJ* 4, no. 1 (1973): 41–64.

For more recent treatments of Vermigli's doctrine of predestination, particularly within the framework of his Aristotelian scholasticism:

John Patrick Donnelly, *Calvinism and Scholasticism in Vermigli's Doctrine of Man and Grace*, Studies in Medieval and Reformation Thought 18 (Leiden: Brill, 1976), esp. 3–41, 116–49.

Frank A. James III, *Peter Martyr Vermigli and Predestination: The Augustinian Inheritance of an Italian Reformer*, Oxford Theological Monographs (Oxford: Clarendon, 1998).

idem, 'Peter Martyr Vermigli: At the Crossroads of Late Medieval Scholasticism, Christian Humanism and Resurgent Augustinianism,' in *Protestant Scholasticism: Essays in Reassessment*, ed. Carl R. Trueman and R. Scott Clark (Carlisle: Paternoster, 1999), 62–78.

J. C. McClelland, 'The Reformed Doctrine of Predestination: According to Peter Martyr,' *SJT* 8, no. 3 (1955): 255–71.

Richard A. Muller, *Christ and the Decree: Christology and Predestination in Reformed Theology from Calvin to Perkins*, Studies in Historical Theology 2 (reprint; Grand Rapids: Baker Academic, 1988), 57–75.

For studies on the debates regarding infra- and supralapsarianism in the Reformed tradition:

Joel R. Beeke, *Debated Issues in Sovereign Predestination: Early Lutheran Predestination, Calvinian Reprobation, and Variations in Genevan Lapsarianism* (Göttingen: Vandenhoeck & Ruprecht, 2017).

J. V. Fesko, *Diversity Within the Reformed Tradition: Supra- and Infra-lapsarianism in Calvin, Dort, and Westminster* (Greenville, SC: Reformed Academic Press, 2001).

For an exposition of the Reformed confessions on the doctrine of predestination:

Jan Rohls, *Reformed Confessions: Theology from Zurich to Barmen*, trans. John Hoffmeyer, Columbia Series in Reformed Theology (Louisville: Westminster John Knox, 1998), 148–66.

For treatments of the extent or design of the atonement in Calvin and later Calvinism:

Brian G. Armstrong, *Calvinism and the Amyraut Heresy: Protestant Scholasticism and Humanism in Seventeenth-Century France* (Madison: University of Wisconsin Press, 1969).

W. Robert Godfrey, 'Reformed Thought on the Extent of the Atonement to 1618,' *WTJ* 37, no. 2 (1975): 133–71.

Richard A. Muller, *Christ and the Decree: Christology and Predestination in Reformed Theology from Calvin to Perkins*, Studies in Historical Theology 2 (reprint; Grand Rapids: Baker Academic, 1988), 33–35.

Roger Nicole, *Moyse Amyraut (1596–1664) and the Controversy on Universal Grace: First Phase (1634–1637)* (PhD diss., Harvard University, 1966).

Peter L. Rouwendal, 'Calvin's Forgotten Classical Position on the Extent of the Atonement: About Efficiency, Sufficiency, and Anachronism,' *WTJ* 70, no. 2 (2008): 317–35.

G. Michael Thomas, *The Extent of the Atonement: A Dilemma for Reformed Theology from Calvin to the Consensus (1536–1675)*, Paternoster Biblical and Theological Monographs (Carlisle: Paternoster, 1997).

For interpretations of the Reformed tradition that seek to contrast Calvin with later Calvinism:

Brian G. Armstrong, *Calvinism and the Amyraut Heresy: Protestant Scholasticism and Humanism in Seventeenth-Century France* (Madison: University of Wisconsin Press, 1969).

Basil Hall, 'Calvin against the Calvinists,' in *John Calvin: A Collection of Distinguished Essays*, ed. G. E. Duffield, trans. G. S. R. Cox and P. G. Rix, Courtenay Studies in Reformation Theology 1 (Grand Rapids: Eerdmans, 1966), 19–37.

R. T. Kendall, *Calvin and English Calvinism to 1649* (Oxford: Oxford University Press, 1979).

For a compelling refutation of Calvin against the Calvinists:

Paul Helm, *Calvin and the Calvinists* (Edinburgh: Banner of Truth, 1982).

Richard A. Muller, 'Calvin and the "Calvinists": Assessing Continuities and Discontinuities between the Reformation and Orthodoxy,' Part 1, *CTJ* 30, no. 2 (1995): 345–75, and Part 2, *CTJ* 31, no. 1 (1996): 125–60.

idem, *The Unaccommodated Calvin: Studies in the Foundation of a Theological Tradition*, Oxford Studies in Historical Theology (New York: Oxford University Press, 2000), 3–8.

idem., *Christ and the Decree: Christology and Predestination in Reformed Theology from Calvin to Perkins*, Studies in Historical Theology 2 (reprint; Grand Rapids: Baker Academic, 1988), esp. 175–82.

Carl R. Trueman, 'Calvin and Calvinism,' in *The Cambridge Companion to John Calvin*, ed. Donald K. McKim (Cambridge: Cambridge University Press, 2004), 225–44.

CHAPTER 6

Jacob Arminius, 'Declaration of Sentiments of Arminius, delivered before the States of Holland,' in *The Works of James Arminius*, trans. James Nichols and William Nichols, 3 vols. (reprint; Grand Rapids: Baker, 1986), 2:580-732.

Peter Y. De Jong, ed., *Crisis in the Reformed Churches: Essays in Commemoration of the Great Synod of Dort, 1618-1619* (2nd ed.; Grandville, MI: Reformed Fellowship, Inc., 2008).

Richard A. Muller, 'Grace, Election, and Contingent Choice: Arminius' Gambit and the Reformed Response,' in *The Grace of God, the Bondage of the Will*, vol. 1: *Biblical and Practical Perspectives on Calvinism*, eds. Thomas R. Schreiner and Bruce A. Ware (Grand Rapids: Baker Books, 1995).

Keith Stanglin and Thomas H. McCall, *Jacob Arminius: Theologian of Grace* (Oxford: Oxford University Press, 2012).

CHAPTER 7

Karl Barth, *Church Dogmatics*, vol. II/2: *The Doctrine of God*, eds. G. W. Bromiley and T. F. Torrance (Edinburgh: T & T Clark, 1957).

Michael T. Dempsey, ed., *Trinity and Election in Contemporary Theology* (Grand Rapids: Eerdmans, 2011).

Fred H. Klooster, *The Significance of Barth's Theology* (Grand Rapids: Baker, 1961).

Bruce L. McCormack, 'Grace and Being: The Role of God's Gracious Election in Karl Barth's Theological Ontology,' in *The Cambridge Companion to Karl Barth*, ed. John Webster (Cambridge: Cambridge University Press, 2000).

Stephen N. Williams, *The Election of Grace: A Riddle without a Resolution?* (Grand Rapids: Eerdmans, 2015).

CHAPTER 8

Willem J. van Asselt, J. Martin Bac, and Roelf T. te Velde, eds., *Reformed Thought on Freedom: The Concept of Free Choice in the History of Early Modern Reformed Theology* (Grand Rapids: Baker Academic, 2010).

Millard Erickson, *God the Father Almighty: A Contemporary Exploration of the Divine Attributes* (Grand Rapids: Baker Books, 1998).

Ron Highfield, 'The Function of Divine Self-Limitation in Open Theism: Great Wall or Picket Fence?,' *JETS* 45, no. 2 (2002): 279-99.

Richard Muller, *Divine Will and Human Choice: Freedom, Contingency, and Necessity in Early Modern Reformed Thought* (Grand Rapids: Baker Academic, 2017).

John Sanders, *The God Who Risks: A Theology of Providence* (Downers Grove, IL: InterVarsity Press, 1998).

CHAPTER 9

Sinclair Ferguson, 'Blessed Assurance, Jesus is Mine: Definite Atonement and the Cure of Souls,' in *From Heaven He Came and Sought Her: Definite Atonement in Historical, Biblical, Theological, and Pastoral Perspective*, eds. David Gibson and Jonathan Gibson (Wheaton, IL: Crossway, 2016).

John Murray, 'The Free Offer of the Gospel,' in *Collected Writings of John Murray*, vol. 4: *Studies in Theology, Reviews* (Edinburgh: The Banner of Truth Trust, 1982).

J. I. Packer, *Evangelism and the Sovereignty of God* (Downers Grove, IL: InterVarsity Press, 1961).

B. B. Warfield, 'The Development of the Doctrine of Infant Salvation,' in *The Works of Benjamin B. Warfield*, vol. 4: *Studies in Tertullian and Augustine* (reprint; Grand Rapids: Baker Book House, 1981).

Glossary

Arminianism: A theology associated with the teaching of Jacob Arminius, a Dutch Reformed theologian who inverted the order of election and grace, making the former subsequent to the latter so that God decrees to save all who repent, believe, and persevere. Divine election is thus made conditional upon God's foreknowledge of the persevering faith of those who respond properly to the gospel call.

Arminius, Jacob (1560-1609): A Dutch Reformed minister and professor at the University of Leiden who argued for a substantially different view of predestination than that which prevailed among the Reformed during the sixteenth century. His revision of the doctrine of election provoked considerable controversy within the Dutch Reformed churches, as well as other Reformed churches throughout Europe, that led to the convening of the Synod of Dort. See *Arminianism; Synod of Dort (1618-1619)*.

assurance: The believer's infallible certainty of being in the state of God's grace and persevering therein unto eschatological salvation. This comes about through the use of the means of grace, the preaching of the gospel and the reception of the sacraments.

Augustinianism: A theology associated with Augustine (354-430) that most commonly refers to his anti-Pelagian position wherein he maintained that fallen sinners are dead in their sins and, therefore, can only be saved by a mighty work of God's prevenient grace. The influence of Augustine's teaching has continued to assert itself throughout the history of the church up to the present.

concupiscence: The loss or privation of original righteousness, and a positive cause of sin.

concurrence: That work of God that belongs to the order of creation and providence by which He continually supports the operation of all secondary causes and enables all acts of contingent being to occur, whether good or evil. Accordingly, God is immanent in every act of His creatures.

379

conditional predestination: Jacob Arminius' doctrine that God elects to save those whom He foreknows will respond in faith to the gracious summons of the gospel and elects not to save those whom He foreknows will respond to the gospel call in unbelief and impenitence. Though God absolutely and antecedently wills to save all sinners who are fallen in Adam, His decree respecting the salvation of actual persons is conditioned upon their free decision to embrace the gospel promise.

covenant of grace: The gracious bond between the offended God and the offending sinner in which God promises salvation in the way of faith in Christ and the sinner receives this salvation by believing.

creation: That external work of God by which He has produced everything out of nothing and has imparted to all things their nature.

creationism: A view of the origin of the soul as a direct act of God. The Pelagian accusation that Augustine's doctrine of original sin would make God the author of sin assumes that he espouses a creationist viewpoint, and expresses a common complaint against this view in the history of theology.

decree of God: The free determination of God's rational will concerning everything outside Him that will be and how it will function. The decree of God is eternal, one, universal, efficacious, and immutable.

double predestination: God's election of some to salvation and His non-election or reprobation of others to punishment. God's purpose of election ordinarily contemplates the whole human race in its fallen condition. For this reason, Paul compares the human race to a 'lump of clay' from which God is free to make 'one vessel for honorable use and another for dishonorable use.' The implication of this language is that God is not only free to show mercy to some and not others, but He also acts justly when He 'endures with much patience vessels of wrath prepared for destruction.' For Paul, however, the primary emphasis lies upon the marvel of God's rich mercy toward all whom He wills to save, not upon the corollary truth that God justly with-holds His mercy from others whom He leaves in their sin.

effectual calling: An act of God whereby all whom He has predestined unto eternal life are effectually brought out of a state of sin and death to grace and salvation in Jesus Christ by His Word and Spirit. This effectual calling is of God's free and special grace alone and not from anything at all foreseen in sinners. Sinners are regenerated by the Holy Spirit in order to answer this call and to embrace the grace offered and conveyed in it.

election: God's pre-temporal, gracious self-determination to grant salvation to those who are the chosen objects of His favor. God elects to save His people in Christ, who is accordingly the foundation, executor, and source of the salvation that He is pleased to grant them. God does not elect His people to salvation without also electing Christ as the One through whom His purpose of election will be accomplished. Furthermore, He does not elect those who are blameless, but rather elects His people in order that they might become holy and blameless before Him.

Five Arminian Opinions: A statement consisting of the five articles that the Arminian party presented to the Synod of Dort (1618-1619) as a summary of their opinions regarding the five main heads of doctrine adopted by the Synod. These opinions were: 1. election is conditional on a person's response, being grounded in God's foreknowledge; 2. Christ died for each and every person but only believers are saved; 3. a person is unable to believe and needs the grace of God; but 4. this grace is resistible; 5. some true believers may fall away and not persevere in a state of grace unto eschatological life.

Five Points of Calvinism: The 'five points of Calvinism,' commonly so-called, are really five 'counter-points' to the errors of the Arminians or Remonstrants (see *Five Arminian Opinions*). Today, they are often known in English-speaking circles by the acronym, 'TULIP' (**T**otal depravity, **U**nconditional election, **L**imited atonement, **I**rresistible grace, and the **P**erseverance of the saints). Unfortunately, this acronym is of recent vintage, changes the order of the five points, and also employs terminology (especially in the case of 'total depravity,' 'irresistible grace,' and 'limited atonement') that does not adequately express the Reformed view.

foreknowledge: God's exhaustive knowledge of all that will actually take place in accordance with His will. In Romans 8:29 and 11:2, God's foreknowledge is His prior (pre-temporal) commitment to treat those whom He predestines with special favor. The focus of God's foreknowledge in this passage is not something that certain persons do in response to the gospel call. Rather, the object of God's foreknowledge is consistently those persons whom God beforehand distinguishes as the special recipients of His favor. God's foreknowledge is the basis and occasion for His gracious predestination. And this foreknowledge and corresponding act of fore-ordination are what undergirds His acts of calling, justifying, and glorifying.

free knowledge: God's knowledge of all actual things that exist or take place by virtue of His will. It concerns His knowledge of all that He wills to become actual. From out of all possibilities, God freely wills that some things become actual, and His knowledge of such is therefore a free knowledge. Since God's free knowledge is His knowledge of the actualities that He wills to exist, it is often termed God's 'visionary or definite knowledge' (*scientia visionis et definita*), or His 'voluntary knowledge' (*scientia voluntaria*).

general calling: A term applied to the universal offer of the gospel, which is made to all without distinction through the preaching of the word of God. It is either accepted by faith or rejected in unbelief.

infralapsarianism: The view of God's decree to elect or not elect to salvation as 'below' (*infra*) or logically subsequent to His decree to permit the fall into sin (*lapsus*). The objects of God's decree are conceived as created and fallen sinners (*homo creatus et lapsus*). The order of the elements in God's decree in the infralapsarian scheme is as follows: 1. the decree to glorify Himself in the creation of the human race; 2. the decree to permit the fall; 3. the decree to elect some of the fallen human race to salvation and to pass by others and condemn them for their sins; 4. the decree to provide salvation for the elect through Jesus Christ.

libertarianism: The view that the human will is free in relation to the call of the gospel, so that the will to believe or not to believe is wholly self-caused and independent of God's decree of predestination.

middle knowledge: God's knowledge of things intermediate between His necessary and free knowledge. In addition to God's necessary knowledge of all possibilities and His free knowledge of all actualities that He wills and effects, God also knows those things that depend on the liberty of created choice or pleasure. Whereas God's free knowledge contemplates those things that He knows by virtue of His having freely willed them to be, God's middle knowledge concerns those acts of free creatures that occur wholly by virtue of their own free and independent choices. Since Arminius bases God's decree to elect some to salvation solely upon His foreknowledge of their faith and repentance in response to the gospel, he introduces the idea of middle knowledge to explain how God can foreknow the actual choices of creatures who have the power to believe or, to the contrary, disbelieve.

monergism: The idea that salvation is accomplished by the sole agency of God so that it is the work of His grace alone apart from the independent co-operation of sinners.

necessary knowledge: God's knowledge of all things that He must know, which includes the knowledge of Himself and all possibilities. Because God's necessary knowledge logically precedes, and therefore does not depend upon, an act of His will, it was often termed God's 'knowledge of simple intelligence' or His 'natural and indefinite knowledge' (*scientia simplicis intelligentiae seu naturalis et indefinita*).

original sin: The doctrine that Adam's sin entailed the hereditary corruption of all his posterity, as well as their liability to condemnation and death. Thus, all human beings are born and conceived in sin, subject to condemnation and death, and in need of regeneration and renewal by God's prevenient grace.

particularism: The election of particular individuals as the special recipients of God's saving grace. While it is certainly true that the reach of God's mercy is universal in that it encompasses the salvation of many from all nations, Jew and Gentile alike, God's election to save is always particular, and not universal, in its scope.

Pelagianism: A theology associated with Pelagius who denied that God's grace underlies, or is prevenient to, the salvation of all believers who embrace the gospel promise of Christ. There are four main features of Pelagius' teaching: 1. his basic conviction that what God commands in His righteous law must be within the reach of human ability, which means all human beings retain the power of free will to obey the commands of God's law; 2. his insistence that, because human beings are in principle capable of keeping God's law in its entirety, they are able to live without sin; 3. his repudiation of the doctrine of original sin so that Adam's sin is not transmitted to his posterity by any form of hereditary corruption, but solely by way of 'imitation'; 4. his attenuated view of God's grace in salvation that involves no interior or transformative work, but externally bestows a created ability to choose to do good or evil, forgives past sins that cannot be undone, encourages and instructs in His holy law, and provides a good example of obedience in Christ.

perseverance: A gift of God's grace whereby He preserves those whom He wills to save in the way of faith unto salvation in glory.

preceptive will of God: The will of God's precept, which is revealed in the law and in the gospel. It has reference to the duties which God prescribes to man, represents the way in which man can enjoy the divine blessing, and can be frustrated.

predestination: The aspect of God's providence that pertains to His good and gracious will to grant salvation to the elect from among the fallen human race. In the strictest sense, predestination focuses especially on God's gracious election, which displays His undeserved mercy toward those whom He is pleased to save from the fallen human race, and not on His determination to leave others in their lost condition. Whereas gracious election especially displays God's mercy, God's determination not to save the nonelect displays His justice.

preterition: God's passing by or determination to leave some from among the fallen human race in their fallen condition, and to punish them justly for their sins.

prevenient grace: The grace of God that comes before conversion and any response of fallen sinners to the gospel call. With God's prevenient grace, all sinners are dead in their trespasses and sins, and unable to do any saving good. In Augustinianism, God's prevenient grace is effectual to the salvation of the elect. In Pelagianism, semi-Pelagianism, and Arminianism, God's prevenient grace is always resistable and ineffectual.

providence: The work of God, subsequent to His creation of all things, whereby He sustains and governs all things, and concurs in the free, non-coerced actions of all moral creatures.

redemptive history: The unfolding of God's eternal purpose to elect His people to salvation in Christ. In the Old Testament, this purpose is realized through the election of Israel as God's chosen people, and the election of particular individuals as the special recipients of God's saving blessings. In the New Testament, God's purpose finds its fulfillment in Jesus Christ, the Chosen Servant through whom God's promise to bless all the families of the earth is fulfilled.

Remonstrants: After Jacob Arminius' death in 1609, the Arminian party in the Dutch Reformed churches prepared a summary statement of their position. On January 14, 1610, more than forty representatives who championed Arminius' views gathered in Gouda. These representatives drew up a *Remonstrance* or petition in which their case was set forth and defended. After complaining that their cause had been misrepresented by their opponents, and then appealing to the state to exercise its authority to settle the controversy, this *Remonstrance* presented the Arminian position in a series of five articles (see *Five Arminian Opinions*). The teaching of the Remonstrants was condemned at the Synod of Dort (1618-1619).

reprobation: The decree of God whereby He has determined to pass by some with His regenerating and saving grace and so manifest His justice in them by punishing them for their sin.

secret will of God: The will of God's decree, which is largely hidden in God. It pertains to all things which God wills and are, therefore, certain to come to pass, whether necessarily, contingently, or freely.

semi-Pelagianism: The term is a relatively modern expression, which was first officially used in the Lutheran Formula of Concord (1577). It refers to a teaching that surfaced late in the controversy with Pelagius as a kind of 'half-way' house between a full-blown Pelagianism and Augustine's robust doctrine of predestination. It rejects the idea that faith is a gift of God's grace granted to those toward whom God chooses to show mercy and effectively call through the gospel. Rather, it teaches that faith, as the initial response to and acceptance of God's grace, finds its sole cause in a free, indeterminate act of the human will. Salvation, therefore, begins, and ultimately depends upon, the co-operation of the human will with the grace of God (see *synergism*).

supralapsarianism: The view of God's decree to elect or not elect to salvation as 'above' (*supra*) or logically prior to His decree regarding the fall. The objects of God's decree are conceived as uncreated and unfallen sinners (*homo creabilis et labilis*). The order of the elements in God's decree in the supralapsarian scheme is as follows: 1. the decree to glorify Himself through the election of some and the nonelection of others; 2. the decree to create the elect and the reprobate; 3. the decree to permit the fall; 4. the decree to provide salvation for the elect through Jesus Christ.

synergism: The idea that salvation is accomplished by the dual agency of God and man, so that in order for man to be saved he must co-operate with God's grace.

Synod of Dort (1618-1619): An international Synod held in Dordrecht, Netherlands in 1618–1619 because of the serious disturbances in the Dutch Reformed churches by the rise and spread of Arminianism. The Synod condemned the Remonstrant Articles and produced the *Five Articles Against the Remonstrants*, also called the *Canons of Dort*. See *Remonstrants; Five Arminian Opinions*.

traducianism: A view of the origin of the soul that regards the soul to be transmitted (*traduced*) through the mediate act of human procreation.

Scripture Index

387

Subject Index

Death in Adam, Life in Christ

The Doctrine of Imputation

J. V. Fesko

- First study in the R.E.D.S series
- History & exegesis of imputation
- Exploring the Biblical roots of sin and salvation

The doctrine of imputation is the ground in which salvation is rooted. It is often seen as superfluous or splitting hairs, and yet, without it, redemption automatically becomes reliant on our own works and assurance of salvation is suddenly not so sure. J. V. Fesko works through this doctrine looking at its long history in the church, its exegetical foundation, and its dogmatic formulation. In exploring imputed guilt from the First Adam alongside the imputed righteousness from the Second, this volume offers a helpfully well-rounded explanation of the doctrine.

ISBN: 978-1-78191-908-8

Cracking the Foundation of the New Perspective on Paul

Covenantal Nomism versus Reformed Covenantal Theology

Robert J. Cara

- Second title in the R.E.D.S doctrine series
- Critiquing the New Perspective on Paul
- Covenantal Nomism versus Reformed Covenantal Theology

The New Perspective on Paul claims that the Reformed understanding of justification is wrong – that it misunderstands Paul and the Judaism with which he engages. The New Perspective's revised understanding of Second Temple Judaism provides the foundation to a new perspective. This important book seeks to show that this foundation is fundamentally faulty and cannot bear the weight it needs to carry, thus undermining the entirety of the New Perspective on Paul itself.

ISBN: 978-1-78191-979-8

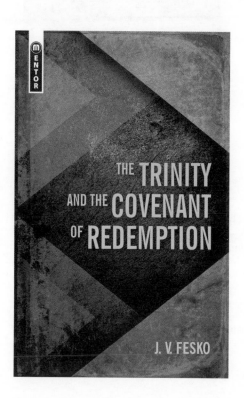

THE **TRINITY**
AND THE **COVENANT**
OF **REDEMPTION**

J. V. FESKO

The Trinity And the Covenant of Redemption

J. V. Fesko

- The covenant of redemption.

- First in a three part series on Redemption, Grace and Works.

- Important resource for reformed thinkers.

When Christians reflect on the gospel, their attention is rightly drawn to the cross and empty tomb. But is this it? Or is there much more to the story? In a ground–breaking work, J. V. Fesko reminds us that the great news of this gospel message is rooted in eternity, whereby a covenant was made between the persons of the Trinity in order to redeem sinners like you and me. J. V. Fesko, in the first of a three part series on covenant theology featuring Redemption, Grace and Works, aims to retrieve and recover classic Reformed covenant theology for the church.

ISBN: 978-1-78191-765-7

Christian Focus Publications

Our mission statement –

STAYING FAITHFUL

In dependence upon God we seek to impact the world through literature faithful to His infallible Word, the Bible. Our aim is to ensure that the Lord Jesus Christ is presented as the only hope to obtain forgiveness of sin, live a useful life and look forward to heaven with Him.

Our books are published in four imprints:

CHRISTIAN
FOCUS

Popular works including biographies, commentaries, basic doctrine and Christian living.

CHRISTIAN
HERITAGE

Books representing some of the best material from the rich heritage of the church.

MENTOR

Books written at a level suitable for Bible College and seminary students, pastors, and other serious readers. The imprint includes commentaries, doctrinal studies, examination of current issues and church history.

CF4•K

Children's books for quality Bible teaching and for all age groups: Sunday school curriculum, puzzle and activity books; personal and family devotional titles, biographies and inspirational stories – because you are never too young to know Jesus!

Christian Focus Publications Ltd,
Geanies House, Fearn, Ross-shire,
IV20 1TW, Scotland, United Kingdom.
www.christianfocus.com